TRAVELER

# greece

# NATIONAL GEOGRAPHIC
## TRAVELER

# greece

Mike Gerrard

National Geographic
Washington, D.C.

# CONTENTS

Pages 2–3: Santorini at dusk; Left: Church square, Olympos, Karpathos

# TRAVELING WITH EYES OPEN

Alert travelers go with a purpose and leave with a benefit. If you travel responsibly, you can help support wildlife conservation, historic preservation, and cultural enrichment in the places you visit. You can enrich your own travel experience as well.

To be a geo-savvy traveler:

- Recognize that your presence has an impact on the places you visit.

- Spend your time and money in ways that sustain local character. (Besides, it's more interesting that way.)

- Value the destination's natural and cultural heritage.

- Respect the local customs and traditions.

- Express appreciation to local people about things you find interesting and unique to the place: its nature and scenery, music and food, historic villages and buildings.

- Vote with your wallet: Support the people who support the place, patronizing businesses that make an effort to celebrate and protect what's special there. Seek out shops, local restaurants, inns, and tour operators who love their home—who love taking care of it and showing it off. Avoid businesses that detract from the character of the place.

- Enrich yourself, taking home memories and stories to tell, knowing that you have contributed to the preservation and enhancement of the destination.

That is the type of travel now called geotourism, defined as "tourism that sustains or enhances the geographical character of a place—its environment, culture, aesthetics, heritage, and the well-being of its residents." To learn more, visit National Geographic's Center for Sustainable Destinations at *www.nationalgeographic.com/travel/sustainable*.

# greece

## ABOUT THE AUTHOR

**Mike Gerrard** is an award-winning travel writer (Travelex Travel Writers Award, Outdoor Writers; Guide Awards for Excellence in Photojournalism and Features; and the British Guild of Travel Writers award for "Best U.K. Feature") who first visited Greece in the late 1960s and fell in love with the country at first sight. He has been back every year since, sometimes several times, and has written guides to Athens, the Greek mainland, the Greek islands, Crete, and Corfu. His travel journalism has appeared in newspapers and magazines worldwide, including *The Times* in London and *The Washington Post*. To research a piece for *The Times* he tried being a Greek waiter for a week on the island of Zakynthos and, as a result, he now gives bigger tips.

# Charting Your Trip

Known as the cradle of European civilization, Greece has much more to offer than ancient remains, though it has these in abundance: the Acropolis, ancient Olympia, and Knossos, to name just three. But it also has the beaches and beauty of the Greek islands, where the welcome is as warm as the summer sunshine. It has dramatic natural scenery in places like Crete and the Pindos Mountains, many of these places hardly known to visitors.

### How to Visit in One Week

If it's your first visit to Greece and you only have a week, there's good news and there's bad news. The bad news is that you can only skim the surface of what this magnificent and fascinating country has to offer. The good news is that, whatever you choose, you're assured an excellent time.

Any journey should start and end in Athens, and not only because that's where the main international airport is. Since the cleanup and refurbishment for the 2004 Olympics, Athens has become a wonderful place to visit. Much of the downtown Plaka and Acropolis areas are easily walkable, and the excellent subway system will whisk you anywhere you want to go.

Two to three days in this unique and ancient city would enable you to visit not only the two essentials of the Acropolis and the National Archaeological Museum, but some of the city's other fine museums as well. The latter tend to get overshadowed by the main museums, but the Benaki Museum, the Cycladic Art Museum, the newly improved Museum of Byzantine and Christian Art, and the Islamic Art Museum are all fine examples of modern museums at their best.

Within easy reach of Athens is the ancient site of Delphi, on the edge of the Parnassos Mountains. Along with Olympia and Knossos, this is one of the country's prime sites. It isn't only that it is historically fascinating, but its location at the head of a valley filled with olive trees is magical. It's an easy day trip from Athens by tour bus, but you could do it yourself by renting a car

The intricate detailing on the Dervani Krater depicts scenes of Dionysos.

and leaving in the afternoon, staying overnight in the town of Delphi, and being at the site when it opens and before the day's crowds.

No trip to Greece would be complete without taking in at least one of the Greek islands. With Athens as a base, this is also straightforward. The four main Argo-Saronic Islands are all within easy reach of the Greek capital, and although you could visit one or two of them in the course of one day, a better option is, as with Delphi, to plan to stay overnight. With the good ferry connections from Pireas, you could start on Egina, stopping at the Temple of Aphea (older than the Parthenon) before catching another boat to the walkable island of Poros. Another possibility is the artist haven of Idra. Wherever you stop, allow time to relax, dine on fresh fish by the water's edge, and unwind into the Greek experience.

## If You Have More Time

Many European visitors take a two- or three-week vacation in Greece and the Greek islands every year, such is the hold the country has on people. This happens mostly in summer, making the popular islands extremely crowded. With time at your disposal, so many possibilities open up. Athens and Delphi are still a must, but instead of limiting yourself to the islands closest to Athens, you can indulge yourself with a week or more on whichever other island(s) strike your fancy.

### NOT TO BE MISSED:

## In-flight Reading

Greek myths are so omnipresent that at least a cursory understanding is necessary to appreciate most of the country. But if you grew up within the Western world, you already know more than you think. And if not, relax, the flight to Greece is long, and there are always layovers. The following is a brief reading list to get you up to speed:

For diehard myth fans, nothing beats the classics—works by Homer, Euripides, Sophocles, Aeschylus, and others from ancient Greece—but for the sake of brevity, a single volume or collection will suffice and provide clarity. Thomas Bulfinch's *Mythology* is the standard modern rendering of these myths. First published in 1855, it is erudite, thorough, and still the benchmark. More recent is Edith Hamilton's *Mythology* (1998), which, due to its relative ease, is more widely read than Bulfinch. To understand the cultural importance of myth, read Joseph Campbell's *The Hero with a Thousand Faces*, first published in 1949.

Astipalea castle and its church overlook the sea.

## Is Haggling Acceptable?

If you're in a tourist shop in Athens and quoted a price for something that you think is too high, you might offer a lower price and see what the shopkeeper says. In local markets you might make an offer, or ask for a good price if you buy more than one item. Perhaps some vendors will come down in price, but you don't normally get into the offer and counter-offer bargaining process—save that kind of to-and-fro haggling for neighboring Turkey. However, to save a few dollars, or euros, ask about breaks on taxes for international visitors. Also, in local markets cash tends to go over better than credit cards.

**The Greek Isles:** With numerous flights and fast ferries from Pireas, the port for Athens, the option of island-hopping opens up. It's one of the most liberating experiences, to be on the deck of a ferry reluctantly leaving one paradise but heading for a new destination and adventures unknown. It takes a little planning and research, but any of the island groups will reward exploration.

The largest island, Crete, offers the best of everything in one place: beaches both busy and quiet, mountains for hiking, attractive harbor towns like Hania and Rethymno, a proud people and culture, music and good food, and numerous archaeological sites of which Knossos is merely the biggest and best known.

The Cyclades are probably the prettiest island group, with two special gems, Santorini and its black sand beaches and Mikonos known for its nightlife. The ancient Cycladic civilization flourished here, producing dazzling works of art. The Dodecanese offer lots of variety, from busy Rhodes to smaller islands like Tilos and Halki. The most southerly of the island groups, they are especially wonderful in spring.

The Ionians are harder to get around, so you may want to focus on Corfu, a scenic island with plenty of variety. Close to Italy, its buildings show influences of the Byzantine, Venetian, French, and British past.

**The Mainland:** There's even more variety on the Greek mainland; so you may choose to turn your back on the islands completely. A week in the Peloponnese could include ancient sites such as Olympia and Mycenae, pretty towns such as the old capital, Nafplio, beaches as good as any on the islands, and the rugged scenery of the Mani or the mountains. Or from Athens after your visit to Delphi you could continue north into the most dramatically beautiful part of Greece, the Pindos Mountains and Macedonia. This is an area for outdoor lovers, walkers, and wildlife watchers.

Eastern Macedonia includes Greece's second largest city, the vibrant Thessaloniki, with the nearby holiday resorts of Halkidiki and the "Monks' Republic," Mount Athos. Farther east still, the region of Thrace is the part of Greece that borders on its neighbor Turkey. It's a much less-explored part of the mainland, and will give you the feeling that you're discovering that mythical thing, the "real Greece." ∎

## Being Polite: The Top Ten Phrases

Greek is not a language that many visitors speak, and any attempt to do so is usually greeted with enthusiasm and appreciation. Try to remember a few simple phrases:

| | |
|---|---|
| *Parakalo* | Please |
| *Efharisto* | Thank you |
| *Signomi* | Excuse me |
| *Kali mera* | Good morning |
| *Kali spera* | Good evening |
| *Kali nichta* | Good night |
| *Kala* | Good |
| *Ne* | Yes |
| *Ohi* | No |
| *Endaxi* | Okay |

Note: you usually say *"kali mera"* throughout the day, and switch to *"kali spera"* as it gets toward evening. *"Kali nichta"* is a phrase you only use when bidding someone good night, knowing you won't see them again that night.

## When to Go

Greece is a year-round destination, so if you can only travel in midsummer or midwinter, you'll still enjoy your visit. However, August is best avoided, not only because it is the peak vacation month and therefore the most crowded, but also because temperatures can soar to well over 100°F (38°C), and Athens in particular can be very uncomfortable.

In midwinter there may be rain and temperatures around 50°F (10°C), but equally you may get clear blue skies and temperatures of 20°F (-6°C). The best time to visit is in the spring and the fall, when the weather is comfortably warm, there is little rain, and fewer vacationers means the naturally hospitable locals have time to talk to visitors. In the springtime wildflowers will be blooming and the landscape lush. If you wish to visit mountainous regions, late May onward is when the snow starts to melt and paths become passable again.

An especially good time to visit is during Easter week, when there are many celebrations: Easter is the most important festival in the Greek calendar. However, it only occasionally coincides with the dates of Western Christian Easter as it is determined by a different system, so check the dates ahead of time.

# History & Culture

Minoan mural from 1600 B.C.

The much photographed Roussanou Monastery in Meteora was founded about 1288.

# Greece Today

**What is Greece? Greece is the Parthenon, standing above Athens, a monument to the country's ancient history. Greece is also deep blue skies and turquoise seas, and white houses stacked like cubes on a hillside above a harbor, enticing modern tourism to the islands. But Greece is much, much more than those things.**

It is a country with a unique culture and language, a landscape that is among the least explored in Europe, and a people who are the most hospitable in the world.

Of course many visitors have time to see only the tourist centers and can't explore off the beaten track. Even so, they will still find that special quality encountered nowhere but in Greece. No one's heart can fail to be lifted on arriving in the country's busy capital and finding the skyline dominated not by skyscrapers but by a building more than 2,500 years old—and not merely old but one of the most beautiful ever constructed. The first sight of the Parthenon, no matter how familiar it is from postcards and prints, will fill you with excitement.

> The first sight of the Parthenon, no matter how familiar it is from postcards and prints, will fill you with excitement.

A brief visit allows you to take in some other of Greece's highlights, such as the treasures of the National Archaeological Museum (one of the very few national museums that does not contain foreign works), and a trip to the ruins of Delphi, one of the most magical sites in the world. A leisurely cruise through the islands might take you to the Old Town of Rhodes, and the harbor that the Colossus of Rhodes allegedly bestrode, and to the reconstructed ruins of the Royal Palace at Knossos on Crete, the center of the mighty Minoan civilization. There will also be time for one of the greatest and simplest pleasures that Greece has to offer—a delicious meal outdoors at the water's edge, and at a price as cheap as you'll find in any Western country.

Those with more time will be torn between idling the days away on one tiny island, getting to know the local people—who will be as interested in you as you are in them—and exploring several islands to see how they subtly differ. Rent a car to explore the mainland and you will be made welcome in towns where few tourists venture. Plan to see the great classical sites such as Delphi and Olympia first thing in the morning or last thing in the afternoon—you will probably have them virtually to yourself. Go walking in the mountains, visit the lakes and other places that only the Greeks know about, and you will truly feel yourself to be a privileged traveler in this special land. Be prepared to take plenty of photos, because everywhere you turn, you'll see charm, beauty, and vivid local color.

## Greek Character

Although it has become a cliché to describe a country as being "a land of contrasts," it is certainly true that the Greek character is full of contrasts. On the one hand, Greeks think nothing of cheating their own government—in fact it is seen

**Athens's Plaka is full of street cafés and shops for the casual stroller.**

**The Church of the Holy Apostles and the Temple of Hephaistos in Athens**

as something of a national sport—and even pulling a fast one on their next-door neighbor, yet the vast majority are wonderfully honest in their dealings with strangers. Regular visitors will tell you of countless experiences of Greek honesty: When bags have been left behind in a restaurant and dutifully handed in to the owners; when wallets have been dropped and someone has come running after to return it without thought of reward; when a busy bar owner has said "come back and pay tomorrow" when rushed off his feet.

That is not to say that the entire Greek nation is made up of angels. There are thieves in Athens, yet nowhere near as many as in other Western capitals, and there are waiters who will try to shortchange you, or add up the bill in their favor. But for every one of those there are ten Greeks who would willingly pay for your meal rather than see you cheated.

There is a Greek word *xenoi*, which is one of the first things you must understand when visiting the country. It is a word with a dual meaning, both "stranger" and "guest" simultaneously. A stranger is automatically a guest in their country, their town, their home. Visit a Greek home and you will experience a hospitality that can be overwhelming. Admire a painting on the wall and you may find yourself taking it away with you as a gift. Walk in the country and you might be given fruit to eat by a farmer, or beckoned to someone's house for a drink or a slice of bread and cheese.

The Greeks love nothing more than a good argument. This is, after all, the birthplace of philosophy and discourse, and in *kafenion* (cafés) throughout the land you will still find men arguing ferociously, slamming the table and gesticulating wildly. It might be about the next elections, or it could just as easily be about the price of honey or fish these days. The discussions always seem more violent than they are, as if about to boil over into a fist fight, but that is merely the Greek passion for argument.

Greece is a male-dominated society, which is why it will be men and not both sexes sitting in cafés putting the world to rights. Cafés are male places, where few Greek women would care to venture. That is not because they are insalubrious places, just that it is not the custom. Foreign women can venture in alone or with company and will not feel threatened, as the Greeks make exceptions for visitors. There is still a vast chasm between the role of women in a city like Athens, where it is common to see them in positions of authority and men seem comfortable with this, and in rural Greece, where the sex roles are still very firmly defined and the woman's place is in the home.

## Family

It is in the home where the women wield the power. No man would admit it in public, where he plays the strutting head of the household, yet Greek women are fearsomely strong characters. The family is vitally important to the Greek people, particularly in rural areas. Children live at home until they are married. Even when married, the couple may live with one set of parents until they can afford a house of their own. When one grandparent dies, the other moves in with the rest of the family, as it would be unthinkable to allow an elderly person to live alone.

You will see very few beggars outside Athens, and those that you do see are most usually economic migrants who have come into Greece illegally. Greek families look after their own. People with mental or physical disabilities can find themselves shunned, however, as if bringing some kind of shame on the family. It is fairly common for them to be put into a home, although within the broader family of, say, a village, you will often see someone with mental disabilities provided with a simple job such as sweeping the street and treated like any other member of the society.

## Religion

Religion and family are very much tied together. About 97 percent of Greeks are Greek Orthodox, although not necessarily devout. Sunday morning services are a focal point and a time when communities get together. The services are interminably long, and few Greeks attend the whole three hours or so that a service lasts. They call in for a while, then leave, have a chat outside the church, and maybe go back later if they feel like it. Visitors are quite welcome at the services as, like the Greeks themselves, services are both casual and formal at the same time.

### Dining Etiquette

Greeks, like most Mediterranean people, eat later than northern Europeans and North Americans. If you want to secure a table at a busy or fashionable restaurant, you stand a better chance if you ask for an early time. If you arrange to meet Greek people for a meal then the actual starting time may be later than stated, as they usually have a flexible attitude to time-keeping. Only in a trendy restaurant where it's hard to get a table would you expect people to arrive more or less on time. Children usually dine with adults, as eating out is a family affair and the family is a very strong unit in Greece. However, the children will often be put at a separate table of their own, alongside the adults. That way everyone is happy.

### Feast Days & Festivals

There are numerous feast days around Greece, as every saint's day is celebrated in every church named after that saint—and there are a lot of saints and a lot of churches in Greece. When the local saint's day is celebrated, you can expect fireworks—often literally—as well as parades, parties, shows, and maybe a day or two when the stores will be closed.

> Every saint's day is celebrated in every church named after that saint ... you can expect fireworks, parades, parties, and shows.

Most Greek celebrations revolve around the church and are occasions for eating, drinking, dancing, and music. A feast often starts on the eve of the day itself with a church service, and afterward there may be a huge meal, frequently followed by music and traditional dancing. The next day they often see no reason not to do it all over again. Festivals often involve parades that include children, bands, and dance groups. After the parade there is another huge communal meal and more music and dancing as the spirit takes them. The Greeks like to party and need little encouragement to make sure the celebrations go on as long as possible. The visitor will always be warmly welcomed to join in.

For dates of public holidays, see page 340.

### A Relationship with the Sea

Greece has always been a maritime nation, and much of its past wealth has come from shipping dynasties, of which the Onassis family is probably the best known. It was inevitable that a country, which includes about 2,000 islands should develop a knowledge of the sea. Travel by ferry is as natural to a Greek islander as using a train or plane in other countries. Despite that, many Greeks do not make good sea travelers. While visitors head for the sun decks, most Greeks make straight for the lounge, where they find space to lie down and often look the worse for wear when the journey is over.

Fishing is a mainstay of many Greek towns and villages, in the islands or along the country's rugged coastline. Most fishermen work individually rather than as part of a large fleet, catching enough for their family, the local market, and any restaurants they might supply. Most fishing takes place at night, and during the day a characteristic sight is fishermen by the harbor mending their yellow nets. You will no doubt see some of them pounding octopuses against the rocks to tenderize them before taking them to a local restaurant or home to the family. And don't be surprised when you come across a clothesline with raggedy-looking handkerchiefs—look closer and you'll see tentacles.

## Rural Greece

Greece is very much a rural country and until the advent of tourism its economy was as dependent on agriculture as on fishing and the shipping trade. The overwhelmingly predominant crop is olives—a prime export of a people who themselves consume more olive oil per capita than any other country in the world.

Olive groves dominate the landscape. To give an idea of the scale of things, the single island of Corfu has an estimated three million olive trees. There are other crops, of course, including tobacco and cotton in Thrace. Almost every household in the country has its gnarled but abundantly fruitful olive trees and its vine-covered patio, and even the smallest family might well produce enough grapes to make its own wine.

This is not to claim that Greece is the epitome of a rural idyll. By the standards of Western Europe it is a poor country, and many people hold down two or even three jobs just to survive. Greece's rural past has been thrown into conflict with some aspects of the modern world. Farming here has been naturally organic and the land maintained with care. However, the gains to be made from tourist development are creating environmental conflicts. Short-term gain may be long-term loss. Nowhere is this better illustrated than with the turtles nesting on Zakinthos (see pp. 329, 330–331). ∎

**On Karpathos, a single-room dwelling preserves the traditional way of life.**

# Food & Drink

**Greek cooking is steeped in 3,000 years of history and, due to its geographical location, combines Eastern and Western cuisines with good, simply prepared food that is delicious. Eating out is one of the highlights of any visit to Greece.**

Greek food is best when kept simple. Take a cut of lamb, or a fish caught just that morning, grill it slowly over charcoal, serve it with a slice of lemon and a crisp salad, and nothing tastes as good.

Greek wine has improved immeasurably in the last few years, and where once there was little choice, now Greek wines are winning international competitions. Retsina, the unique resin-flavored white wine, accounts for only 15 percent of domestic wine sales.

## Dining Habits

Like other Mediterranean peoples, Greeks eat late—around 2 p.m. for lunch and 9 p.m. for dinner, though resorts will cater to visitors at earlier times.

Popular hors d'oeuvres include dips such as *taramosalata* (cod's roe pâté), *tsatsiki* (yogurt and cucumber), and a mixed dish of different items, known as *meze*. The most famous traditional Greek dish is probably moussaka, which is layers of potato, ground meat, and eggplant. Fish is widely available (see p. 385 for the most common fish, and their Greek names). Lamb is the most popular meat, but you will find chicken, pork, and beef as well. Recently, a modern, more sophisticated take on traditional Greek cooking has attracted the attention of foodies.

## Having a Drink

The preferred Greek apéritif is ouzo, an aniseed-based drink that turns milky when mixed with water. Greeks drink it straight, but it is always served with a glass of water to cleanse the palate. After dinner, people often move on to a café for a Metaxa, which is a brand-name synonymous with brandy. It is usually available in three-star, five-star, or seven-star varieties, the last being the smoothest. Another strong after-dinner drink is raki. This is like Italian grappa, and can range from the rough to the smooth. But be warned, it always has a high alcohol content.

Many Greeks drink beer with a meal instead of wine, and there is usually a choice of two or three types. The most popular European beers are Amstel and Heineken, both light lager-type beers suited to a hot climate. The major Greek brand is called Mythos, which has a slightly nutty taste.

Be careful how you refer to coffee. What you might elsewhere describe as Turkish coffee is here called Greek coffee. It is very concentrated, and served in a small cup without milk. It is normally served with sugar already boiled into the coffee, when it is known as a *metrio* (medium). If you want extra sugar ask for a *glyko* (sweet); coffee with no sugar at all is a *sketo*. If you want an American-style cup of coffee, ask for a Nescafé. Greeks also love a *frappé,* a refreshing, cold milky coffee served in a tall glass. ■

**Fresh fruits and vegetables from the market form the basis for many Greek dishes.**

# History of Greece

Several places claim to be the cradle of civilization, but Greece can certainly claim to be at least the cradle of European civilization—the arts, philosophy, architecture, and democratic politics. It has been written of Athens that "wherever you set your foot, you encounter some memory of the past," and this by none other than the Roman writer Cicero (106–43 B.C.).

## Stone Age

In many countries the Paleolithic period, dating roughly from 2.5 million B.C. to about 9000 B.C., provides the richest and most fascinating archaeological pickings. Yet in Greece comparatively little has been found from this period. This apparently late start makes the sudden flourishing of culture in Greece from about 3000 B.C. onward appear all the more extraordinary.

The oldest significant Greek find from the Stone Age is a single pre-Neandertal skull discovered in a cave 30 miles (50 km) southeast of Thessaloniki. The cave of Kokkines Petres (Red Stones) also contained remains of prehistoric animals, and was found not by archaeologists but accidentally by villagers from nearby Petralona in 1959.

It is known that there were settlers in Greece as early as 200,000 B.C., probably coming from the Middle East, and these were concentrated in northern Greece, and on the fertile plains of Thessaly. Three caves farther west in the Louros Valley in Epiros have produced evidence to indicate that they were inhabited by about 40,000 B.C. The oldest known farming communities in Greece, and therefore in Europe, have been dated to about 7000–5000 B.C., again in Thessaly and Macedonia, where remnants of pottery and mud-brick houses have been found. The earliest settlements on the island of Crete—for example, the tombs found in the Cave of Trapeza, high on the Lesithi

A stone fragment with Linear B script

Plateau—and on some of the Aegean islands, have also been dated to this period, with indications that trade between the communities was flourishing. The ancient past of Greece looks set to keep scholars occupied well into the future.

## Minoans

The Cycladic culture flourished from about 3200 B.C. onward in the islands of the Cyclades group in the Aegean. Large numbers of statues and figurines dating from about 2800 B.C. have survived, mostly found in burial tombs. These graceful and elegant creations with their deceptively simple, stylized lines and smooth pale marble curves have influenced many 20th-century artists and can still cause gasps of admiration in anyone seeing them for the first time, knowing they are almost 5,000 years old.

**The Minoan civilization reached its peak around 1500 B.C., by which time trade, in pottery, wine, oil, jewelry, and other goods, was flourishing in places such as Egypt and the Middle East.**

Greek culture truly flourished for the first time, however, with the Minoan civilization. It owes its name to the English archaeologist Sir Arthur Evans (see pp. 284–285), who excavated the Royal Palace at Knossos on Crete and named the civilization which created it after Minos, the legendary king of Crete. (Scholars now believe that minos was a title, like king, rather than an individual's name.)

The first palace at Knossos was built around 2000 B.C., and its vast scale is a vivid pointer to the wealth and power of the people who created it. At that time Crete dominated trade in the Eastern Mediterranean, as strategically placed then as it was during World War II. There were other Minoan cities at Argos, Tiryns, and Mycenae, all close together in the Peloponnese on the Greek mainland, as well as on Rhodes, on Kithera (off the southern coast of the Peloponnese), and in the Cyclades. The civilization reached its peak at around 1500 B.C., by which time trade in pottery, wine, oil, jewelry, and other goods was flourishing in places such as Egypt and the Middle East.

Evans believed that it was the mighty eruption on the island of Santorini in 1500 B.C., and the resultant tidal wave that washed over Crete, that brought a premature end to the Minoans. In fact their civilization ended in about 1450 B.C., but his theory has so strong a hold that the Santorini eruption is often dated to 1450 B.C. because of it.

We do not know for sure why the Minoan civilization ended. It may have been a revolution by the people themselves against the overly powerful priests and rulers, or it may have been some kind of natural disaster. Or maybe there was an invasion by an unknown power, or even by the Mycenaeans. What we do know is that the Mycenaeans became the dominant people in the Aegean.

## Mycenaean Age

Work by the German archaeologist Heinrich Schliemann (see pp. 112-113) revealed that the city of Mycenae was founded in about 2100 B.C. It was settled by some of the waves of migrants who were then passing into Europe from the Indian subcontinent, but quickly fell under the control of the Minoans, whose center of strength was at Knossos on Crete. Due to the mix of myth and history conjured up

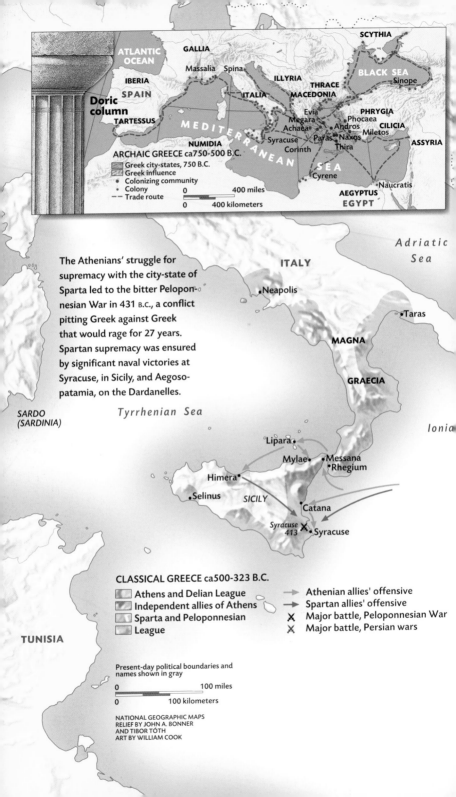

## ARCHAIC GREECE ca750-500 B.C.

ATLANTIC OCEAN

GALLIA

SCYTHIA

Massalia    Spina

IBERIA
SPAIN

ILLYRIA

BLACK SEA

Sinope

**Doric column**

ITALIA

THRACE

MACEDONIA

PHRYGIA

TARTESSUS

M E D I T E R R A N E A N

Evia
Megara
Achaea
Syracuse
Corinth

Phocaea
Andros
Paras  Naxos
Thira

Miletos

CILICIA

ASSYRIA

NUMIDIA

S E A

Cyrene

AEGYPTUS
EGYPT

Naucratis

Greek city-states, 750 B.C.
Greek influence
• Colonizing community
• Colony
- - - Trade route

0        400 miles
0        400 kilometers

---

Adriatic Sea

ITALY

The Athenians' struggle for supremacy with the city-state of Sparta led to the bitter Peloponnesian War in 431 B.C., a conflict pitting Greek against Greek that would rage for 27 years. Spartan supremacy was ensured by significant naval victories at Syracuse, in Sicily, and Aegosopatamia, on the Dardanelles.

•Neapolis

•Taras

MAGNA

GRAECIA

SARDO
(SARDINIA)

*Tyrrhenian Sea*

Ionia

Lipara•

Mylae•  •Messana
•Rhegium

Himera•

Selinus•

*SICILY*

•Catana

Syracuse
413  ✗•Syracuse

## CLASSICAL GREECE ca500-323 B.C.

TUNISIA

Athens and Delian League

Independent allies of Athens

Sparta and Peloponnesian

League

→ Athenian allies' offensive
→ Spartan allies' offensive
✗ Major battle, Peloponnesian War
✗ Major battle, Persian wars

Present-day political boundaries and names shown in gray

0        100 miles
0        100 kilometers

NATIONAL GEOGRAPHIC MAPS
RELIEF BY JOHN A. BONNER
AND TIBOR TÓTH
ART BY WILLIAM COOK

# Warfare & Empire

The fifth century B.C. was a time of glory and strife in Greece. Athens was entering its Golden Age in 495 B.C., with the development of a lasting political structure as well as a flourishing arts scene (see p. 29). At this time the Greeks, at the head of the Delian League, triumphantly fought off attacks from the Persians, following up the famous victory at Marathon in 490 B.C. with further success at Mycale and Plataea in 479 B.C.

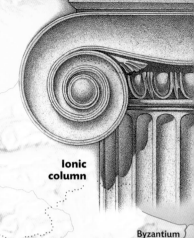

Ionic column

ILLYRIA

MACEDONIA

• Epidamnus

MACEDONIA
Amphipolis 422 ✕
THRACE
Sindos• •Thessaloniki

• Apollonia
ALBANIA
Spartolus 429 ✕ CHALKIDIKE ✕ 430-32
Aegospotami 405 ✕
Byzantium •
✕ Cyzicus 410 ✕
✕ Cynossema 411
• Troy
TROAS
TURKEY

THESSALY
GREECE
EPIROS
Olpae 426 ✕
Thermopylae 480
Artemisium 480 ✕
Aegean Sea
Assos
Agia Paraskevi•
LESVOS
AEOLIS
Arginusae ✕ 406
PERSIAN EMPIRE
• Phocaea

Corfu •

ea
Aegitium 426 ✕
Delphi •
BOEOTIA
Delium
Thebes ✕ 424
Plataea 431 ✕
SKYROS
EVIA
Eretria •
Lefkadi •
Megara Marathon 490
Plataea 479
IONIA
Notium 406 •
• Ephesus
ACHAE
Corinth•
PELOPONNESE
Olympia •
Mantinea 418 ✕
ARCADIA
Vasses•
MESSENIA
Sphacteria 425 ✕
Salamis 480 ✕
ATTICA
Lavrion •
Vravron •
Pireas
Tenea
Athens •
Taygetos
• Sparta
LACONIA
• Delos
PAROS
SAMOS
Mycale 479 ✕
Lade 494
Halicarnassus •
• Miletos
Rhodes •
RHODES

The period 750–500 B.C., sometimes known as the Archaic period, was characterized by considerable emigration from Greece—the spread of an empire. Colonies grew up to the west around the shores of the Mediterranean, and east along the coast of Turkey, boosting trade and spreading Greek culture far and wide. In the wars that were to follow, eastern colonies sided with Athens to form the Delian League, while western colonies remained neutral.

CRETE
• Knossos

MEDITERRANEAN SEA

by Homer (see pp. 326–327), Schliemann believed that he had located the burial place of the legendary king of Mycenae, Agamemnon.

There are some things we can be sure of. Thanks to the existence on clay tablets of fragments of writing referred to as Linear B (which was also found at Knossos), we know that the Mycenaeans spoke an early dialect of Greek. We also know that by about 1400 B.C. when the Minoan civilization had declined, for whatever reason, the Mycenaeans came into the ascendancy and took over the wealth, trade, and control of the eastern Aegean, which the Minoans had previously enjoyed.

There is no question that Mycenaeans possessed that wealth and power. At Mycenae itself many gold and silver objects were found, some of incredible beauty and obviously of enormous value, the best of these being among the highlights of the collection at the National Archaeological Museum in Athens (see pp. 82–85). In addition, the Mycenaeans controlled several other cities, such as nearby Tiryns, Pilos on the west coast of the Peloponnese, and even as far as Troy in western Turkey (see sidebar below).

The site at Tiryns, just a few miles south of Mycenae, also contained a large palace complex, with grand halls and entrance gates. Until Evans uncovered the Minoan palace at Knossos, the site at Tiryns was the best-preserved example of such a "royal palace" known to exist.

Although strong, the Mycenaean culture was comparatively short-lived, flourishing for only 200 years. Its power waned about 1200 B.C., and, as with the Minoans, no one knows why. It may have been wiped out by some natural disaster, or by the arrival of a new enemy—the Dorian tribes from the north.

## Dorian Age

The collapse of the Mycenaean civilization was the beginning of Greece's "dark ages." There were several factors behind this, not least of them the invasion by the Dorian people from northern Greece in about 1200–1100 B.C. They occupied Corinth, then moved in and took control of Mycenae, Sparta, and Argolis.

The warlike Dorians lacked the culture that had made the Minoans and Mycenaeans so great. The Dorians simply suppressed the beliefs of the people they conquered in lands that in time included most of the Greek mainland, Crete, the Dodecanese, parts of southern Italy, Sicily, and into the Middle East. Despite this, the sea trade that had made previous rulers so rich dwindled under these ruthless people.

---

## Mycenaeans at Troy

In the *Iliad,* Homer tells how Agamemnon, king of Mycenae, took his troops to Troy and was among the heroes of the ten-year siege of the city. Troy eventually fell to the Greeks, thanks to the ruse of the wooden horse.

To overcome the strong winds that were delaying his troops' journey home, Agamemnon sacrificed his daughter to the goddess Artemis, then returned to Mycenae in triumph, bringing with him the Trojan princess Cassandra. In the *Oresteia* by Aeschylus (see p. 61), he is killed in his bathtub by his wife, Clytemnestra, and her lover.

There certainly were powerful kings at Mycenae, but whether one of them was named Agamemnon is another matter, and whether it was his death mask that Schliemann found is even more debatable.

---

**The massive 13th-century B.C. Lion Gate guards the entrance to the palace at Mycenae.**

Greece has always depended on its maritime trade, right through to the shipping dynasties of the 20th century, so with its disappearance the country suffered badly. Trade over land had always been difficult because of the mountain barriers of the north and the constant disputes with the Turkish people to the east. The sea was vital. Under the Dorians, the Greeks lost not only their trade but also communication by sea with their immediate neighbors, and cultural exchanges suffered as much as commerce. The people became inward-looking and had to rely on farming to survive.

It is easy to imagine how difficult that time must have been. Even today Greece is not a rich country; it relies heavily on the finance generated by tourism and maritime trade and the money sent back to Greece from Greeks settled overseas.

## Classical Greece

Out of the darkness there eventually came light, and the first signs of what was to become the greatest period in Greek history. Because Greece had been so insular, people focused on their own communities, and this led to the emergence of the city-states from about the ninth century B.C. onward. They functioned totally independently of each other, forming alliances, trading, and going to war just like separate nations.

Eventually the two strongest city-states to emerge were Athens and Sparta. Sparta had been a Dorian stronghold, and from descriptions of its harsh and militaristic way of life it is easy to see where the word "spartan" came from. The Athenians were much more cultured, and by the fifth century B.C. all male Athenians who were not slaves had the vote. The importance of this, at such an early date, can be appreciated when you consider that as recently as the second half of the 20th century there were countries where citizens did not have the vote.

Athens also had military might, as victories over the Persians at Marathon, Mycale, and Salamis showed, and it was this city rather than Sparta that flourished in the sixth and fifth centuries B.C., the era we know as classical Greece.

> **During the Golden Age of Pericles in Athens, the Parthenon was built, drama flourished, and many democratic ideas were introduced.**

This was also known in Athens as the Golden Age of Pericles. Pericles (circa 495–429 B.C.) was an Athenian statesman who introduced revolutionary ideas and encouraged the arts and architecture. During his reign the Parthenon was built, drama flourished (see p. 106), and many democratic ideas were introduced. Pericles initiated the idea that people who worked for the state should be paid for their labor, that free male citizens should have the vote, and that the citizens should decide who governed them. The word "democracy," so close to the

heart of all Americans, derives from the Greek *demokratia*–control by the people.

The arts also flourished in Athens at this time, with dramatists such as Aeschylus and Aristophanes (see pp. 60–61) to the fore. Poetry was already established, notably in the works of Sappho (see pp. 234–235). The great philosophers Socrates, Plato, and Aristotle were pushing back the boundaries of debate.

Rivalry between Athens and Sparta continued and resulted in the Peloponnesian War of 431–404 B.C. Sparta had long dominated the city-states of the Peloponnese, and together they launched attacks on Athens, with Sparta victorious in 404 B.C. In the following year the Athenians revolted and threw the Spartans out of Athens, returning to their cultured and independent way of life.

But there was another threat on the horizon, one that would come not from the Peloponnese, but from the opposite direction: Macedonia to the north.

**Seventeen-century painting depicts "The Siege of Troy."**

## Alexander the Great & the Macedonian Empire

In 382 B.C. at Pella, then the capital of Macedonia, Philip II was born and would be crowned king of Macedonia in 359 B.C. He himself became a powerful enough leader, but his son, Alexander the Great, changed the face of that part of the world forever.

It was obvious from the nature of Greece at that time, with its warring city-states, that it was vulnerable to outside attack, although not even the might of the Persian

**Alexander the Great defeated the Persian king Darius III in 334 B.C.**

army had been able to take control. The Greeks had always somehow managed to raise enough forces to repel any potential invaders, only to return to internal fighting afterward. Philip II and Alexander were going to be attackers of a very different order, as Greece—and the rest of the civilized world—was about to discover.

Philip II had been a prisoner in Thebes at a time when it was the most powerful of the Greek city-states. He observed the workings of their army, and on his return home he adopted Theban military tactics. Macedonia then centered on the fertile plains north of Athens; it was an independent but vulnerable kingdom inhabited by Greek-speaking people. Philip II pulled the Macedonians together, then began to attack neighboring territories, both in the east toward Chalkidiki and on into Thrace, and to the south toward Athens. He at first made a peace pact with Athens, but it did not last long and in 338 B.C., at the Battle of Chaeronia, he defeated the combined armies of the Athenians and his old role models, the Thebans.

In 336 B.C. Philip was assassinated as he prepared to invade Persia, and it is uncertain whether Alexander had a hand in this. Philip was buried at Vergina, between Pella and Mount Olympus. The discovery of his royal tomb in 1977 was one of the greatest archaeological finds in 20th-century Greece. His intact skeleton and the golden treasures buried with him are now on display in the Archaeological Museum at Thessaloniki. Philip was without question one of the most powerful rulers of his time. His power, however, was nothing compared with that of his son.

Alexander was only 20 when his father was assassinated and, as the new ruler of a newly powerful small empire, he was naturally very vulnerable. He did what many great rulers before and since have done: He killed any potential enemies in his own camp. He regained control of Thessaly, which had rebelled against the Macedonians, did the same against Thrace, and then again, in ruthless fashion, against Thebes, burning the city to the ground and imprisoning its luckless inhabitants.

With these swift, strong, and brutal actions, Alexander quickly established himself as a powerful ruler of the then Greek world. He took command of the Macedonian troops, and in 334 B.C. led an army of some 35,000 across the Hellespont (now the Dardanelles). Although outnumbered, they defeated the Persian army, allegedly with the loss of only 110 of their own men. Alexander treated the Persians as mercilessly as he had treated the plotters in his own camp and the rebellious Greek states. His leadership inspired his men, and although frequently outnumbered, they continued to defeat the Persians and pushed on into the Middle East and Egypt.

Though he had by this time complete control of the eastern Mediterranean, Alexander was still not satisfied and headed for India, where he won more victories but at the cost of great numbers of men. He was back in Babylon in 323 B.C., turning his attention to more conquests, when a fever laid him low. He died 11 days later.

It is said that Alexander had a vision not merely to conquer the world but to unite East and West in one large, harmonious empire. Certainly the cities he founded were all civilized and cultured places, and he fervently spread Greek culture and language while taking an interest in the cultures of the lands he conquered. Had Alexander lived, the empire would undoubtedly have expanded even farther, but it was almost inevitable that upon his death no one man could take his place and keep the empire together.

> **It is said that Alexander the Great had a vision not merely to conquer the world but to unite East and West in one large, harmonious empire.**

## Roman Greece

With the death of Alexander, his empire quickly disintegrated, some of the remoter places claiming their independence while three separate areas were still nominally under Macedonian control: Egypt, Persia, and Macedonia/Greece itself. The consequent breakup produced a series of wars and resulted in loss of power for the individual Greek city-states. This so-called Hellenistic Period lasted from the death of Alexander in 323 B.C. right up until a new power emerged. This was the Roman Empire.

The king of Macedonia was now Philip V but his army was nowhere near as strong as its predecessors, and it was defeated in a battle against the expanding Roman might in 200 B.C. Within less than ten years Rome had taken control of what had been Macedonian Greece, but within this territory the Greek city-states such as Athens, Sparta, and Thebes were allowed to maintain their independence. It was a situation that could not last. The city-states were effectively run by Rome anyway; although they joined forces and rebelled against Roman rule, their disparate nature could never be a match for a combined Roman force. In 146 B.C., the Roman Empire took control of the city-states, removing their independence and creating instead a new Roman province called Macedonia.

Apart from the loss of independence, the change was not too detrimental to Greece. The people were allowed to retain the Greek language, and Roman culture boosted rather than diluted Greek culture. Christianity was introduced and became the dominant religion. Under enlightened emperors such as Hadrian, Athens was reborn as a center for the arts, architecture, and politics. Hadrian's Arch, Hadrian's Library, and the Theater of Herodes Atticus in Athens are but a few examples of Rome's positive influence on Greek life. Compared with the later Turkish occupation, it was virtually a return to the Golden Age.

## Eastern (Byzantine) Empire

By the fourth century A.D., the Roman Empire had lost much of its power and had grown so big that it was divided into two, the Western Empire with its headquarters naturally in Rome, and the Eastern Empire, ruled from the "new Rome," modern Istanbul.

Emperor Constantine the Great (circa 280–337) moved the capital of the Eastern Empire to the site of the ancient Greek city of Byzantium, which became Constantinople, which in turn became Istanbul. Work on building the city began in 326, and was completed four years later. It was at first a blend of Greco-Roman culture, but the shift of the empire's center eastward meant that there was an inevitable increase in Oriental influence on life there. Byzantine culture became a blend of Roman Christian and Greek culture with the exoticism of the east.

The focus emphatically shifted from Athens to Constantinople, which blossomed as Athens had done during its Golden Age. Anti-Greek feeling developed, resulting in the eradication of all traces of the old Greek paganism, the closing of the Oracle at Delphi (regarded as the center of the world by the Greeks), and the ending of the Olympic Games, that representation of the Greek spirit. Greece became of little account, and when parts of it were invaded by Slavonic tribes it was of no great concern to what was now referred to as the Byzantine Empire.

Constantinople resisted all attempts to capture by outside forces, and the empire lost little of its territory at this time. The Byzantine Empire continued long after the Western Empire had disappeared, invaded by Goths in 476. The Byzantine Empire remained a force for almost a thousand years, until the Crusaders captured Constantinople in 1204. Many Greeks to this day believe that at some time in the

## Lord Byron & Greece

Support for the Greeks during their War of Independence was widespread in Europe. Volunteers made their way to Greece to fight alongside the resistance movement, many of them from Germany. But the most famous volunteer was the poet Lord Byron (1788–1824). That a young English nobleman and celebrated author should side with the ordinary Greek people was a terrific boost for the cause. Byron even gave his life in the struggle for independence, although not in battle: He died of a fever. The impact of his death was immense.

A Byzantine-style mosaic gleams down from the ceiling of Nea Moni convent on Hios island.

future, Istanbul will return to being Greek Byzantium (a notion that does nothing to help the precarious Greek-Turkish relationship). Given what happened next on Greek territory, such strength of feeling is understandable.

Between the end of the Byzantine Empire and the arrival of the Turks, the Greek people were subjected to waves of other invasions, notably during the Crusades. The Normans arrived on Corfu in 1081 and proceeded to establish themselves there and on the mainland, while in the early 13th century the Venetians and the Franks also occupied large parts of Greece. This resulted in two centuries of squabbling for supremacy, settled only when Turkey took over the vast majority of Greek territory in 1453.

## Turkish Occupation

The Greeks still resent the long period when they were ruled by the Ottoman Empire and when a mosque was built inside the Parthenon, which was itself left to decay. Furthermore, it was during this period that Lord Elgin, then British ambassador at Constantinople, obtained the Elgin Marbles (see p. 55) from the Turkish rulers and shipped them back to Great Britain.

Constantinople fell into Turkish Muslim hands in 1453, the year the Greeks regard the occupation as beginning, even though it was a few more years before the Turks began to infiltrate what is modern Greek territory. When they did, it was with a vengeance. Most of Greece fell into their hands, bar the Ionian islands off the western coast, the Cycladic islands in the Aegean, and small parts of Crete and the mainland.

This was a time of mixed fortunes for the Greeks. Some did well, where the Turks effectively handed over control to a local chieftain, happy that he should make his fortune, as long as he paid his dues to Constantinople and subdued the local populace. In other areas, where a tyrannical Turkish ruler was imposed, entire towns and villages were slaughtered if they offended him. While this was going on, Turkish culture was being introduced, and it lingers on in places such as Ioanina, the capital of Epiros, in Thessaloniki, and, of course, in Thrace, the Greek region closest to Turkey.

The Turks kept control of their empire quite comfortably for more than 300 years. Only toward the end of the 18th century, and into the beginning of the 19th, did moves toward forcibly regaining independence begin to be made.

> The War of Independence began on March 25, 1821, at the Monastery of Ayia Lavra when Archbishop Yermanos of Patra first hoisted the Greek flag in defiance of the Turks.

## War of Independence

Several events spurred the fight for independence. One such occurrence was on Crete in 1770 when the Russian Orthodox Church came to the aid of its Greek Orthodox brothers in a failed attempt to overthrow the Turkish government. Not long after came the French Revolution, which encouraged ordinary Greeks to believe that they, too, could overturn tyrannical rulers.

In 1821 the War of Independence began. On March 25 at the Monastery of Ayia Lavra, just outside Kalavrita near the north coast of the Peloponnese, Archbishop Yermanos of Patra hoisted the Greek flag in defiance of the Turks. The monastery is now a place of pilgrimage on that same date each year, to celebrate the start of the fight to throw out the Turks. After centuries of subjugation, the fight would be won before the decade was out.

Britain, France, and Russia sent official aid to the Greek forces, while the Turks got help from their fellow Muslims, the Egyptians, after promising them Crete and other Turkish territory if victorious. The end of the war came after an accidental naval encounter in Navarino Bay, off the southwest coast of the Peloponnese. The Turkish-Egyptian navy was annihilated, and when soon afterward the mighty Russian Bear declared war directly on Turkey, the Turks capitulated over Greece and agreed to the country's independence. When this was officially formalized in 1830, under the guarantee of Britain, France, and Russia, it was an act of immense importance to the Greek people.

## Post-Independence & the Balkan Wars

Although the Greeks had won their freedom, this was not the start of a peaceful period for the new nation. For one thing, when the various parties involved drew up the boundaries for the new Greece, the result was a long way from being what the people had hoped for. The large regions of Epiros and Macedonia on the mainland remained in Turkish hands, as did the islands of the Dodecanese, while the Ionian islands off the western coast became a British Protectorate. The Greeks had every right to feel that justice had not been done.

Sadly the result was internal conflict, which eventually erupted into a full-blown civil war in 1831, when the former resistance leader and the new country's first president, Ioannis Kapodistrias, was assassinated by two fellow Greeks. The Western powers quickly stepped in again and in 1832 turned Greece into a monarchy under an imposed ruler, King Otto I, who came from Bavaria. Otto was only 17 years old and proved to be a poor choice. The newly liberated Greeks, optimistic for their future, had a double complaint: They had been given a territory much smaller than the present Greece, and Otto handed key positions of power to fellow Germans. Greece appeared to have exchanged one oppressor for another.

In 1862 Otto faced a revolt by his army and civilians alike, and was officially deposed with the cooperation of the Western powers, who provided a replacement in King George I, from Denmark. Greece's second king proved a much better and more popular choice. He returned to the people land that had been seized by the Turks—something Otto had resisted doing—and he pressed further Greek territorial claims against Turkey. By 1878 Thessaly and part of Epiros had been regained as Greek territory.

Further inroads into what was still Turkish territory were much less successful. In 1895 the Cretans revolted against their Ottoman rulers. The revolt was only partially successful. In 1898 Crete was given a high commissioner on behalf of the European powers. The island was eventually reunited with Greece in 1913.

Macedonia proved to be a greater problem. In 1917 Greece attacked Turkish forces in Macedonia, and was overwhelmed by the resultant retaliation, disaster being averted only by the intervention of the other European powers pressing Turkey to desist.

**Young citizens don traditional dress and join in the fun of an Independence Day parade.**

## Balkan Wars

The First Balkan War took place in 1912–1913, a complicated catalog of alliances and old enmities. Greece was not the only country to claim Macedonia from the Turks, as its northern neighbors (Romania, Serbia, and, most of all, Bulgaria) also had their territorial eyes turned toward it—with some historical justification. An up-

rising by Bulgarians living within Macedonia resulted, bizarrely, in the Greeks offering to come to the aid of the Turks. As the fighting intensified, and Turkey sent in troops with a view to getting rid of all the warring parties, the latter united and Turkey was defeated by a combined force of Greek, Bulgarian, Serbian, and Montenegrin armies. Greece reclaimed parts of Macedonia, and Turkey finally ceded Crete to the Greeks.

Hot on the heels of the First Balkan War, a second war in the region erupted that same year, 1913, but lasted only a month. This time Greece and Serbia allied against Bulgaria, which was no match for them.

Greek involvement in World War I was equally complicated. Prime Minister Venizelos was keen to support the British side, but King Constantine I, who was married to the sister of the German kaiser, insisted on neutrality. Veni-

**Constantine I (r. 1913–1917, 1920–1922) re-gained the throne for a short period before a second abdication in favor of his son.**

zelos went from Athens to Greece's second city, Thessaloniki, and set up a government in opposition. Unsurprisingly, the British and the French recognized Venizelos' government.

All appeared to be going well for Greece, as its troops under Venizelos fought on the side of the Allies and the king was forced to abdicate, handing the throne to his son Alexander. After the war, Greece reclaimed Thrace from the Bulgarians and Turks, and also islands in the Aegean that Turkey had continued to occupy.

Venizelos, however, made one claim too many. Instead of settling for what Greece had been given, he also staked a claim to the territory of Smyrna on the Turkish Aegean coast, which was indeed mainly inhabited by Greeks. In 1919 Greek troops landed there. Initially they made inroads, but the Turks under their powerful and forward-looking new leader, Kemal Ataturk, fought off the Greeks and drove them out of Smyrna. They also slaughtered the remaining Greek population and destroyed the city.

The result of all this was that Ataturk had the upper hand, and the infamous "Exchange of Populations" took place in 1923. Turkey, a vastly bigger country than Greece, received about 400,000 Turks back from Greece, but in return about 1.3 million Greeks living in Turkey were forced to leave. This immediately added about 25 percent to Greece's population—for the most part poor, dispossessed refugees. They may have added to the music and culture of Greece, but their arrival had a devastating effect on the economy, which took a long time to recover given the general state of world affairs in the 1920s and 1930s.

## World War II & the Greek Civil War

It is said that Greece's entry into World War II began with a single word: *Ochi*–
No. This was allegedly the response by Prime Minister General Metaxas (1871–
1941) to the request from Mussolini to allow Italian troops to pass through
Greece. Mussolini's ultimatum was delivered on October 28, 1940, and Metaxas's
curt reply to the Italian foreign minister in Athens propelled Greece into the war.
That response is commemorated every year on October 28, a public holiday
known as Ochi Day. It's a good story, but in fact the response would have been
delivered in French, the language of diplomacy, and is thought to have been *"C'est
la guerre*–It's war."

War it was, and despite initial resistance in the mountains of northern Greece, Italian
troops eventually moved down from Albania and, with naval support from Germany,
had occupied Greece and most of its islands within little over six months. By this time
General Metaxas was dead, and the king and his government were in exile.

Greek resistance continued, however. It was focused on the National Liberation
Front (EAM, its Greek initials), which worked alongside the British secret services
against the occupying forces. There were some successful heroics, but sadly, too, the
Communist-dominated EAM was divided into two warring factions fighting for control
of a peacetime Greece. When the war ended for the rest of Europe in 1945, Greece
plunged into a bitter civil war, which lasted until 1949. One side of that story is told in
the book *Eleni* by American-Greek author Nicholas Gage, which recounts the dreadful
events in his family's village in the mountains of northern Greece.

The dispute arose when the British occupying forces formed an interim government
with the EAM. The British wanted to see a return of the monarchy and tried to reduce
the influence of EAM, which went down badly with the men who had been risking their
lives for Greek freedom.

In 1946 a right-wing government was elected, and in 1947 a vote was taken in favor
of reinstating the monarchy. By this time the Communists were marginalized, with the
help of significant U.S. support for the right-wing government. EAM found itself again

### Under German Occupation

Greece suffered terribly in World War II,
and the full horrors of the years of
occupation have never been fully told.
About half a million Greeks died of
starvation, many of them on the streets
of Athens, and some of these appalling
stories are depicted in the city's War
Museum (see pp. 75–76). Many more
were the victims of atrocities, and the
dreadful events that took place are still
remembered by the older generation.

The Greek Jewish population was
particularly hard hit, and in some towns
and cities where there had been only
a small Jewish population, it was completely wiped out. Even in Thessaloniki,
which at one time had the largest Jewish
population in Europe, their numbers were
reduced from 60,000 before the war to a
few hundred afterward. In all, 87 percent
of Greek Jews were killed.

In some parts of Greece, however, the
war had less of a direct impact, especially
on those islands where the occupying
forces were Italian, who were not far removed in temperament from the Greeks
themselves and were likely to establish a
working relationship with them.

fighting a resistance movement, but this time against fellow Greeks and their allied support. The conflict was every bit as bloody as more recent Balkan wars. Eventually the right-wing forces emerged with a precarious victory.

These events may have taken place half a century ago, but be circumspect in discussing the war and its aftermath. For some people the memories are as vivid as yesterday.

## The Colonels

It is hardly surprising that after the turbulence of the last few centuries, followed by a series of wars large and small in the first half of the 20th century, Greece did not immediately settle down to a period of peace and stability.

In the 1950s Cyprus became a trouble spot, where Greek terrorists were active on an island governed by the British but which they felt was territorially Greek. The granting of independence to the island was a compromise solution that would prove to have disastrous consequences.

In the 1960s a series of changes in leadership, both politically and in the monarchy, led to increased divisiveness. Greece, for all its history of resistance fighters and a frequent sense of anarchy, has traditionally had a right-wing ruling party. The more moderate rule by Prime Minister George Papandreou (1888–1968) was seen as far too liberal by many, and run-ins with the monarchy over who should have control of the army (among other things) resulted in Papandreou resigning in 1965.

This strong character was followed by several ineffectual leaders, and on April 21, 1967, a right-wing military junta led by a group of colonels seized control of the country. It was the kind of rule more familiar to Central American republics: mass arrests, torture, disappearances, martial law, news censorship, and clampdowns on civil liberties. After the moderate Papandreou, the country was now ruled by a hard-line right-winger, Colonel George Papadopoulos (1919–1996). King Constantine II (born 1940) was exiled after a failed attempt to overthrow the junta.

**With Andreas Papandreou's death in 1996, Greece lost one of its most prominent politicians of the 20th century.**

The colonels brought about their own downfall, however, in attempting to seize control of Cyprus. Instead of succeeding, there was a counterinvasion by Turkish troops who took over 40 percent of the island, where they remain to this day. The Greek Army mutinied against its own leaders. The colonels had already demonstrated their ruthlessness at home when they killed a number of students demonstrating against the regime at the Athens Polytechnic on November 17, 1973. No one has ever established the number of students killed that day (still commemorated in Greece), but the Polytechnic still bears the bullet holes, as the nation bears the scars of the colonels' junta.

## After the Colonels

Once democracy was returned to Greece, the country entered a much more stable and prosperous period, which included a huge boom in tourism and membership in the European Union.

After the defeat of the colonels, former Prime Minister Constantine Karamanlis returned from his exile in Paris and won a good majority for his New Democracy party

**Greek partisans, noted for their fierce tenacity, celebrate liberation in 1944.**

(Nea Dimokratia) in the first democratic elections. However, one of his defeated rivals, Andreas Papandreou (1919–1996), the son of George Papandreou, with his new PASOK Socialist party, played a center-stage role in Greek politics for the next two decades. Karamanlis held a referendum on the monarchy, and a sizable majority of the people voted against the return of the exiled king.

Karamanlis himself had seven years of power before PASOK and Papandreou were voted overwhelmingly into office in 1981 to form the first left-wing government in Greece in almost 50 years. Papandreou embarked on a campaign of populist reforms, including equal rights for all, increases in pensions, the right to have a civil marriage in a church-dominated society, and other similar measures. However, the cost of some of those reforms meant that the economy suffered, so Papandreou did not enjoy universal popularity. PASOK promised removal of U.S. air bases and withdrawal from NATO, but these promises were never fulfilled.

Two elections in 1989 proved inconclusive and provided only coalition governments. Then, in spring 1990, the New Democracy party was returned with the slenderest of majorities. This swing back to the right lasted less than four years, and in October 1993 Andreas Papandreou returned as prime minister at the age of 74.

With Papandreou's death in 1996, Greece had lost one of its most prominent and influential politicians of the 20th century. In March 2004 the president of the New Democracy party, Kostas Karamanlis (the nephew of Constantine Karamanlis), was elected prime minister. Greece had once more swung back to the right. The new Karamanlis government brought in strict economic measures, and while these naturally proved unpopular with the Greek public, they did bring the country steady economic growth. ∎

# The Olympics: A Look Back

It just seemed right that the Olympic Games be held in Greece—what with the original games first held in Olympia in 776 B.C. and taking place for more than a millennium after, and the modern games being revived in Athens in 1896. So when Athens was awarded the privilege to host the 2004 games, the country became a hotbed of excitement and activity.

The first revival of the Olympic Games in 1896, held in Athens

Athens underwent a massive makeover that included new sports venues and upgraded transportation systems. The Olympic Stadium at Maroussi was the main venue, with Killimarmaro—the 1896 stadium—the venue for archery and the close of the marathon. All this, for a centuries-old tradition.

In Ancient Olympia, the early games were little more than local sprinting races. Later, events such as horse racing and wrestling

were added, as well as poetry and music contests. The competitors began to come from farther afield.

During the games of 720 B.C., it was decided that athletes should compete in the nude, and for this reason female spectators were banned. Nevertheless, crowds of some 20,000 would gather on the raised terraces overlooking the track in Olympia, which has survived to this day. It is still the place where the Olympic flame is kindled, using the rays of the sun, and from where the flame is conveyed to herald the new competition. During opening ceremonies, the Greek team leads the procession of competing nations in honor of their ancestors.

After being revived in 1896, the modern games have been held every four years—with the exceptions of 1916, when the games were scheduled to be held in Berlin, and 1940 and 1944, during the World Wars.

Though the games are supposed to be apolitical, world events are inseparable. About one-third of the competing nations, including the U.S., withdrew from the Moscow Olympics of 1980, protesting the Soviet invasion of Afghanistan. It was almost inevitable that the U.S.S.R. would withdraw from the 1984 Olympics in reprisal, which were held in Los Angeles (the host nations are decided six years ahead).

World events continue to have an impact on the Olympics: In the aftermath of the September 11 attacks on the World Trade Center, security for the Athens Olympics was unprecedented, with more than 45,000 security personnel on duty—far outnumbering the 10,500 competitors.

Despite such problems—and there were equivalent controversies right back at the very start of the games—more countries take part each year. Look at the statistics: The 1896 Olympics were held among 13 nations, with just nine sports represented and a grand total of 42 events. Today, some 186 nations are affiliated with the International Olympic Committee, which is based in Lausanne, Switzerland, and 201 nations were represented at the 2004 Olympics, competing in 28 sports ranging from rowing to track & field to table tennis.

A museum in the town of Olympia tells the full story of the games, both ancient and modern (see p. 131).

## Pentathlon Pointers

While the only sport in which you can compete in Olympia today is outrunning the hordes of tourists, centuries ago men—no women, please!—came to win honor at the Ancient Olympiads. One of the most important events, added to the roster in 708 B.C., was the pentathlon, which combined discus, javelin, jumping, running, and wrestling. The exact order in which the events were held is unknown, but ancient texts reveal that wrestling was last in the lineup. The ultimate victor needed to excel in speed, strength, skill, and endurance, accounting for each event's own peculiarities.

For the discus throw, the athlete stood facing the opposite direction of his intended target—a 40- to 60-degree delineated area—holding the discus along its outer edge with the tips of his fingers; he then quickly rotated 540 degrees and released it, flinging it as far as possible within the marked area. The javelin was made of wood with a metal tip, and had a leather handle attached in the middle for increased accuracy. For the long jump, the Olympians used lead or stone weights, called *halteres*, to help lengthen their jump: By swinging the halteres backward mid-jump, the shift of momentum carried them farther.

The fundamentals of running were very much the same for the ancient athletes as they are today, but the foot events were not always so streamlined: The *hoplitodromos*, for example, required competitors to race in 40 to 60 pounds (18–27 kg) of military armor. Ancient wrestling, too, was somewhat similar to today's, except the men were nude. Biting and genital grabbing were not allowed, although wrestlers did find a strategic edge by coating themselves in lard.

# The Arts

It is almost impossible for any kind of creative artist to throw off the shackles of history, of Greek myths and legends, of the long shadow cast by centuries of Orthodox religion. Most artists at some stage, be they writers or painters or jewelers, will explore that heritage in their own work, albeit by sometimes giving it a modern interpretation.

## Visual Arts

Ancient Greece excelled at sculpture. Greek statues often combine power and strength with grace and agility. The first statues were produced in the Archaic period, about the eighth and seventh centuries B.C. when trade with Egypt was flourishing. Egyptian statues were brought to Greece and at first merely imitated. You can see the similarities: upright bodies, arms by the side, hands held rigidly attached to the body. Soon, however, the pupils were excelling their tutors, and within a century the Greeks were adding their own flourishes, giving the bodies movement, and making them more realistic. Back in Egypt, the statues remained exactly as they had always been.

> Ancient Greece excelled at sculpture. Greek statues often combine power and strength with grace and agility.

To see the developments in Greek sculpture, take a stroll through the centuries in the National Archaeological Museum in Athens (see pp. 82–85), where a knowledgeable guide will talk you through the ages and take you to the highlights of the collection. Some of the greatest Greek work is not in its homeland, of course. In addition to the thorny question of the Elgin Marbles (see p. 55), the Louvre alone boasts both the Venus de Milo and the Winged Victory of Samothrace.

The issue of the Elgin Marbles is important to Greece because temple friezes such as these are not merely works of art in themselves but integral parts of the temples for which they were made. The finest sculptors were hired, and friezes were usually complete narratives, working their way around the temple, depicting such legends as the Battle of the Gods and Giants, which adorned the Siphnian treasury at Delphi.

Vase painting was another traditional Greek skill, which also often told a story, and many fine examples reside in museums throughout the country. This art is especially important, as it tells so much about the lives of the ancient Greeks. The most striking style is the combination of red and black colors. At different periods either the figures or the background would be carved from the clay, and the rest of the scene painted in black or dark brown. Vase painting was at its height in the fifth century B.C., when it attracted the best artists, who all wanted to work in this new, exciting medium. It could be said to have laid the groundwork for the representational art that was later to flourish throughout Europe.

In the more modern visual arts, one area where Greece is very strong is that of photography. Greece has often been said to have the best light in the world for

**Modern buildings like the Syntagma Metro station provide bold new space for public art.**

photography, with the clarity of the Aegean and its deep blue skies and blinding white houses inspiring its photographers to explore their land most thoroughly and effectively. Greek traditions are captured by the native photographer's lens in a way that the traveler passing through can never hope to attain. Young photographers to watch out for include Nick Apostolopoulos (born 1955), whose sports photography has won a Fuji Award, and Andreas Zacharatos (born 1961), whose award-winning work varies from jazz in Athens to rural landscapes.

Greece has not had an abundance of painters of international renown. Its one artist known throughout the world was dubbed El Greco, The Greek, when he went to Spain. Domenikos Theotokopoulos, El Greco (1541–1614), was born in Iraklio on Crete but did his greatest work in Italy and Spain, and is more accurately thought of as a Spanish artist.

A Greek artist whose work is well worth investigating is the naïve painter, Theophilos Hadzimichalis (1873–1934), known as Theophilos. He was a prolific worker and examples of his work can be seen in many places, including the Folk Museum in Athens and in the house in which he lived, now a museum, just outside Mitilini on Lesvos (see p. 236). He was an eccentric, prone to wearing traditional Greek costumes, often penniless, and prepared to paint murals on taverna walls in exchange for a meal or a drink. Though unsophisticated, his work has a vibrancy and energy that leaps from the canvas.

## Architecture

If there is one artistic skill that towers above all others in Greek history it is that of architecture. Take one look at any of the better-preserved temples, such as the Parthenon or the Temple of Aphaia on Egina, and you know that ancient Greek craftsmen were masters.

Greek temples were originally influenced by Egypt, but quickly took on a style and grace all their own. This was in part due to the building materials available. While the Egyptians worked in stone and created a somber grandeur from it, the Greeks were using limestone and, later, marble to create structures of grace and light.

If anyone knows anything at all about Greek architecture it is that there are two main "orders" or types of columns, Doric and Ionic. The name Doric comes from the Dorians (see p. 26), and is most easily identified because the columns do not stand on a base. They rise straight from the floor and are usually closer together than in the Ionic style, giving a more claustrophobic feeling. The style spread throughout Greece and

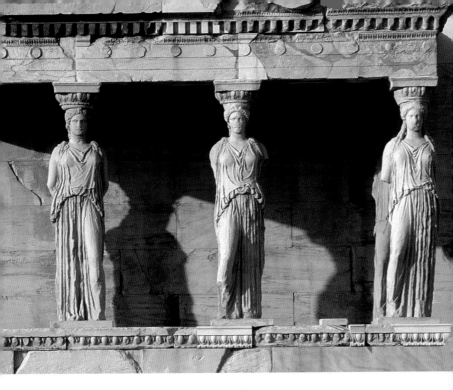

Copies of the original six graceful caryatids, each well over 6 feet (2 m) high, support the southern portico of the Erechtheion, facing the Parthenon in Athens.

into southern Italy and Sicily, and an outstanding example—though imagination will be required to appreciate it today—is the Temple of Zeus at Olympia (see p. 130).

The Ionic style comes not from the Ionian islands off the west coast but from Ionia, the ancient name for western Asia Minor, where modern Turkey now is. Ionic columns are placed farther apart and are also generally narrower than Doric columns, creating a greater sense of space on temple frontages. They are also usually placed on a small base, and their capitals are more ornate than the plain Doric style. Good examples are at Ephesus in Turkey, in the area where the name originated, and on the Erechtheion on the Acropolis in Athens.

The most famous piece of Greek architecture in the world, the Parthenon on the Acropolis, combines both Doric and Ionic columns. To get a fuller sense of its original beauty, see the small-scale model in the National Archaeological Museum in Athens. To understand some of the drudgery needed to create the temple's beauty, look for displays about its construction in the New Acropol is Museum (see pp. 58–59).

If the workers provided the 90 percent of perspiration that is needed to produce great works of art, then it was the architect Pheidias who provided the 10 percent of genius or inspiration that is also required. Pheidias was the great sculptor of his day. He also produced the statue of Olympian Zeus that stood at the center of Olympia and the giant statue of Athena Nike that served as the centerpiece of the Parthenon itself.

Temples became churches, and the other great aspect of Greek architecture, visible from the tiniest rural village to the very center of urban Athens, is the Byzantine church. These red-tiled buildings may be big or small, but all have certain elements in common.

The altar in a Byzantine church is always to the east, and always concealed behind the screen known as the iconostasis. In front of this there are three main aisles, and above the central aisle, in the largest open part of the church, is the main dome. This is invariably decorated with a painting of Christ Pantokrator, or Christ All Powerful, gazing down unremittingly on the congregation. Another icon of Christ will usually be found over the main door to the church, to greet you as you enter. The interiors of Byzantine churches are always elaborately decorated with mosaics and friezes, the walls hung with icons and votive offerings—a real assault on the senses, especially during services when the air is filled with the smell of incense and the sound of holy chanting.

A look at Athens today may leave you wondering what became of Greece's glorious architectural heritage, and it is true that few modern buildings stand out. Some of the finest were influenced by German architects in the 19th century, notably Ernst Ziller. Among other buildings, Ziller was responsible for the magnificent 1896 Olympic Stadium.

**The eight-stringed *bouzouki*, a long-necked mandolin, traditionally accompanies singing and dancing in Greece.**

## Music

Greece is one of the few countries in the world that has not succumbed to Western pop music. Turn on a radio at random and you can almost guarantee that the first music you hear will be distinctly Greek. It may be modern Greek pop music, but it will still have that unique sound born of the bouzouki (the mandolin-like stringed instrument that epitomizes Greek music) and the influences of Asia, with definite echoes of Indian music.

That's not to say that young Greeks are not aware of the latest rock bands and trends. They are. And you will have no trouble finding indoor and outdoor discos, outdoor rock concerts in summer, and clubs where blues, rock, and jazz are just as good as back home. But young Greeks grow up with the music of Greece in their blood ... and certainly in their ears, for wherever you go in Greece you will hear music: in tavernas and bars, on ferries, in buses, escaping through the windows of houses and cars.

Every region, every island has its own folk music, although not much of it is truly native as the imported oriental influences are ubiquitous. Everywhere you will come across official music and dance festivals (the two are virtually inseparable in Greece), as well as impromptu sessions when the chairs are pushed back and the mood of the music simply takes over.

*Rembetika* is the blues of Greece, with a blend of jazz. As with those types of music, it is created from various influences yet combines them all to produce a style that is unique. No one is sure where the name came from, but the music came to Greece with the exchange of populations that took place in 1923 (see p. 36). Greeks who had been living in Turkey—most of them born there—brought back with them the distinctive oriental music that was popular in cafés and bars. The people who returned were for the most part desperately poor, many of them forced to live in primitive conditions around Pireas, the port of Athens. Here drinking dens grew up where musicians and singers would meet, their music expressing the poverty of their lives and their feelings of alienation. In this way the Greek blues was born.

Rembetika lives on, just like the blues in America, because it expresses heartfelt feelings that are both particular to a certain class of people and at the same time universal. If you want an insight into the Greek soul, seek out one of the rembetika clubs in Athens and spend an evening watching and listening. If you do not understand the words, you will understand the sincere sentiments being expressed. Be prepared for a late night, too.

## Greek Instruments

The music of Greece is unique and homegrown, both in style and in the instruments used. The following instruments form the backbone of traditional Greek sound: The lyre—a relative of the harp, famous for accompanying Orpheus into Hades—has relinquished the lead role it enjoyed in antiquity. However, its descendant, the lute, known on Crete as the *laouto*, is still a Greek mainstay. Similar string instruments include the *tamboura* and the *outi*. In addition, you'll seldom see a band without a tambourine, called either a *defi*, *dachares*, or *tsaboutsas*, depending on where you are in Greece. Finally, a unique woodwind is the *zoumas*, known elsewhere as the *shawm*.

The most famous Greek musician of contemporary times is undoubtedly Mikis Theodorakis (born 1925), best known for his sound track music for the 1965 movie *Zorba the Greek*. No one will get through a visit to Greece without hearing either the title track of *Zorba* or that of another famous Greek movie, *Never on a Sunday*, whose music won an Academy Award for composer Manos Hadjidakis (1925–1994). Theodorakis's music—at least in those days—was known as Entechno. This has nothing to do with modern Techno music but is a fusion of the folk and rembetika styles that produced a new type of music with a more contemporary feel without losing the sounds of the past.

Theodorakis studied at the Paris Conservatoire, but became critical of the Greek classical musical establishment—and the Greek establishment generally. When the colonels came to power in 1967, two years after *Zorba*'s success had made Theodorakis a Greek musical hero, he was imprisoned and his music was banned for being subversive.

Greece produced a composer of international standing in Iannis Xenakis (1922–2001). Also an architect, he worked as assistant to the innovative French architect Le Corbusier (1887–1965) from 1948 until 1960. Xenakis's work showed a corresponding interest in the mathematical and harmonious elements in music. He founded the School of Mathematical and Automatic Music in 1966. He sometimes worked with Greek themes, such as providing music for a production of the *Oresteia*, but Xenakis moved to France in the late 1940s, and became a French citizen in 1965.

Restored theaters like Epidavros have brought classical Greek drama to new audiences.

## Literature

The influence of Greece on the literature of the world has been profound and the past resonates down through the centuries. Modern literature has its roots in Homer (see pp. 330–331), and those roots still nourish the literary tree. Arguably the greatest novel of the 20th century was *Ulysses*, by the Irish writer James Joyce (1882–1941), who based the plan for his complex and experimental book on Homer's *Odyssey*.

It could be said that the Greeks invented travel writing too, as the first such book was *Hellados Periegesis (Description of Greece)* by the historian and traveler Pausanias, who lived in the second century A.D. and provided this guide for Roman visitors to Greece's classical sites. It is as useful today as it was then, as indeed are many books by historians that give us literary accounts of life in ancient Greece, notably the *Histories* by Herodotus (circa 484–425 B.C.) and the *History of the Peloponnesian War* by Thucydides (circa 460–400 B.C.).

Herodotus has been called the Father of History, and his book is regarded as the first major work of nonfiction, slightly predating Thucydides's *History of the Peloponnesian War*. It includes sections on the Persian Wars (490 and 481–479 B.C.) but also illuminates life in those days with accounts of legends, customs, beliefs, traditions, and everyday events that bring the period vividly alive once again.

The value of Thucydides's book is immense for several reasons, not least because of the chronicle it gives of the war itself. Though Thucydides participated in the war as an

Athenian commander, he also saw the value of recording events, and of trying to give an objective rather than partisan account. He interviewed combatants and quotes the speeches of the leaders in a manner that serves as a template to this day.

The great Greek poets from Homer to Elytis are dealt with elsewhere (see pp. 238–239), as are the great dramatists Aeschylus, Sophocles, and Euripides (pp. 60–61) and modern novelist Nikos Kazantzakis (see p. 278). But Greece has many other fine writers, less known to the outside world simply because of the language they write in. The enterprising Athenian publisher Kedros has published a superb series called "Modern Greek Writers," translating its works into English for the first time.

Greek writers still grapple with the big themes, as shown by Dido Sotiriou (1909–2004) in her novel *Farewell Anatolia*. A best seller in Greece since it was published in 1962, the book recounts the forced exchange of Greek and Turkish populations in 1923. Its publication in a Turkish translation in 1970 was welcomed as providing a greater understanding of the suffering on both sides, and in 1990 the author was awarded the highest literary award in Greece, the prize of the Academy of Athens.

Eugenia Fakinou (born 1945) is another female writer whose books deal with what it means to be Greek. Her first novel, *Astradeni*, has been in print since it was published in 1982. It tells a tale familiar to many Greeks, of a family forced by circumstance to leave its island home to move to Athens in search of a better life. The young girl who tells the story, Astradeni, depicts the changes with the bold, simple gaze of a child.

Petros Abatzoglou (1931–2004) wrote several novels and collections of stories, but for an outsider perhaps the most interesting is *What Does Mrs. Freeman Want?* It

# EXPERIENCE: It's Greek to You

Travels in Greece are enormously more pleasurable if you can speak at least a little of the language. Greek is one of those languages, like Dutch, that is not spoken very widely, and so many visitors know little or none of the language, and rely on Greeks speaking English or some other language to get by. But in the more remote and beautiful parts of Greece, many of the people you would want to speak to don't speak anything but Greek. If you're catching a bus, the destination on the front may be written in the Greek alphabet, and if you're driving you'll find plenty of road signs in Greek only. You could literally be lost without some Greek.

Any knowledge of Greek is not only welcomed by the locals, it broadens your understanding of the people and the country hugely. And there's probably no better way to learn the language than in a total-immersion course in Athens. You'll find plenty of companies that provide such courses, including the **Language Travel Company** (*www.the languagetravelcompany.com*), which offers courses for all levels including business speakers as well as for Ancient Greek scholars, and the **Hellenic Language School Alexander the Great** (*www .alexander-edu.org*), with locations in Athens, Thessaloniki, and Chania, Crete.

Most people, though, will want to take the conventional Modern Greek course, fitting it in with sightseeing that itself affords plenty of opportunity to practice the language. Students can take 10, 20, or 30 lessons a week, and can opt to stay with a Greek family—which could be a learning experience in more ways than one.

gives the Greek perspective on a pair of English tourists, who come to soak up the sun while the book's narrator observes them and soaks up the ouzo.

## Cinema

Movies as varied as *For Your Eyes Only, Shirley Valentine, The Magus, Captain Corelli's Mandolin,* and *Boy on a Dolphin* have all been shot in Greece. Several Greek movies have won Academy Awards in various categories including, not surprisingly, music.

First and foremost must be *Zorba the Greek,* made by director Michael Cacoyannis in 1964 and starring Anthony Quinn in the title role. The first notable modern Greek movie had been four years earlier with *Never on a Sunday,* which picked up five Oscar nominations, including best director for Jules Dassin, who also starred in the movie, and best actress for Melina Mercouri. It won an Oscar for best song—the irresistible title tune written by Greek composer Manos Hadjidakis.

The most distinguished contemporary Greek moviemaker is Theo Angelopoulos, born in Athens in 1935. He first came to prominence in 1974 with *Traveling Players,* the story of a group of actors moving physically through Greece but also temporally through Greek history. Angelopoulos's 1986 movie, *The Bee-Keeper,* also tells of a journey through Greece, this time a retired schoolteacher transporting his bees on a truck and forging a relationship with a young hitchhiker along the way. Its feel for Greece's landscape, people, and history make it a movie that should not be missed by anyone seeking to understand the country.

Angelopoulos won the Palme d'Or at Cannes in 1998 for *Eternity and a Day,* the most prestigious award any Greek moviemaker has ever achieved. His most recent movie, *The Weeping Meadows* trilogy, is one of Greece's most expensive film productions. ∎

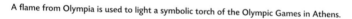

**A flame from Olympia is used to light a symbolic torch of the Olympic Games in Athens.**

From the Parthenon and the treasures of the National Archaeological Museum to the bustle of the city streets

# Athens

Ceremonial guard, or *Evzone*

# Athens

Athens is steeped in history. You will want to visit its Parthenon, of course, but don't overlook the other ancient sites and museums, many of which have undergone a marvelous makeover. Then take a break from culture and stroll the Plaka district, the old but touristy part of town—or just wander. Regular visitors know that the streets of Athens are full of wonderful treasures.

Almost four million people—one-third of the Greek population—live within the greater Athens area. This is a busy metropolis whose main problems are an excess of traffic and, in summer, the consequent *nefos* (smog).

The 2004 Olympic Games in Athens was a great incentive for change. Suddenly all those half-completed projects that had been lingering for years have come to fruition, such as the Syntagma subway station and Omonoia Square. The city's face-lift has revived many of the neglected building facades, and sidewalks have been enhanced with pink marble. And the steady expansion of the Metro subway system, the introduction of "green" buses, new trams, and trolley services are helping to eradicate the old problem of pollution.

The nefos is a result of Athens's attractive location, with hills on three sides trapping the smog—a situation similar to that in Los Angeles. The Aegean lies to the south, beyond the port of Pireas, which merges with Athens. Anyone who feels that central Athens is busy should try spending some time in the bustle and chaos of its port. Little wonder that the sleepy islands are of such appeal. But spend just a short time in Athens, and its charms start to surface. ■

## NOT TO BE MISSED:

# Acropolis

*Akro poli* means "upper city," and many Greek towns have an acropolis. Athens has the most famous, capped as it is by the Parthenon. Whether you see it in daylight when approaching from the airport, at night from your hotel balcony, or up close when you visit, the Parthenon dominates Athens, a constant reminder of the Golden Age of ancient Greece.

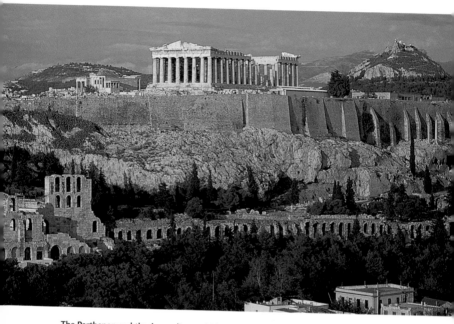

The Parthenon and the Acropolis on which it stands loom over modern Athens.

**Acropolis**

🅜 Map p. 52

☎ 210/321-0219
Museum:
210/323-6665

💲 $$

🚇 Metro: Akropoli

**Visitor Information**

✉ Athens Tourist Information, Amalias 26

☎ 210/331-0716

You can reach the entrance to the Acropolis by walking up one of the two approaches to the western end. The more atmospheric of the two is through the Plaka district where you will spot occasional handwritten signs directing you up the steep streets. Local storekeepers are used to being asked directions as the route is not always obvious. The only approach from Dionysiou Areopagitou, a street recently pedestrianized for visitors, is easier to follow.

Evidence of a settlement on the southern slopes of the Acropolis dates the first habitation in Athens to about 3000 B.C. The buildings that remain date mainly from the fifth century B.C., when ancient Athens reached its pinnacle during the Golden Age of Pericles (see pp. 28–29). Pericles hired the finest workmen of the day, including the master sculptor Pheidias. He was the main artistic director of the **Parthenon,** a temple and the first building to be raised on the site. The great architect Iktinos was probably responsible for its overall design and construction.

It is now well known that the Parthenon has no straight lines in its construction, the apparent symmetry created by gently tapering columns and steps. The building is designed using repeated ratios of 9:4, for such aspects as the gap between columns in relation to the width of a single column, or the width of the building in relation to its height. Originally the focus of the building was a 40-foot-high (12 m) golden statue of the goddess Athena, after whom the city is named. A model of the Parthenon as it would have looked then can be seen in the National Archaeological Museum (see pp. 82–85).

The building took nine years to construct, was finished in 438 B.C., and is made from marble quarried locally. Flecks of iron in the marble give the building its wonderfully warm golden glow in evening light.

For the last few years the Parthenon has been roped off to prevent visitors from destroying the precious marble. The sheer number of feet and hands of those who come to admire, and not vandalize, has had to be curtailed. The skyline is usually marred by the sight of a crane, but this is vital reconstruction and preservation work, as in places some of the marble has cracked and needs to be bound together.

Several other buildings on top of the Acropolis are worthy of a closer look. To the right soon after you enter is the small **Temple of Athena Nike,** added in 427–424 B.C. to celebrate victories by the Athenians in their wars with the Persians. Athena Nike means Athena of Victory. (The Parthenon was dedicated to another aspect of the goddess: Athena Promachos, Athena the Champion.) In 1686 the temple was destroyed by the Turks then occupying Greece. It has been reconstructed twice, most recently in 1936–1940.

The Turks wreaked havoc on the Acropolis, building a mosque inside the Parthenon, which was left to fall into ruin before parts of it were sold off to Lord Elgin (see Elgin Marbles, below). They also used the building as a weaponry store, which resulted in

## Elgin Marbles

In 1801 Thomas Bruce, the Earl of Elgin, was British ambassador to the Porte, the Turkish government that was then in control in Athens. The Turks were using antiquities from the crumbling Acropolis for building materials. Lord Elgin was allowed to save some stones and sculptures, which he ended up selling to the British Museum in 1816. The most famous of these, friezes from the Parthenon, are the Elgin Marbles.

Every Greek envisions the marbles being returned to their proper home. The plan is to place them in a special gallery in the New Acropolis Museum. Only time will tell whether the gallery will ever see its controversial appointees.

further damage when the arsenal exploded after being fired upon. Over to your left as you approach the Parthenon is the **Erechtheion,** added between 421 and 395 B.C. It is said that the first olive tree in Athens sprouted here when the goddess

## The Acropolis

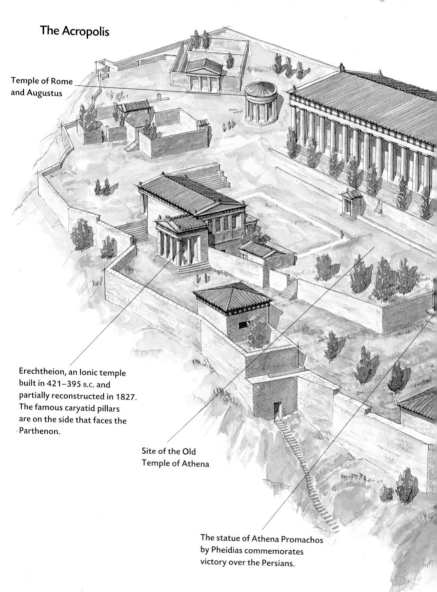

Temple of Rome and Augustus

Erechtheion, an Ionic temple built in 421–395 B.C. and partially reconstructed in 1827. The famous caryatid pillars are on the side that faces the Parthenon.

Site of the Old Temple of Athena

The statue of Athena Promachos by Pheidias commemorates victory over the Persians.

Athena touched the ground with her spear. An olive tree has been kept growing here since 1917 as a symbol of this. The building includes the Porch of the Caryatids, where the supporting columns have been sculpted in the shapes of six maidens. Those now on the site are copies: Five of the originals are in the Acropolis Museum, the other was carried off by Lord Elgin. The **museum** at the far end of the site had an impressive collection, but most of it has been moved to the newer New Acropolis Museum, which is located south of the Acropolis (see pp. 58–59). ■

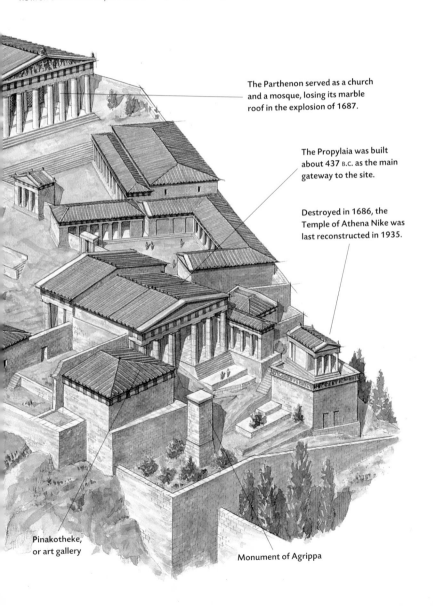

The Parthenon served as a church and a mosque, losing its marble roof in the explosion of 1687.

The Propylaia was built about 437 B.C. as the main gateway to the site.

Destroyed in 1686, the Temple of Athena Nike was last reconstructed in 1935.

Pinakotheke, or art gallery

Monument of Agrippa

# South of the Acropolis

The approach to the Acropolis from the south side (the usual route if you arrive by bus) is a walk up a modern pathway that snakes up through trees and behind the most prominent building on the southern slopes, the Herodes Atticus Theater.

A carving at the Theater of Dionysos shows signs of corrosion by weather and pollution.

**Herodes Atticus Theater (Teatro Irodou Attikou)**

🅰 Map p. 52

✉ Leoforos Dionysiou Areopagitou

🕒 Only open for special performances

Ⓜ Metro: Akropoli

Unlike the Acropolis buildings, the **Herodes Atticus Theater (Teatro Irodou Attikou)** dates from the Roman period and was built in A.D. 161–174 by a businessman from Marathon with the grand name of Tiberius Claudius Atticus Herodes. The theater, restored in 1955, seats 5,000 people and is still used during the Athens Festival

from June to September.

Farther along to the South below the Acropolis, the unrestored **Theater of Dionysos (Teatro Dionysiou)** provides a great contrast to the grandlooking Herodes Atticus Theater next door. Bear in mind that the remains that appears here are only part of a large complex, which seated 17,000 spectators at its height. The original Greek theater, built in 342–326 B.C., was much expanded during the Roman period.

The Dionysos was used for a multitude of purposes—most notably for gladiatorial fights and annual drama contests. When you look at the stage here, you are looking at the place where drama was born. This is where Sophocles and Aristophanes first had their works produced—although not on the remains that stand today, which date from Roman times. Among those remains are marble thrones for dignitaries, and marble flooring put in by Emperor Nero in the first century A.D. Walk back toward the rock of the Acropolis to see the unusual chapel of the Lady of the Caves, inside a cave in the rocks.

Across from the Theater of Dionysos is Athens's latest star attraction, the **New Acropolis Museum** (www.newacropolis museum.gr/eng/). The museum wasn't yet ready for visitors at the time of writing, with the opening scheduled for the spring of 2009, but from the outside it already looks stunning. The opening has been delayed several times already because, this being Athens, yet more archaeological remains were discovered while the foundations were being dug. The museum sits on the site of what was found to be a prehistoric Athenian settlement, and these new discoveries were left as found on the site, and will be visible through glass floors and walkways that were hastily incorporated into a new design for the basement.

Higher up the building, space is being left in the hope that one day the Parthenon Marbles, currently held in the British Museum and known there as the Elgin Marbles, will be returned to their home city. At the very top, a glass atrium will provide views of the Parthenon and the rest of the Acropolis. On other floors will be displayed the contents of the old Acropolis Museum, and more of the archaeological collection for which there was previously insufficient display space.

To the west of the museum is the hilly park known as the **Pnyka.** The entrance is almost opposite the Herodes Atticus Theater, and here is where the **Acropolis Sound and Light Show** (tel 210/928-2900, $$$) is held. Few visitors realize that the seating is in the actual place where the Assembly of Athens used to take place in the days of Pericles, when 18,000 people would gather to hear the city's finest speakers and to debate issues affecting the citizens.

Life wasn't always so gloriously democratic, however, as a sign pointing to the "Prison of Socrates" indicates. This somewhat shabby-looking place claims to be the site where the philosopher Socrates (circa 470–399 B.C.) was imprisoned after his arrest for "corrupting the youth of Athens" with his radical teachings. He was sentenced to death and obliged to drink deadly hemlock, although this actually took place in a prison on the site of the Agora. His imprisonment in a cave on the Pnyka is most likely a piece of folklore. ∎

### Theater of Dionysos (Teatro Dionysiou)

- Map p. 52
- Leoforos Dionysiou Areopagitou
- $
- Metro: Akropoli

### New Acropolis Museum

- Map p. 52
- Makriyianni/ Areopagitou
- 210/321-0219
- Metro: Akropoli

### Pnyka

- Map p. 52
- Metro: Akropoli

---

## Big City, Small-Town Feel

Many cities are described as being like collections of small villages, but Athens is a Greek village magnified. Human touches are everywhere: flowers in pots, neighbors chatting, people doing each other favors, an old lady stopping for a few minutes in church.

The very prominence of the churches is testament to the fact that this is an unusual city, a modern capital perhaps, but still a city on a human scale. Tiny Byzantine chapels force the city's traffic patterns to detour around them, in an era when other metropolises would have long since demolished such obstacles to efficiency and the free flow of traffic.

The homogeneity of the population in Athens, its very Greekness, is also extraordinary. There are rapidly growing ethnic populations, such as Albanians, others from the Balkans, and newcomers from the Asian subcontinent. But when you are in the Greek capital, you could be in no other city in the world.

# Greek Drama

**Ancient Greece was the birthplace of modern drama. The fifth century B.C., known as the Golden Age of Pericles (after the great Athenian statesman Pericles), was a time when the arts, architecture, and politics all flourished in Athens, with the dramatic arts high on the agenda.**

The very word *drama* derives from the Greek verb for "to do," and the dramatic form developed in the sixth century B.C. from an acting out of stories or songs. It is thought

**Agave unknowingly kills her son in Euripides's *The Bacchae*.**

that drama originally derived from a choral tradition in which choirs would sing hymns in honor of the gods—but hymns that included some kind of narrative or story. On one occasion, a choral leader named Thespis (hence, "thespian") stepped out from the chorus and began to make the hymns more dramatic and active.

The chorus remained an essential part of early Greek plays. The chorus was made up of a group of observers who interpreted and commented on the action as it unfolded, as if the audience could not understand it for themselves. The plays were written in verse, and alternated the performance of scenes with choral interjections. Gradually, as the art developed and the possibilities of drama were explored, the chorus became less important.

The works of many of the playwrights from those early days are still performed all around the world—and during the summer season in an original setting at the magnificent old theater at Epidavros (see sidebar opposite), as well as in Athens at the Herodes Atticus Theater (see pp. 58–59).

Three writers dominated the developing drama of tragedy in ancient Greece: Aeschylus, Sophocles, and Euripides. Aeschylus (ca 525–456 B.C.) introduced a dramatic feature that might seem simple now but was revolutionary at the time: a second character on the stage. Until then all plays had been monologues, the telling of tales in the Homeric tradition. Now poetry and drama began to mingle.

Aeschylus drew on his experiences as an Athenian soldier (he fought at the Battle of Marathon in 490 B.C., for example), especially in plays such as *The Persians* and *Seven Against*

*Thebes.* The best known of his works that have come down to us are *Prometheus Bound,* which is the only surviving part of an original trilogy of plays, and the *Oresteia,* a complete trilogy about the doomed family of King Agamemnon.

One of the great rivals of Aeschylus was Sophocles (ca 496–405 B.C.), another Athenian tragedian. The innovation of Sophocles was

The most famous works of Euripides include *Medea, Electra,* and *The Bacchae,* all of which are still performed today. Euripides was an early example of an artist whose works became even more popular after his death than when he was alive.

But it wasn't all tragedy at this time. Many humorous and satirical plays were also being written during this great Athenian

---

## EXPERIENCE: See a Play at Epidavros

Most visitors to Epidavros see it during the day, when the site's ancient theater is empty apart from the visitors wandering around. The setting is spectacular at any time, but it's much better to see the theater used as it was intended, for the staging of drama.

If you're staying nearby, or in Athens or Nafplio, then you can attend plays in the theater during the Hellenic Festival (*www.greekfestival.gr*) in July and August. Modern plays are staged as well as ancient Greek classics, and visiting companies might include such illustrious names as the National Theatre of Greece and the National Theatre of Great Britain. Some-

times productions of opera and dance are held here.

Tickets can be bought at Epidavros or the Festival box office arcade in Athens (*Panepistimiou 39, Syntagma metro*). If you don't have your own transport, don't worry: Festival-goers can ride one of the special buses that run from Athens and Nafplio, aboard which the Festival spirit gets into full swing. A second venue at Epidavros, the Ancient Epidavros Little Theatre (dating back to the fourth century B.C.), stages events during the Festival as well; however, it is much smaller than the main theater, so be sure to buy tickets for the right venue.

---

that he introduced a third character into his dramas and started to play down the previously important commentary role performed by the chorus. In short, Sophocles wanted to let the action speak for itself. The greatest of his seven major surviving works is undoubtedly *Oedipus, the King,* a masterwork from any age of drama, let alone from an art form still in its infancy.

The third towering figure of those days is Euripides (ca 480–406 B.C.), who devised much more intricate plots than his predecessors had and allowed his characters to speak in a more natural dialogue. The technique brought him much criticism at the time, but it was a breakthrough in the development of drama.

golden age. Another Athenian, Aristophanes (ca 450–385 B.C.), was the outstanding playwright in this genre. Humor usually has the shortest of shelf lives, but the plays of Aristophanes, including *The Birds* and *The Frogs* (in which he spoofs his fellow dramatist Euripides), continue to be performed all over the world. However, Aristophanes' most famous comedy, with a theme that has been borrowed over and over again down the ages, is *Lysistrata,* in which the women refuse to make love to their men until the men agree to stop making war.

The dramatic art was treated as seriously in historic times as it is today, and the first work of literary criticism, *Poetics,* was written by Aristotle in the fourth century B.C.

# North Slopes of the Acropolis

Visitors who approach the Acropolis from the northern side may seriously doubt the validity of the handprinted signs, arrows, and scribbling on the walls that directs them to one of the most significant historical sites in the world. There are no prominent official signs pointing the way as you might expect, but continue up steps, past postcard sellers and cafés, and you'll reach the Acropolis.

Alfresco dining beneath the plane trees in the Plaka

Follow the signs and you will eventually get there, but you could miss one of the most delightful parts of Athens: **Anafiotika.** This quaint area is like an authentic, self-contained little village in the heart of the city. It nestles between the Plaka area and the rocks of the Acropolis. The dazzling whitewashed houses with brightly painted blue doors give the impression that you are in a village in the

Cyclades. The roar of the traffic is left behind, and the paths are so narrow that there is scarcely room to squeeze through.

The people who first lived here came from the island of Anafi, in the Cyclades. They were brought to Athens by King Otto soon after he ascended to the Greek throne in 1832. He wanted a palace built by the country's best craftsmen and was assured that the workers on Anafi were the best that money could buy. He commissioned them to construct his palace. When they realized they would be based in Athens for several years, they re-created their island home right here at the foot of the Acropolis. Don't leave Athens without seeing this charming side of the city.

## Agora

As you walk down from the Acropolis to the north, the large site of the **Ancient Agora,** or marketplace, spreads out below you to the left. After the Acropolis itself and the National Archaeological Museum, this is the next essential visit for those interested in the city's history. The area was originally a cemetery, and many tombs are still visible, but it began to be used as a market place around the sixth century B.C. It expanded to become the center of Athenian life for several hundred years, packed with stalls and shops, and crowds just as talkative as modern Athenians.

Two major buildings on the site merit close attention: the **Temple of Hephaistos (Hephaisteion)** and the Stoa of Attalos. The temple is clearly visible above the trees in one corner of the Agora, looking like a miniature Parthenon. It is also known as the Thissio, a name given to the surrounding area of Athens, including the nearby subway station. The temple was built in 449–444 B.C., so it predates the Parthenon. In fact it marked the start of the city's development that became known as the Golden Age. Hephaistos was the god of many things, including fire, art, and metallurgy, and the temple was built in the metalworkers' quarter of the city. It rivals the Parthenon as one of Greece's best-preserved temples.

On the far side of the Agora is the **Stoa of Attalos (Stoa Attalou).** A stoa is a roofed colonnade, and this two-story building is unique in Athens, as it is the only one that has been fully restored. Reconstruction of such buildings is a thorny subject, as some people prefer to see them left just as they were found. There is no doubt that this restoration was splendidly

---

## Tips on Tipping

Tipping is a much less formal affair in Greece than in some countries, especially the United States, where you would have to receive very poor service not to give a generous tip. In Greek restaurants the service charge is included in the bill automatically, so there is no need to add anything to it. It is common, however, to leave some spare change on the table for those who clear the dishes, or if you have had exceptionally good service and wish to acknowledge that. Hotel porters and chambermaids will always appreciate a tip, but if you don't have the right change, it doesn't matter. Similarly with taxi drivers—you can tell them to keep the change, if the amount is suitable, but if you don't, then that's okay, too.

---

### Ancient Agora

- 🅰 Map. p. 52
- ✉ Adhrianou 24
- ☎ 210/321-0185
- 🕐 Closed Mon.
- 💲 $$
- Ⓜ Metro: Monastiraki

### Temple of Hephaistos (Hephaisteion)

- 🅰 Map p. 52
- ✉ Pelopidha/ Eolou
- ☎ 210/321-0185
- 🕐 Closed Mon.
- 💲 $
- Ⓜ Metro: Monastiraki

### Stoa of Attalos

- 🅰 Map p. 52

**Roman Forum
(Roman Agora)**
🄰 Map p. 52
✉ Pelopidha/
Eolou
☎ 210/324-5220
🕐 Closed Mon.
💲 $
🚇 Metro:
Monastiraki

**Tower of the
Winds
(Naos Aiolou)**
🄰 Map p. 52
🚇 Metro:
Monastiraki

carried out, in 1953–1956, by the American School of Archaeology in Athens, generously funded by John D. Rockefeller, Jr.

The stoa was first built in the second century B.C. by Attalos, king of Pergamon, but was burned to the ground in A.D. 267. Inside it today is a small but fascinating museum, with a collection that brings to life the people and society of the Agora. It includes a wide range of artifacts, from a child's toilet to important historical items, such as one of the voting machines that citizens used to elect the city's officials.

## Roman Forum

Just over 100 yards (100 m) east of the Ancient Agora is the interesting but less impressive Roman Forum, also known as the **Roman Agora,** or marketplace. It was originally an extension of

the earlier Greek Agora, and was built by Julius Caesar (r. 59–44 B.C.) and Emperor Augustus (r. 44 B.C.–A.D. 4). While it looks scruffy in comparison with other sites nearby, it contains one of the most unusual and distinctive Athenian landmarks, the **Tower of the Winds (Naos Aiolou).**

The marble tower was built in the second half of the first century B.C., to the design of a Syrian astronomer named Andronikos of Kyrrhos. The tower stands 39 feet (12 m) high and measures 26 feet (8 m) across, and its Greek name is *Aerides,* which means "the Winds." Its Pentelic marble glows as golden as the Parthenon itself under the last rays of the setting sun. It has eight sides and several functions.

Each side faces one of the eight main compass points, and a decorative frieze at the top of

The pepperbox Tower of the Winds found new purpose in the sixth century as a chapel.

each represents one of the eight winds of mythology. The North Wind, for example, is Boreas, warmly clad and with billowing cloak; his brother Notos, the South Wind, brings rain, which he pours from a pitcher of water. Another brother is Zephyros, the West Wind, scattering flowers, while the Northeast Wind, Kaikias, brings hailstones. Beneath Boreas and Apeliotes (the East Wind), small holes allow some light into the tower. All eight sides once had a sundial below the friezes.

The tower also originally had a water clock, driven by a stream of water which flowed down from the Acropolis. All that remains today is a water channel on the floor inside. The water was let into a cylinder at a predetermined rate, and the time could be told by examining the level of the water as it slowly filled the cylinder.

The tower may also have been used as an early planetarium, with a device inside for recording the movements of the sun, the moon, and the five planets that were known and visible at that time.

The other notable building within the Roman Forum is the **Mosque of Fethiye Tzami,** built in 1458 and therefore the oldest in Athens, but today only in use for storage. Another Islamic building stood opposite what is now the public entrance to the Roman Forum. This was a *medresse,* or school, where Muslim students were taught the Koran. It later became a prison, and a tree in the grounds was used for public hangings, but the building was almost completely destroyed after the prison closed down.

At one time **Hadrian's Library (Vivliothiki Asriianou)** stood on the edge of the Roman Forum, but it is now separated from the site by several streets. It was

**INSIDER TIP:**

**Keep in mind that Greeks dine late; never before 9 p.m., often later. For the best restaurant, taverna, *psistaria,* or *ouzerie* atmosphere, turn up about 9:30 p.m. And it is perfectly acceptable to sit and talk for an hour or more after you have finished eating.**

—NICHOLAS TURLAND
*National Geographic field scientist*

built around A.D. 132 by Emperor Hadrian, mainly to house his vast collection of books, the extent of which can be gauged by the fact that this was the largest building he erected in Athens. The library had a pool and a garden surrounded by a walled courtyard 400 by 270 feet (122 by 82 m), and containing no less than 100 columns. There is not much to see there now apart from the remaining east wall, but archaeologists have been working on the site for some years, and visitors should eventually be able to enter the library. A notable feature will be the recesses in the stone where the books—in the form of rolled-up manuscripts—were stored. ■

**Hadrian's Library (Vivliothiki Asriianou)**

🅰 Map p. 52
🚇 Metro: Monastiraki

# Monastiraki

Centered on the square of the same name, Monastiraki is one of the most vibrant and exciting shopping areas of Athens. This Greek flea market with its shops and stalls sells everything from holy icons to old copies of *Playboy*. Bordering the pleasant, pedestrianized Plaka district (see p. 68), Monastiraki is a rough and ready hubbub of activity.

Modern temples to the passion for shopping dwarf a Byzantine church in Monastiraki.

**Monastiraki**

Map p. 52

Monastiraki Square (Plateia Monastiraki) is not at all reminiscent of the peaceful monastery that once stood on this site and gave the place its name. A new subway station has quickly become one of the city's busiest. The station also created a hub of excitement when antiquities were uncovered during its construction. The pieces are showcased as found, behind glass panels (see p. 81).

Walk westward away from Plaka and you enter the **flea market.** Hundreds of shops line the main street and the side streets, many aimed at the visitors who spill over from the Plaka. The farther you go the more varied the shops become. If you want to find a genuine Greek coffeepot or a traditional bouzouki, this is the place to come. There are shops selling clothes, CDs, books, videos, antiques, paintings, postcards, musical instruments, electrical appliances, kitchen equipment—you name it. Shopping here has the flavor of a Middle Eastern bazaar. Shopkeepers will try to coax you in, but usually in a jovial way. Pickpockets can be more of a problem, so be vigilant.

The biggest crowds and best spectacle are on a Sunday morning, when the market expands, extending as far as the Kerameikos cemetery and beyond. The crowds can be so intense that everything comes to a halt in a human traffic jam. It is all very good-natured, with the occasional scene of Greek drama thrown in.

Try to visit the cemetery of **Kerameikos,** but if you are in a hurry then Sunday morning is not the best time. The name comes from the potters of the ancient city. Keramos was the patron deity of potters: hence, ceramics. The cemetery is a peaceful haven, with much greenery and wildlife. It first served as a burial ground in the 12th century B.C., and many old tombs still remain, most notably along the central Street of the Tombs. Take a look, too, at the incredibly moving grave inscriptions in the site's small museum.

Walk back along Ermou away from Kerameikos, past Monastiraki Square, and you reach another, much more peaceful and graceful square known as Cathedral Square—Plateia Mitropoleos. There are in fact two cathedrals here, the little and the large. The **Little Mitropolis (Mikri Mitropoli)** to the right is a charming, tiny church dating back to the 12th century and dedicated to Agios (St.) Eleftherios. Its cavelike interior is usually lit by the glow of votive candles, and it exudes an air of peace and spirituality. Outside delicate carvings grace its walls. Next door is the **Great Mitropolis (Megali Mitropoli),** which is Athens's cathedral, constructed in the mid-19th century. Note the detailed and colorful mosaics

stretching above the impressive entrance. The cathedral is used on formal occasions, such as for funerals of distinguished Athenians.

Next door to Monastiraki, to the north of Ermou and west of Amerikis, is the district of **Psirri.** This was already an up-and-coming area before the Olympics effect of 2004 kicked in and helped modernize many parts of Athens. Psirri today is unrecognizable from the rather run-down corner of Athens it once was, and where there used to be builders' merchants and auto repair shops there are now fashionable *ouzeries* and restaurants, bars, and clubs.

Here too is now one of the city's best small museums, the **Benaki Museum of Islamic Art,** which houses all the Islamic items that used to be on display at the main Benaki Museum (see pp. 74–75), and many more that there was no space for. It's a

**INSIDER TIP:**

Visit the Monastiraki market on Sunday to absorb the local colors, sounds, and smells.

—EVA VALSAMI-JONES
*National Geographic field scientist*

collection of truly exquisite items, and not to be missed.

West of Psirri is Gazi, the latest inner-city area to be transformed. A onetime gasworks has been turned into **Technopolis,** the kind of cultural center that would grace any capital city, housing changing art and photography exhibitions, with evening concerts too. ■

**Kerameikos**

- Map p. 52
- Ermou 148
- 210/346-3552
- Closed Mon.
- $
- Metro: Kerameikos

**Benaki Museum of Islamic Art**

- Map p. 53
- Asomoton 22
- 210/325-1311
- Closed Mon.
- $$
- Metro: Syntagma or Evangelismos

**Technopolis**

- Map p. 52
- Pireos 100
- 210/346-0981
- Metro: Thissio

# Plaka & Around

Plaka is the warren of streets that meander to the north and east at the foot of the Acropolis. It is the prime visitor area of Athens, and you will be surrounded by picture postcards, souvenir shops, and restaurants trying to attract your custom. Many of the buildings are old and beautiful. The streets are mainly pedestrianized, there are some good eating places, and the atmosphere is lively, day and night.

Enjoying the Plaka with a view of the Acropolis beyond

**Museum
of Popular
Instruments
(Mouseio Ellini-
kon Mousikon
Organon)**

🅰 Map p. 71

✉ Diogenous 1–3

☎ 210/325-0198
or 210/325-
4119

🕐 Closed Mon.

🚇 Metro:
Monastiraki

The area expanded in the 19th century, and was home to many well-to-do Athenian families. They built grand neoclassical mansions, several of which have been turned into museums or stores and can therefore be enjoyed both inside and out.

An essential stop on a stroll round the area is the **Museum of Popular Instruments (Mouseio Ellinikon Mousikon Organon)**, housed in a mansion that was built in 1842. Its courtyard is used in summer for outdoor concerts.

Inside on three floors are some of the 1,200 or so musical instruments amassed over the years by the Greek musicologist Fivos Anoyanakis (born 1915). It is a museum that is both fascinating and fun, telling the story of Greek music in an entertaining manner. Headphones allow you to listen to many of the exhibits being played. In one wing is the museum gift shop, which has one of Athens's best collections of Greek traditional music on CD.

Another mansion, dating from 1884, houses the **Kanellopoulos**

Museum (Mouseio Kanellopoulos). Inside is a collection of ceramics, statues, jewelry, and general art and craft work built up by Athenian collectors Paul and Alexandra Kanellopoulos. Exhibits cover the years from the 3rd century B.C. to the 19th century A.D., ranging across civilizations (Minoan, Mycenaean, Roman, Persian, Egyptian, and Phoenician). Items include exquisite jewelry, and erotic vases, and the museum makes a good stopping-off point on the way up to or down from the Acropolis.

The other principal museum in Plaka that all visitors should try to see is the **Museum of Greek Folk Art.** It is somewhat chaotic, and crammed in—rather like Athens itself—but like the city it is fascinating, with intriguing nooks and crannies. The five floors contain a wealth of material, and there is usually an additional temporary exhibition to see.

Highlights include examples of the work of the primitive painter Theophilos (see p. 44), including an entire painted room transported from a house on the island of Lesvos. Displays of work by, and costumes of, the Sarakatsani nomads (see p. 157) are here too, alongside a large collection of other folk costumes covering most of the island groups and the main regions of the Greek mainland. For anyone interested in embroidery or clothing generally, the museum is a must. A small shop sells samples of work as well as books on the folk arts.

Sampling the food is the other

(continued on p. 72)

### Kanellopoulos Museum (Mouseio Kanellopoulos)
- ▲ Map p. 52
- ✉ Panos/Theorias
- ☎ 210/321-2313
- 🕐 Closed Mon.
- 💲 $
- Ⓜ Metro: Monastiraki

### Museum of Greek Folk Art (Mouseio Ellinikis Laografias)
- ▲ Map. p. 52
- ✉ Kydathinaion 17
- ☎ 210/322-9031
- 🕐 Closed Mon.
- 💲 $
- Ⓜ Metro: Syntagma

---

# EXPERIENCE: Learn to Dance in Athens

Dora Stratou (1903–1988) was one of the most significant figures in Greek dance in the 20th century. She wrote books about traditional dances, issued records, made films, conducted interviews, and was a one-woman crusade to preserve and promote the various forms of dance from all over Greece. Her name lives on in the Dora Stratou Theatre, near the Acropolis, where her acclaimed dance troupe performs regularly to the delight of Greeks and visitors alike.

Greeks are born dancers. It's an important part of their tradition, as anyone who has ever been to a local feast will attest. Everyone from toddlers to grandparents gets up on the dance floor and joins in the many different Greek dances that exist. Visitors to Athens can do more than just watch the show, however, as the Stratou also conducts workshops in

Greek dance (in English) throughout the summer.

The workshops go far beyond merely learning a few steps, which anyone can do at any "Greek night" throughout the tourist resorts. Here, for four hours each afternoon, you learn the history and traditions of dance, attend lectures, see the 3,000 or so costumes that the Stratou has in its wardrobe, watch visiting dance groups, and learn the dances that are going to be performed in that evening's show. For dancers and would-be dancers, it's a chance to become Greek from the feet up.

Contact the Dora Stratou Theatre (*Scholiou 8, Plaka, 10558 Athens, tel 210/324-4395, fax 210/324-6921, www .grdance.org, closed weekends*). Cost for a week's tuition begins at around 120 euros ($180).

# Walk: Plaka Highlights

Plaka's shops, restaurants, and nightlife make the district one of Athens's most popular with visitors. It also has some fine churches and examples of neoclassical architecture, with several of these mansions now housing museums. This short walk takes in a variety of Plaka's many delights.

Dealers at Monastiraki's Sunday flea market provide a vast array of collectibles.

## NOT TO BE MISSED:

Museum of Greek Folk Art • Center for Popular Arts and Traditions • Museum of Popular Instruments

From **Syntagma Square (Plateia Syntagmatos)** ❶ (see pp. 72–73), face away from the Parliament Building at the top, walk across to the far left corner, and turn left along the right-hand side of Filellinon, the one-way street taking traffic away from the square. Walk a little way along here until you see the **Church of St. Nikodemos (Agios Nikodimos)** on the left (also known as Agia Triada). This is the main Russian Orthodox church in Athens, built in the 1850s, although there has been a church on this site since 1031. Almost opposite the church, turn right, where you see a sign for the folk art museum.

The street you enter, Kydathinaion, is one of the main Plaka streets, and it starts to get busy just beyond the **Church of St. Sotira (Agia Sotira)** on the right. This is the main

## Dealing with the Summer Heat

The heat in Greece, particularly in July and August, can be intense. In Athens and in the Aegean islands in particular, temperatures can reach the 90s (32°C+). The obvious solution is to do what the Greeks do: Stay out of it, though that isn't easy if you're on vacation and want to be sightseeing. But you should at least try to take breaks from the heat in order to keep your body temperature down. Avoid alcohol during the day, which can dehydrate you. Drink lots of water. Use sunscreen and wear a hat. It pays to cover up, too. After all, desert-dwellers wear flowing robes with long sleeves, not shorts and a T-shirt.

church of the Plaka district, and dates from the late 11th or early 12th century. Note the fountain in the courtyard, for a long time the only source of water in this area. On your left is the **Museum of Greek Folk Art (Mouseio Ellinikis Laografias)** ❷ (see p. 69), and farther along on your right the **Hellenic Children's Museum (Elliniko Paithiko Mouseio,** tel 210/331-2995), worth seeing if you have children with you, since it is more of an activity center than a traditional museum.

Continue down Kydathinaion a short way and look on your right for the street named Geronta. At the far end of Geronta is the **Center for Popular Arts and Traditions (Kentro Laikis Technis kai Paradosis,** tel 210/322-0826) ❸; you may wish to make a detour to see the collection of Greek folk art inside this Plaka mansion. Farther down Kydathinaion is the intersection with Adrianou; cross over and walk up Thespidou Street. On the right you will find the **studio of George Savakis,** a Plaka artist who has painted many murals in the local tavernas as well as scenes of Plaka life. You can buy an original as a distinctive souvenir.

Return to Adrianou, go left and walk down into the heart of the Plaka. After about 300 yards (275 m) and beyond a small intersection, look on the left for the small stepped street called Mnissikleous. Walk up here and take the first right onto Diogenous. At the far end of this street on your right is the mansion that now contains the **Museum of Popular Instruments (Mouseio Ellinikon Mousikon Organon)** ❹ (see p. 68).

Continuing along Diogenous brings you out at the **Roman Forum** ❺ (see pp. 64–65). Turn right and walk around the Agora, and just about opposite the entrance take a right turn down Eolou. Pass the bottom of Adrianou on your right and take the next left onto Pandrossou Street, another of the Plaka's shopping streets. This will bring you out in **Monastiraki Square (Plateia Monastiraki)** ❻, on the edge of the Athens **flea market** (see p. 66), where there is a Metro station.

----

Ⓜ See area map p. 52
▶ Syntagma Square
⬌ 1 mile (1.5 km)
⏱ 30 minutes
▶ Monastiraki Square

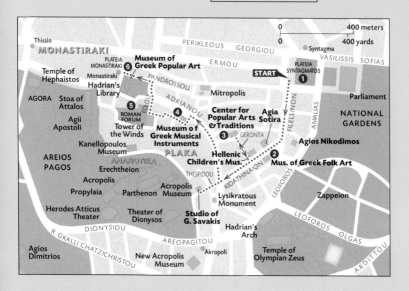

**Syntagma Square
(Plateia
Syntagmatos)**
🅐 Map p. 52
🚇 Metro:
    Syntagma

essential ingredient of any visit to Plaka. Half the premises seem to be tavernas, bars, or cafés, with a number of them distinguished by someone standing at the doorway trying to persuade you inside. As a rule, it is best to avoid such places.

Square and the Greek Parliament Building, or **Vouli,** stands here. Built as the royal palace, it was completed in 1842, and King Otto I proclaimed Greece's first constitution from its balcony.

## Eleusis

**Final resting place for the souls of the heroic, the Elysian Fields marked one end of the Sacred Way that ran to the Parthenon in the heart of Athens.**

**Suburban Eleusis is not very Elysian today, located as it is in an industrial area to the northwest of the city whose main link is now a freeway that runs straight into Athens. Only the foun-**

**dations of the site remain, but models and artifacts in the museum (Gioga/Iera1, tel 210/554-6019, $$) located here help to create a picture of the unusual sect that worshipped at Eleusis. Little is known about the cult, except that up to 30,000 people attended its rituals, and the cult lasted for some 2,000 years, having been established as early as 1500 B.C.**

The better restaurants appeal to locals year-round and have no need to pay someone to fill their seats—their reputation does it for them. There are several basement restaurants in Plaka, which are very basic affairs but with good value and lots of fun, and their walls often covered with lively murals by local artists.

Plaka wakes up slowly, but it is the perfect place for an outdoor lunch or an evening's entertainment, starting with a stroll, taking in a typical Greek meal, moving on to some music, and ending late with a coffee and a brandy in the warm night air.

### Syntagma Square

Syntagma (**Plateia Syntagmatos**) is the heart of Athens. The name means Constitution

In front of the Vouli and marking the boundary of the square is the **Tomb of the Unknown Soldier.** Its permanent guard, Greek soldiers known as Evzones, are there in their colorful traditional costumes of red beret, dark tunic in winter or red vest in summer, short white kilt over white leggings, and red wooden shoes adorned with huge pom-poms. The best time to visit is at 11 a.m. on Sundays for the main Changing of the Guard ceremony, but if you can't make it, you can see the guards change on the hour in an elaborate routine.

Along one side of the square, the **Grande Bretagne Hotel** is normally used by dignitaries who might be visiting the Parliament, and by other celebrities. Over the years guests have included actress

Elizabeth Taylor, composer Richard Strauss, and Sir Winston Churchill.

Another prestigious hotel is the King George Palace, which, like the Grande Bretagne, looks down on the center of Syntagma Square. This pedestrianized area is another beneficiary of the investments made in the city for the 2004 Olympic Games, with a smart new Metro station bringing people more easily into the heart of the city by public transport rather than the dreaded car. Several cafés stand round the edge of the square, their shady awnings providing a retreat from the sun and a relaxing place to take five in the city center.

## National Gardens

The National Gardens **(Ethnikos Kipos)** are laid out beside the Greek Parliament Building, formerly the royal palace, making a peaceful and shaded retreat. Created in the 1840s, the gardens are still a focal point in Athens, with the modern Presidential Palace right behind them. They are also known as the Royal Gardens, because they were created at the same time as the palace.

The gardens were the creation of Amalia, wife of King Otto I. The queen brought no less than 15,000 seedlings from Italy to landscape the grounds.

At 40 acres (16 ha), the National Gardens are not quite big enough to get lost in but still a good size to explore, with plenty of park benches if you want to relax or enjoy a few moments of solitude. It's a popular spot with working Athenians who

come here to eat a sandwich at lunchtime or read the daily paper. You might see nannies with babies in strollers visiting one or other of the children's playgrounds. The gardens also have a children's library, with books in several languages—worth knowing about if you're traveling with a family and encounter a rainy day. Small ponds in the gardens are filled with terrapins, which can be observed sunning themselves on rocks, or resting with their tiny heads peeping out above the surface of the water.

Graceful marble statues line the footpaths, and there are fountains and quiet cafés. At the south side, a grand 19th-century building called the Zappeion is now a conference center, but was originally built as an

**Icons such as this depiction of the Crucifixion can be highly stylized yet remain remarkably vivid.**

exhibition hall by Greek-Romanian cousins, Evangelos and Konstantinos Zappas. The café alongside, an Athenian institution recently refurbished to its former glory, is the ideal place to stop for a frappé, ouzo, or *mezedes*.

**National Gardens (Ethnikos Kipos)**

▲ Map p. 52

✉ Leoforos Amalias

🚇 Metro: Syntagma

**Benaki Museum (Mouseio Benaki)**

Map p. 53

Vasilissis Sofias/ Koumbari 1

210/367-1000

Closed Tues.

$$

Metro: Syntagma

## Benaki Museum

Antoine Emmanuel Benaki (1873–1954) was a Greek cotton trader from Alexandria, Egypt. He spent much of his

**INSIDER TIP:**

**Step in and explore Athens's Mediterranean Grocery at 1 Sofokleous Street or 11 Artidou Street for a wide variety of local products.**

—PENNY DACKIS
*National Geographic publicist*

vast wealth amassing a varied collection of historical artifacts, now displayed on several floors of the neoclassical mansion that was once his family home. The Benaki Museum's **(Mouseio Benaki)** collection, built up over a 35-year period, reflects his eclectic tastes, ranging from the 3rd century B.C. to the early

20th century. He eventually donated it to the Greek state on condition that it be put on public display in a museum.

The eclectic collection is ordered roughly chronologically, starting with statues dating back to the fifth century B.C. On the second floor artifacts from the Greek islands and Asia Minor have pride of place.

Greek culture and crafts feature on the third floor, including jewelry, wooden carvings, ceramics, and a sizable collection of Greek costumes. There are also Mycenaean jewelry and many religious items, such as early Gospels, church vestments, and some exquisite icons. Lord Byron's desk is a star exhibit (see p. 32). Another major piece, which combines both beauty and grandeur, is the reception room taken from a 17th-century Egyptian palace.

Paintings on the fourth floor include works by El Greco. One of the earliest paintings, from the third century A.D., is a delicate, wonderfully lifelike portrait of a

The streamlined body of a modern jet fighter stands outside the War Museum.

young man painted onto linen by an Egyptian artist.

The museum has been recently renovated, and special exhibits of modern artists and photographers take place throughout the year. Don't miss the rooftop snack bar.

## War Museum

The War Museum (**Polemiko Mouseio**) catches the eye as you walk along Vasilissis Sofias because outside is a display of Greek military equipment, including tanks that date back to World War I and several fighter planes, including a venerable Tiger Moth. Steps lead up to the exhibits, so that you can inspect their interiors.

War has always played a major part in Greek history, from as far back as the Trojan Wars almost up to the present day. This museum is one of the few good things to come out of the warlike rule of the colonels in 1967–1974. It was intended to reflect glory on themselves and the army, but the propaganda element is minimal and the museum has become an unlikely attraction—well worth allowing a few hours to look around.

Inside, over several large floors, the theme of war is given the broadest possible interpretation, and the exhibits are arranged chronologically. Military conflict in ancient times is represented in the displays by copies of dramatic carvings from the Temple of Vasses (see p. 129) and other statuary. The vast collections of rifles, swords, and other weapons might lack variety, but your imagination will surely be stirred by

exhibits such as models of Greek castles and fortified towns. Other models show the reenactment of significant battles from Greek history—and there are certainly plenty of those to draw on.

From more recent times there are displays covering the War of Independence, including interesting exhibits showing the role of the Greek Resistance heroes. There are also very moving accounts of the way Greece was affected by World War II,

## War Museum (Polemiko Mouseio)

- Map p. 53
- Leoforos Vasilissis Sofias 22/Rizari 2
- 210/729-4464
- Closed Mon.
- Metro: Syntagma

## Athens Nuisances

Athens has its annoying characters, like any other big city, though probably fewer of them than most. You might find people trying to pick you up—both men and women—but once you realize that this is the case, and it's not just someone being friendly, then you should be persistent in your refusals. This usually works. It may also be that the friendly approach in the street is the beginning of an effort to get you into a particular hotel, shop, or bar. A common approach is to ask you what the time is, usually in English. This is almost always followed by more questions, and an attempt to befriend you. A good ploy is simply to play dumb from the start, and pretend you don't speak whatever language they are using to address you.

## National Gallery (Ethniki Pinakothiki)

Map p. 53

Vasileos Konstantinou 50

210/321-1010

Closed Tues.

Metro: Evangelismos

especially on the streets of Athens, and in the bloody Civil War that followed it.

## National Gallery

The National Gallery of Greece (Ethniki Pinakothiki) is housed in a modern building a short walk east of the War Museum on Vasilissis Sofias, near the intersection with Vasileos Konstantinou and close to the Hilton Hotel. It has a sculpture garden as well as extensive indoor displays.

Greece has never, as a nation, had money to invest in major works of art, so the gallery relies largely on the work of local artists, few of international renown.

An advantage of this concentration on the work of Greek artists is that you can learn a great deal, in one go, about the talent that exists within the country. Many of the paintings are conventional landscapes, and some with historic views are

fascinating if you have visited areas such as Meteora or the smaller islands. In among the ordinary are some extraordinarily vivid works: Look for the name of Nikos Hadjikyriakos-Ghika, who signs himself "Ghika," one of Greece's most prominent modern artists. The work of Greece's primitive school, as typified by Theophilos (see p. 44), is also well represented here.

There are works on display by important artists such as Cézanne, Breughel, Caravaggio, Picasso, Braque, Rembrandt, and Dürer, but they are on the whole smaller and lesser-known works such as engravings and sketches. The most famous Greek painter is, of course, El Greco (see p. 44), and five good examples of his work are displayed in the gallery.

Unfortunately the gallery is frequently closed while temporary exhibitions are being mounted or removed, and the main rooms are usually inaccessible when the tem-

## EXPERIENCE: Learn Icon Painting

If you want to learn how to paint religious icons, consider a taking a class on Patmos, the island in the Dodecanese where St. John is said to have written the Book of Revelation. Courses show you how to first sketch a design on paper, then transfer it to wood. You'll learn about mixing paints and making traditional ones from natural ingredients, including minerals and plants. That most precious of minerals, gold, is applied to the painting in the form of gold leaf, to create the halo around a saint's head. Icon painters even use special brushstrokes to create the effects they are

looking for—you'll learn the techniques needed to execute the light and shade effects of a good icon painting.

There are certain set rules and traditions that dictate how icons are painted, and students will learn these by visiting local churches and monasteries and studying some of the ancient icons on display. Finally, you will need to master the writing of your name in Byzantine script to autograph your work, before a protective lacquer coating is applied to help preserve the icon for centuries to come. For details, contact AegeanScapes (www.aegeanscapes.com).

porary galleries are being worked on. However, the temporary shows can be excellent, including touring exhibitions by internationally known artists, and displays that concentrate on specific aspects of Greek art, such as theater design or Byzantine art.

## Byzantine Museum

The revamped Byzantine Museum **(Vizantino Mouseio)**, whose new extension opened in 2007, has gone from being a small museum of well preserved religious icons to one of the city's brightest attractions. The underground wing is an astonishing architectural feat and an attractive home for the extended collection.

Special exhibitions are now displayed in one of the museum's former homes, a Florentine villa built in the 1840s by the French Duchesse de Plaisance (1785–1854), who fell in love with Greece as soon as she visited it. The attractive courtyard, built around a fountain and containing lots of flowers and orange trees, is still there. The museum's extension has enabled the atmosphere of the buildings to be retained by the simple—if challenging—means of going underground.

Despite being below ground, the new galleries are spacious and well lit. The first gallery sets the whole collection in context by telling the story of the Byzantine Empire, and the displays throughout have long and informative display panels.

The journey begins with the pre-Byzantine art of the Christian era, and moves on to display icons,

"Apollo Grocery" by Nikos Hadjikyriakos-Ghika resides in the museum's 20th Century–After the War collection.

jewelry, ceramics, illuminated manuscripts, Bibles, frescoes, embroideries, and sculptures. The galleries come to a close with the fall of Constantinople in 1453. Audio tours are also available, though at the time of writing they were only in Greek. Other languages are being added. There are also statues and other displays which the visually impaired can touch.

The improvements and expansion of the museum are not yet finished either. New items are still being drawn from storage and put on display, with plans to house a special exhibit of the breathtaking illuminated manuscripts. There is also an ongoing archaeological dig at the site, which is believed to be the location of Aristotle's famous **Lyceum,** where he taught some 2,500 years ago. ∎

**Byzantine Museum (Vizantino Mouseio)**

- 🅰 Map p. 53
- ✉ Vasilissis Sofias 22
- ☎ 210/367-1000
- 🕐 Closed Mon.
- 💲 $
- Ⓜ Metro: Evangelismos

# Kolonaki & Lykavittos

As you approach the district of Kolonaki from Syntagma, you are aware that you are entering a more upscale area of Athens. There is an increasing number of galleries, antiques shops, and fashion stores, as well as far more well-dressed young people, frequently posing in sidewalk cafés with their mobile phones, and ladies with their lapdogs. The hill of Lykavittos can be seen from everywhere in central Athens, and a visit there is a must.

Belltower at the summit of Lykavittos

**Kolonaki**
🅰 Map. p. 53

**Museum of Cycladic Art**
🅰 Map p. 53
✉ Neofytou Douka 4
☎ 210/722-8321
🕐 Closed Tues. & Sun.
💲 $
🚇 Metro: Syntagma or Evangelismos

## Kolonaki

If you walk toward Kolonaki along Neofytou Douka you will come to the splendid **Museum of Cycladic Art (Mouseio Kykladikis kai Archais Ellinikis Technis),** one of the city's most important but lesser-known highlights. This modern museum, opened in 1986, houses a collection of art from the Cycladic islands (see pp. 240–255) that dates back 5,000 years. It was originally amassed by late Greek shipowner Nikolas Goulandris,

and donations from other specialists have made this the finest such collection in the world.

There are vases and glassware, as well as other sculptures in the museum, but it is the extensive range of Cycladic figurines that steals the show. The best works were produced at the height of the Cycladic civilization—about 3000–2000 B.C.

The Cycladic figures—statues and face masks—are known for their graceful simplicity and are wonderfully displayed here, with subtle lighting bringing out every nuance of their shape and texture. You will immediately see how the figures inspired modern artists, including Spanish artist Pablo Picasso (1881–1973) and British sculptor Henry Moore (1898–1986), but most notably the Italian painter and sculptor Amedeo Modigliani (1884–1920).

If you feel tempted to buy a copy of one of the works, the well-stocked gift shop has some excellent reproductions.

The collection is extensive enough to cover four floors, and in 1992 a new wing was opened in the nearby Stathatos Mansion, connected to the original museum by an unusual covered glass walkway. The new wing has some rooms with period furniture to show what the mansion was like when built in 1885; others contain overspill from the main museum, some with the Greek art owned by the Athens Academy, and there's also space for temporary exhibitions.

The **American School of Classical Studies (Gennadeion)** is also in Kolonaki. It opened in 1926 and is of interest mainly to scholars for its vast archive of some 24,000 books. However, the attractive neoclassical building is open to the general public and worth seeing for the landscape paintings on the walls, including some by English poet Edward Lear (1812–1888), and the collection of items that once belonged to Lord Byron (see p. 32).

## Lykavittos

The dominant feature of this part of town is the hill known as Lykavittos, or Lykabettos. At 909 feet (277 m), this is the highest hill in Athens and naturally provides superb views over the city. The best are toward the Acropolis and beyond that to Pireas and the Aegean Sea—and even to the island of Egina if the air is clear.

Lykavittos can be reached on foot or by **cable car.** The walk to the top is pleasant but tiring, the path zigzagging through scented pinewoods. While you don't have to be super-fit to walk, think twice in the height of summer. The cable car leaves from the top of Plutarchou Street and operates until after midnight in summer, reflecting the popularity of the spot for locals and visitors alike.

At the top of the hill is the whitewashed 19th-century chapel of **Agios Georgios,** or St. George. (His feast day is celebrated on April 23, and ceremonies are well worth attending if you happen to be in Athens at the time.) Near the chapel, the excellent Orizontes Restaurant offers some of the best views in the city, particularly when the Parthenon is illuminated at night. There is also a café partway down Lykavittos, for a restorative coffee or glass of ouzo.

On the far side of the hill from Kolonaki, the modern, open-air **Lykavittos Theater** stages some of Athens's biggest concerts—everything from classical music and dance to modern rock bands. ■

**American School of Classical Studies (Gennadeion)**
- Map p. 53
- Souidias 54
- 210/725-8829
- Closed Aug.
- Metro: Syntagma

**Lykavittos**
- Map p. 53

**Cable car**
- Aristippou/ Plutarchou
- $
- Metro: Syntagma

---

## Shop Hours

The Greeks have a casual attitude to most things, including time-keeping and shop opening hours. If you arrange to meet a Greek person for a drink at 8 p.m., don't be surprised if he or she turns up half an hour later. Absolute punctuality is not considered that important in everyday life. Small family-run shops will often not display any opening hours. They usually open early in the morning, and will stay open till they feel it's time to close and there won't be any more

customers. Also, don't be surprised to walk into a shop at lunchtime and find it seemingly deserted. The owners are probably taking a break, and may well send out one of their young children to take care of the customers. Some shops will also close when there's a local feast day, often the night before the feast itself. In Greece it's assumed that everyone knows what's going on locally, so the temporary visitor might well lose out.

# Around Omonoia Square

Plateia Omonoias means Harmony Square, which must rank as one of the greatest misnomers in the city. It is the second most important square in Athens after Syntagma Square, but unlike Syntagma, where traffic circles the square in a one-way system with a large pedestrian area in the center, Omonoia is simply where six main roads intersect, with several minor roads also feeding traffic into the maelstrom.

Some streets around Plateia Omonoias are pleasantly uncongested.

**Omonoia Square
(Plateia
Omonoias)**

Map p. 52
Metro: Omonia

However, work on the new Metro line was recently completed and Omonoia is beginning to look like its old, more harmonious self. There are fountains in the center and seating that looks down Athinas to the Acropolis.

Omonoia is like Athens itself: At first an overwhelmingly noisy and polluted place, but once you get used to the noise and the crowds, a different picture starts to emerge. If you do a complete circuit of the square you will pass newsstands where the world's

press is available and vendors sell lottery tickets, fast food, cheap watches, smuggled cigarettes, and much more. There are also busy cafés where you can soak up the real Athens atmosphere. And as a landmark for negotiating the city, Omonoia can't be beat.

If Syntagma is the European face of Athens, then Omonoia is quite definitely the Balkan/ Middle Eastern face. It is loud and bustling, full of traders and cheap goods, and emphatically full of life.

At night the square becomes Athens's equivalent of an older

Times Square or London's Soho. Illegal immigrants cluster in Omonoia and surrounding streets, selling imported goods or fake designer gear, but by and large the area is safe because it is so busy, with plenty of people about late into the night. At night Omonoia also becomes the red-light district, with a few sleazy movie theaters showing erotic movies in the streets just off the square. However, this is so low-key that many visitors might not even notice it.

One of the liveliest places is a few blocks down Athinas, heading south from Omonoia Square— the **Central Market (Kentriki Agora)**. The market is housed in a 19th-century building of glass and metal, and, although it is the city's main meat and fish market, many other goods are on display, too. If you are interested in seeing the fish that are hauled in daily from the waters of the Aegean, then this is the place to come.

The Central Market is busy from early in the morning through the afternoon. In the evening it livens up again as there are several *ouzeries* (where you can sample a variety of ouzos along with snacks) and *rembetika* (see p. 47) music clubs in this area.

This is a good place to visit before a picnic or if you're taking a trip to the islands and want to stock up for the ferry ride—Greek ferries always provide basic snacks, but little more. Here you will find cheeses and olives, bread and fruit, fresh herbs and spices, along with flowers and vegetables. If you are looking for a souvenir, there are nuts and ouzos. In short, if you can eat it, then you'll find it here.

Athinas itself is an unofficial employment exchange. In the early morning you may see painters and decorators standing with their buckets and ladders, hoping to pick up a day's work. They add yet another shade to a colorful area. ■

## The Largest Archaeological Dig

Contractors knew that when they began digging new sections of the Athens Metro system in the 1990s, they ran the risk of encountering significant archaeological remains. But they never guessed the extent of their finds. The discoveries they unearthed from beneath the city included an ancient bathhouse, metalworking shops, aqueducts, roads, city walls, and cemeteries. Some artifacts even dated from the Neolithic era. To avoid disturbing important sites, the contractors had to completely relocate one new Metro station and, elsewhere, change part of the route. They also had to resort to manual digging rather than their usual tunnel-boring machines. Excavated remains—many of museum quality—are now displayed behind glass panels at several new stations in the city center, including Syntagma and Monastiraki. Traveling on the Metro in Athens is truly taking a trip through ancient Greece.

# National Archaeological Museum
## (Ethniko Archaiologiko Mouseio)

This collection of the best treasures from Greek civilizations down the centuries forms the core of one of the world's great museums. If you do only two things in Athens, go see the Parthenon and visit this awesome collection of artifacts. The museum was spiffed up for the 2004 Olympic Games, its exhibits updated and minor damage from a September 1999 earthquake repaired.

A slender-necked amphora from about 750 B.C., discovered in Athens

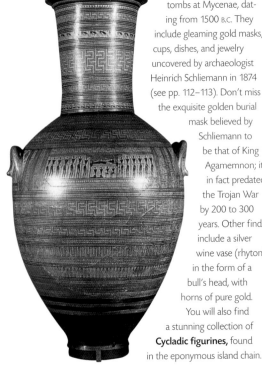

To see everything properly, plan to visit the museum twice as there is too much to take in on one long visit. If your time is limited, take a guided tour, available in several languages.

Head first for the **Mycenaean Collection,** the treasures from the royal tombs at Mycenae, dating from 1500 B.C. They include gleaming gold masks, cups, dishes, and jewelry uncovered by archaeologist Heinrich Schliemann in 1874 (see pp. 112–113). Don't miss the exquisite golden burial mask believed by Schliemann to be that of King Agamemnon; it in fact predated the Trojan War by 200 to 300 years. Other finds include a silver wine vase (rhyton) in the form of a bull's head, with horns of pure gold. You will also find a stunning collection of **Cycladic figurines,** found in the eponymous island chain.

Dating from 2000 B.C., they possess an uncanny modern nature.

The museum's **sculptures** are equally impressive. Seek out the rudely exuberant statue depicting the gods Pan and Aphrodite, dating from the first century A.D. He clearly has lascivious designs on this naked goddess, while she preserves her modesty with one hand and wields a shoe in defense in the other one. Also lovely are the remnants of a colossal cult statue of Zeus, found in 1916, and some delicate plaques of dancing girls from the Theater of Dionysos (see p. 58).

The **bronzes**—including some of the museum's largest works—possess an overpowering majesty, none more so than the huge figure of the sea god Poseidon. Arm stretched back in muscular grace, he is about to throw a trident, though some believe the figure is actually Zeus, preparing to throw a thunderbolt. The expression on his face has enabled experts to date the statue to about 460–450 B.C.

The more delicate "Jockey Boy" is one of the museum's most famous bronzes. The powerful horse and its tiny rider may or may not have been intended as one work—it

NATIONAL ARCHAEOLOGICAL MUSEUM

was found in pieces—but the result is dramatic and full of movement. The figures were discovered, like the bronze of Poseidon, in the sea off Cape Artemision and date from the second century B.C.

Another brilliant piece is the

## INSIDER TIP:

**When shopping for local souvenirs, you'll find a great variety in the Plaka, but an even better place to look can be the museum shops.**

—PENNY DACKIS
*National Geographic publicist*

"Youth of Antikithera," a 6.5-foot-high (2 m) bronze statue of a nude young man that combines delicacy and power. Some believe it's the work of the famous sculptor Euphranor. The statue once held a spherical object in his right hand—perhaps an apple, which would make him Paris. The sculpture was found in the waters off the small island of Antikithera in 1900 and dates from the Hellenistic period.

The **collection of Egyptian art** reminds the visitor of the ancient Greeks' close trading ties with the Egyptians. Among the works to admire are an alabaster statue of a pharaoh, dating from 2575–2155 B.C.; a granite statuette of Ramses II, dating from 1290–1224 B.C.; and a stone stela from 664–525 B.C. with hieratic text.

The museum boasts two

private collections: the **Eleni Stathatou Jewelry Collection** and the **Karapanos Collection.** The latter includes many artifacts from the site at Dodoni, near Ioanina in Epiros (see pp. 164–165), including lead tablets containing questions for the oracle there. The jewelry collection includes beautiful work in turquoise, silver, bronze, and glass, ranging in time from the Bronze Age to the Byzantine era. Worth checking out are the museum's temporary exhibits; there have been some impressive shows put on here in recent years.

Coin enthusiasts will want to see the **Numismatic Museum.** Located in the 1878 mansion of Heinrich Schliemann—and known as the Palace of Troy—its 600,000 coins range from ancient Greece through Roman and Byzantine periods up to the present day.

**National Archaeological Museum (Ethniko Archaiologiko Mouseio)**

- 🅰 Map p. 52
- ✉ Oktovriou 28/ Patission 44
- ☎ 210/821-7724
- 🕐 Closed Mon. before 1:00 p.m.
- 💲 $$
- Ⓜ Metro: Omonia or Victoria

## Greek Coins

**The old Greek currency, the drachma, in existence since at least 1100 B.C., was replaced by the euro in January 2002. It was not a universally popular move, especially as consumers saw prices rise due to "rounding up" on the new exchange rates, but the drachma is no longer found. It lives on, though, on the 1 euro coin, which cleverly depicts on one side an old 4 drachma coin from the fifth century B.C. The 2 euro coin also has an ingenious design from Greek mythology, showing Zeus as a bull abducting Europa—after whom Europe and ultimately the euro was named. Other coins depict Greek ships, from old triremes to a modern tanker, and famous Greek politicians including Venizelos and Kapodistrias.**

# National Archaeological Museum

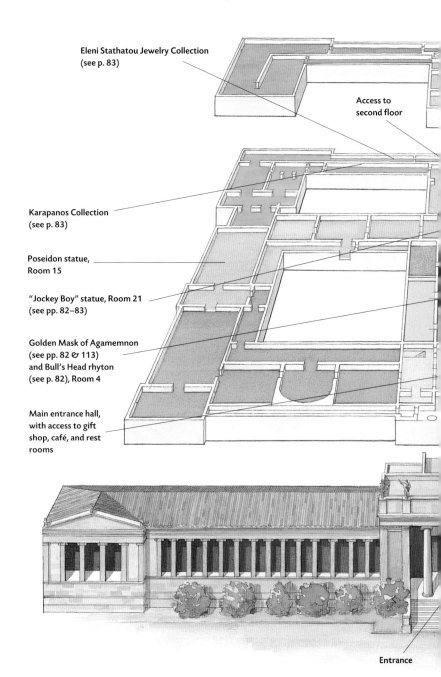

Eleni Stathatou Jewelry Collection
(see p. 83)

Access to
second floor

Karapanos Collection
(see p. 83)

Poseidon statue,
Room 15

"Jockey Boy" statue, Room 21
(see pp. 82–83)

Golden Mask of Agamemnon
(see pp. 82 & 113)
and Bull's Head rhyton
(see p. 82), Room 4

Main entrance hall,
with access to gift
shop, café, and rest
rooms

Entrance

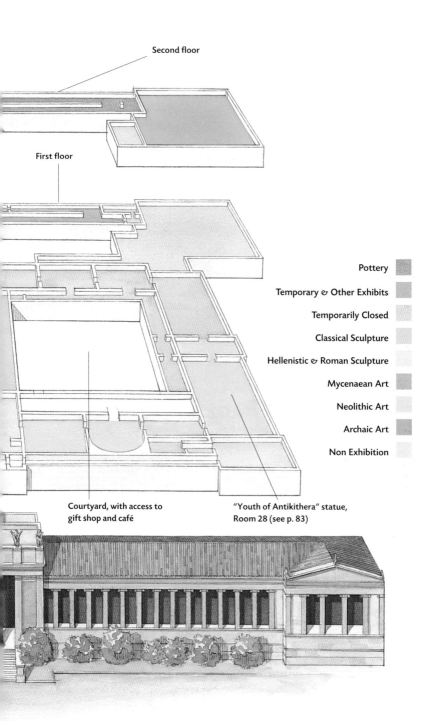

Second floor

First floor

Pottery

Temporary & Other Exhibits

Temporarily Closed

Classical Sculpture

Hellenistic & Roman Sculpture

Mycenaean Art

Neolithic Art

Archaic Art

Non Exhibition

Courtyard, with access to
gift shop and café

"Youth of Antikithera" statue,
Room 28 (see p. 83)

# Pireas

For many visitors, Pireas is all that they see of Athens, as they fly into the airport then take a ferry straight to one of the islands. Yet Pireas has a cosmopolitan character and charm of its own, along with handsome public buildings, chaos, and traffic and noise—all you expect of a busy harbor. It has been a major port since about 500 B.C. and is still one of the largest in the Mediterranean.

Greece's biggest port, Pireas has harbored boats since ancient times.

**Pireas**

Ⓜ Map p. 91

At the southern end of the subway line connecting with central stations Monastiraki and Omonoia, Pireas is easy to reach from downtown Athens.

If you are looking for a ferry, make sure you know the departure point first, and allow yourself plenty of time to find it. The layout of Pireas can be confusing, because of the indentations made by the various harbors, and it is easy to become disoriented. Kentriko Limani is the main ferry port,

with upscale shops and restaurants close by. Different harbors serve different parts of Greece, and some are a long way from each other and from the Metro station.

The bustle of life here was well illustrated in the 1959 movie *Never on a Sunday,* which starred Melina Mercouri as a local prostitute. This side of life is also described in some of the *rembetika* songs (see p. 47), which originated here and can still be heard in the late-night clubs

INSIDER TIP:

When selecting fresh fish in a restaurant by weight, ask how much it is going to cost before you order. Some species of fish can be shockingly expensive.

—NICHOLAS TURLAND
*National Geographic field scientist*

that flourish in the back streets, a world away from the tourist areas of central Athens.

Pireas has its cultural highlights too, with a small but rewarding archaeological museum, and a naval museum. The prize exhibits in the **Archaeological Museum** were all found in the harbors around here. In 1930 a collection of stone statues was discovered in a sunken ship used to transport the pieces from a Greek workshop to Italy. In 1939 the harbor also yielded up huge, magnificent bronze statues of Artemis, Athena, and Apollo.

The **Naval Museum of Greece (Nautiko Mouseio Elladhas)** overlooks the Zea Marina Harbor and is easily recognized by the old submarine that stands at the entrance. Greece has an illustrious maritime history, and this collection of over 2,000 items covers a great deal of it, from the early days of the elegant triremes with their three levels of rowers, to the lone fisherman with his little caïque, and the vast luxury liners of shipping dynasties. The whole story is told in a rich mix of paintings, photographs, maps, flags, uniforms, artifacts, and fascinating scale models of ships and boats.

Part of the museum is made from remains of the so-called Long Walls, or Legs, barriers constructed between 493 and 456 B.C. to fortify the harbors, but largely destroyed in 86 B.C. The walls, which also connected Pireas with Athens, were begun by the Athenian statesman and soldier Themistocles (circa 523–468 B.C.), and were enhanced by Pericles during the Golden Age of Athens, when Pireas was already a major port.

Pireas has a number of upscale restaurants, especially around the harbor of **Mikrolimano,** where luxurious yachts tie up beside fishing caïques. Fresh fish is the dish to have, but it won't be cheap. The harbor makes a great place for an alfresco lunch, and is especially popular on Sundays, or for a romantic evening meal, with a view of the bobbing yachts, the twinkling lights, and the blue Aegean Sea beyond. ■

**Archaeological Museum**

- ✉ Harilaou Trikoupi 31
- ☎ 210/452-1598
- 🕐 Closed Mon.
- 💲 $
- 🚇 Metro: Piraeus

**Naval Museum of Greece**

- ✉ Akti Themistokleous

## Keeping in Touch

If you want to stay current on the news back home, major cities and most tourist spots sell daily newspapers from several European countries. Some are on sale on the day of publication. U.S. newspapers will probably only be found in large cities like Athens and Thessaloniki. Cable TV networks mean that you will be able to see the news on CNN or the BBC in larger hotels, and a surprising number of cheaper hotels, too.

# More Places to Visit Near Athens

If you are based in the heart of Athens, you might like to get out of the city and explore farther afield. It might take some effort to get to these suggested places, by a combination of subway, bus, taxi, or ferry, but each is worth seeing.

## Kaisariani Monastery

Look southeast from downtown Athens and you will see the slopes of Mount Hymettus, which lies about 3 miles (5 km) away. A bus or taxi ride brings you to the 11th-century monastery of Kaisariani. The main attractions at the monastery are its frescoes. Some of these date back as far as the 12th century, but most are from the 16th and 17th centuries.

The monastery is still functioning and inhabited, and is open to visitors. Forest fires have scarred the hills around Athens, but the landscape here remains lush and green, thanks to the nearby Ilissos River. The river once supplied Athens with fresh water, and the spring at its source was named after the emperor Hadrian. It is called the Imperial Spring, and the Greek word for imperial is *kaisariane*.

☎ 210/723-6619 ⑤ $ 🚌 Bus: 234

## Kifissia

The suburb of Kifissia is at the northern end of the Metro line, and well worth a day's exploration. It is a prosperous and fashionable area, with a slightly cooler climate even though it is only 906 feet (276 m) above sea level. The **Goulandris Natural History Museum** (*Levidou 13, tel 210/801-5870*) is worth exploring for its vast collection of Mediterranean plants, but Kifissia is also simply a pleasant area to stroll around and enjoy the parks and the grand old mansions.

**Tourist Police** ☎ 210/808-1464 or 210/808-1465 🚇 Metro: Kifissia

## Paiania

Beyond Kaisariani, about 11 miles (18 km) east of Athens stands the village of Paiania. Known as the birthplace of Demosthenes (284–322 B.C.), the Athenian statesman who was said to be the greatest Greek orator of them all, the main attraction of the village today is the unusual Vorres Museum (which is named after the owner of the museum, Ian Vorres). The museum exhibits traditional Greek folk art alongside contemporary works in renovated buildings, with a delightful sculpture courtyard.

Also accessible by road from the village is the Koutouki Cave, which features a guided tour through its strangely shaped stalactites and stalagmites.

**Vorres Museum** ✉ Diadochou Konstatinou 1 ☎ 210/664-4771 🕐 Closed Aug.
**Koutouki Cave** ☎ 210/644-2108 ⑤ $$

## Salamina

The Argo-Saronic islands (see pp. 218–223) are undoubtedly the most popular places for one-day trips from Athens, yet the largest of them is almost unknown outside Greece. It sits closest to Athens in the Bay of Salamis, and is probably neglected by visitors because of its very proximity to the city. Many Athenian commuters choose to live here, and although the main town and the port are fairly unattractive, Salamina has several small, quaint fishing villages, a 17th-century monastery, some beautiful old mansions, and a small beach resort at Selinia.

It was in this bay that the Battle of Salamis took place in 480 B.C., when a large Persian fleet was defeated by a smaller but speedier Greek fleet. The fast-moving Greek triremes were able to maneuver quickly among the bulkier Persian warships and inflict great damage.

🅰 Map p. 91  ⛴ Ferry from Pireas

Treasures beyond the capital city, from isolated ruins and temples to glorious beaches and enchanting villages

# Around Athens

Sun-weathered shutters, Attica

# Around Athens

Most visitors to Athens see only the downtown area before moving on. Yet it is easy to get a fuller Greek experience simply by traveling a few miles to explore the areas immediately around the city. You will have to pass through the apparently endless, sometimes industrial, suburbs first, but the reward is the chance to have some classical sites all to yourself, particularly if traveling out of high season.

Wildflowers bring color to the UNESCO-listed monastery ruins at Dafni, on the outskirts of the city.

It can be unnerving to drive in central Athens since, despite attempts to cut vehicle numbers downtown, the volume of traffic is still high and signs are poor. If you wish to see Attica (the region around Athens), it is better to rent a car at the airport, to the east of the city, and head straight off from there. Alternatively, many of the best attractions are easily reached by public transportation, and it is surprisingly inexpensive to rent a taxi by the day.

A short trip out to Akra Sounion, where there is one of the most gloriously located temples in all of Greece, is an absolute must. Many Athenians go there to watch the sun set and enjoy a drink with a view out over the beautiful blue Aegean. The coast that runs from Pireas to Akra Sounion also boasts the closest beach resorts to the capital—not as peaceful and beautiful as beaches on the islands perhaps, but a reasonable (and quick) escape from the stresses of city life in Athens. Farther afield, places such as Marathon will spring to life when you realize that you are standing where that historic battle took place (see pp. 96–97). And simply wandering around places like Marathon and Vravron will give you a very different perspective from the hustle and bustle of the capital. ■

Area of map detail

## NOT TO BE MISSED:

**Watching a glorious sunset at Cape Sounion  93**

**The tasty local bread in Markopoulon  94**

**Dining at one of Rafina's waterside fish restaurants  95**

**The famous burial mound at Marathon  96–97**

**Spectacular beaches at Vouliagmeni  98**

**The scenic road to Evia  98–99**

**The remote site of Rhamnus  100–101**

**A visit to the Archaeological Museum at Vravron  102**

# Akra Sounion & the East Coast

Athens is blessed with beaches on its doorstep and beautiful islands just a short boat ride away from Pireas. Visitors should do what the Greeks do and head for the beach playgrounds in the suburbs as summer temperature soar. You'll be in good company as everybody wants to cool off, and it reveals a different side to the capital more famous for its classical sites.

The Temple of Poseidon promises spectacular sunset views.

**Akra Sounion**
🅰 Map p. 91

**Temple of Poseidon**
🅰 Map p. 91
☎ 229/203-9363
🕐 Closed Mon.
💲 $

For a day out from the city, the first major resort to the east, less than 30 minutes from downtown Athens, is **Glyfada,** which merges with **Voula** to the south.

While neither is the peaceful beach resort you might hope for, if you are traveling with children and they want a day on the beach, this strip of the Apollo Coast will provide them with sea, sand, and entertainment, and parents can enjoy a seafood lunch at a waterfront restaurant. Flight noise from the airport can be a drawback.

As you head south along the coast and farther from Athens, the resorts are quieter and more spread out. Whether you travel along here by bus or in a rented car, there is no mistaking the magnificent spectacle of the temple that stands proud on the 200-foot (60 m) headland of Akra Sounion.

The **Temple of Poseidon** on the headland was built in 444 B.C. out of gray marble mined just a few miles away in the quarries at Agrileza. Of the original 34 columns, 15 are still standing to their full height, one of them bearing the initials of the British Romantic poet, Lord Byron (see p. 32). Byron visited the site in 1810 and carved his signature on the column nearest the entrance; unfortunately you won't be able to get close enough to see. The remains of the temple are now roped off to prevent further damage by the thousands of people who come here every year.

The temple stands on the remains of an even older building, thought to have dated back to 490 B.C. The present temple is dedicated to the god of the sea, Poseidon, and there could be no more fitting setting for it than this cape overlooking the Aegean Sea. The temple may have been designed by the same (unknown) architect responsible for the elegant Temple of Hephaistos in the Agora site in Athens (see p. 63).

Cape Sounion is famous for its impressive sunsets, which give breathtaking vivid bloodred and fiery orange colored skies, the stuff of many a postcard. There is a café here, so you can enjoy the sunset in comfort. Below the promontory is a beach with accommodations, if you choose to stay. Your best chance for avoiding the crowds in this lovely spot is to be here first thing in the morning.

The largest island near the cape is Kea, one of the smaller Cycladic islands and the closest of that group to Athens. Look west toward the setting sun to see the island of Egina, in the Argo-Saronic group (see pp. 218–223). Beyond it you should be able to see the east coast of the Peloponnisos.

Heading north from Cape Sounion up the east coast of Attica brings you to **Lavrion.** This small town may not look

## Lavrion
Map p. 91

## Ferry Service

Greece has an excellent ferry service, as you might expect from one of the world's great maritime nations. There are services to Greece from Italy, notably from Bari, Brindisi, Ancona, Trieste, and Venice, and from Dubrovnik in Croatia. A high-season journey between Italy and Greece costs from around $70 oneway for a foot passenger, up to around $150 for a car.

For travel to the islands, there are usually several ferry choices, as well as a growing network of faster (and more expensive) hydrofoil services. Many smaller boats also operate between neighboring islands and run excursion trips in the summer. Even if you don't want the full excursion, these can sometimes be more convenient options than the larger com-

mercial ferry services, and an individual running his own boat will be open to bargaining. The shoulder seasons *(Oct.–Nov., & April–May)* are slightly cheaper.

There are numerous rival ferry companies, and schedules change constantly. For up-to-date information, contact the Greek National Tourist Organization *(7 Tsoha, tel 210/870-7000, e-mail: info_central@gnto.gr, www.gnto.gr, 8 a.m.–3 p.m. Mon.–Fri.);* at its Information Desk at 26 Amalias *(tel 210/331-0392, e-mail: info@gnto.gr, 9 a.m.–7 p.m. Mon.–Fri., 10 a.m.–6 p.m. Sat.–Sun. & holidays);* or at its Information Desk at the airport arrivals hall *(tel 210/353-0445, e-mail: venizelos@gnto.gr, 9 a.m.–7 p.m. Mon.–Fri., 10 a.m.–4 p.m. Sat.–Sun. & holidays).*

**Porto Rafti**
🗺 Map p. 91

**Markopoulon**
🗺 Map p. 91

**Koropi**
🗺 Map p. 91

prosperous today, but the port is gearing up to play a big role as a yachting and cruise hub. Huge silver mines here helped to finance the building of Periclean Athens; they also provided the wealth that paid for the powerful Athenian navy that defeated the Persians and established Greece as one of the great maritime nations. The mines closed in the 19th century, and a small mineralogical museum in Lavrion tells their story.

Farther up the coast is the more attractive—and today more prosperous—resort of **Porto Rafti.** Its lively fishing harbor, good restaurants, and bars make it a popular weekend retreat for Athenians.

Just off the coast in the harbor—one of the finest in Greece—is the island that gives the port its name: Rafti. There is a huge marble statue of a seated woman here, made in Roman times and used over the years as a safety beacon for ships. It is known as "the Tailor" (raftis in Greek) because it is thought that the statue's hands (one arm is now missing) once held a pair of scissors. It is also possible that the missing arm once held either bunches of fruit or sheaves of wheat, as a symbol of fertility. It was from here that the first fruits from the mainland were sent every year to the sacred island of Dilos (see p. 247).

If you decide to head inland to **Markopoulon** instead of taking the coastal road to Vravron (see pp. 101–102), you will find yourself in a busy market town that prospers thanks to its fertile setting and proximity to Athens.

Vineyards spread out around the town. Several tavernas provide an authentic Greek lunch (you'll find no tourist menus here), and plenty of bakeries sell the local bread, for which Markopoulon is widely

**INSIDER TIP:**

**Types of Greek honey vary according to the trees or bushes the bees visit—*thymaria* (thyme), *elato* (alpine pine), orange, or lemon. Taste it, enjoy it, and have some shipped to yourself at home; it's easier than trying to carry it through Customs.**

—PENNY DACKIS
*National Geographic publicist*

known. There are also some small chapels that you can visit. Ring the bell for admission or ask the first person you see how to find the key-holder.

A diversion slightly farther west takes you to **Koropi,** which is even bigger and also noted for its extensive wine production. Koropi is particularly famous for its production of retsina, the unique white wine of Greece that is flavored with pine resin. The resin was originally introduced into the winemaking process in ancient times as much for its preservative qualities as its flavor. On the southeast outskirts of the town is the church of the Metamorphosis Sotiras, which dates back to the tenth century and is therefore one of the oldest churches in Attica.

## Rafina

The port of Rafina, on the eastern coast of Attica, about a 40-minute bus ride from central Athens, is increasing in size and importance since the new airport was built east of the city. It means that many foreign visitors will find it more convenient to head for Rafina, rather than Pireas, the traditional gateway to the Greek islands. Rafina already serves the islands of Evia and the northeast Aegean, and many more islands in both the Cyclades and Dodecanese groups.

The heart of the town is the old fishing harbor, which remains wonderfully picturesque but has been enhanced by the addition of many excellent seafood restaurants, most with rooftop terraces overlooking the boats bobbing in the water below. Here you will find Athenians escaping the city's pace, especially on weekends, and demanding the best fresh fish—it can get very crowded down here on weekends.

Around the harbor you will also find the main ferry departure point. Away from the city center, coastal developments serve as a reminder that Rafina is a popular resort in its own right. There is no shortage of pleasant affordable hotels, places to swim, and watersport opportunities. Several small beaches lie either side of the resort, and the coast is dotted with vacation villas for Athenian residents. Beyond beaches, little remains from the old settlements that have always existed here.

Inland from the harbor and slightly uphill is the large main square, where you can escape the noise of the harbor and feel you are in any Greek town, with children playing while grandmothers watch them. How long Rafina will retain its charms once the new airport is in full swing remains to be seen.

To the north of Rafina is another resort, **Mati,** slightly quieter and without the bustle of busy ferries.

From the slopes behind Mati a fabulous view takes in the Bay of Marathon. Nearby is a good bathing beach, Agios Andreas. If you are taking a ferry to or from Rafina, where hotels can be fully reserved well ahead, it is worth thinking about staying at Mati and taking a taxi to or from Rafina. ■

**Rafina**
Map p. 91

**Mati**
Map p. 91

**Rafina is a busy harbor for both ferries and fast hydrofoils to the islands.**

# Marathon

The word "Marathon" has passed into the language of the world, and while the approximate story of how a Greek village came to give its name to a long endurance race is well known, the details of that story may be less familiar.

The athletic grace of long-distance runners is captured on a vase dating from 470 B.C. Much of what we know of sport in ancient Greece comes from such vivid records.

**Marathon**
 Map p. 91

In 490 B.C. the Athenians were under attack and heavily outnumbered by the Persian army. No exact figures are available, but it is estimated that as many as 25,000 Persian troops were fighting 10,000 Athenians. The Athenians had their backs not to the wall but to the pass of Thermopylae in the mountains on the east side of Athens, defending it from the enemy who had been thus far victorious in their progress through Greece. Persian warships brought their army ashore here, and they thundered onto the Plain of Marathon and toward the outnumbered Greeks.

The people in Athens knew that their fate was being decided by soldiers on the plains of Attica, and waited anxiously for news of the battle. The Athenians duly fought for their lives and defeated the Persian armies. The heroic nature of the victory is indicated by the fact that some 6,400 Persians are thought to have been killed, while the Athenians lost only 192 men.

News of the victory was carried back to Athens by one of the soldiers, Phedippides, who ran all the way from Marathon to the Acropolis in his full armor. After relaying the information he promptly died on the spot from his exertions.

The present-day marathon race of 26 miles 385 yards (42.195 km) commemorates that brave feat (though the 385 yards were added in the 20th century), and each October the Athens Open International Marathon is run over the probable route the soldier took—minus the full armor—and ends in the Panathenaic Stadium.

What we know of the Battle of Marathon comes from the Greek historian Herodotus, who recorded the events some 50 years after they occurred. The Athenian dead were buried under a simple earthen mound only 33 feet (10 m) high but 590 feet (180 m) in circumference. Its very simplicity makes it all the more striking. The **burial mound** is about 2.5 miles (4 km) south of the modern town of Marathon, down a road that is off to the right if you are heading toward Marathon itself. The site was originally marked by a gravestone that showed a soldier fallen in battle. This can now be seen in the National Archaeological Museum in Athens (see pp. 82–85), with a copy on display at the site.

If you continue toward Marathon, a left turn takes you to the **Archaeological Museum.** Recently renovated and well worth seeing, the small collection displays items found on the field of battle and on the estate of the wealthy arts patron Herodes Atticus (A.D. 101–177), who came from this area. The finds include statues, urns, gravestones, an unusual bronze mirror, and part of the memorial erected by the Greeks at the time to celebrate the victory at Marathon.

Behind the museum you can climb to the **Mound of the Plataians,** discovered in 1970. Allies of the Athenians, the Plataians joined in the Battle of Marathon. They lost 11 of their own soldiers, including a ten-year-old boy. The dead Plataians are buried here in this mound.

**Marathon** itself is a fairly ordinary small town, worth a stop if you need to buy provisions but otherwise unremarkable. A short drive to the west of Road No. 83 takes you past the impressive **Lake Marathon.** The reservoir owes its existence to a marble dam that was built in 1925–1931 to trap the waters coming down from the Mount Parnitha range; until the 1950s it was the main water supply for all of Athens.

If your interest in the historical significance of this place has drawn you here, you can round off your visit by heading for some pleasant small beaches along the coast, the best being at Skhinias. If you merely want to cool off with a dip in the Aegean, you can walk from the burial mound to the coast and find some small stretches of beach to relax on. ■

**Archaeological Museum**

☎ 229/405-5155
🕐 Closed Mon.
💲 $

---

# EXPERIENCE: Enter a Marathon Race to Athens or a Spartathlon to Sparta

One way of understanding how the Greeks feel about their heroes of the past would be to enter the annual Athens marathon. Fortunately, it's held at a cooler time of the year, on a Sunday in early November, when there is less risk of suffering the same fate as the original marathon runner, Phedippides; he collapsed and died from exhaustion after running the 26 miles (42 km) from Marathon to the center of Athens. The modern race is, of course, the only marathon in the world to cover the original marathon route, and attracts more than 3,000 runners keen to race from Marathon to the end point, the Panathenaic Stadium. For information, visit *www.athensmarathon.com.*

If the marathon isn't challenge enough for you, try the Spartathlon, which is held in September every year. This race commemorates another running feat during the same Greek battles against the Persians, when a messenger from Athens was dispatched to Sparta to recruit reinforcements to help the Greeks fight off the invaders. He allegedly arrived the next day, having covered a distance of almost 153 miles (246 km). For information, visit *www.spartathlon.gr.*

# Drive: Exploring Attica

The region of Attica that surrounds Athens offers visitors a picture of Greece in miniature. It has high hills, beach resorts, small villages, old churches, and a number of interesting classical sites.

## NOT TO BE MISSED:

Akra Sounion • Markopoulon • Marathon burial mound & Archaeological Museum • Rafina

Taking in the best of Attica's attractions, this route begins in downtown Athens and winds along the coast, finishing at Halkida, the gateway to Evia; anyone who wishes to return to Athens could do so at Marathon, which would shorten the route and the time slightly.

From central Athens, follow Leof. Syngrou southwest to Highway 91. Turn left and head south. This coastal route, with the Aegean to your right, is a welcome relief after Athens's bustle. South of the suburban sprawl you'll come to **Vouliagmeni ❶**, a popular beach resort and escape from the city. Stroll along its sandy beaches, enjoy windsurfing, sailing, or scuba diving, or just relax at an outdoor café. A small **Temple of Apollo** is just south of town.

Continue south along the coastal road. After awhile the impressive ruined **Temple of Poseidon ❷** (see pp. 92–93) comes into view, atop the headland of Akra Sounion and visible from miles away. If you time it right, you'll be treated to one of the area's famous sunsets.

Having visited the cape, return to Highway 91 and turn right. Almost immediately, the road changes its number to 89. It heads north now, sticking to the Attica coast before veering inland through the fertile interior toward the small town of **Markopoulon ❸** (see p. 94). Here you can stretch your legs and stock up on provisions, if you like.

On leaving Markopoulon, retrace your route to Highway 89 and turn left. Almost

immediately, turn right onto Highway 85, which brings you—after about 12.5 miles (20 km) and another pleasant section of coastal driving—to the port and resort of **Rafina ❹** (see p. 95). If you follow the signs for "Ferries" you should be able to find somewhere to park near the harbor, where you can enjoy a lunch or dinner in one of the many waterside restaurants.

Return to Highway 85 and continue north to the smaller resort of Nea Makri, passing vacation homes and villas along the way. At Nea Makri, join Highway 83 and turn right toward **Marathon** (see pp. 96–97), the legendary site of the Battle of Marathon in 490 B.C., in which the Athenian army defeated the Persians. The route taken by the messenger sent to Athens to share the news of victory—running 26 miles and dying upon delivery of his message—forms the basis of the modern-day marathon race. The Athenian dead were buried under a simple **burial mound ❺** (Tymfos Marathona). Watch for the sign about 2.5 miles south of Marathon; a road to the east of Highway 83 will take you there. Farther north on Highway 83 and to the left is the small but worthwhile **Archaeological Museum** (see p. 97).

From the town of **Marathon,** continue on the winding Highway 83, until you reach the village of Agios Stefanos. Here a right turn will take you to the main Athens–Thessaloniki highway, which is known as Highway 1 but also, confusingly, in certain places as the E75.

Turn right onto the main road and, after about 25 miles (40 km), look for a right turn marked for Evia and **Halkida ❻** (see pp. 208–209), the main town and entrance point for the island of Evia, reached across a bridge from the mainland. Alternatively, when you join Highway 1 you can turn left, which returns you to central Athens.

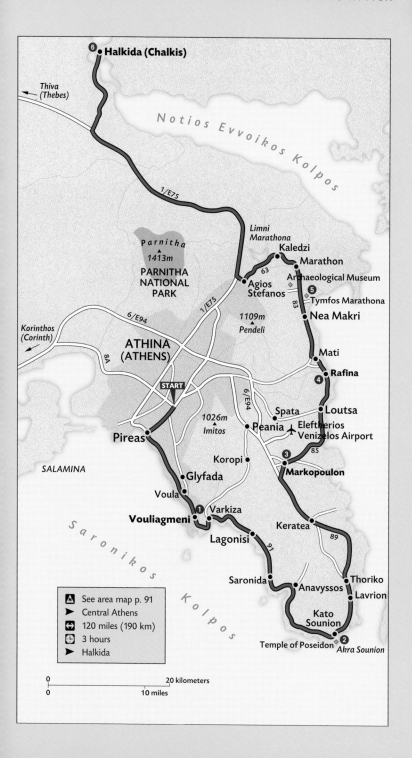

**6 Halkida (Chalkis)**

Thiva (Thebes)

*Notios Evvoikos Kolpos*

1/E75

Limni Marathona

Kaledzi

Marathon

Parnitha 1413m

PARNITHA NATIONAL PARK

63

Archaeological Museum

Agios Stefanos

83

**5** Tymfos Marathona

1/E75

1109m Pendeli

**Nea Makri**

Korinthos (Corinth)

6/E94

**ATHINA (ATHENS)**

8A

Mati

**Rafina**

**4**

**START**

6/E94

Spata

**Loutsa**

1026m Imitos

Eleftherios Venizelos Airport

Peania

85

**Pireas**

Koropi

**3**

**Markopoulon**

*SALAMINA*

**Glyfada**

Voula

**1** Varkiza

**Vouliagmeni**

Keratea

89

**Lagonisi**

*Saronikos Kolpos*

91

Saronida

Anavyssos

**Thoriko**

**Lavrion**

Kato Sounion

Temple of Poseidon   *Akra Sounion* **2**

See area map p. 91
Central Athens
120 miles (190 km)
3 hours
Halkida

0 — 20 kilometers
0 — 10 miles

# Rhamnus & Vravron

The classical site of Ancient Rhamnus is one of the most remote and, for this reason, also one of the most appealing in Attica. While not as isolated, Vravron (also known as Brauron) is well worth allowing time to explore thoroughly. Lying about 5 miles (8 km) northeast of Markopoulon, it incorporates a sizable archaeological site and an interesting museum, as well as a modern village. The site and museum are close to each other, and the village is only a few hundred yards away if you want to walk.

Part of the colonnaded stoa at Vravron, famous for its quiet setting

### Rhamnus

Map p. 91

### Rhamnus

You will need a rental car or taxi to get you to Rhamnus, since there are only a few buses a day from Athens to the nearest village, Kato Souli, and from there it is a long walk to the site.

You will be glad you made the journey, and will possibly even have the place to yourself. You might wonder why it is kept open, with so few visitors, but archaeologists have been working here since 1975 and only a small area is open to everyone. It is hoped that in the near future, when the archaeological work is complete, more of the site will be opened up to the public and access improved.

Largely overgrown by nature in an appealing way, the remains at Rhamnus are scattered over a hillside above the sea. Wandering through the ruins you are accompanied by butterflies and lizards that scuttle into cracks in the stones. The name of the site comes from a prickly shrub that grows in this area, called *ramnos* in Greek.

There is in fact very little to see, so it helps to know something about the background to the site in order to appreciate it for more than just its tranquillity and as an idyllic picnic spot. Nemesis, the Greek goddess responsible for dispensing good or bad luck to us mortals, was worshipped here.

(The gods always eventually got their revenge on those who had offended them, hence the expression "to meet your nemesis.")

Some of the Persian forces are said to have landed here before their defeat at Marathon, a defeat sometimes blamed on their theft of a marble block from the **Temple of Nemesis,** on which they intended to commemorate their victory. What remains today are mainly foundations, but the sixth-century B.C. temple can be clearly identified.

## Vravron

Unusually, Vravron is located at the foot of a small hill rather than on top. On the crown of the hill is a pretty little Byzantine chapel dedicated to St. George—**Agios Georgios.** The village and site are in a valley surrounded by agricultural land, an attractive area with abundant wildlife. The people are welcoming, as they are not yet overrun by visitors.

The story of this site is a fascinating one. Its main focus is the mysterious **Sanctuary of Artemis,** of which only the foundations remain today. Artemis is the Greek equivalent of the Roman goddess Diana, the daughter of Zeus and the twin sister of Apollo. She was the moon goddess, as well as the goddess of childbirth, the harvest, hunting, and wildlife. Every four years a festival would take place at Vravron in which young girls would dress as bears and dance. Aristophanes refers to the dance in *Lysistrata,* but like the one that centered on Eleusis (see p. 72), we do not know exactly what took place or why.

In his play *Iphigenia at Tauris,* Euripedes (see p. 61) relates events at Vravron. Iphigenia, the daughter of Agamemnon and Clytemnestra, was held responsible for a strong wind that prevented the Greek ships from sailing to Troy prior to the Trojan Wars. The wind was sent in retribution for the killing of one of the wild animals that Artemis protected, probably a bear. Agamemnon agreed to the sacrifice of his daughter on the altar of Artemis at Vravron so that the ships could set sail.

According to Euripedes, the goddess spared Iphigenia because she would not allow her altar to be stained by human blood,

### Vravron
- Map p. 91
- ☎ 229/902-7020
- 🕐 Closed Mon.
- 💲 $

---

## Driving Etiquette

Greeks are, by and large, fairly cavalier drivers. Men like to show off and drive at speed, even though the police have quite a large presence on the roads. If an oncoming car flashes its headlights at you, and you don't appear to be doing anything wrong, then it's probably to warn you that there's a police car or speed trap up ahead of you, waiting to catch you out. Another reason for the use of headlight flashing is when two cars are approaching an intersection or narrow road at the same time. In some countries the flash is an invitation to you to come through, but in Greece it means "get out of my way, I'm coming through."

**Archaeological Museum**

☎ 229/902-7020

🕐 Closed Mon.

💲 $

and substituted a deer for the sacrifice instead. Iphigenia went on to found the sanctuary here, dedicated to Artemis.

In other versions of the story, Iphigenia was sacrificed. Her alleged grave was discovered here, south of the stoa (a colonnaded building) and next to the remains of the **Sacred House,** where the

evidence from the site points to the existence here of stables, a gymnasium, and other buildings, but these have not yet been properly uncovered.

The nearby **Archaeological Museum** displays finds from the site and elsewhere, and is intriguing despite its comparatively small size. It includes a scale model

Her companion deer identifies the goddess Artemis on this carved relief.

priestesses of the Artemis cult stayed during the festivals.

By the fourth century B.C., the area here had flooded, and the communities that had arisen all disappeared. The village of Vravron eventually reestablished itself, but it was not until 1946 that work began on uncovering the site of ancient Vravron, work that continued until 1963. It revealed the remains of a fifth-century B.C. temple and, next to it, a **stoa** that may be even older; inscriptions describe it as "the Parthenon of the Bears."

Beside the stoa are the remains of one of the oldest stone bridges you will see anywhere in the world. The structure dates back to the fifth century B.C. Other

of the temple that gives a vivid impression of how the site must have looked in its prime; it's worth the effort to see.

Among the more important exhibits is a decorated stirrup jar from about 1200–1000 B.C. that was found in the late-Mycenaean cemetery at Perati. A beautifully detailed statue that has been dated to the fourth century B.C. depicts a young girl clutching a rabbit. Several other statues and busts date from the same period, and there is a fascinating collection of pottery and jewelry. A votive relief of Artemis, from Vravron, also dates from the fourth century B.C. It shows the goddess seated, welcoming pilgrims of all ages. ∎

Three "fingers" of land projecting into the Mediterranean and separated from the rest of Greece by the Corinth Canal

# Peloponnisos (Peloponnese)

Olives are a Greek staple.

# Peloponnisos

**Many visitors choose to return again and again to the massive peninsula of the Peloponnisos (Peloponnese), and it is an area with enough variety to invite weeks or even months of exploration. The landscape is impressively wooded and mountainous, and around its edges are wonderful beaches, as fine as any on the Greek islands.**

The 16th-century Bourtzi tower marks the entrance to Methoni's harbor.

It has some of the most important archaeological sites in the world—Epidavros, Mycenae, and Olympia to name only the best known. There are also cosmopolitan old towns such as the former Greek capital, Nafplio, as well as unspoiled mountain villages where you might be the only visitor.

The name goes back into ancient history, as this is the "island of Pelops." Pelops was the son of Tantalus, one of the sons of Zeus. When the gods came to dine at Tantalus's home, he killed his son and boiled him in a cauldron to feed to them—he wanted to see if the gods truly were omniscient. They were, and they restored Pelops to life, punishing Tantalus by leaving him hanging from a tree, with a raging thirst and hunger. Every time he tried to drink or eat, the water and food moved away from him, although both were "tantalizingly" close.

The Peloponnis has played a central role in more recent history, too. This was the heartland of the War of Independence in the 19th century, where the Greek flag was first raised in defiance of the Turks, and where the capital was based before it was moved to Athens.

It is not quite an island—a narrow isthmus, just 3.5 miles (6 km) wide, joins the Peloponnisos to the mainland, yet in resorts such as Koroni and Methoni, with their busy tavernas and long, sandy beaches, you could believe yourself on an Aegean island. In the interior, however, the older traditions of mainland Greece linger, with a mountain scenery that appeals to walkers and nature lovers. In fact, the province of Arcadia gave its name to a fictional rural paradise.

Historians will never want to leave. Aside from the famous sites already mentioned, there are lesser-known but equally exciting treasures to discover, such as the Byzantine ruins of Mystras, and the rock at Monemvasia, which has an entire village hidden from the mainland. ∎

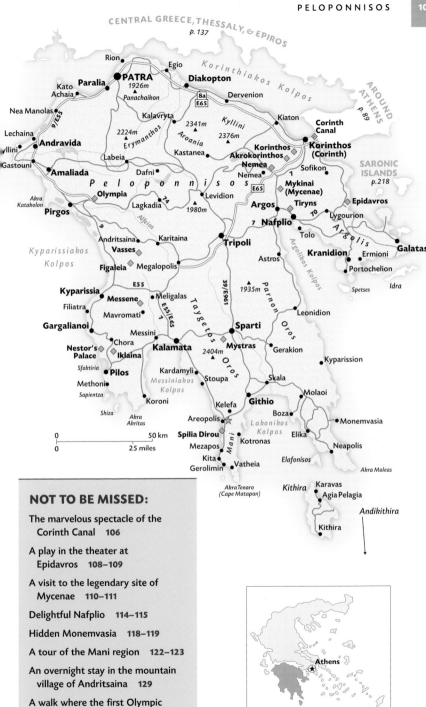

CENTRAL GREECE, THESSALY, & EPIROS
*p. 137*

*Korinthiakos Kolpos*

Rion
Egio
**PATRA**
1926m
*Panachaikon*
Kato
Achaia
**Paralia**
Nea Manolas
Kalavryta
Dervenion
**Diakopton**
Kiaton
**Corinth Canal**
Lechaina
2224m
Erymanthos
2341m
Aroania
2376m
**Korinthos**
**Akrokorinthos**
Sofikon
**Korinthos (Corinth)**
Yllini
**Andravida**
Labeia
Kastanea
**Nemea**
Nemea
Gastouni
**Amaliada**
Dafni
*P e l o p o n n i s o s*
Akra
Katakolon
**Olympia**
Lagkadia
Levidion
1980m
**Mykinai (Mycenae)**
**Argos**
**Tiryns**
**Epidavros**
Lygourion
**Pirgos**
*Alfeios*
**Nafplio**
Tolo
Andritsaina
Karitaina
**Tripoli**
Astros
**Kranidion**
Ermioni
**Galatas**
*Kyparissiakos Kolpos*
**Vasses**
**Figaleia**
Megalopolis
Portochelion
*Spetses*
*Idra*
**Kyparissia**
E55
Meligalas
1935m
Leonidion
Filiatra
**Messene**
Mavromati
*Taygetos Oros*
*Parnon Oros*
**Gargalianoi**
Messini
**Sparti**
**Nestor's Palace**
Chora
**Iklaina**
**Kalamata**
2404m
**Mystras**
Gerakion
Kyparission
*Sfaktiria*
**Pilos**
Kardamyli
Stoupa
Skala
Methoni
*Sapientza*
Koroni
*Messiniakos Kolpos*
Molaoi
*Shiza*
Akra
Akritas
Kelefa
**Githio**
Boza
**Monemvasia**
Areopolis
*Lakonikos Kolpos*
Elika
**Spilia Dirou**
Mezapos
Kotronas
Neapolis
Kita
Vatheia
*Elafonisos*
Gerolimin
*Akra Maleas*
*Akra Tenaro (Cape Matapan)*
*Kithira*
Karavas
Agia Pelagia
*Andikithira*
*Kithira*

0        50 km
0        25 miles

## NOT TO BE MISSED:

The marvelous spectacle of the
Corinth Canal   106

A play in the theater at
Epidavros   108–109

A visit to the legendary site of
Mycenae   110–111

Delightful Nafplio   114–115

Hidden Monemvasia   118–119

A tour of the Mani region   122–123

An overnight stay in the mountain
village of Andritsaina   129

A walk where the first Olympic
athletes gathered   130–131

Athens

Area of map detail

# Corinth

**The Corinth (Korinthos) Canal is one of the great sights of Greece. With luck, you might be there when a ship is being steered between the narrow, sheer walls, which stretch away in the distance to link the Gulf of Corinth with the Aegean Sea.**

### Corinth (Korinthos)
🅼 Map p. 105

### Ancient Corinth & Archaeological Museum
🅼 Map p. 105
☎ 274/103-1207
💲 $$

### Akrokorinthos
🅼 Map p. 105

Roman Emperor Nero (A.D. 37–68) first mooted the idea of cutting a canal through the isthmus so ships could sail from Italy into the Aegean without going around the Peloponnisos. He performed the first symbolic excavation in person, using a silver shovel, but the task was never completed. Ships continued to sail up the Gulf of Corinth, unload their cargoes, and have them carried the 3.5 miles (6 km) to a ship waiting on the far side, rather than risk the stormy circuit.

It was not until 1893, after a total of 12 years' work, that the 75-foot-wide (23 m) **Corinth Canal** was finally cut through, enabling boats to sail directly to Pireas. The canal is still used, although less these days, as supertankers cannot squeeze through.

A few miles beyond the canal is **modern Corinth (Korinthos),** which detains few visitors except as a refueling stop. It is an agricultural service town, although it is interesting to note that it is a center for the Greek currant industry; the word "currant" actually derives from Corinth.

Ancient Corinth comes to life as you walk around the well-preserved remains, dominated by a fifth-century B.C. Temple of Apollo. With its massive Doric columns, this was one of the buildings that the Romans left when they redeveloped the city as their

provincial capital in 44 B.C.

The city was once home to 300,000 citizens and 460,000 more who were slaves—about the population size of modern Dallas. The smaller buildings are the ones that speak of the history: the remnants of shops, houses, and administrative buildings. The **Peirene Fountain** was a gift from Herodes Atticus, the wealthy Athenian, patron and friend of the Romans, and the spring beneath it still supplies water to the modern town of Corinth.

The **Archaeological Museum** on the site has a good display of remains found there. Some lovely mosaics, mostly dating from the second-century A.D. Roman period, are a good indication of the city's wealth at that time. Domestic vases, pottery, and jewelry give the collections a more human scale.

Overlooking the lower city from the hilltop 2.5 miles (4 km) away was **Akrokorinthos,** or Upper Corinth. Its walls and spectacular views are the chief reasons to visit. When you see the position the city commands, you realize its strategic importance and why it has been refortified by every wave of invaders, Venetians, Franks, and Turks. The walls run for 1.25 miles (2 km) around a 60-acre (24 ha) site, where you can find the remains of chapels, mosques, houses, fortifications, and the still working Turkish Fountain of Hatzi Mustafa. ∎

# EXPERIENCE: See the Nemean Games

Everyone knows the Olympic Games, but there were several other regular sporting events held by the ancient Greeks, including the Nemean Games. Like the Olympics, these too live on, although without the worldwide fame of the Olympics. However, unlike the Olympics, anyone can apply to join in the Nemean Games.

Both the participants and judges dress in ancient garb at the Nemean Games.

Nemea is in the northwest Peloponnisos, between Corinth and Argos. Here the original Nemean Games took place, and here they are re-created every four years, usually in June, the next due in 2012. The original games were, like the Olympics, held in honor of Zeus, and have been dated back to the sixth century B.C.

They have not, though, adopted the Olympic practice of requiring contestants to run naked. If you wish to participate, you will do so wearing a conventional ancient Greek outfit of *chiton*, or tunic, and *zoni*, or belt, as will the judges and other officials. The games were revived in 1994 by archaeologists and volunteers from the University of Berkeley, California, who were working on the site of ancient Nemea, on the Temple of Zeus. They became interested in the games that were held there, and inevitably someone wondered if they might be revived, like the Olympics but on a smaller, local scale.

Some 10,000 people turn up at Nemea for the two-day event, and hundreds participate in the races, which are divided according to sex and age, with 12 participants in each race. The races are all over a standard length of 100 meters. The original Olympic Games only had one running event, which was to run the length of the stadium, but gradually other events were introduced. The Nemean Games stick to the original notion of just one standard-length race for all.

Athletes assemble in the locker room, or *apodyterion*, which has only partly survived, so a tent of the same size is erected over the top to complete the building. A judge dressed in black enters to collect each group of runners, and as in the old days he will be carrying an olive branch. This is not a symbol of peace, but to be used to beat anyone who breaks the rules or disobeys his orders.

You then race in the same stadium and on the same track that was used more than 2,500 years ago. At the original games the winners were awarded a wreath made from wild celery leaves from Argos, but today's winners receive a palm branch, a ribbon, a pin, a T-shirt, and a place at the victors' dinner.

To join in the games, you must register two months before the event—contact the Secretary, the Society for the Revival of the Nemean Games (*P.O. Box 2000, GR-205 00 Nemea, Greece, http://socrates.berkeley. edu/~clscs275/Games%20 folder/society.htm*).

# Epidavros

The ancient theater at Epidavros (Epidaurus) is one of the most wonderful sites in all of Greece. Renowned for its perfect acoustics, the theater is still used for modern performances during the Athens Summer Festival. Few people can resist testing the acoustics on their friends at the back of the theater, so be prepared to make your speech!

Craftsmen continue to renovate and restore the site.

**Epidavros**

🅰 Map p. 105

☎ 275/302-2009

💲 $$

Because much of Epidavros appears overgrown, many visitors do not take the trouble to explore it, leaving after a quick visit to the theater. Yet there are signs leading you to the various remains, and if you arm yourself with a map, and can pay a prior visit to the museum, you'll thoroughly enjoy your exploration.

The **theater** was built in the fourth century B.C., and has 55 rows of seats able to hold 14,000 people. The stage is 65 feet (20 m) in diameter. It is hard to believe that the theater lay buried and undiscovered until excavations started in the late 19th century. It was finally restored in 1954, and it is worth noting that the first 34 rows of the auditorium are all original. Audiences look out across

the site of ancient Epidavros to the mountains beyond. See a performance if you get the chance.

## Around the Site

There is more to Epidavros than the theater, which was not built purely for aesthetic reasons or to celebrate drama. The site was dedicated to the god of healing, Asklepios, the son of Apollo. He learned his skills from the centaur Charon; he was so gifted at healing that he was thought to have the ability to bring people back from the dead. They were proven wrong when he was killed by a thunderbolt from Zeus, who feared Asklepios was becoming too powerful.

There was a **temple** at Epidavros dedicated to Asklepios, which contained a statue of the god made out of gold and ivory. While little of the temple is visible today, Epidavros is undergoing long-term excavation work and may eventually be revealed as an even more important site than it is already known to be.

People brought their health problems to Epidavros, where medical practitioners were based, and the **museum** on the site contains examples of the medical instruments used. Drama played a part as a kind of catharsis (purging) in some of the healing processes recommended in those days. The museum also contains records of cures alleged to have taken place here, as well as more conventional vases and statuary recovered during the excavations.

There are also the remains of guesthouses, a bath, and a gymnasium, showing that physical exercise was as important in some cures at that time as it is today. The Greeks were firm believers in a healthy mind in a healthy body. This small nation gave the world not only the greatest philosophers but also the Olympic Games and the father of medicine, Hippocrates.

Another important building is the circular **tholos**, designed by the same architect, Polykleitos, who was responsible for the theater. Its purpose is not certain. It may

have housed the sacred serpents used in some rites, or been a place where those rites were carried out. One theory suggests that it worked as shock therapy for the mentally ill, who were made to crawl through the concentric passages inside, until they found themselves in the central area in pitch darkness, surrounded by snakes—treatment guaranteed to produce a shock if not a cure.

Near the tholos and about 400 yards (365 m) northwest of the theater are the remains of the fifth-century B.C. **stadium;** some of the seating and the starting and finishing lines for races are visible. It would have been used during the major festival in honor of Asklepios, held every four years. ■

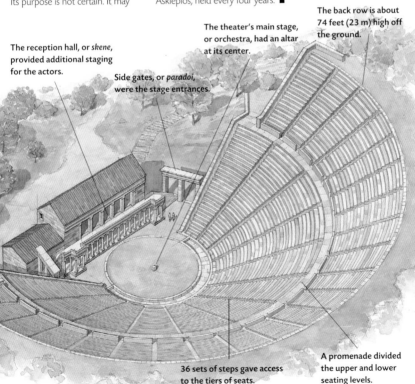

The reception hall, or *skene*, provided additional staging for the actors.

Side gates, or *paradoi*, were the stage entrances.

The theater's main stage, or orchestra, had an altar at its center.

The back row is about 74 feet (23 m) high off the ground.

36 sets of steps gave access to the tiers of seats.

A promenade divided the upper and lower seating levels.

# Mycenae

Without doubt, Mycenae (Mykinai) is the most important historical site on the Peloponnisos. The great palace of Mycenae was known as the House of Atreus after the ruler of that name, the son of Pelops (who gave his name to the Peloponnisos, see p. 104). The ruined complex lies just over a mile (2 km) outside the modern village of Mycenae, which straddles the Nafplio–Athens main road, and is clearly signed.

Containing many of the best royal tombs, Grave Circle A has been included within the city walls.

**Mycenae**
- Map p. 105
- 275/107-6585
- $$

The first thing you see as you approach, on your left, is the **Treasury of Atreus.** This beehive tomb is an impressive structure, especially considering that it was built without a scrap of mortar. Pass down a long corridor into the main tomb, where the acoustics are startling.

Try speaking aloud to experience this yourself. Take a look, too, at the hefty lintel over the entrance door, which is 26 feet (8 m) long and weighs almost 120 tons.

Greek dramatists tell the grisly story of the curse on the House of Atreus. Atreus's wife was seduced by his brother, Thyestes. In revenge, Atreus murdered two of Thyestes's sons, boiled them, and served them to their father at a banquet. He then showed Thyestes the severed heads of his sons, to let him know what he had eaten. From then on, Atreus and his descendants—who included Agamemnon, Menelaus, and Orestes—were cursed by the gods.

The Treasury is often referred to as the Tomb of Agamemnon, and although it was indeed a royal burial tomb, there is no evidence to support this attribution. The spot that Schliemann (see pp. 112–13) believed to be the tomb of Agamemnon is at the main site, farther along the road. The Treasury dates to the 14th century B.C. and so would have been used before the time of Agamemnon.

The first thing to strike visitors arriving at the main site is the famous **Lion Gate,** the carved lintel which straddles the entrance. Built in the 13th century B.C., it is 12.5 feet (3.75 m) wide at the base and almost 11 feet (3.5 m) high. Note the grooves in the floor, which were made by chariots, and the holes for bolts at the side to keep the doorway firmly shut when required.

When you pass through the gate, to your right are the circular remains of the **royal tombs.** In Grave Circle A, as it is known, six graves were discovered, containing a total of 19 bodies. This is where Schliemann found the glorious golden burial mask that he believed was buried with King Agamemnon. In all, 30 pounds (14 kg) of gold in the form of masks, jewelry, crowns, and other items were discovered

**INSIDER TIP:**

Mycenae's popularity means that at the height of the tourist season it seems as if everyone is visiting at the same time. But, join the crowd!

—MIKE GERRARD
*National Geographic author*

here, and this treasure haul is one of the major attractions at the National Archaeological Museum in Athens (see pp. 82–85).

You need to use a certain amount of imagination, and maybe have a map, to make the most of a visit to the rest of Mycenae. There are plenty of foundations to see, and the picture that emerges is of a large royal palace, with huge walls, and an extensive community living just outside the walls and serving the royal court. The walls themselves were up to 46 feet (14 m) thick, and were called the Cyclopean Walls, as people later could not understand how they had been built, if not by the one-eyed giants known as the Cyclops.

The royal palace was destroyed by fire in 1200 B.C.; the burn marks can still be seen on the foundation stones that remain. A century later, the site was abandoned and left to decay until its rediscovery by Schliemann in 1874. As you wander around today, you can see the remnants of bedchambers, royal apartments, baths, a grand reception hall, and a throne room. ■

## Cyclops

The huge, one-eyed Cyclopes are often maligned, especially due to Odysseus' encounter with the hungry Polyphemus, but they have a presence in classical mythology. They play a pivotal role in Homer's *Odyssey* and also appear in Hesiod's *Theogony*; in the latter the Cyclopes, banished to Tartarus, are said to have fashioned Zeus's thunderbolts, Artemis's bow, and Poseidon's trident. And Perseus's helmet of darkness? They made that, too.

Quite the résumé, but one has to ask:

How did the concept of a race of one-eyed giants make it into the collective imagination? In 1914, paleontologist Othenio Abel posited that the skulls of prehistoric elephants might have had something to do with it, as they appear to have only one eye socket, which is actually the nasal cavity. Whether that is the case or not, the myth of the Cyclopes lives on, their name even being used to describe a medical condition: Cyclopia is a congenital defect found in one out of every 16,000 live births.

# Heinrich Schliemann

**German-born archaeologist Heinrich Schliemann (1822–1890) devoted his life to pursuing the treasures hidden in the Greek earth. If at times he let his theories override the evidence, he was still a great enthusiast who discovered many of Greece's finest ancient treasures—even if they were not always exactly what he believed them to be.**

Schliemann was an intriguing man. After making his business fortune partly as a military contractor in Germany, Holland, and Russia during the Crimean War, he became a U.S. citizen while living in California in 1850s. He moved to Greece at age 46 to devote the rest of his life to archaeology. More specifically, he had been fascinated since childhood by the works of Homer, and their mingling of myth and history. Did such places as Troy and the Palace of Odysseus actually exist? Schliemann resolved to find out.

He began by looking for Troy, scene of Homer's *Iliad*. In 1870 he began digging at Hissarlik, close to the Turkish Aegean coast, which he had identified as the probable location of the city. He found evidence of several cities having existed on the site, and declared that the second earliest of them, where there were traces of burning, was Homer's Troy. It is now known that if, in fact, Troy was

located there, it was one of the later levels that Schliemann had already dug through and destroyed in the process of excavation. Whatever the truth of the find—it has never been established for sure, and probably never can be—Schliemann certainly uncovered an important historical site.

From Troy he moved in 1874 to explore at Mycenae (see pp. 110–111). He was seeking the tombs of the ancient Mycenaean kings and was determined to find the tomb of Agamemnon, to prove that this character actually existed. Schliemann uncovered a stunning golden burial mask, and confidently announced to the king of Greece in a famous telegram: "I have gazed upon the face of Agamemnon." In fact, later dating established that it could not have been Agamemnon, even if the king had been a historical rather than a legendary character. Schliemann never let the opinions or evidence of experts divert him from his own strongly held views.

**Opposite:** Although the formal education of Heinrich Schliemann ended at age 14, he went on to make extraordinary archaeological discoveries. His Greek wife, Sophia, is shown (opposite right) wearing gold jewelry from Mycenae.
**Above:** Schliemann believed this gold death mask to be Agamemnon's; in fact it dates from the 16th century B.C. and so is too old to be the legendary king's.

It was inevitable that Schliemann would move on to Ithaca, to look for historical evidence of the existence of Odysseus and his palace, and other sites described in Homer's *Odyssey*. It was equally inevitable that he would find something that he identified as those sites, but again there is still no absolute proof that he was right. He did further important work at Tiryns, near Mycenae, and also hoped to excavate at Knossos on Crete, another location mentioned by Homer, but he could not agree to the price being asked for access to the land.

Despite his great knowledge and enthusiasm, Schliemann was perceived by other archaeologists as an amateur and an upstart. Nevertheless, it cannot be denied that he uncovered large and significant sites that other archaeologists had missed.

# Nafplio, Tiryns, & Argos

Nafplio is the most delightful town in all of the Peloponnisos. Much of its charm stems from the medieval architecture of its old town, dating from the second Venetian occupation (1686–1715), not to mention its looming castles and watery vistas. Less well known than Mycenae, but much of it better preserved, Tiryns is worth visiting for an hour or two. One of the earliest inhabited towns in Greece, Argos has some remains worth investigating.

Rooftop view over Nafplio

**Nafplio**

🗺 Map p. 105

**Visitor information**

✉ Tourist Office, 25 Martiou

☎ 275/202-4444

**Palamidi Fortress**

☎ 275/202-8036

💲 $

## Nafplio

There are several reasons for visiting Nafplio, not least the town's location by the water with views across a gulf to the mountains of the eastern Peloponnisos. The narrow streets and pristine whitewashed houses of the old town are reminiscent of a Greek island, and it has excellent restaurants. Nafplio's appeal is enhanced by two high fortresses dominating the low buildings of the town. You can reach the **Palamidi Fortress** either by climbing up 999 steps,

which is not for the fainthearted, or by an easier but longer route by road. The views from the top make the effort worthwhile. The main fortress is Venetian and dates from the 18th century, although inside the primary walls there are remains of three smaller fortresses to explore.

The **Its Kale fortress,** whose name is Turkish for "inner castle," is slightly less dramatic. This was the site of Nafplio's original acropolis, and several castles have stood here over the centuries. There are few remains to see, but it is a pleasant place for a short stroll. Another good walk leads around the headland on which the fortress stands.

On an islet in the bay is another, smaller fortress known as the **Bourtzi.** Built in the 15th century, at the time of the Venetian occupation, it owes its importance to the deceptive waters here. They look deep, but in fact there is only one navigable passage into Nafplio. The Bourtzi guards could block this by stringing chains across from the islet to the town. Among the fortress's various functions over the years, it was the home of the town's executioner until 1930 and later a luxurious hotel. At the moment it simply stands there, empty and undeniably picturesque.

Nafplio's museums are all worth a visit for different reasons. On the main square, Plateia Syntagmatos, is the **Archaeological Museum** (*tel 275/202-7502, closed Mon., $*), housed in an elegant 18th-century former Venetian warehouse. The highlight of its collection is a suit of bronze armor that has survived virtually intact from Mycenaean times (about 1500 B.C.). Many items here were found at the nearby sites of Tiryns (see below) and Mycenae (see pp. 110–111).

The **Folklore Museum** in Nafplio is one of the best in the country. Run by the Peloponnesian Folk Foundation, it has extensive displays of colorful traditional costumes from all over the region; signage for exhibits is well done in both Greek and English. A wide collection of farming and domestic artifacts provides information about the rural life of the region. Lovely examples of local handicrafts, made by those who keep the folk traditions alive, are sold in the first-rate gift shop.

The **Military Museum** is full of authentic weaponry and documents. There is a large collection of moving—and occasionally harrowing—photographs, portraying the impact of World War II on Greece. There is also an interesting collection of artifacts relating to the War of Independence, with which Nafplio is closely linked. The town served as the capital of a newly independent Greece from 1829 to 1834.

Greece's first president, Ioannis Kapodistrias (1776–1831), lived in Nafplio and also died there, assassinated outside the church of **Agios Spiridon** by two villainous chieftains from the Mani region of the southern Peloponnisos. You can see the bullet holes on the wall of the church. Three years later, in 1834, Athens was made the new capital of modern Greece.

## Tiryns

At the time of the Mycenaean civilization (about 1400–1200 B.C.), Tiryns stood on the shores of the Aegean guarding Mycenae and neighboring Argos from attack. Since then the sea has retreated, leaving Tiryns stranded a few miles inland, and easily reached off the Athens road 2 miles (4 km) west of Nafplio.

Homer described Tiryns as having mighty **walls,** and these are still the first thing you notice in the town. Their remains—rebuilt in the 13th century B.C.—are 2,300 feet (700 m) in length, up to 26 feet (8 m) wide, and 33 feet (10 m) high, although they originally stood twice this high. The

**Folklore Museum**

- ✉ Vasilissis Alexandrou 1
- ☎ 275/202-8947
- $ $
- 🕐 Closed Tues.

**Military Museum**

- ✉ Leoforos Amalias 22
- ☎ 275/202-5591
- 🕐 Closed Mon.

**Tiryns**

- 🗺 Map p. 105

---

## Sparta

The word "spartan" has passed into the language to denote the tough and austere regime for which Sparta's soldiers were renowned in the days when their city-state was Athens's great rival. Although it is a thriving city today, there is little to detain you for more than an hour or two as you track down the scattered remnants of the past. These include a theater and some temple remains, with a small Archaeological Museum (*Ayios Nikonos, tel 273/102-8575*).

**Royal Palace**
☎ 275/202-2657
$ $

**Argos**
▲ Map p. 105

**Archaeological Museum**
✉ Plateia Agiou Petra
☎ 275/206-8819
🕐 Closed Mon.
$ $

site is better preserved than Mycenae but lacks the resonance of the royal tombs, and thus has not been as well excavated or cared for. Some parts are off-limits to visitors, as much to protect people from accidents as to protect the remains from damage.

Arriving at the site is impressive: You climb the entrance ramp that any attackers would have had to negotiate, with its sharp turn at the top. The thick gateway here, which would have matched the famous lion gate at Mycenae, has not worn so well, and its distinctive carvings have not survived.

Little remains of the **royal palace,** aside from foundations. However, with a floor plan,

A narrow vaulted passage runs through the massive stone walls of Tiryns.

available from stores in modern Mycenae (don't wait until you get to the site), it is possible to make out sections such as the royal apartments. A bathroom is easily distinguishable, its floor made up of one immense flat stone. The stone staircase that leads down to a postern gate has survived, virtually intact, for almost 3,000 years.

## Argos

Argos is at a crossroads, where the Nafplio–Athens and Tripoli–Athens roads meet, and is a changing place for those traveling by bus. It has all the facilities you might want, such as banks, stores, post offices, and gas stations.

Its **Archaeological Museum,** close to the main square, has finds from both Mycenae and Tiryns. The best of these are now in the National Archaeological Museum in Athens (see pp. 82–85), but Argos can boast a bronze helmet and breastplate that date to Mycenaean times and excellent collections from the later Roman period.

The importance of Argos in historic times can be seen at the site of **ancient Argos,** only a short walk from the center of town along the Tripoli road. The principal attraction is the theater, which is bigger than Epidavros, with steeply ascending seating for 20,000 spectators. It was built toward the end of the fourth century B.C. but was twice modernized by the Romans. The site also has the remains of a Roman bath, theater, aqueduct, and large drainage channels, which indicate the size and importance of the settlement that grew up here.

Above the site a path leads to the fortress where the original Argos acropolis was situated before being replaced by a medieval castle (although some of the walls date back to the sixth century A.D.). It is a steep climb, so you may prefer to drive the circuitous route instead. At the top there are breathtaking views to the Aegean, north toward the Gulf of Corinth, and south across the Peloponnisos. ∎

# EXPERIENCE: Join an Archaeological Dig

Iklaina is a mountain village of about 300 to 400 people, located in the southwest corner of the Peloponnisos. It's less than 9 miles (14 km) inland from the coastal resort of Pilos. Pilos is a small but attractive harbor town, guarded by two medieval castles and standing on one of the most impressive natural harbors on the Peloponnisos: Navarino Bay.

Known to all Greek students because the Battle of Navarino Bay, **Pilos** was a pivotal sea battle in October 1827 in Greece's War of Independence against the Turks. It is also mentioned in Homer's *Odyssey* as the place where the palace of King Nestor—wise counselor to Agamemnon—was located. This has been proven true, and Nestor's Palace is an archaeological site that can be visited just along the coast.

Little **Iklaina** has its claims to fame, too, but fewer people know about these as its secrets have not yet been fully revealed. Iklaina, surrounded by dusty-red hills and overlooking the Ionian Sea, has been inhabited since the Late Bronze Age, about 1600–1100 B.C. Although mentioned by Homer in his writings, it wasn't until the excavations by the Athens Archaeological Society in the 1950s that finds from the Bronze Age were uncovered.

### Iklaina Archaeological Project

While many organizations sponsor archaeology trips to Greece, the early work at Iklaina has been continued in recent years by the Iklaina Archaeological Project at the University of Missouri–St. Louis. In addition to providing students the opportunity of spending a semester in Greece through its large Greek Studies program, anyone can join the project's annual summer trips. During the summer participants help with the ongoing excavation work at Iklaina.

A visit to a site like Iklaina provides volunteers with an appreciation of life in Mycenaean times. It provides a vast amount of rich historical information buried beneath its soil.

By literally getting your hands dirty, you will learn about the layers of history that lie beneath the surface of Greece. It will also help to give something back to a country that is rich in remains, but economically poor by the standards of many Western countries.

By joining in an archaeological dig (training is provided for those with little or no experience), you learn not only about the civilization you are investigating, through evening lectures and other activities, but you also learn about archaeology itself, and how it helps us understand the past.

Trips include visits to other Mycenaean sites, including **Mycenae** itself and other places of interest nearby, such as ancient **Olympia** and the attractive fortress town of **Nafplio,** which was the capital of

Archaeological search involves detail work.

Greece before Athens.

There are usually two trips to choose from each summer, each lasting 17 days or so and costing around $4,800 for the program fees and tuition. For more information, visit the **Iklaina Archaeological Project** at *www.iklaina.org* or contact project director, Professor Michael B. Cosmopoulos *(Department of Anthropology, University of Missouri–St. Louis, St. Louis, MO 63121, tel 314/516-6241, fax 314/516-7235, e-mail: cosmopoulos@ umsl.edu).*

# Monemvasia

It is astonishing that the name of Monemvasia is hardly known outside Greece, because it is one of the most extraordinary towns in the whole country. The result is that it remains delightfully unspoiled. Those who venture here can regard it as a special place that few other visitors see.

The medieval village of Monemvasia provides solitude to the few who visit.

**Monemvasia**

🗺 Map p. 105

**Visitor Information**

✉ Tourist Police

☎ 273/106-1941

A huge mountain of a rock stands offshore, linked to the mainland by a single stretch of road. This is Monemvasia, known as the Gibraltar of Greece. When you approach it for the first time you may feel that, yes, it is an impressive sight—but once you have seen it, what then? Well, then you walk or drive across the road to the entrance; if you drive, be prepared to leave your car outside. The name Monemvasia means "single entrance." To discover the secrets of this remarkable island you must walk through the single doorway, as into a medieval castle. The doorway is only wide enough to accommodate a loaded donkey.

## Entering the Town

As you pass through that entrance, you feel that you are stepping back into the 15th century, when Monemvasia was a busy Byzantine city of some 50,000 people. Today its permanent population stands at a mere 50, leaving it full of ghosts and echoes of the past. A few of the old houses have been renovated and turned into hotels, and a handful of others are now restaurants and gift shops. But development has been on a very small scale, and the atmosphere remains unique. The hotels are small, so if you want to stay in the old town and experience the full flavor of Monemvasia, then make reservations. There are also several small, simple hotels in the modern town across on the mainland.

The rock became an island when it was severed from the mainland by an earthquake in A.D. 375, and the old town was founded when the first road was built in the sixth century. It became a vitally important port, controlling the passage of ships traveling around the southern Peloponnisos between Italy and Constantinople. With its one entrance and sheer sides, the rock was virtually impregnable, and the only time it fell was in 1821 during the War of Independence, when Turkish occupiers were trapped here and besieged by the Greeks. After five months, the people inside were reduced to eating grass, rats, and even, it is reputed, each other, before they surrendered.

Dining on the island today is, you'll be glad to know, more sophisticated. Whether you visit by day or in the evening, allow time to wander through the streets—not just the main streets but the backstreets, where crumbling churches and houses create a picture of what life used to be like here.

Immediately on your left as you go through the entrance gate is the house where the respected Greek poet Yannis Ritsos (1909–1990) was born. At the far end of the village, look for the church of Panagia Chrysafitissa. Its original date is uncertain, but it was restored by the Venetians in the 18th century. Its bell hangs from an acacia tree. Close by is the larger church of Agios Nikolaos, built in 1703. All this is in what is known as the **lower town.**

The approach to the **upper town** at the top of the rock is by a zigzag stone path that leads to another entrance, still with its original iron gates. All that remains of the upper town, however, is the 13th-century church of Agia Sofia, alone at the very top of the site. Make the effort to reach it because the views along the coast are very impressive. ■

## Remote Islands

**Elafonisos, a small island perched between Kithira and the Greek mainland, is the nearest approach to a desert-island paradise that you will find in Greece. Elafonisos has some glorious, long, white sandy beaches and just one village with a few small pensions that are open only during the summer months.**

**Andikithira, halfway between Kithira and Crete, is even more remote, with fewer than 200 permanent inhabitants, a collection of ruins, a few beaches, and two villages. Accommodations in Andikithira are not only primitive but few and far between. The island is definitely a place where you can get away from it all—but rough seas might mean that it's some time before you get back.**

# Mani

Of the three peninsulas that jut southward from the mass of the Peloponnisos, the central "finger" is the Mani. Its tip at Akra Tenaro (also known as Cape Matapan) is the southernmost point of the Greek mainland—and the legendary entrance to Hades (Hell). Even without such associations, you know that when you enter the Mani you are entering a special region.

Dramatically overlooking Akra Tenaro and the sea, Vatheia's tower houses compose an exemplar of local architectural history.

The landscape becomes much more barren and rugged in the Lower Mani, where you will start to see the distinctive stone tower houses that hint at the violence of life here in the past.

The remoteness of the Mani meant it was always a place of escape or refuge, and the families who settled here in the 15th century became very clan-like, fighting bitterly for the best areas of land. The Nyklian family were dominant. At first they alone had the right to build onto their properties the characteristic tall, square stone towers, which were used for both defense and attack. The taller the tower, the easier it was to fire down on enemies through the narrow slits of windows.

Eventually other families began to build towers, each trying to build as high as possible. If one family offended another, or killed someone, then a feud began, heralded by the ringing of church bells and a retreat by the respective families into their towers. Such feuds often lasted for years and down generations, as the sense of honor was great. There was no difficulty in keeping the tower houses supplied—women were protected and could continue to bring food into the towers for their men. The only hiatus in the feuding came at harvest time, when a truce was called. A feud could only be ended by total annihilation or capitulation by one party. The last recorded feud of this kind took place in 1870 at Kita, and was stopped only by the intervention of the Greek Army.

**Kita** is one place where the tower houses survive, and there are several clustered dramatically together in the village of **Vatheia,** in the very south of the Mani. But you will see others as you travel

**INSIDER TIP:**

**Don't miss the southern tip of mainland Greece, the deepest part of the Mani. Walk to Cape Tainaro lighthouse, past an ancient mosaic floor exposed in the landscape and the remains of a classical temple converted into a church.**

—NICHOLAS TURLAND
*National Geographic field scientist*

around, sometimes just a single tower in an isolated village.

There is much more, however, to the Mani than feuds and a barren landscape. Several delightful fishing villages welcome visitors in summer, such as **Stoupa** and **Kardamyli.** In a churchyard just outside the latter is the grave of British travel writer and novelist

Bruce Chatwin (1940–1989), who loved the area.

## Around the Mani

The northern region, known as the Outer Mani, is dominated by the mountain range of **Taygetos,** a defiant spine of rock climbing to a height of 7,885 feet (2,404 m). The lower slopes offer wonderful walking, as well as a scenic backdrop of pine forests, but to venture farther, seek advice from local guides.

The main town of the Inner Mani, the more southerly half of the peninsula, is **Areopolis.** This town provides all the facilities you might want, including a few hotels, but it is not the best place to be based for any length of time. On the coast a few miles south of Areopolis is one of the region's main attractions, the **Spilia Dirou,** or Diros Caves. You can combine a 30-minute boat ride into the underground cave network with a short exploration on foot of the Alepotripa Caves. Both have dramatic stalactites and stalagmites. Those in the Diros Caves are enhanced by the echoey, damp atmosphere and the striking reflections in the water.

The main town on the east coast of the Mani is **Githio,** actually the capital of the whole area but very different from it in style. It is a busy and prosperous little port, with several good restaurants around its attractive harbor. With the remains of a Roman theater, beaches on its outskirts, and a choice of accommodations, it is a good place to relax while you make forays into the unique Mani region.

**Kardamyli**
Map p. 105

**Areopolis**
Map p. 105

**Spilia Dirou**
Map p. 105
273/305-2222
$$$

**Githio**
Map p. 105
**Visitor Information**
20 Vass. Georgiou, 232 00
273/302-4484

# A Drive Around the Mani

You could spend several days exploring the Mani, discovering its unique culture and a landscape that is harsh but compelling. In spring the wildflowers add dashes of color, yet in winter it can be austere. This drive takes in the highlights if time is limited, and can be done in half a day—but allow a full day if possible. It begins in the main west-coast town of Areopolis (see p. 121) and ends in Githio, the principal town on the east coast.

Before you set off on this rural drive, make sure you have a full tank of gasoline as there are few filling stations in this quiet area. From **Areopolis ❶** head south on the unnumbered local road following the signs for the **Spilia Dirou ❷** (Diros Caves, see p. 121). These caves are 5 miles (8 km) south of the town. Follow the signs and turn right, just past a left turn. (You will emerge here after a circular tour of the Inner Mani, see p. 121.) The caves are 2.5 miles (4 km) down the road. They are worth visiting, but you will need to have plenty of time, especially in high season when waiting time increases and you can enter the caves only on the organized boat tour.

Retrace your route and return to the main road to continue south, avoiding any turns. Even if you do accidentally take a wrong turn, most will eventually return you to the main road anyway, as they are either deadends or loops through villages.

On this western part of the route, known as the Shadowed Coast, look for the peninsula's characteristic square **tower houses.** You might consider stopping in a few of the villages you pass through, many of which have beautiful old Byzantine chapels.

One circular detour off the main road you should take is about 6 miles (10 km) beyond the turnoff for Spilia Dirou, where you come to an intersection. Here you turn right toward Agios Georgios and on to the tiny, quiet village of **Mezapos ❸.** From Mezapos a short walk gives you a view across the sea to the 13th-century Byzantine fortress at **Tigani,** or "frying pan" (named for its shape). If you continue driving

## NOT TO BE MISSED:

**Spilia Dirou • Mezapos**
**Tigani • Vatheia**

along this road you will circle around and rejoin the main road, where you turn right to resume your original drive route.

When you reach the village of Alika, look for a right turn marked for **Vatheia ❹**; take this to look at the cluster of stone tower houses that dominate this otherwise tiny settlement. Here you will have to turn around and retrace your route back to the main road. (If you're feeling adventurous, drive on to the southernmost tip of the Mani and admire the hill of Akra Tenaro—aka Cape Matapan— at closer quarters.)

At the main road, turn right again to continue along the only road, which swings north and takes you up the east coast of the Inner Mani. You travel through several remote villages and past some quiet beaches—and pleasantly off the beaten track. The road eventually swings left and back across the peninsula to rejoin the main west coast road south of Areopolis.

Turn right here and the road becomes Highway 39, which you follow all the way back across the peninsula. The route passes to the south of the Taygetus Mountains, winding up and over until, after about 15 miles (25 km), you arrive at the small port of **Githio ❺** (see p. 121), the main settlement on the Mani's eastern coast. ∎

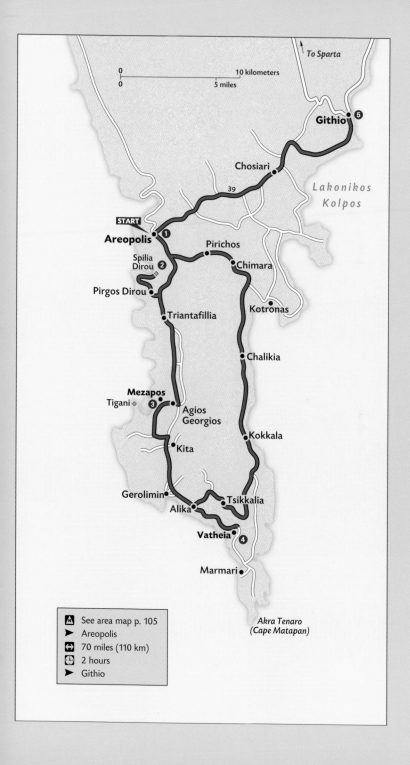

To Sparta

Githio ⑤

Chosiari

*Lakonikos Kolpos*

39

**START**

Areopolis ①

Spilia Dirou ②

Pirgos Dirou

Triantafillia

Pirichos

Chimara

Kotronas

Chalikia

**Mezapos** ③

Tigani

Agios Georgios

Kita

Kokkala

Gerolimin

Alika

Tsikkalia

**Vatheia** ④

Marmari

*Akra Tenaro (Cape Matapan)*

See area map p. 105
Areopolis
70 miles (110 km)
2 hours
Githio

0 — 10 kilometers
0 — 5 miles

# Mystras

A wander around this magical ruined Byzantine city is a sheer delight. Its setting is spectacular, with a hill rising from a plain at the edge of the Taygetos Mountains, which thrust down into the Mani. Atmospheric ruins sprawl over the top and slopes of the hill, with enough remaining to give a good idea of what it must have been like for the 42,000 people who lived here in the 15th century.

Majestic Mystras dates from Byzantine times.

**Mystras**
- Map p. 105
- ☎ 273/108-3377
- $ $$

The city was founded in 1249 by the Franks, who had taken control of Greece at the start of the 13th century. It owes its existence to Guillaume II de Villehardouin, who planned Mystras as the third of his strongholds in this region, alongside Monemvasia and Tigani in the Inner Mani. He saw Mystras as a replacement for nearby Sparta, which lies in the plain. Mystras fell to the Byzantine in 1262, but the new town that grew up in and around the fortress began to flourish. It developed as a notable center of artistic excellence, attracting painters from as far afield as Italy and Constantinople.

There are two entrances to the site. Approaching from Sparta, you first come to the lower entrance. The second entrance is at the top of the hill, and both have parking. There is no particular advantage to either of them, although if you don't enjoy a lot of climbing you might wish to explore the lower slopes first, before driving up to the top and looking around there. Whichever you choose, a map is essential to make sense of the labyrinth of paths, and even so you can't avoid some doubling back.

If you begin at the bottom and turn right you come almost at once to the **Mitropolis,** the cathedral, which dates to 1309, making it the oldest church in Mystras. Inside are some 14th-century frescoes and, conspicuous on the floor, a stone with the Byzantine double-headed eagle carved into it. On this spot the last Byzantine emperor, Constantine

XI Paleologus, was crowned in 1443.

Beyond the Mitropolis is the convent of **Pantanassa,** whose few remaining nuns are the only people still living in Mystras. They sell refreshments and their own handicrafts at busy times of the year. Not surprisingly, the church of this working convent is the best preserved of all in Mystras. Built in 1365, it was the last to be constructed in this hillside walled town.

Turn left at the bottom entrance to reach the **Perivleptos Monastery.** The church here has particularly fine 14th-century frescoes around the dome which, in accordance with Byzantine convention, carries an image of Christ Pantokrator.

## Kastro

The dominant feature at the top of the site is the castle, or Kastro, though first you come to the Palace Chapel of Agia Sofia with its stunning marble floors. Below here it is possible to walk around the castle keep, which gives wonderful views over the ruined city. This dramatic spot is where the German writer and scientist Goethe (1749–1832) set the meeting between Faust and Helen of Troy in his famous play, *Faust.*

In addition to the Kastro, there is also the **Despots' Palace.** The first Byzantine rulers here were the Despots of Morea, Morea being the name of this whole region of Greece. The palace has survived well over the centuries but has been closed for extensive renovations for several years. One wing dates from the original Frankish days; another was added in the 14th century. This section includes a throne room that was used for the coronation of several Byzantine kings. ■

## EXPERIENCE: Cherry-picking & Jam-making in the Southern Peloponnisos

The Greeks have a sweet tooth, as anyone who has sampled baklava or one of their other favorite desserts will know. What visitors may not know, unless they've been invited to visit someone in their home, is that it's a tradition in some places to welcome guests with a glass of water and a spoonful of something sweet, like jam. It's all the more hospitable if the jam is homemade—and it usually is.

Trekking Hellas *(www.trekking.gr)* offers cherry-picking trips that teach you how to make cherry marmalade and more about this Greek tradition. The three-day excursion starts and ends in Athens, and takes visitors to a village called Arna, about three to four hours away in the southern Peloponnisos. Arna is in the foothills of Mount Taygetus, and the first night is enjoyed dining in the village square, in the shade of the biggest plane tree in Greece.

The next day is spent picking cherries, in season, and then washing them in the old cistern, pitting them, and generally getting everything ready for the jam-making process. The third and final day includes the making of both marmalade and the traditional Greek cherry sweet jam, which will then be bottled, labeled, and taken back with you to Athens. For other trips, visit *www.agrotravel.gr.*

# Messenian Peninsula

The towns of Koroni and Methoni stand like twin sentinels on either side of the Messenian peninsula in the southwestern Peloponnisos. Once known for their fortresses, they are better known today as beach resorts. The rest of the region has a range of minor but interesting archaeological sites.

Taking it easy on the beach at Koroni. Boat repair and repainting is usually done in the winter.

**Koroni**
🗺 Map p. 105

**Methoni**
🗺 Map p. 105

The two towns were known as the "eyes of Venice," as their respective forts kept close watch over the shipping movements between Italy and Greece. The castle at **Koroni** was begun in 1206 and its imposing walls still stand, now sheltering the convent of Timiou Prodromou and some private houses. It is a charming place to wander around in the evening. The town below the fort, an attractive jumble of houses, dates only to circa 1830. Its main appeal for vacationers is the magnificent mile-long (1.6 km) sandy beach.

Contemporary with the fort at Koroni, the **Methoni** fortress juts out into the sea, with water on three sides. A moat protects the fourth side. It is a forbidding stronghold, conveying a feeling of abandonment as you walk around inside the walls and see the remnants that are still standing. In contrast to the inhabited fortress at Koroni, in Methoni you find only the ruins of houses, a cathedral, a Turkish bath, and some underground passages.

Methoni also has a good beach, and is altogether a much busier resort than Koroni. Yet at its heart are still the attractive whitewashed houses, with their colorful bougainvillea and hibiscus flowers trailing from the balconies.

## Nestor's Palace

In Homer's *Odyssey*, as the hero Odysseus is endeavoring to get home to the island of Ithaca, his son Telemachus visits the palace of King Nestor to try to get news of his father. Here Telemachus is bathed by Nestor's daughter, Polycaste. Naturally, a bathtub has been found on this site, alleged to be that of the palace of King Nestor, and adding substance to the legend.

An early visit to the **Archaeological Museum** located in the nearby village of **Chora** is recommended. Finds from the palace are on display here with good explanations and help to make more sense of your visit to the site itself.

### Kalamata

**Because of its busy airport and its size—the biggest city in the southern Peloponnisos—Kalamata is more often a place for visitors to set out from than a place to stay. It has long been famed for the quality of its olives and olive oil, however, which are exported to countries all around the world. Visitors to Kalamata should certainly try to buy some of the olives locally. The most attractive part of the city is around the castle, with the Archaeological Museum close by.**

At first sight the remains of this Mycenaean palace are not particularly impressive. Yet it has much of interest, and the small scale of the palace helps bring alive the people who lived here.

The bulk of the site consists of foundations little more than a few inches high; however, with the aid of a plan it is possible to rebuild the palace in your mind. The task is made easier by its fabulous setting, on top of a promontory overlooking the sea and olive groves.

Nestor's Palace was only discovered in 1939, and so has not been subject to the over-enthusiastic interpretations of the likes of Heinrich Schliemann. Exploration continues, using the most modern archaeological techniques. One of the most exciting finds so far is several hundred tablets inscribed with the script known as Linear B, which Sir Arthur Evans had also found at the Minoan site at Knossos on Crete, thereby proving a link between the Minoan and Mycenaean civilizations. Ironically the tablets were preserved by being baked in the very fire which destroyed the palace around 1200 B.C.

## Messene

Ancient Messene is said to have been built in a mere 85 days in 369 B.C. as the brand-new capital of the Messenian people. This westernmost of the Peloponnisos's three peninsulas is named after them. Like other sites, it owes its appeal to its location as much as to what has actually survived here. It is found just outside the village

**Nestor's Palace**

⬛ Map p. 105
🕐 Closed Mon.
💲 $

**Archaeological Museum**

✉ Chora
☎ 276/303-1358
🕐 Closed Mon.
💲 $

**Messene**

⬛ Map p. 105

**Megapolis**

 Map p. 105

of Mavromati, on the slopes of Mount Ithomi (2,600 feet/800 m) at the northern end of the peninsula, and is referred to as Ithomi on road signs.

If you are driving, take the road to Meligalas to pass through the huge and dramatic Arcadia Gate, part of the original city walls. Some 5.5 miles (9 km) of wall have so far been unearthed, and excavations at the site are ongoing. You can see the foundations of a temple to Artemis here, along with the remains of the acropolis on top of Mount Ithomi, and a fountain in the Sanctuary of Asklepius, which still provides water to the modern village.

## Megalopolis

Farther north on the road towards Tripoli are the ruins of ancient Megalopolis, the "big town," on the edge of the modern town that retains that name. Little of the town remains, but to get some impression of its former glory, know that the theater here could easily seat some 20,000 people, making it bigger than the theater at Epidavros and even the Theater of Dionysos in Athens.

Megalopolis was built at about the same time as Messene, 371–368 B.C., and by the same person, the Theban leader Epaminondas. His aim was to have a series of defensive cities to keep the Spartans at bay. But Megalopolis never prospered, and even today has an abandoned air. Its overgrown state makes a welcome contrast to sites where everything is mapped and labeled. ■

## National Flag

The distinctive blue and white flag of Greece seems ideally suited to this country of deep blue skies and almost blindingly bright whitewashed houses. The blue and the white have been Greek colors for centuries, although the modern design was adopted only in 1833, a year after Otto of Bavaria was made the first king of an independent Greek state (see p. 35). Before this, the flag was a simple white cross on a blue background, a design that was adopted again between 1975 and 1978 and which is still occasionally seen.

The nine horizontal stripes on the flag are highly significant. They represent the nine syllables of the motto of the freedom fighters who fought against Turkish rule in the War of Independence: *"Eleutheria i thanatos!—Freedom or death!"*

Over the years the shade of the blue stripes has changed from light to dark and back to light again. The flag you see today was finally settled upon on December 21, 1978.

Greece is a country with a keen sense of patriotism, and you will see the flag flying everywhere, all year-round.

# Andritsaina & Vasses

Heading northwest from Megalopolis, a winding road leads up into one of the most picturesque and unspoiled mountain settlements in all of Greece: Andritsaina. On its way the road
passes Vasses and its temple, one of the most dramatically situated in Greece.

Old mountain towns like Andritsaina seem almost untouched by the modern world.

Andritsaina was an important market town during the Turkish occupation and is still a focal point for the smaller, isolated villages around, with old men whose eyes have seen a great deal of history now sitting in cafés to watch the world go by.

There are places to stay overnight here if you don't mind something simple, but most visitors make only a brief stop before heading out into the mountains, to see the **Temple of Vasses,** also known as Vassae or Bassae. This is one of the most remote and impressive classical sites, standing at a height of 3,711 feet (1,131 m), with little around it to distract the eye.

The temple was dedicated to Apollo and built by the Figalians, the local people, as thanks for protection from a plague. The site of ancient Figalia was west of here, scattered around the modern village of Figalia. Vasses is one of the best preserved temples in Greece, in an even better state of preservation than the Parthenon. It was once thought it might have been designed by Iktinos, the Parthenon's architect. Now it seems likely that it predates it, and was probably completed by 425 B.C.

It will be more impressive when restored. Until then it is protected from the elements by a vast tent, although even this creates a novel experience. ∎

**Andritsaina**
 Map p. 105

**Vasses**
 Map p. 105

# Olympia

The modern Olympic Games date back little more than a hundred years, but the original games were first held nearly 3,000 years ago, beginning in 776 B.C., and took place every four years for more than a millennium. A visit to the actual stadium where those games were held—and where the Olympic flame to herald the start of the modern athletic contests is lit—is, for many, a dream come true.

A double row of columns marks the boundary of the square sports arena, or *palaestra*.

**Ancient Olympia**
- Map p. 105
- ☎ 262/402-2517
- $ $$

**Visitor Information**
- ✉ Tourist Office
- ☎ 262/402-3100

**Archaeological Museum**
- ☎ 262/402-2529
- $ $$

**Museum of the Games**
- ☎ 262/402-2544
- $ $$

The town marked the 2004 homecoming of the games with a multimillion-dollar face-lift, including a new ring road, pedestrianization of the main street, footbridge to reach the ancient site, riverside walks, cultural center, two new museums—and the holding of one event, the shot put, at the ancient site.

But none of this can compare to the experience of walking down the entrance tunnel, beneath the third-century B.C. arch and out into the arena at **Ancient Olympia,** and imagining the roar of the crowds.

You see much more of the site before reaching the stadium itself, however, revealing what a vast

complex it was—the equivalent of today's modern Olympic villages.

At the center of the site was the **Temple of Zeus,** constructed in the fifth century B.C. Only the bases of the columns remain, although some fallen columns have been left in sections where they crashed to the ground, helping to give a picture of the place not only in life but also as it fell into decay.

The temple contained a huge statue of Zeus, which was made in the group of buildings whose foundations are in front of the temple, on the side away from the stadium. One of these buildings is marked as the **Studio of Pheidias,** the sculptor who crafted the statue. Across the path from here are the remains of the **Leonidaion,** the guesthouse used for distinguished visitors.

Behind the Leonidaion is the **Bouleuterion,** the meeting house where the equivalent of the modern International Olympic Committee would gather. It was also where the athletes swore to uphold the Olympic rules. From here the athletes made their way into the stadium, passing rows of statues portraying past athletes who had broken the rules. Paid for by fines levied on these disgraced athletes, the statues recorded each person's name, father's name, and hometown. Cheaters were not taken lightly.

There was also, naturally, a section where the heroes of the games were honored. Close to the modern-day entrance is another building of note. The **Temple of Hera** is smaller than the Temple of Zeus. Dating from the seventh century B.C., it was rebuilt in the sixth century B.C. and is almost as old as the games themselves.

## The Museums

Opposite the site of Olympia, the renovated **Archaeological Museum** houses finds from the site, one of Greece's finest collections. Pride of place, in the main hall, goes to the sculptures and friezes that adorned the Temple of Zeus. Tools from the workshop of Pheidias are displayed in another room. Displays on a more human scale include items used in the games themselves, such as discuses, part of a starting block, and the stones used by the weightlifters. Don't miss the elegant marble statue of Nike by Paionios, from the fifth century B.C.

Also worth visiting, the **Old Archaeological Museum** is now in a renovated neoclassical house at the end of the main street. Located a block behind the main street, the **Museum of the Games** focuses on the modern games and host cities with medals, torches, posters, and more.

## EXPERIENCE: Tapestry-weaving Lessons

You can try your hand at tapestry-weaving by taking a course near ancient Olympia in the western Peloponnisos, which includes time off to visit the site of the original Olympic Games. Included in the package is transport to and from Athens, six nights accommodation in a Class A Guesthouse, most of your meals, and 16 hours of tuition in tapestry-weaving on your own frame loom.

The course is relaxed, with lots of free time, and not for those who want an intensive workshop. But for beginners seeking to combine some tapestry-weaving and learning about dyes with the chance to explore the area, this is ideal. As well as seeing Olympia you'll have the chance to go walking in the gorge of the Ladonas River, where you will collect wildflowers that produce some of the dyes.

One morning is spent cooking the traditional local sourdough bread, and making a pie using fresh herbs collected locally. There are also visits to monasteries and to villages where few tourists venture, but by the end of the six days you will have produced your own tapestry to take away with you. For more information, visit *www.trekking.gr* or *www. agrotravel.gr.*

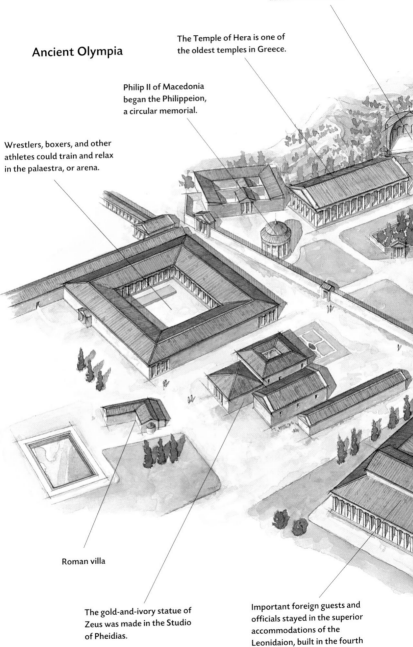

The Exedra of Herodes Atticus, an elaborate drinking fountain, dates from A.D. 160.

The Temple of Hera is one of the oldest temples in Greece.

## Ancient Olympia

Philip II of Macedonia began the Philippeion, a circular memorial.

Wrestlers, boxers, and other athletes could train and relax in the palaestra, or arena.

Roman villa

The gold-and-ivory statue of Zeus was made in the Studio of Pheidias.

Important foreign guests and officials stayed in the superior accommodations of the Leonidaion, built in the fourth century B.C.

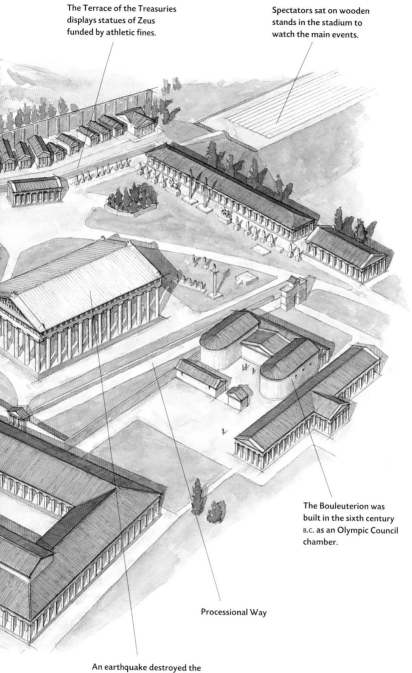

The Terrace of the Treasuries displays statues of Zeus funded by athletic fines.

Spectators sat on wooden stands in the stadium to watch the main events.

The Bouleuterion was built in the sixth century B.C. as an Olympic Council chamber.

Processional Way

An earthquake destroyed the Temple of Zeus 1,100 years after its construction in the fifth century B.C.

# Patra

The largest city in the Peloponnisos and the third largest in Greece, Patra (or Patras) is chiefly attractive to visitors for its port, which allows access to other areas. It is the second largest port after Pireas, with connections to Italy and to several of the Ionian islands, as well as train connections to Athens and bus connections to many parts of the Greek mainland.

Agios Andreas, the modern church of St. Andrew, houses the head of the saint.

**Patra**
🇦 Map p. 105
**Visitor Information**
✉ Amalias 6
☎ 261/046-1740

From just outside Patra at Rion, a short ferry ride transports you across the Gulf of Corinth to northern and western Greece. A bridge to speed up the journey is under construction.

Nevertheless, if you decide to spend a night here, there are plenty of hotels and enough diversions to keep you amused for a few hours. The downtown is at **Plateia Psila Alonia,** where sidewalk cafés invite you to sit and watch the drama of everyday street life unfold. At the southern end of the waterfront is the large Byzantine-style modern church of **Agios Andreas** (St. Andrew), built in 1979 on the spot where the saint is said to have been

martyred. You may be surprised to find that inside is the head of the saint, which was returned to Patra from Rome in 1964.

The most attractive part of Patra is the **upper town,** around the slopes of the ancient acropolis where the mainly Byzantine **castle** now stands. The ruins are in a pleasant park and worth the climb. From here you can see north across the Gulf of Corinth, south to the mountains of the Peloponnisos, and across the Ionian Sea to the islands of Zakinthos and Kefalonia. A few blocks south of the castle is the Roman **Odeion** (theater), which has been restored so that it can now be used for modern performances. ■

# More Places to Visit Around the Peloponnisos

## Kalavryta

Few foreign visitors make the journey to Kalavryta, about 20 miles (32 km) southeast of Patra, but to the Greeks it is a place of pilgrimage. In 1821 at the **Monastery of Agia Lavra,** 4 miles (6 km) outside Kalavryta, the Archbishop of Patra raised the Greek flag in defiance of the Turkish occupiers, signaling the start of the War of Independence. The small mountain town is likely to be filled with Greek visitors at any time of the year, but on the anniversary of that event, commemorated every March 21, you will be unable to move.

The monastery itself had to be rebuilt after World War II. In a terrible act of reprisal, Nazi forces killed the entire male population of Kalavryta—1,436 men and boys—then burned down the town and, in the ultimate act of contempt, also burned down the monastery where the rebellion had begun. A mural in the reconstructed town commemorates that event, and one of the clock towers on the main church remains forever fixed at 2:34 p.m., the time of the massacre.

The journey to Kalavryta can be one of the most uplifting travel experiences in Greece. A **rack-and-pinion railway** runs from the coastal town of Diakofto, on the Gulf of Corinth, and climbs slowly for 14 miles (22.5 km) along gorges, by cliff faces, through woods and 14 tunnels, alongside rivers, and across bridges, bringing you through breathtaking scenery to Kalavryta at 2,480 feet (756 m).
🅼 Map p. 105  ☎ 210/513-1601 for railroad timetable details  🆂 $

## Kithira

Kithira is an island that sits on its own at the foot of the Peloponnisos and is awkward to reach. There are daily flights from Athens, and in summer several ferries or hydrofoils per week from the Peloponnisos. Outside the short peak season of June–September, ferry service is limited, and cancellations frequent because of the notoriously rough seas.

In part Kithira owes its fortunes, or lack of them, to those rough seas. The difficulty of negotiating these waters was a prime reason for the opening of the Corinth Canal in the late 19th century (see p. 106). Before then, boats would call at Kithira regularly, bringing welcome trade and income. With the opening of the canal, that trade ceased almost completely. Since then the island's population has fallen to about 3,000 people. Although few visitors reach the island there are numerous attractions—and you'll have them all to yourself if you're lucky.

The capital is **Chora.** Whitewashed buildings cluster on a hillside above the harbor, leading up toward the domineering walls of a hugely impressive **fortress,** which seems almost as big as the town again. The castle was begun by the Venetians in the 13th century and expanded in the late 15th century—you can see the date of 1503 inscribed there. Within its walls is the church of the Panagia Myrtidiotissa, with a straight drop to the sea behind it, and a view of the islet of Avgo, one of several places claiming to be the birthplace of Aphrodite. Inside the castle there is also a very small **Archaeological Museum** (tel 273/503-1739, closed Mon.).

Below Chora is the harbor cum resort of **Kapsali,** which is as close as the island gets to a developed resort. It has an adequate beach of pebbles and sand, but to get to the best sandy beaches you will have to explore. Public transportation is limited, and you really need to rent a car or make use of the taxi service to get around. There are excellent beaches at Diakofti on the east coast, Limiona on the west, and Plateia Ammos in the very north.

To get to Plateia Ammos, you pass through the beautiful unspoiled hill village of **Karavas,** from where a road leads down to the island's main port at **Agia Pelagia.** Several hotels here cater for the travelers who might need to stay overnight before moving on. Farther south again is the site of the island's former capital at

**Paleochora,** now deserted. Its ruins stand 650 feet (200 m) above the sea—a haunting place, and an essential visit if you are on the island. A thriving Byzantine town with some 72 churches, Paleochora had been the island capital since 1248. Although the town was designed to be invisible from the sea, the renowned pirate Barbarossa attacked and destroyed it in 1537, killing many and taking 7,000 captive. Today only half a dozen churches survive among the ruins.

🗺 Map p. 105

## Pilos

Boats bob and fishermen mend their nets in this appealing harbor—familiar scenes in the Greek islands. The attractive town of Pilos, on the west coast of the Peloponnisos, makes a good base for a few days or even longer. Waterfront restaurants serve the freshest of food, and one end of the harbor is dominated by the castle, built originally by the Turks in 1572 but added to by the Venetians and the French. Parts of the structure are run-down, but, with the beautiful church of Agios Sotiros sitting within its walls, the castle is a good place to explore.

Pilos commands the southern entrance to Navarino Bay (Ormos Navarinou), which is almost sealed off from the rest of the Ionian Sea by Sphaktiria Island. It was in this bay that one of Greece's most significant sea battles took place. On October 20, 1827, a fleet of 26 Greek and allied warships approached the bay, where 82 Turkish and Egyptian ships were waiting. The intent was to negotiate, but one of the Egyptian ships fired a cannon, after which a full-scale battle took place. No fewer than 51 Turkish ships were sunk, while the Greeks lost none. The resulting dominance of the waters was in no small way responsible for Greece winning its independence from Turkey in 1828.

🗺 Map p. 105

## EXPERIENCE:
# Volunteer with Birds of Prey in Greece

The small island of Andikithira, located between Kithira and Crete, is an important passing point for migrating raptors. The observation and recording of the birds is just one of several projects run by the Hellenic Ornithological Society for which they are always seeking volunteers. This offers a great opportunity for ornithologists and other nature lovers to study Greek birds of prey at close hand and, by providing statistics, assist the Ornithological Society to help the Greek bird population.

Periods for which volunteers for this particular project are needed are from March to May and late August to October. You will need to take a sleeping bag, though accommodation in a recently restored guesthouse is provided, along with basic food supplies. The guesthouse sleeps ten, and you have to be prepared to mix in with the cooking. You need to stay at least 15 days, and work for seven to eight hours a day, though this varies depending on the number of volunteers.

For the raptor program you will spend several hours each day in an observation post, and while it will obviously help if you know your European birds of prey already, you can also volunteer for the training program, for which no previous skills will be expected of you.

The cost is €30 for nonmembers of the Hellenic Ornithological Society, and you must make your own way to the destination. For more information, contact the society (*Vas. Irakleiou 24, GR-10682, Athens, Greece, tel & fax 210/822-7937 or 210/822-8704, www.ornithologiki.gr; also at Kastritsiou 8, GR-54623, Thessaloniki, Greece, tel & fax 231/024-4245).*

From the mountains of the north to the Gulf of Corinth and from the blue Ionian Sea in the west to Macedonia in the east, the most diverse and exciting region of the country

# Central Greece, Thessaly, & Epiros

Modern icons for sale

# Central Greece, Thessaly, & Epiros

If you had to choose a single area of Greece that encapsulates all that is best about the country, it would have to be this central region. Modern beach resorts such as Parga dot the west coast, and important historical remains, such as those at Dodoni, are found farther inland. In Delphi, the region also has the most important historic site outside of Athens.

The lakeside town of Ioanina is popular with Greeks but often overlooked by visitors. Its setting, beside a deep lake and with a mountain backdrop, is breathtaking.

This is a mountainous region, including the dramatic Pindos range and the Parnassos farther south, both favored by avid walkers in search of fresh air and unspoiled beauty. The Pindos Mountains include an area known as Zagoria, where villages built of stone and slate are linked to each other by centuries-old paths cut out of the harsh surroundings.

This region also has the magnificent Vikos Gorge, the second longest in Europe after the Samaria Gorge in Crete, but visited by a few hundred people rather than thousands every day. East of here you climb into the Pindos, where the roads may be blocked by snow in winter but in summer give access to awesome scenery and very special mountain villages—including Metsovo, home to some of Greece's last remaining nomads.

Across these mountains and back down in the plains of Thessaly (Thessalia), you find a place unlike any other in the world. This is Meteora, where ancient monasteries cling to the tops of rocks that thrust up out of the plain.

Heading east to the coast again, you find the picture-postcard scenery of a Greek idyll, with sandy beaches, fresh fish, and friendly people. It's all there on the Pilion peninsula, the legendary relaxing place of the Greek gods and a favorite with Greek vacationers. It is, however, still something of a secret to foreign visitors. ∎

**NOT TO BE MISSED:**

Area of map detail

MACEDONIA & THRACE    p. 167

2917m
Olympus

6/E92

Meteora
Kalabaka

Elasson

Tirnavos    1 E75

Zarkos    6/E92    Larissa

Trikala    Pineios

Pyli    T H E S S A L Y    Kanalia

Karditsa    Makrinitsa    Agios
    Ioannis

1551m    Tsagkarada

Limni    Farsala    Volos    Vizitsa    Milies
Tavropou
    Neo Monastiri    Pilion

Kastania    Pagassitikos
    Kolpos

Domokos    3/E65    Almyros    Trikeri    Platania

Fragkista    2315m    Makrakomi    Sourpi    Agia
    1726m    Kiriaki

38/E951    Othrys

Karpenissi    Lamia    Glifa

Acheloos    Texniti Limni    Spercheios    EVIA
    Kremaston    p. 203

C E N T R A L
    G R E E C E    Vorios Evvoikos Kolpos

Evinos    2510m    1 E75    Arkitsa

Agrinio    Lidorikion    PARNASSOS
    NAT. PARK    Malesina

Limni    Amfissa    3    Kifisos
Trichonida    2457m
    Corycian Cave

Messolongi    E65    Delphi    Arachova    Livadia

Nafpaktos    Galaxidion    Osiou    Aliartos    3/E962
Adirrion    Louka

    Thisvi    Thiva
    (Thebes)

Korinthiakos    AROUND ATHENS

PELOPONNISOS    Kolpos    p. 89
    p. 103

# Gulf of Corinth

The spectacular drive along the northern shore of the Gulf of Corinth (Korinthiakos Kolpos), looking across the blue waters to the mountains of the Peloponnese, is one of the best in Greece. Behind you rise the imposing Parnassos Mountains. The road heading west, when it joins the coast beyond Delphi, links a series of appealing little coastal towns, all delightful stopping-off points.

The Gulf of Corinth shines in late afternoon.

**Gulf of Corinth**
 Map p. 139

**Galaxidion**
Map p. 139

**Nautical &
Historical
Museum**
✉ Mouseio 4
☎ 226/504-1795
💲 $$

**Nafpaktos**
Map p. 139

The first of these is **Galaxidion,** its houses radiating from a headland and painted in white and pretty pastel colors. The dome of the church is clearly visible as you approach the town, in pride of place on the headland, and dedicated to Agios Nikolaos, the patron saint of sailors. The fine 19th-century mansions that line the waterfront—along with many good tavernas—indicate the importance of shipping to the town. To learn about Galaxidion's past, visit the new **Nautical and Historical Museum,** an enjoyable summary of the town's history.

The next town of note as you head west along the coast is **Nafpaktos,** which is also built around a headland, this time crowned by a 15th-century **Venetian fortress.** Take a walk to the top for views along the coast and across the gulf. The castle walls extend to the sea and around the harbor, with one of the old gates leading to the town's beach.

The medieval Venetian name for Nafpaktos was Lepanto, and this was the scene of the last major sea battle to be fought with ships propelled primarily by oars, in 1571. The Battle of Lepanto was between the Turks, who occupied Greece at that time, and an attacking fleet made up of a Christian alliance from several European nations. The Turks lost the battle but did not lose Greece. One notable casualty was the Spaniard Miguel de Cervantes Saavedra (1547–1616), the author of *Don Quixote,* who lost his left hand in the fight.

From Nafpaktos it is a short drive southwest to **Andirrion,** from where the ferries leave for the short sail across the Gulf of Corinth to Rio, just outside Patra on the Peloponnese side. A road bridge is also under construction. The main reason for visiting Andirrion is to explore the remains of the Franco-Venetian castle that stands guard over this stretch of water—known to the Greeks as the Little Dardanelles—and matches another castle on the far side.

Beyond Andirrion the road swings inland and crosses a slightly flatter landscape as it heads for the marshes and salt pans that surround the town of **Messolongi.** This is where Lord Byron died of a fever, and his statue stands in the town's **Garden of Heroes.** Beneath the statue, erected in 1881, is buried the poet's heart.

Close to the garden is the **Gate of the Exodus,** through which you'll probably pass on your way in or out of Messolongi. In 1826, two years after Byron's death, the town was besieged by Turkish forces. In a desperate bid for freedom, an estimated 9,000 men, women, and children broke out through the gate, leaving their fellow citizens to destroy the town rather than let it again fall into Turkish hands. The rebels fled into the hills, but they were caught and every one of them killed. The bodies of those people left behind are also buried in the Garden of Heroes, under a small, plain mound near Byron's statue.

Byron died at a house on Odos Levidou that was destroyed during World War II. A memorial garden marks the spot. There is a small **museum** you will want to visit if you are especially interested in the War of Independence; its collection includes an original copy of the patriotic poem by Solomos that became the Greek National Anthem, "Hymn to Freedom." ∎

**Messolongi**

🅰 Map p. 139

**Visitor Information**

✉ Tourist Police

☎ 263/102-7220

## "Mad, Bad, and Dangerous to Know"

That was the description given to British poet Lord Byron (1788–1824) by one of his lovers, Lady Caroline Lamb. The sixth Baron Byron also had a memorable love affair with Greece, and it was while traveling there that he wrote one of his most famous works, *Childe Harold's Pilgrimage.* Byron felt so strongly about the country that in January 1824 he joined Greek rebels fighting the Turkish rulers in the War of Independence. In only three months he was dead, after contracting a fever in Messolongi, which was then much more swampy than it is today. A statue in the town commemorates the poet, and scarcely a Greek city exists without a Byron (Vyronos) Street somewhere.

# Osiou Louka

**The monastery of Osiou Louka (Blessed Luke) stands alone in an olive-filled valley surrounded by mountains, just a few miles down a side road off the Athens–Delphi road. The saint to whom it is dedicated was a Greek hermit, not the more famous Gospel-writer. He died in A.D. 953 and is buried in a crypt at the monastery.**

Osiou Louka dates from the 11th century.

**Osiou Louka**

A Map p. 139

☎ 226/102-4088

$ $

The chapels here are among the best examples of Byzantine architecture in Greece, and have some of its finest preserved frescoes. Despite its isolated position, Osiou Louka is usually busy, not just because of the frescoes or reverence for St. Luke, but because it makes a convenient second stop on one-day trips from Athens to Delphi.

St. Luke was probably born in Delphi in A.D. 896, to parents who had fled from Egina to escape the Saracens. Known to be spiritual and somewhat other worldly, Luke left home in his teens to seek solitude. He gained a reputation as a healer, and was soon credited with miraculous cures. Eventually Luke settled in the nearby village of Stiri, and the first church on the site of the monastery was built

between 941 and 944 and dedicated to St. Barbara.

By this time Luke had also developed a gift for prophecy, and among his predictions was one that Crete would be liberated by an emperor named Romanos. In 961, eight years after Luke's death, Crete was taken from its Arab rulers by the Byzantines under Emperor Romanos and, in recognition of Luke's prophecy, Romanos built a larger church alongside that of St. Barbara.

The first thing to greet you when you arrive at Osiou Louka is a glowing gold mosaic of the saint on an arch over the entrance gate into the monastery proper. The church built by Romanos has been replaced by one built in 1020, known as the **Katholikon.** It is an awesome experience to enter the tall building, with its marble walls, and see the light slanting in from high windows onto the ancient frescoes, some of which date back to the original building of the church at the start of the 11th century. However, many of the frescoes were repainted after an earthquake in 1659 damaged the monastery.

The finest of the mosaics is reckoned to be "The Washing of the Apostles' Feet," in the narthex high up to your left as you enter the main, western door. It is a striking work, not only for the bright gold and other colors that remain, but for the very human expression on the faces of the Apostles. It helps to have binoculars with you to get a good look.

Beneath the Katholikon is a crypt with the body of St. Luke. More frescoes dating back to the 11th century are here, although it is difficult to fully appreciate them as the light is kept low, both out of reverence to the remains of the saint and also to help preserve the frescoes.

In an unusual arrangement, the smaller church of the **Theotokos** (the God-Bearing, referring to the Virgin Mary) is connected to the larger church. The Theotokos is thought to have been built in the years 997–1011, so it is slightly older than the Katholikon. Its mosaics are easier to see, most being on the floor. Note, too, the elaborate exterior brickwork.

The monastery has outbuildings that can be explored, as well as a museum containing finds from the site, and shops indicating the popularity of the place for pilgrims. Don't miss the terrace, which gives wonderful views across farmland and groves of olives and almond trees to the Elikonas Mountains beyond.

Only a handful of monks still live here, and the daily round of visitors is a necessary interruption to their monastic life. Lucky is the visitor who arrives here to find the tranquillity that the monks themselves seek out, and can perhaps share it with them, if only for a while. If you want to enjoy the place in as peaceful a way as possible, arrive early or late in the day to avoid the crowds. If that is not possible, don't avoid it—it is still a magical place at any time. ∎

## Icons

Icons have become universal in our modern world, but the specific meaning goes back to the Greek *eikon,* meaning an image of a person. In some churches that is all it is: an image or depiction of the saint or other holy person. In Eastern Orthodox religions like the Greek Church, however, the image itself is sacred. When you visit churches and see worshippers kneeling before an icon, or kissing it, they are communicating directly with the person portrayed. Icon painting in Greece goes back to the earliest days of Christianity and continues to the present. Greeks still buy them, both large ones for the home and small ones for their cars, and they make unusual souvenirs.

# Delphi

The ancient Greeks considered Delphi the center of the world, and to the modern visitor looking to travel beyond Athens, it should be the center of any itinerary. The site lies on the southern slopes of the Parnassos Mountains, looking out over a wide valley filled with olive trees that falls away toward the coast. Even without the wonders of the ancient site, it would be unforgettable.

The beautiful rotunda, or tholos, in the Sanctuary of Athena was a fourth-century-B.C. shrine.

**Delphi**
- Map p. 139
- 226/508-2313 (site & museum)
- $$

**Visitor Information**
- Tourist Office, Town Hall
- 226/508-2900

At no time of year is Delphi empty of visitors so, if you have your independence and are not reliant on an organized tour, it is worth staying at least one night in either modern Delphi or the next village along, **Arachova**. This will ensure that you can be at Delphi early in the morning or toward the end of the day, and enjoy its marvelous sights in relative peace.

When you visit Delphi you are part of a tradition that goes back over 3,000 years. In the 12th century B.C., the first pilgrims began to come here to seek advice from the Pythia, the most famous oracle of the ancient world. They continued to do so in large numbers until the fourth century A.D. The traditional time to visit was on the seventh day of the month, when anyone could ask questions of the oracle for guidance on matters large or small. From tablets and fragments that have been found here and at other oracles, it can be seen that concerns through the ages have changed little. People wanted to know if their partner was faithful, whether they could trust a friend, or whether to take a particular job.

The oracle was not one particular person, but a woman (usually over age 50) deemed to have been given the powers of prophecy by the god Apollo. The Pythia was attended by priests, who interpreted her prophecies. It is thought that when called upon to prophesy she might have gone into a drug-induced trance, resulting in utterances that needed a great deal of translating, so making the priest's job a vital one.

The **Rock of the Sibyl,** which stands on the spot where she was consulted, is marked to one side of the paved **Sacred Way.** This path leads up through the site to the remains of the **Temple of Apollo,** which dates from the fourth century B.C. (an earlier building is known to have existed here in the sixth century B.C.). The temple was discovered by French archaeologists exploring here only in 1892, and since then six of the temple's fallen Doric columns have been re-erected to try to give a sense of the grandeur of the building.

Above the temple is the **theater,** which has survived remarkably from the fourth century B.C., when it was built to hold 5,000 spectators. Beyond the theater, where comparatively few visitors

## EXPERIENCE: Join in a Local Feast

The Greek calendar is filled with feasts, most of them religious ones celebrating saints' days, but that doesn't mean they are somber, sober affairs. The Greeks know how to have a good time, and if you hear of anything taking place while you are visiting, you should try to attend.

These feasts are once-a-year affairs. The more rural a place is—the tiny islands, the mountain villages—the better time you'll have. For example, the village of Arachova near Delphi celebrates the feast of St. George in a big way. Known in other parts of the world as a dragon-slayer, St. George is the patron saint of shepherds, an important figure in this rural mountain community. The feast also celebrates the Greek victory over the Turks in 1826 to gain their independence.

The events, which go on for three days, begin on April 22 with a church service to celebrate Greek liberation, which includes the blowing of trumpets and the firing of a cannon. Prayers and services continue in the church for the next three days. Outside there are athletics events, commencing with one in which the old men of the village (anyone over 70) compete in a race to chase the Ottomans up the hill on which a local battle took place.

There are also wrestling, jumping, and shot-putting competitions, as well as traditional music and dances. Anyone who has reason to thank St. George offers a lamb, which is blessed by the priest and then slaughtered, the blood being used to mark crosses on the foreheads of children. It's a reminder to a new generation never to forget their roots and their village, the sacrifices made by previous generations to ensure freedom, and the place of the church in their lives.

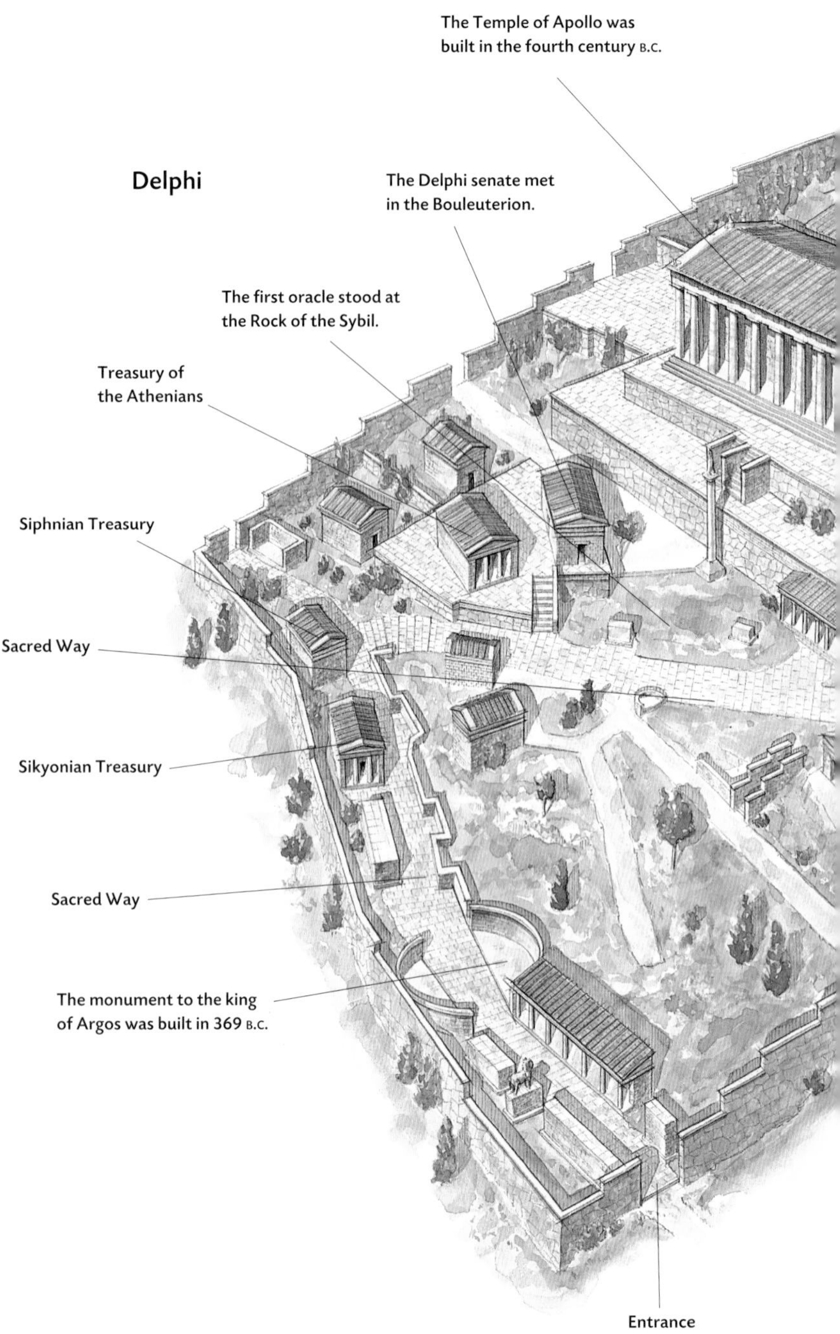

The Temple of Apollo was
built in the fourth century B.C.

# Delphi

The Delphi senate met
in the Bouleuterion.

The first oracle stood at
the Rock of the Sybil.

Treasury of
the Athenians

Siphnian Treasury

Sacred Way

Sikyonian Treasury

Sacred Way

The monument to the king
of Argos was built in 369 B.C.

Entrance

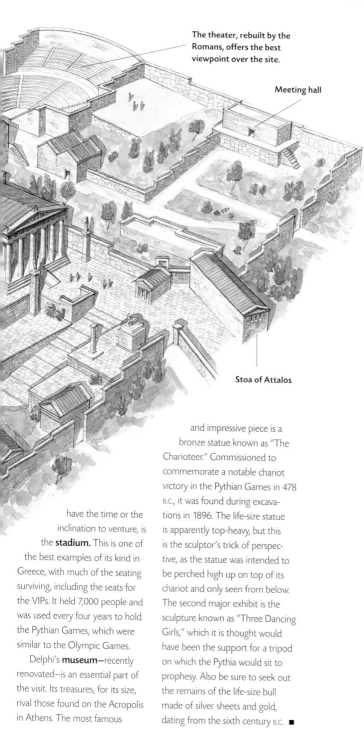

The theater, rebuilt by the Romans, offers the best viewpoint over the site.

Meeting hall

Stoa of Attalos

have the time or the inclination to venture, is the **stadium.** This is one of the best examples of its kind in Greece, with much of the seating surviving, including the seats for the VIPs. It held 7,000 people and was used every four years to hold the Pythian Games, which were similar to the Olympic Games.

Delphi's **museum**—recently renovated—is an essential part of the visit. Its treasures, for its size, rival those found on the Acropolis in Athens. The most famous

and impressive piece is a bronze statue known as "The Charioteer." Commissioned to commemorate a notable chariot victory in the Pythian Games in 478 B.C., it was found during excavations in 1896. The life-size statue is apparently top-heavy, but this is the sculptor's trick of perspective, as the statue was intended to be perched high up on top of its chariot and only seen from below. The second major exhibit is the sculpture known as "Three Dancing Girls," which it is thought would have been the support for a tripod on which the Pythia would sit to prophesy. Also be sure to seek out the remains of the life-size bull made of silver sheets and gold, dating from the sixth century B.C. ■

# Parnassos Mountains

Behind Delphi rise the dramatic Parnassos Mountains. Their highest point is the 8,061-foot (2,457 m) Mount Liakoura, or Wolf Mountain. You are unlikely to see wolves today, as roads make the top easily accessible, and skiers, hikers, and mountain bikers now flock here. Nearby Gerontovrachos, or Old Man's Rock, looms slightly lower at 7,989 feet (2,435 m).

The views are dramatic, but Mount Parnassos and other nearby peaks are easily accessible by road.

**Parnassos National Park**

Map p. 139

Much of the area is protected as **Parnassos National Park,** established in 1938. This makes it one of the first national parks in Europe and, with the one around Mount Olympus, the oldest in Greece. It is dominated by forested slopes of Cephalonian fir. Between the trees there are beautiful meadows, colored with alpine flowers in the spring. Only the occasional wolf makes a visit these days, when driven down by especially harsh conditions in the mountains, but there are foxes, badgers, squirrels, and even wild boars. The

**INSIDER TIP:**

*Formaela* (Arachova's local cheese) is best served roasted with some drops of lemon.

—PENNY DACKIS
*National Geographic publicist*

Parnassos Mountains are home to several species of vulture and eagle, including golden eagles.

## Arachova

Despite being just 7 miles (12 km) from Delphi, this delightful mountain village is little affected by tourism. Beyond the souvenir shops lining the main road the traditional life of Arachova goes on, as you will see if you spend a night or two there and join the local people in their evening *volta*.

Away from the main road you find narrow streets of traditional houses, and the tavernas serve hearty mountain food. The region is known for its cheeses and robust wine. Roadside stores are filled with woolen rugs known as flokatis, excellent for keeping out the cold mountain air in winter.

From Arachova it is easy to make forays into the lower slopes of the Parnassos range, either by hiring a local guide or simply arming yourself with a good map. Always keep a watchful eye on the weather, which can change quickly. Let someone at your hotel know where you are going and when you expect to be back.

## Delphi

The modern village of Delphi is another good base, not only for visiting the classical site (see pp. 144–147), which is within walking distance, but for venturing into the mountains. Hotel and restaurant prices are a little higher than at Arachova.

A popular walk leads up to the **Corycian Cave,** which was once the scene of frenzied orgies when it was held to be sacred to Pan, the god of fertility. Today you will need a flashlight, not for illuminating any such activity but rather to see the stalactites and stalagmites inside the cave and to read the inscriptions carved into the walls. Check local conditions before setting off, and note that the cave is not usually accessible November–April.

From December to April the ski season is in full swing. The main center is at **Fterolakkas,** a 15-mile (24 km) drive from Arachova. Here you will find a restaurant and a chairlift to take you up to 6,200 feet (1,900 m), from where a ski lift takes you higher up the slopes. Snow gives way to colorful wildflowers in spring. ∎

## EXPERIENCE:
## Go Skiing

Greece is not renowned as a great skiing destination, and while the facilities here are certainly not in the same league as France, say, the scenery in places can match anything anywhere in Europe. The resorts themselves also have a more homey charm, precisely because they are not as well known and not as super-smooth—or as expensive—as their counterparts in the Alps and elsewhere.

The Greek season runs roughly from January to April, depending on the snow conditions, of course. Featuring 17 downhill runs, the best-known resort is the **Parnassos Ski Centre** (*www.parnassos-ski .gr*). About 110 miles (180 km) northwest of Athens, close to Delphi. Because it's quite near Athens, it's one of the busier resorts. **Mount Vermio** (*tel 0332 71234*) near Veroia, about 62 miles (100 km) from Thessaloniki has just eight runs. There are several other ski resorts in Macedonia, Thessaly, and central Greece, and two small resorts in the Peloponnisos You can get details of these and other ski information from the Hellenic Skiing Federation (*Karagiorgi Servias 7, 10563 Athens, tel 210/323-4412*). There is also an information leaflet, *Mountain Refuges and Ski Centres,* which should be available from Greek tourist offices.

# Volos & the Pilion Peninsula

Tradition holds that the Pilion peninsula is where the Greek gods used to go to enjoy themselves by relaxing, eating, and drinking. Today it's where modern Greeks go to do the same, joined by an increasing number of discerning visitors. The region's highlights include beaches, unspoiled mountain villages, forests, good walking, orchards, and abundant fruit and vegetables that make for a unique and excellent cuisine.

Makrinitsa, a traditional village, clings to the mountain slopes.

**Volos**

🅰 Map p. 139

**Visitor Information**

✉ Thessaly Region H.Q., Plateia Riga Fereou, Volos

☎ 224/102-3500 or 224/102-4915

In Greek mythology the Pilion was home to the centaurs, those creatures who had the upper torso and head of a man and otherwise the body of a horse, and were known for their lusty, drunken ways. The exception was the wise and good centaur Chiron, who was tutor to the young Jason. In later life Jason undertook a quest for a famous trophy, the Golden Fleece,

in order to claim his rightful kingdom. He set off on the heroic quest with his company of Argonauts from **Volos,** the city that marks the gateway to the Pilion.

Volos is now an industrial city and a major port from where visitors head into the Pilion itself—and one of four cities that hosted soccer during the 2004 Olympics. The principal reason to linger in Volos might be to visit the **Archaeological Museum,** an excellent example of its kind, with the best of the treasures from two nearby archaeological sites, Dimini and Sesklo.

Leaving Volos, enter the green and densely wooded Pilion, where your first port of call, depending upon which route you take, may well be **Makrinitsa,** one of 24 villages scattered across the mountain. This village was founded in the 13th century by refugees fleeing from Constantinople. Its steep, cobbled streets and protected status mean that you will have to leave your vehicle outside the village and proceed on foot. Several traditional mansions have been well restored, and some of these are now available as stylish hotel accommodations. There are tavernas serving gourmet food, a number of old churches to explore, and a monastery, as well as a wonderful view over Volos and the bay on which it stands.

**Vizitsa** is a similar village farther south in the Pilion, and should also not be missed. Vizitsa, too, has mansions restored for use as guesthouses and memorable eating places. It can be busy during the daytime, but at night it is more like the peaceful, traditional mountain settlement it has always been.

To reach Vizitsa, turn off the road at the larger village of **Milies,** where there are more attractive old mansions, as well as churches to visit and the small **Milies Folklore Museum.** The village is connected to Ano Lechonia

## The Greatest Soccer Match in Greek History

On July 4, 2004, the perennial soccer underdog, the Greek national team, surprised the world when it beat host country Portugal 1–0 in the final of the Union of European Football Association's (UEFA) Euro 2004. The odds of them winning were 80 to 1. Impressively, the team also beat Portugal in the opening round—the first time a double win had ever happened. (The last time the Greek national team had even qualified for the series, in 1980, it failed to win a single game.) Angelos Charisteas scored the winning goal, and team captain Theodoros Zagorakis was named best player of the championship.

by a steam train on summer weekends, offering an exhilarating way to enjoy some of the Pilion's lovely scenery.

If you're looking for a beach, head for **Agios Ioannis,** an attractive small resort at the end of a steep, zigzagging road coming down from the Pilion's hills. It has a good beach with water sports and several restaurants serving Pilion cuisine.

South from Agios Ioannis is the inland village of **Tsagkarada.** Sprawling over a wide area of the northeast coast, it keeps a distinctly village feel. Its main claim to fame is the biggest and oldest plane tree in Greece, reputedly a thousand years old and with a massive trunk 59 feet (18 m) in circumference. This whole area is covered in forests of plane and oak, with apple and cherry orchards, and old stone houses, their terraces draped in vines.

Farther south still is a small bump at the end of the peninsula, called **Trikerion.** It is much quieter than the rest of the Pilion, and its local architecture takes on Cycladic style. The beautiful fishing village of **Agia Kiriaki** is everything you ever dreamed a Greek fishing village could be. Boats are still made here by traditional methods in the boatyard. Although there's no beach, just a few rooms to rent and a few places to eat, the village still makes an idyllic location to spend a few days. It is connected by road and tracks to the even more peaceful hilltop village of Trikeri. Regular boats leave in summer for the Sporades, if you wish to move on into the Aegean. ∎

## Archaeological Museum
- ✉ Athanasaki 1. Volos
- ☎ 224/102-5285
- 🕐 Closed Mon.
- 💲 $

## Milies
- 🅰 Map p. 139

## Milies Folklore Museum
- ✉ Mileai
- ☎ 242/308-6602
- 🕐 Closed Mon.– Tues. & Nov.– March
- 💲 $

# Meteora

Meteora is one of the most extraordinary places in the world. The name means "rocks in the air," which is a simple and accurate description. A series of sandstone rocks rise from the surrounding plain of Thessaly like tall lumps of clay on a potter's wheel. They were formed some 30 million years ago beneath the sea, and it was the pounding of the water on the sandstone that created these Daliesque shapes, left high and dry when the sea retreated.

A primitive chair lift offers a perilous alternative to climbing hundreds of steps.

**Meteora**

⛰ Map p. 139

☎ 243/202-2649

🕐 Varies with monastery & season, so check ahead.

💲 $$

It is hardly surprising the rocky pinnacles reaching for the sky were seen as places of religious retreat. The first to seek solitude was probably a man named Barnabas, who moved into a cave on one of the rocks in A.D. 985. A colony of hermits seems a contradiction in terms, but that is what developed around Meteora, until a monastery was eventually founded in 1336.

That first monastery, **Megalo Meteoro,** was begun by a monk named Athanasios on a 1752 foot (534 m) pinnacle. Athanasios came here from Mount Athos (see pp. 186–187), and his hermit's cave can still be seen outside the monastery. Other monks and

monasteries followed, until at one time there were 24. Today only 13 monasteries remain, of which six are open to the public. To give the remaining monks and nuns some solitude, all six do not open at the same time. Check locally for the current opening hours, as they can change at short notice.

How did the monks build these monasteries on top of sheer cliff faces? It was only in recent times that paths were cut into the rocks to create greater access for people, and at the **Monastery of Varlaam** you can still see the winch formerly used to haul both supplies and visitors up in a basket at the end of a rope. One theory is that kites were flown over the rocks, trailing strings tied to light ropes, which in turn were used to haul up stronger ropes to build the first rope ladders to the summits. No one knows for sure, but what was created is absolutely amazing.

Visiting the monasteries is easiest by car. The nearest accommodations are in the village of Kastraki, or slightly farther away in the town of Kalambaka. From here you can walk to the nearest monastery, **Agia Triada,** in about 30 minutes. Or you can take one of the several daily buses to the farthest monastery, **Metamorphosis,** and walk or get a later bus back again. ■

# Metsovo

**To travel from the plains of Thessaly into the western region of Epiros (Epirus) involves a drive over the highest road pass in Greece, which is 5,599 feet (1,707 m) high and often closed in winter. Nearby is the lovely mountain town of Metsovo, full of character and atmosphere, reflecting the independent spirit of the people who live high in these hills. Some are settled Vlach nomads (see pp. 156–157), although a few hill dwellers retain the old nomadic lifestyle.**

Metsovo is very much on the tourist trail, as it is a ski resort in winter and popular with walkers in summer, but it has lost none of its charm.

It has developed a distinctive and hearty cuisine including pungent sheep's cheeses, game, and robust red wine, and there are plenty of restaurants in town offering you a chance to taste these specialities. Stores sell wine, honey, and cheeses—great for gifts or a picnic lunch. Other souvenirs

**INSIDER TIP:**

**The high mountains can be cold and windy, especially at night. If you are hiking or camping, take some extra layers of clothing, a waterproof jacket, a flashlight, a map, and a compass.**

—NICHOLAS TURLAND
*National Geographic field scientist*

reflect the cultivation of arts and crafts in the area, especially in embroidery, silverware, and in the carving of wooden shepherd's crooks. Some older men still wear their traditional dark blue or black pleated costumes, not unlike the kilted outfit of the Greek Army, complete with their pom-pommed shoes.

Metsovo has flourished for many years, thanks to judicious tax benefits under the Ottoman rule because of its position at the head of this vital mountain pass.

Merchants prospered under these conditions, and some of their grand mansions can still be seen; one such, the **Tositsa Mansion,** is open to the public. The Tositsa family was prominent in Metsovo and a famous benefactor, not just locally but across Greece. The family *archontiko* (mansion) has been preserved as a museum, to give visitors an indication of the sumptuous lifestyle. Three floors are elegantly laid out with expensive furniture, rugs, silverware, jewelry, and local folk costumes. Entry to the museum is via guided tour, offered every half hour.

The Averoffs were another wealthy and influential local family with a magnificent vision for Metsovo. The three-story **Evangelos Averoff Gallery** is one of the many treasures they left behind. The gallery displays the family's collection of modern 19th- and 20th-century Greek art. They also founded the village's cheese making industry. ∎

**Metsovo**
- Map p. 138

**Tositsa Mansion**
- Tositsa
- 265/604-1084
- Closed Thurs.
- $

**Evangelos Averoff Gallery**
- Off central square
- 265/604-1210
- Closed Tues.
- $

# Pindos Mountains

The Pindos is one of the mightiest mountain ranges in Greece, stretching from its northern borders west to the Ionian Sea, south to Metsovo, and east into Macedonia. The range encompasses two national parks, the second longest gorge in Europe, and some of the highest mountain peaks in the country.

Mount Smolikas—one of the wildest areas left in Europe—looks across to the Pindos Mountains.

**Pindos Mountains**

🏔 Map p. 138

One area of the Pindos is protected in the **Vikos-Aoös National Park,** which was created in 1973 and covers the area around the Vikos Gorge. The larger **Pindos National Park** was created in 1966, in part to protect the Balkan and black pines that have covered these mountain slopes for thousands of years. Here you find Greece's remaining wolves and bears (see Bears opposite), as well as deer, wild boar, wildcats, and chamois. There are dice snake and nose-horned vipers, too, so watch out if walking in remote areas.

When not watching the ground, scan the skies for the birds of prey that survive here, including the goshawk, Egyptian vulture, golden eagle, imperial eagle, and griffon vulture.

These are rugged and potentially treacherous mountains, so consider a guide. The peaks are generally covered in snow from October until May, and when the snows melt the waters come cascading down the rivers. Paths normally easy to follow in midsummer can become dangerous.

The ultimate challenge for experienced trekkers is **Mount**

**Smolikas,** which at 8,459 feet (2,637 m) is Greece's second highest peak after Mount Olympus. Reaching the summit requires several days, good preparation, and your own camping equipment or reservations for the mountain huts that provide shelter. Greece's footpath network is not well marked; often the only directional signs are blobs of red paint dabbed onto rocks.

The northern sector of the mountains are remote and will satisfy anyone looking for a more rugged mountain experience. The accommodations may be simpler than elsewhere, but the hospitality more than compensates.

The small town of **Konitsa,** a few miles from the Albanian border, is a popular center for walkers. There are a handful of hotels and eating places here, and a chance to hire local guides for exploring this remote corner. Konitsa has a beautiful setting, overlooked by Mount Trapezitsa and in turn overlooking the Aoös River, a river-kayaking destination.

Konitsa was badly damaged by an earthquake in 1996, and some of its older buildings were destroyed. The old bazaar area survived, however, as did the small Turkish quarter, and both add spice to the lively but remote town.

From Konitsa it is possible to walk south to climb **Mount Gamila** (8,134 feet/2,497 m). This requires a night's stay at the mountain hut at Astraka, and you can take in a visit to the mountain lake of Drakolimni. Alternatively, heading east takes you to Mount Smolikas via the mountain hut at Naneh and another mountain lake, Drakolimni (Dragon's Lake).

The road running northwest from Konitsa heads to Albania, which is still sensitive due to the recent Balkan conflicts, so you may be required to show your passport before being allowed to proceed. The reward for your adventure will be a visit to the village of **Molivdoskepastos,** right by the border and providing unrivaled views into Albania and back toward the Pindos peaks of Smolikas and Gamila. Venture here and you have truly reached one of the most remote corners of Greece. ∎

## Konitsa
⚠ Map p. 138

---

## Bears & Wolves

In the mountains of northern Greece, some magnificent wild creatures survive—despite the Greek fondness for hunting and the farmers who kill anything that might threaten their often meager livelihood. The most splendid—and rarest—of these wild animals are the European brown bear *(Ursus arctos)* and the European silver wolf *(Canis lupus).*

Sadly, you are unlikely to see either species as they are seriously endangered, but it is hoped that increased ecological awareness in Greece has come in time to save them. There are thought to be fewer than 200 bears, and perhaps a few hundred wolves, mostly concentrated in the national parks in northern Greece: Vikos-Aoös, Pindos, and Prespa.

# Greece's Nomads

Few visitors realize, when lying on an Aegean beach or enjoying a meal in a five-star hotel in Athens, that Greece is still home to small groups of nomads whose cultural roots go back thousands of years. There are not many left these days—it is a way of life that is dying out everywhere—but they are still to be found in the more remote parts of Epiros, around the mountain town of Metsovo, and in the depths of the Pindos Mountains.

The long-legged mountain sheep are valued for their milk yield as well as for their meat and fleece. You'll hear the "tonk" of sheep bells all over the Greek countryside.

The largest group is the Vlach, whose name is linked to the Romanian region of Wallachia. They were shepherds who led a nomadic existence, wandering throughout central and eastern Europe and down into the Balkans, traveling to wherever they could find the best grazing for their sheep.

The Vlach "capital" has always been Metsovo (see p. 153), close to the highest road pass in Greece, on the road between Meteora on the Thessaly plains, and Ioanina, the main town in Epiros. Many Vlach live in Metsovo today, but they have settled into houses and no longer live as shepherds. Although their way of life is dying out, it is still possible to catch a last glimpse of a proud and independent people.

Some maintain their traditional way of life, taking their flocks of sheep down to warmer climes and better grazing in winter, and back up again into the cooler Pindos Mountains in summer. Although nomads, these shepherds live in houses, simply migrating from one base to another over the year, unlike the Sarakatsani (see below) who carry their tents with them. In older times, a wealthy Vlach shepherd might have had as many as 10,000 sheep, though today the handful of flocks that remain and are moved between winter and summer pastures number only a few hundred.

No one knows for sure where the Vlach came from. One theory suggests that they were descendants of Roman legionaries, who were stationed or settled in central Europe. Another theory is that the Greek Vlach are native to the area, and the origins of their nomadic lifestyle go back to the Roman occupation, when the local mountain people would have been put to work as shepherds or as guards on the Via Egnatia. This road connected Rome with the more distant parts of its empire, going through the Pindos Mountains, through Meteora, on to the important Balkan port of Thessaloniki, and beyond that all the way to Constantinople (Istanbul). When the Romans eventually left, the nomadic way of life would have continued.

The Romans left behind aspects of their language. The Vlach people have their own tongue, which still has many linguistic connections to Latin and Italian. In fact, Vlach were often employed as interpreters when the Italian army occupied these mountains during World War II.

**A Vlach shepherd. Many believe that the Vlachs are descendants of Roman Legionaires.**

## EXPERIENCE:
# Mushroom-collecting in the Pindos Mountains

France and Italy are known for their fine mushrooms, but Greek mushrooms are of high quality, too. The wild mushrooms of the Pindos Mountains are particularly sought-after. They are nutritious and said to have healing qualities, and a unique taste free from pesticides, fertilizers, or hormones.

You can find this out for yourself by going on a mushroom-collecting vacation on the edge of the mountains, not far from Meteora. A three-day adventure through Trekking Hellas (*www.trekking.gr*) takes place in the beautiful Aspropotamos Valley, four to five hours from Athens. After an introductory talk and slide show on the first evening, the second day is spent out in the forests with a local mushroom expert, identifying and gathering the various species. Then it's back to the traditional tower hotel located deep in the forest, for a meal of mushroom soup, mushroom pie, and veal with mushrooms. On the last day, you are free to visit Meteora, or take a raft trip down the Aspropotamos River. Other trips can be booked through Agrotouristiki (*www.agrotravel.gr*).

The other main nomadic group—rivals to the Vlach—is the Sarakatsani, who were also traditionally shepherds. They occupied the area of Macedonia and Thrace in eastern Greece, and even fewer survive. The Sarakatsani are native Greeks and speak Greek. Some still move their flocks between the plains of Thrace in winter and the Pindos Mountains in summer.

To learn more about the Sarakatsani, and to see their traditional costumes and tents, visit the Folklife and Ethnological Museum in Thessaloniki (see p. 181) and the Museum of Greek Folk Art in Athens (see p. 69).

# Zagorian Villages & the Vikos Gorge

North of Ioanina, as you head toward the Albanian border, you come to Zagoria, one of the most intriguing regions of northern Greece. Forty-six Zagorian villages, with their own distinctive architecture and culture, are linked together by a network of paths that make ideal walking through the superb scenery of the lower Pindos Mountains.

A waymarked track runs through the bottom of the gorge, which is part of the Vikos-Aoös National Park.

One of the great natural features of the area is the **Vikos Gorge,** which runs for 7 miles (12 km) and is only 2 miles (3 km) shorter than the Samaria Gorge in Crete (see pp. 300–301). In places its walls rise 3,117 feet (950 m) sheer from the ground, while elsewhere it opens out to flower-filled meadows, with the opportunity to swim in the Voidhomatis River at the right times of year. If you are reasonably fit and have arranged transport and accommodations, it is possible to walk the gorge in one day.

Extra care must be taken for the gorge is relatively free of other walkers. Traveling at the best times—in early and late summer—you may see only a handful of other people, so a twisted ankle or dehydration could become a serious problem. In winter the gorge may not be passable, and the same applies in April and May, when the mountain snows melt and turn the trickling rivers into thundering torrents. Always take local advice on conditions, and let people know where you are planning to walk.

It would take at least a week just to begin to explore this region. The **Zagorian villages** are fascinating, and the history and the landscape are richly intertwined. The cultural wealth is a result of the region's past poverty. The harsh landscape made it hard for people to scrape out a living here, and many were forced to seek work abroad, but sent money to their families left behind. The Turks, who ruled from Ioanina 31 miles (50 km) to the south, granted Zagoria autonomy, so that the steadily growing wealth from abroad was largely retained, and was used in the 18th and 19th centuries to build houses known as *archontika*. These are modest in size, but grand in comparison to the average mountain home. Some are derelict and romantically crumbling, others are lived in, while some have been restored for use as museums or guesthouses. This corner of the Pindos is not thickly wooded, so the mansions are mostly built from the local limestone, with slate roofs. Often there is space for the animals on the ground floor and a walled yard. They give the small Zagorian villages a very distinctive look.

Some of the villages are now deserted or have just a handful of families supporting themselves by agriculture, but others prosper from the increasing tourism in the area. They are popular with mountaineers, walkers, and more adventurous visitors. The best bases for exploring are the main villages of **Monodendri, Tsepelovo, Megalo,** and **Mikro Papingo.** They have guesthouses, restaurants, and stores, and walking guides are usually available. If you don't have a car, you can reach these villages by the regular bus from Ioanina. ■

**Vikos Gorge**
Map p. 138

## EXPERIENCE: Zagorian Paths

Visitors often overlook the opportunity to walk the trails that connect the bucolic villages of Zagoria. This is a shame, especially during the spring bloom when the paths, which are usually no more than a thin covering of gravel, become carpeted with wildflowers.

Be warned that the trails are narrow, and the bridges along the way are equipped with bells that alert crossers of strong, potentially dismounting winds. The bridges are ancient—first built by traders who had to cross the region during the spring melt when flooding was common. These precarious stacks of stone don't look like they could survive a gust of wind, much less the erosion of the centuries. One of the best preserved is the triple-arched Kalogeriko Bridge, near Kipi.

The best time of year to hike the trails is between April and October. In late summer, the alpine flowers are still blooming, but there are the autumnal charms, too—cool breezes and mellow colors.

The paths are somewhat rough. Boots, or at least good walking shoes, are a must. There are many different walking routes, but it's best to hire a guide. If designated at all, the paths are poorly marked.

For the most part, accommodations along the trails are usually limited to small inns or bed and breakfasts. Each village has several restaurants, almost all of them family owned. **Sherpa Expeditions** (www.sherpa-walking-holidays.co.uk) offers several tours, both self-guided and escorted, throughout the region. Another tour provider is **Trekking Hellas** (www.outdoorsgreece.com), which conducts tours around Zagoria, the Vikos Gorge, and the Pindos Mountains.

# Ioanina

The slim minarets of Ali Pasha's citadel poking above the lakeside trees are a distinctive feature of this beautiful regional capital. Idyllically situated on the shores of Lake Pamvotis, with the Pindos Mountains on the far side beyond the delightful central island of Nissi, it is a lovely place to spend a few days.

Works of art for sale in Ioanina shows Turkish influences.

**Ioanina**

◪ Map p. 138

**Visitor Information**

✉ Epiros Region
   H.Q., Dodonis
   39

☎ 265/104-1868

It is wise not to make too many complimentary remarks around here about Ali Pasha, the murderous tyrant who dominated the city from 1788 until his death on Nissi in 1822, for local feeling still runs high. Ioanina was under the Turkish yoke for almost 500 years, the longest and blackest spell in Greek history, and Turkish influence has survived here more strongly than elsewhere. Yet the name of Ali Pasha is inextricably entwined in the town's history, whether the present citizens like it or not.

Under the Ottomans Ioanina flourished as a center for arts and crafts, notably for silversmiths. Even today, silver from Ioanina is considered to be among the finest in Greece, and you might still find a few craftsmen working in cramped workshops in the back streets. Samples of their best work can be seen in an annex to the **Byzantine Museum,** which is inside the citadel and contains excellent and well-explained collections of Byzantine art. The nearby **Silverwork Hall** includes some exquisite pieces and a reconstructed silversmith's workshop.

Next to the Byzantine Museum is the **Fethiye Tzami,** or Victory Mosque (not open to the public). In front stands the unmarked and untended grave of Ali Pasha.

Also within the citadel, and inside the Aslan Pasha Tzami mosque, is the **Popular Art Museum.** This is worth visiting if only to see inside the mosque, which was first built in 1619, but it also has a good collection of folk costumes, jewelry, and other arts and crafts from the town.

Outside the citadel, the town's **Archaeological Museum** is an essential visit if you plan to go to Dodoni (see pp. 164–165), as many of the finds from that historic site are displayed here.

**INSIDER TIP:**

**Immerse yourself into Greek life by spending an evening in a taverna. Greeks may sit at their local taverna for hours, as much to socialize as to eat.**

—JAMES V. BULLARD
*National Geographic Expeditions*

The other essential visit in Ioanina is to **Nissi,** the island in the lake, reached by a regular ferry service from in front of the citadel walls. The name Nissi is Greek for "island." There is one small, straggling village on the island, where the inhabitants make a living from fishing or tourism. Visitors and locals like to sail across for lunch or dinner on the island, for it has several excellent fish tavernas. However, most of the fish served on Nissi comes from fish farms in the mountains, not from the lake. A unique ingredient is found on the menus of Nissi: frogs' legs. These are so abundant in the area and so tasty that they are even exported to France. Now is the time to give them a try.

A trail goes all the way around the island, which makes for a lovely short walk. Because Nissi is not spoiled it is still good for wildlife, and you might see or hear nightingales, as well as reed buntings, kestrels, woodpeckers, and a variety of waterfowl. Look for signs to the island's only cultural attraction, the **Ali Pasha Museum** (closed some days in winter, $), in the Monastery of Panteleimon. This was built in the 16th century but the present building is a modern reconstruction, the original having been demolished by a falling tree. It was here that Ali Pasha was assassinated, not by the local Greeks but by Turks from Istanbul. Ali's own rulers had become concerned at the power and wealth he had accumulated, and his ambition to create an independent state. Ali was besieged in his citadel but managed to escape to the island in the lake, taking refuge in the monastery. Unsympathetic locals gave away his hiding place, and the Turks shot him through the floorboards from a downstairs room; the bullet holes can still be seen. Ali was beheaded and his head sent to the Sultan in Istanbul to prove that the mission had been accomplished. It is a violent past, at odds with the peaceful nature of the lake today. ■

**Byzantine Museum/ Silverwork Hall**

✉ Inside citadel
☎ 265/102-5989 or 265/103-9580
🕐 Closed Mon. in winter
💲 $

**Popular Art Museum**

✉ Inside citadel
☎ 265/102-0515
🕐 Closed Sat.–Sun.
💲 $

**Archaeological Museum**

✉ Plateia 25 Martiou
☎ 265/103-3357 or 265/108-1554
🕐 Currently closed for renovation
💲 $

# Walking in Ali Pasha's Ioanina

You may be forgiven for thinking in some parts of Ioanina that you have wandered into a Middle Eastern city, or at any rate a Turkish one: Five hundred years of Turkish rule have left a significant legacy. No one had more impact on the town than the evil ruler Ali Pasha, and this walk takes in some of the sites associated with him, beginning with the citadel from which he ruled with an iron hand.

A small ferryboat links Nissi to the mainland.

The walk begins at the main entrance to the **citadel ❶**, which is the second entrance through the thick fortress walls on your right as you walk down Karamanli from Plateia Neomart Yioryiou. A small shrine is in the wall beside the entrance. Go through the entrance and turn immediately left along Ioustinianou. You will pass on the right the **Old Synagogue** (not open to the public), which was built in 1790. Ioanina had a big Jewish community that dated back to the 13th century, but only a few dozen Jewish people survived World War II.

Follow the street past the synagogue until the end, when it bends to the right and leads you toward the Aslan Pasha Tzami mosque.

### NOT TO BE MISSED:

Popular Art Museum
• Byzantine Museum
Silverwork Hall • Island of Nissi
• Ali Pasha Museum

This contains the **Popular Art Museum ❷** (see p. 161). The other rooms around the courtyard are not open to the public, and it was in these that one of the worst episodes of Ali's tyrannical rule took place. He raped the mistress of his eldest son, then threw her and 17 other women into the lake in weighted sacks so that they could not reveal his dreadful crime.

On leaving the mosque by the way you came in, turn left to resume the walk. Keep to the left, just inside the citadel walls, and ignore the sign that points you down "To the Lake" through a gateway. Instead carry on ahead and through the entrance gates into the inner citadel. On the left is a café, and the modern building ahead of you is the **Byzantine Museum ❸** (see p. 160), with the **Fethiye Tzani** (*not open to the public*) to its left, in front of which is the probable tomb of Ali Pasha. The museum's **Silverwork Hall ❹** annex is over to your right, in what was once Ali Pasha's Treasury building.

Return to the gate that gives access to the lake, and take the steps down to the lakeside, turning left until you reach the departure point for the **ferries to Nissi ❺** (see p. 161). The little ferryboats leave every 30 minutes in summer, and every hour in winter, from 8 a.m. to 11 p.m. Take the ferry across to the island. No doubt you'll be in the company of a few other visitors, but for the most part with islanders returning from their errands.

On reaching the island turn left to walk through a small network of streets, following the signs that direct you to the **Ali Pasha Museum ❻** (see p. 161). It has an interesting collection of Ali Pasha artifacts, and you can see the holes left by the bullets that killed him. From the museum you can safely continue on around the rest of the island, which is surrounded by reed beds. There are lovely views across to the Pindos Mountains, and back across the lake to Ioanina, although in places you will be unaware of the busy town's existence.

Carry on along the path, where you may see fishermen mending their nets, until you return to the ferry quay for the boats back to Ioanina.

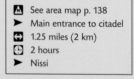

- ⓜ  See area map p. 138
- ➤  Main entrance to citadel
- ↔  1.25 miles (2 km)
- ⏱  2 hours
- ➤  Nissi

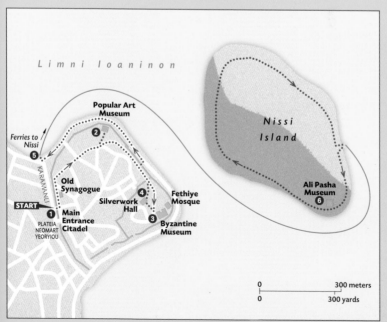

# More Places to Visit in Epiros

## Dodoni

Although the oracle at Delphi is the world-famous one, Dodoni too had its oracle. The Oracle of Zeus is much older, and second in importance only to Delphi. Religious ceremonies took place here at least as early as 2000 B.C. The site, open daily, is beautifully set in a high valley (2,065 feet/630 m) below a range of hills, some 14 miles (22 km) southwest of Ioanina.

Either before or after visiting the site, you should visit the **Archaeological Museum** in Ioanina (see p. 161), where finds from Dodoni are on display. The most interesting of these are tablets on which some of the questions put to the oracle were inscribed. They include such timeless dilemmas as "Am I the father of her children?"

The most impressive feature at Dodoni is its **theater,** which is one of the largest in Greece and dates back to the 3rd century B.C. It was reconstructed in the late 19th century, and again in the 1960s, and is still used in the summer for occasional performances. Its thick walls tower over the visitor. Note the drainage channels around the sides, built by the Romans when the theater was used to stage animal fights and gladiatorial contests. You can still see the pens on either side of the stage where bulls, lions, tigers, and other fierce creatures would have been kept before their release into the arena to the delight of 17,000 yelling spectators.

It was right next to the theater that the Sanctuary of Zeus was located, and the oracle. A good deal is known about the process of consulting the oracle here. A sacred oak tree

A cruise boat plies the clear waters off Parga, a resort town with a richly checkered history.

was completely surrounded by cauldrons on tripods, each one touching the next. The seeker's question was written down on a lead tablet and passed to a priest, who read the question to the oracle. The answer was the priest's interpretation of the noise made by the leaves on the oak tree and the sounds emanating from the cauldrons.

🅐 Map p. 138 ☎ 265/108-2287 💲 $

## Parga

The beach resort of Parga is one of the most attractive and popular along the Ionian coast. There are several good beaches both in and near the town, a choice of excellent fish restaurants, and easy access to Dodoni, Ioanina, and even the Zagorian villages and the Vikos Gorge (see pp. 158–159). You need your own transportation to get to all of these, and Parga makes a good base from which to explore. It is possible to get ferries to the island of Paxi, which in turn gives access to Corfu. It is also not too far from airports at Preveza, for international charter flights, and at Ioanina, for internal flights. Everything considered, it is not surprising that Parga is popular—and finding a room in the height of summer is not easy unless you make a reservation.

For all its appearance as a simple resort town, Parga has had a fascinating history. At one end of the harbor, lined by restaurants and souvenir shops, is an imposing **Venetian fortress** built in 1624, as a date over one of the gates indicates. You can see the symbol of Venice, the Lion of St. Mark, carved into one of the walls in the keep. The town was conquered by the Turks but then taken by the Venetians at a time when the Turkish Empire dominated most of modern Greece. The British then captured it from the Venetians, and in 1819 sold it back to the Turks, where it came under the control of Ali Pasha at Ioanina. Under his despotic rule many of the natives went into exile in Corfu, the families only returning when Parga became Greek again in 1913.

---

### The Tourist Police

The Tourist Police is a specific branch of the police that looks after the interests of visitors. Part of its duty is the inspection of restaurants and hotels, checking facilities and prices, and making sure visitors are not being fleeced. If you have any disputes at all in Greece, over things like hotels, meals, or taxis, then contact the Tourist Police and they will sort the problem out. In smaller places where there are no official tourist offices or large travel agents, the Tourist Police also operates as accommodation finders for visitors. Turn up without a booking and, if you are having trouble finding a room, go visit the Tourist Police and ask for help. You can distinguish them from the regular police because they have a white band on their cap, and the words TOURIST POLICE in English on their shirts and on their shoulder bands. There will be a local phone number to call in each town, which is listed in each chapter of this book in places where there is no official tourist office. If you can't find the local number, then dial 171 and you will be connected to a multilingual assistant who will deal with your inquiry.

---

Beyond the headland is one of the town's best beaches, a long sandy stretch, and there are several more to the north and south of the center. Look for dazzling whitewashed houses in the town, with their vivid dabs of color from bougainvillea, hibiscus, and morning glory plants that cascade down from walls and balconies. Here too are the small hotels, restaurants, and more souvenir shops that mark it out as a tourist resort. Outside the high season (*June–Aug.*) these backstreets are pretty enough to retain their Greek picture-postcard charm.

www.parga.gr 🅐 Map p. 138 ✉ Alexandrou Paga 18 ☎ 268/403-2107

## Efyra

Some 14 miles (22 km) southeast of Parga, on the edge of the village of Mesopotamo, is one of the smallest yet most unusual and haunting ancient sites in all of Greece. A few apparently insignificant buildings stand on top of a small mound that was once an island, when the level of the Ionian Sea was much higher than it is today. This is the **Necromanteion** of Efyra, open daily. The spot was believed to be the source of the mythical River Styx. It was, logically, also the site for the Oracle of the Dead, where people would try to make contact with those who had passed on, by asking questions of the oracle through the priests here. Hallucinogenic drugs were given to the questioners, who were then led through the small maze of passages that can still be seen, into the center of the underground sanctuary to consult with the oracle.

🅐 Map p. 138 💲 $

## Kassopi

Seventeen miles (27 km) southeast of Efyra, on a hillside above the village of Kamarina, is the site of ancient Kassopi. A walk along a path through pine woods leads to what was once an independent city-state. Very little now remains of the city, which was abandoned when its citizens moved to Nicopolis, a few miles to the south, in 31 B.C. But with a little imagination and help from the map posted at the entrance, it is possible to piece together the basic shape of the settlement. The main attraction is the location, which is well worth going out of your way to see.

🅐 Map p. 138 🕓 Closed Mon. 💲 $

## Nicopolis

The ancient city of Nicopolis is 4 miles (7 km) north of Preveza. You'll find that little is immediately visible on the ground today, but an exploration of the overgrown site will start to reveal something of the shape of what at one time was a very significant city.

The name means "victory city," for it was built on the site where the Roman army of Octavian camped before the Battle of Actium in 31 B.C., when they defeated the combined forces of Antony and Cleopatra. It was a victory that was to lead to Octavian becoming the first emperor of Rome, under his adopted name of Augustus, and to the founding here of his victory city.

Some of the walls that remain give an indication of the huge scale of the place; there is also a theater, some remains of baths, and a small museum. The site may have been a good army camping ground but it did not make for the foundation of a successful city, being geographically isolated and with no convenient freshwater supply, as well as subject to subsidence. Nevertheless Nicopolis survived for about a thousand years before being abandoned in 1040.

🅐 Map p. 138 🕓 Closed Mon. 💲 $
🚍 Preveza–Arta Bus

## Perama Caves (Perama Spilaia)

One of the best cave systems open to the public is situated on the outskirts of Ioanina. It was only discovered during World War II when a shepherd was looking for a shelter from bombing raids. The explored part of the caves extends for some miles, with more yet to be discovered in what is believed to be the largest cave network in Greece. Parts of these are open to visitors, but only on a guided tour.

The guides will illuminate and pick out some of the more striking stalactites and stalagmites for you, including natural rock formations said to resemble such objects as the Statue of Liberty, the Leaning Tower of Pisa, and the Sphinx. In all there are around 5,600 feet (1,700 m) of passages open to the public, with the caves extending for several miles under the hillside.

🅐 Map p. 138 ☎ 265/108-1650 💲 $$
🚍 Bus 8

From the Pindos Mountains to the Turkish border, an area of fascinating geographical, historical, and political diversity

# Macedonia & Thrace

Mosaic floor, Dion

# Macedonia & Thrace

Macedonia (Makedonia) is the country's largest administrative district, or prefecture, and it has much to offer the visitor, including Greece's second largest city, Thessaloniki. This lively waterfront city has a wealth of history only rivaled by Athens. East of Macedonia is the long, thin prefecture of Thrace (Thraki), where the Turkish influences are more notable the closer you get to the border.

The west of Macedonia is a remote and rugged region bordered by the Pindos Mountains, where wolves and bears still roam the forests. Here, too, are the beautiful Prespa lakes, surrounded by magnificent snowcapped mountains. Mount Olympus, the home of the gods, provides challenging walking and an opportunity to climb to the highest point in the country.

Historic highlights include sites such as ancient Pella, which has some outstanding mosaics. Vergina, where the Macedonian kings had their royal palace, has produced some of the finest archaeological discoveries in Greece.

Hardly seeming to belong to the 21st century, Mount Athos is known as the Monks' Republic and remains devoted to the contemplative life as it has been for the last thousand years. There could be no greater contrast than the busy beaches and modern

0 | 60 kilometers
0 | 30 miles

BULGARIA

Dytiki Rodopi

Nestos

Anatoliki Rodopi

Kastaneai

**Orestiada**

**Didymoteichon**

alakron Oros
2194m

Falakro

**Drama**      Stavroupolis      **Xanthi**   Iasmos   **Komotini**   1065m   **Dadia**   Souflion
                                                                     Silo    **Forest**   Likofi

**Ne a**                                                                      Aisymi
**ichni**        Doxaton                                              Sapes

**Philippi**   **Chrysoupolis**   Avdira   Lagos   Maroneia               Loutros   E90

Eleftheroupolis                   **Avdira**        **Maroneia**

**Kavala**        Keramoti      Agios             Ferai
                              Haralambos   **Alexandroupoli**

Echinos

Limni
Vistonis

2/E90

T   H   R   A   C   E

Evros

Evros Delta

TURKEY

E90

Kolpos
Kavalas

Asprovalta
Kolpos
Orfanou

**AEGEAN ISLANDS**
p.215

agira
Kolpos
Ierissou

Ouranopolis
Kolpos
Agiou Orous

Ormos Panagias      Athos
                  2033m
Sithonia            Akra Pinnes

Sarti
orto   Toroni
rras
Kolpos
Kassandras

---

**NOT TO BE MISSED:**

Mount Olympus   **170**

The lakeside town of Kastoria
**174–175**

The royal tombs at Vergina   **178**

The mosaics at Pella   **179**

Thessaloniki, Greece's second
city   **180–183**

A boat trip around Mount
Athos   **188–189**

A drive through the Nestos
Valley   **190**

The Thracian feel of Xanthi
**194–195**

The wildlife in the Dadia
Forest   **201**

---

nightlife on the neighboring peninsulas of Chalkidiki, which jut into the Aegean Sea.

Although relations with Turkey have improved in recent years, the border is still a sensitive area, so take care not to wander too far off the beaten track. And there are plenty of beaten tracks to wander off, as Thrace is not only outstandingly beautiful but also contains some of the most unspoiled and unvisited parts of Greece.

In northern Thrace the Rhodope Mountains separate Greece from its Balkan neighbor, Bulgaria. In the extreme east of the region are the Evros Delta and the Dadia Forest, where

wildlife flourishes. There may be no wolves and bears at the eastern extremity of this region, but eagles soar in the sky, and you can feel you are on the very edge of the country. ∎

# Mount Olympus & Dion

The highest mountain in Greece is all the more dramatic because the short range that it belongs to rises sharply from a flat plain and juts straight up into the sky. It is less than 12 miles (20 km) from the top of Mount Olympus (Olympos) to the shore of the Aegean Sea. The main Athens–Thessaloniki highway runs through the plain that stands between mountain and sea, giving motorists the chance to stop and admire the spectacular mountains.

The home of the gods became Greece's first national park in 1937.

**Mount Olympus**
Map p. 168

As you gaze at the peaks you are looking across Mount Olympus National Park, home to deer, boar, badgers, and European wildcats, as well as birds of prey and some 1,700 different plant species. There are oak and beech forests, stretches of Macedonian fir, and a centuries-old rare yew grove near the Monastery of Dionysos.

The entire Olympus range is only 12 miles (20 km) from end to end. The highest point is referred to as either Mount Olympus or Mount Mitikas, but there's no doubt about its height, which is 9,571 feet (2,917 m). It was not scaled by mortal man until 1913.

The Greek gods, of course, got there first. Greeks believed this to be the site of the Battle of the Titans, when the 12 Greek gods led by Zeus defeated the Titans; thus the wild natural forces, represented by the Titans, were tamed by the gods, who introduced some kind of civilization to the world.

Today, anyone who is reasonably in shape and does some advance planning can get to the top, but the six-hour trek means you must spend at least one night on the mountain, either camping out or by making a reservation at one of the two mountain refuges. On no account should the trek be attempted by anyone inexperi-

**Spend a night or nights in the austere mountain wilderness with the benefit of a bed, hot food, and good company. Hike halfway up Mount Olympus to the Greek Mountaineering Club's Spileos Agapitos refuge.**

—NICHOLAS TURLAND
*National Geographic field scientist*

enced, unless accompanied by a local guide.

The base for approaching the mountain and the surrounding park is the busy village of **Litochoron,** which has several hotels and restaurants and is a convenient place for an overnight stop. Here you can stock up on maps, guides, and any equipment you may need.

## Dion

A 9-mile (14 km) drive from Litochoron brings you to the village of Dion, whose name derives from the word *dios,* meaning "of Zeus." At its center is an excellent small **Archaeological Museum** that displays finds from the site of **ancient Dion,** found on the edge of the village. Visiting the museum first will help you understand the site; videos show details of the site's excavation and explain its significance. The guidebook is top of the line, and the superb teaching room on the bottom floor is a must.

Some of the best finds are

statues that were beautifully preserved when the ancient city was covered in mud after an earthquake. It was a considerable city, home to about 15,000 people in the fourth century B.C. when it was regarded as a sacred city by the Macedonians. The remains are mostly from the later Roman era and include a fine example of a Roman bathhouse, a theater, and a stadium. The site is well laid out and well marked. Elsewhere there are the remnants of houses both humble and grand, including a

### What's in a Name?

The breakup of Yugoslavia during the 1990s caused great anxiety among its Balkan neighbors. None felt it more than Greece, especially when one of the former Yugoslav republics declared itself the independent country of Macedonia, the name of the neighboring Greek province. A compromise was reached, and the new country is now called the Former Yugoslav Republic of Macedonia (FYRM).

splendid mosaic remaining in what was once a banqueting hall.

Don't miss the sanctuary to the Egyptian goddess Isis, located across the road from the main area. Copies of original statues from the site stand white against the lush greenery around a small pond. It is a gorgeous spot, with a magical setting between mountains and sea. ■

**Dion**
🅰 Map p. 168

**Ancient Dion**
🅰 Map p. 168
🕐 Open daily
💲 $

**Archaeological Museum**
✉ Dion
☎ 235/105-3206
💲 $

**National Federation of Alpine Clubs (Greek Mountaineering Clubs)**
✉ Milioni
106 73 Athens
☎ 210/364-5904

# Greek Gods

The highest mountain in Greece, Mount Olympus looms spectacularly from a plain close to the Aegean Sea. Sometimes shrouded in mystical mist, it is easy to understand how ancient Greece regarded Olympus as the home of the gods. To tell the full story of the gods would take an entire book, but a few pointers may help to unravel the stories.

**Mount Olympus, throne of Zeus**

The stories were originally oral, passed on in the same way as the Homeric legends of the *Iliad* and the *Odyssey*, by a skilled storyteller to a rapt audience. They were not written down until about the sixth century B.C., and subsequently we have been able to compare similarities in these tales with stories of gods from other countries. In Greece the gods are no longer part of the nation's modern religious beliefs, which are 99 percent Christian, but they are dramatically bound up in the folktales and legends of its prehistory.

Where the stories came from is uncertain, but it is likely that many different strands were involved. One such was Hesiod, an eighth-century B.C. Greek poet who, around the time that Homer was relating his own two epic poems, was responsible for *Theogeny,* a poetic work that tells of "the origin of the gods." Hesiod's *Theogeny* would certainly have been influenced by tales from other cultures of the Near East, as well as by myths and legends handed down by the Mycenaean civilization dominant in Greece in the second millennium B.C.

Athena accepting tributes. The gods expected offerings from mortals and got angry when offended.

The father of the gods was Zeus, who ruled over all the gods from Mount Olympus. Zeus was the youngest son of two of the Titans, children themselves of the heaven and the earth. Zeus seized control of the universe and became the god of the sky, the rain god, and father of all later gods and mortals.

Poseidon, a brother of Zeus, became the god of the sea and was the father of the winged horse, Pegasus. Susceptible to the charms of the water nymphs, Poseidon fathered many children. Another brother, Hades, became the god of the underworld. Zeus' son Apollo, the god of music, agriculture, healing, and prophecy, epitomized civilization. Zeus' favorite child, however, was his daughter, Athena, the goddess of industry, the arts, and wisdom, who gave her name to the city of Athens.

Aphrodite, goddess of love, rose from the waves and became Cupid's mother. Lesser deities were heroes and formed the links between gods and humans, with the qualities of both.

## EXPERIENCE: Mythology

The entirety of Greek culture is mediated through its ancient myths. To approach the country without an elementary understanding of its mythology is a loss for the visitor. Athens has several places to start to explore this world.

While it is chiefly concerned with how the ancient intersects with the contemporary, the **Athinais Cultural Center** (Kastorias 34-36, Votanikos, Athens 104-47, tel 210/348-0000, www.athinais .com/gr) should not be missed. The exhibits, lectures, and performances held in the center's gallery, lecture hall, and theater will help you brush up on facets of Greek culture.

If you'd like more structure, take one of the many courses offered on mythology. **The Greek House** (Dragoumi 7, 145 61 Kifissia, Athens, tel 210/808-5185, www .greekhouse.gr) program mixes language and cultural lessons to give its students a broad understanding of the Hellenic world. There is a placement test to get into the program, but if it's cultural fluency you seek, look no further.

# Kastoria

Visitors to the Greek islands and the mainland resorts may feel that they are seeing the most beautiful parts of the country. But more adventurous travelers who find themselves in towns such as Kastoria will have a different opinion. Unassuming Kastoria has a magnificent location around a headland that juts into Lake Kastoria (also called Lake Orestias).

With its projecting upper floor and big windows, the Immanouil Mansion is one of Kastoria's finest.

**Kastoria**
- Map p. 168

**Byzantine Museum**
- Plateia Dexamenis
- 246/702-6781
- Closed Mon.

Just keep in mind, as you wander around, that it's easy to get disoriented, thanks to Kastoria's maze of cobbled streets and hidden alleyways and the fact that water nearly surrounds the entire town perimeter.

However, getting lost is no bad thing, as some of the town's best features are hidden away, like its numerous **Byzantine churches.** There are 54 of these, some over 1,000 years old, including the ninth-century church of Taxiarkhes tis Mitropoleos. It has superb frescoes, added over the centuries. The tenth-century church of Agios Stefanos has an unusual women's gallery. Most of the churches are usually locked—to see inside you

will either have to be lucky and arrive when there is a service or when the church is being cleaned. Or you can track down the keys at the Byzantine Museum.

Although small, the **Byzantine Museum** is worth seeing for the beautifully detailed and colorful examples of icons from Kastoria's churches. The museum is situated at the top of the town just off the main Plateia Dexamenis. If you ask the way, remember that many local people refer to it as the Archaeological Museum.

The very name of the town comes from the Greek word for beavers, *kastoria*. This animal's fine pelt placed the town at the center of the Greek fur trade from the

17th century onward. Although the local beavers had been hunted to extinction by the 19th century, the furriers continue to import fur today. It is turned into coats, gloves, hats, and other items that you will see for sale in some of the stores, although many items are produced for export.

The town also has a **Folklore Museum** that merits a longer visit, not least for the building that houses it, the 17th-century Alvazi Mansion. It was lived in until 1972, when it was converted into an excellent museum with household items, costumes, agricultural implements, and a restored kitchen and wine cellar. There are also some very good displays on the fur trade.

The wealth that was created by the fur trade led to the building of some more very handsome **mansions.** While the Alvzi Mansion is the only one you can explore inside, there are others that can be viewed from outside, several in the streets within the vicinity of the museum. Look for the Skoutari, Natzi, Basara, and Immanouil Mansions. Typically built of stone on the first floor, they have more elaborate upper floors with wooden balconies, sgraffito plasterwork, and occasionally stained glass in the windows. The living quarters are on these upper floors, while the first floor provides storage, as you will see in the Folklore Museum.

Stroll along the lakeshore—a pleasant walk especially in the spring or autumn when the many trees are at their best—and look for the unusually shaped local boats tied up at the water's edge. The lake is somewhat polluted, but still harbors some wildlife, such as frogs and turtles.

A walk all the way around the headland takes you past another of the town's attractions, the **Monastery of Panagia Mavriotissa.** It is no longer a working monastery, and all that remains are two churches. These date back to the 11th and 14th centuries, and have particularly well-preserved frescoes. ∎

### Folklore Museum
- ✉ Kapetan Lazou
- ☎ 246/702-8603
- 🕐 Closed daily 12–3 p.m.
- 💲 $

## Arcturos Bear Sanctuary

The forests and mountains of northern Greece mark the southernmost boundary in Europe for the endangered European brown bear. The chances of seeing one of these creatures is remote, but a small colony has been created in the Arcturos Bear Sanctuary. Most of the bears have been rescued from captivity, some kept as "pets," and others saved from a cruel existence as dancing bears. The latter were often taken as cubs and had their feet burned while a tambourine was played; as they grew, the Pavlovian reaction would cause them to "dance" when they heard the tambourine. The Arcturos sanctuary was established in 1992 by winemaker Yianni Boutari near his home village of Nympheon, near Florina, and provides a refuge for the bears. A wolf sanctuary has also been established, and much educational and environmental work is undertaken here. Contact Arcturos Bear Sanctuary (*Victor Hugo 3, Thessaloniki, 54625 Greece, tel 231/055-5920, www.arcturos.gr*) or the Arcturos Environmental Centre (*Aetos Florinas 53075 Greece, tel 238/604-1500, closed Wed.*).

# Prespa Lakes

The borders of Albania, Greece, and the Former Yugoslav Republic of Macedonia meet in the waters of the larger of the two Prespa lakes, Megali Prespa. Mikri Prespa is divided between Greece and Albania. This frontier land, perched in the remote northwest corner of Greece, feels untouched by the modern world. The lakes' inaccessibility has made them a haven for wildlife.

Reed beds along the margins of the Prespa lakes provide an important wildlife habitat.

**Prespa Lakes
Information
Center**

⚑   Map p. 168

✉   Agios Germanos

☎   238/505-1211

In the 1970s, no visitor was allowed near this area because the border with Albania was a very sensitive political region. To visit it required advance permission, and you had to be accompanied by a soldier from the Greek Army at all times. For this reason the region is much less known than other parts of Greece, although the world is now gradually discovering that it is a unique, idyllic, and incredibly beautiful place.

Tourists may have been restricted, but that restriction has never applied to the wildlife, and **Prespa National Park** is a vital European breeding ground for many species. Visitors must be sensitive to this at all times, and a thorough exploration of the **Information Center** in the tiny village of Agios Germanos is the best way to start any trip here. It gives a great deal of information about the area in several languages, provides leaflets and walking maps, and sells local produce and crafts. Guided tours of the park can be arranged in advance from here.

It is possible to make a one-day visit to the lakes from somewhere like Kastoria, but if you wish to stay overnight you should make reservations ahead at busy times of the year (Easter and August), as accommodations are limited. There are a few guesthouses in Agios Germanos, which also has the area's only post office. More accommodations are available in the lakeside village of Psarades. Wherever you choose to stay, the accommodations will be simple but pleasurable.

Rare Dalmatian pelicans, of which there are only about 300 breeding pairs remaining in Greece, nest here in the Prespa lakes, although they may fly farther south to the island of Corfu if winter in the mountains is particularly hard and long. Many other bird species live here, including herons, cormorants, egrets, geese, grebes, and the only population in Greece of the goosander. In the skies look for a variety of birds of prey, including the golden eagle, short-toed eagle, booted eagle, and both lanner and

## INSIDER TIP:

**Quench your thirst at one of Greece's many cold, clear springs. Often they are situated along the road and embellished by ornate stone arches. The water is perfectly safe to drink.**

—NICHOLAS TURLAND
*National Geographic field scientist*

peregrine falcons.

Amphibians that live here include several species of frog, toads, newts, and the fire salamander, while there are also 20 species of reptile—including snakes, so be careful when walking—and over 1,300 different plant species. It is a vibrant, rich landscape for wildlife.

The area is also rich in religious culture. In the village of **Agios Germanos,** be sure to see the 11th-century church of the same name, which is adorned with frescoes, some of them original. The church of **Agios Athanasios** in the same village is also worth a visit. To see one of the area's more unusual churches, however, you must take a boat ride out onto Mikri Prespa, which can be arranged at the village of Psarades.

The ruined Byzantine church of **Agios Akhillios** is on the small islet of the same name, where you will also be shown the ruins of a monastery and may meet some of the few families who still live here, eking out a living from fishing and farming.

You can also take a boat trip on the larger lake, Megali Prespa, where the main attraction is the 15th-century church of **Panagia Eleousas,** surprisingly built into the rock near the shore of the lake. Other sights that can be seen only from the water include an icon of the Virgin Mary painted on a rock. The boat trip is in itself a wonderful experience, taking you out into the middle of a large and peaceful lake, surrounded by hills and with those invisible borders stretching across the waters. You feel privileged to be there. ■

# Vergina

One of the most exciting archaeological finds in Greece in the last century took place in 1977, with the excavation of the royal tombs at Vergina, 8 miles (13 km) from the town of Veria. They placed Vergina as the ancient Macedonian capital of Agai, later abandoned for Pella (see opposite).

**Vergina**

 Map p. 168

233/109-2397

Closed Mon. morning

$$

The discovery was made by Professor Manolis Andronikos (1919–1992), who uncovered an entrance to a tomb. Unlike the overconfident Heinrich Schliemann, however, Andronikos did not claim to know in advance what lay inside.

It is believed that what he had found was the burial place of the fourth-century B.C. King Philip II of Macedonia, the father of Alexander the Great. The skeleton was complete and preserved inside a golden funeral casket emblazoned with the emblem of the 16-point Macedonian star.

The find effectively meant a rewriting of the history books, as it had long been thought that the Macedonian kings had been buried at Edessa (see p. 181).

The discovery of the tombs, and the subsequent unearthing of two further royal tombs close by, led to a flurry of activity, and a great deal of archaeological work is still going on, which will add to the excitement of your visit here. A first-class museum was built at Vergina, and you can also view the tombs themselves, which are displayed behind protective glass.

In addition to the royal tombs, this is the site of the **Palace of Palatitsia,** which postdates Philip II and Alexander and was probably built in the third century B.C. as a summer palace for the then king, Antigonus Gonatus. The extent of the site is spectacular. The nearby theater, which is much older, is thought to be the place where Philip II was assassinated in 336 B.C., possibly at the instigation of his son, Alexander (see p. 30). ■

## Whose Bones Are They Anyway?

Ever since a study in 1984, it has been accepted that the skeleton found in the royal tomb at Vergina was that of King Philip II, father of Alexander the Great. The evidence included an apparent head wound above the right eye socket, consistent with the way in which the king is known to have died. However, in 2000 Greek historian Dr. Antonis Bartsiokas claimed that the bones were in fact those of Alexander's half brother, King Philip III Arrhidaeus, who took up the throne on Alexander's death. Dr. Bartsiokas claims that there is no evidence of an eye injury, and that some artifacts found in the tomb dated from after Philip II's death. For the moment, though, Greek academics stick by the original assessment.

# Pella

The unassuming-looking site of Pella is about 27 miles (44 km) west of Thessaloniki, and straddles the main road that runs from northwest Greece. As you approach, it is hard to believe how important this place once was, but it could be regarded as the first capital of a state that approximated to modern Greece.

The original pebble mosaic of "The Lion Hunt" is preserved in the site museum.

Pella was the capital under King Philip II of what was then called Macedonia. When Philip defeated the Greek armies in 338 B.C. (see p. 30), he united under his banner for the first time the various city-states that until then had been almost constantly at war with each other. This created a union that covered much of what is now Greece.

Pella was established in the late fifth century B.C. by King Archelaos (r. 413–399 B.C.), and both Philip II and Alexander the Great were born here. The town was destroyed by the Romans in the second century B.C., and today the overriding reason for visiting Pella is to see the magnificent **mosaics** that have survived there. Some are still in situ, and they date for the most part from about 300 B.C., not long after the death of Alexander the Great. The mosaics are exquisite works of art. Several depict hunting scenes, including naked hunters attacking a lion with clubs and swords, a deer being attacked by a griffin, the hunting of a stag, and an outstanding depiction of the god Dionysos riding a panther.

Many of the mosaics are in the **House of the Lion Hunt,** thought to have been an official building of some kind. It had a dozen rooms ranged around three open courtyards, and was 300 feet (90 m) long and 165 feet (50 m) across. Across the main road is the terrific site **museum,** which has more mosaics as well as statues, ceramics, and other artifacts. ■

**Pella**

- ⬧ Map p. 168
- ☎ 238/203-1160
- ◷ Closed Mon. morning
- $ $

# Thessaloniki

The capital of Macedonia, Thessaloniki is a vibrant metropolis located right on the Aegean, full of history yet very much a modern city, too. It has a large student population, and a walk along the seafront in the evening takes you past rows of bars and cafés, all filled with animated young Greeks.

Modern high-rise condominiums contrast with the ancient White Tower on the waterfront.

**Thessaloniki**

Map pp. 168 & 182

**Visitor Information**

✉ Temporarily in the Port

☎ 231/082-2935 or 231/082-7188

At one end of the waterfront stands an imposing statue of Alexander the Great, whose halfsister gave her name to the city. She was married to King Kassandros, who founded the city in 315 B.C. by amalgamating 25 towns with the town of Therme. After the Romans conquered Greece, they made it the capital of the region of Macedonia prima in 146 B.C.

Thessaloniki lay on the Via Egnatia, the mighty road that linked Rome with its eastern outpost at Constantinople. Its main street today is still called Egnatia. Just off this road, at the eastern end of the city center, you will find the **Arch of Galerius,** erected by the Emperor Galerius (died A.D. 313) in A.D. 303 to commemorate his victory over the Persians six years previously. It is covered in detailed carvings of Galerius' exploits. Almost next door is the **Rotonda,** believed to have been built as a mausoleum for Galerius, although it was never used as such. It has been used as both a church and a mosque in its time, and today houses occasional art exhibitions.

Close by is the city's most famous landmark, the **White Tower,** which you will see on many posters and postcards. It was previously known as the Bloody Tower because it had served as a prison and place of execution. Today it houses a fascinatingly eclectic **Byzantine Museum,** which extends over five floors and brings together many Byzantine objects, including mosaics and jewelry as well as icons. Be sure to walk up to the roof for a good view of the city's extensive waterfront.

The **Archaeological Museum,** a short walk from here and an essential visitor attraction, tells the story both of the Greek region of Macedonia and the city of Thessaloniki. Some of the best displays are from the Roman era, when the city was thriving and prosperous, as is evident from the many Roman remains. The existence here of many well-to-do Roman houses means that a lot of material has survived. Some of the best examples are the impressive floor mosaics, jewels and other decorative items, and household items like vases and plates.

One of the star exhibits is the immense Derveni krater, which dates back to the fourth century B.C. It is a huge 3-foot-high (1 m) ornately decorated bronze vase that was used for mixing wine. Derveni is a significant archaeological site just north of Thessaloniki, and there are many more wonderful items from there that used to be on display here but can now be seen at Vergina (see p. 178). Likewise the finds from Vergina itself have now also been returned to Vergina, leaving the Thessaloniki museum rather depleted but still well worth seeing.

Several smaller museums are also worth visiting. The **Folklife and Ethnological Museum** is housed in a 19th-century mansion east of downtown. It has a good collection of traditional costumes and a large photographic archive, among many other fascinating items. One block back from the waterfront in the center of Thessaloniki is the **Museum of the Macedonian Struggle.** The claim to the name of Macedonia

## Edessa

The waterfalls at Edessa are one of the major attractions for Greek vacationers in the hills of western Macedonia. In the biggest fall, the water plunges 82 feet (25 m) over a precipice and down toward the Macedonian plain. A walkway allows you to go behind one of the falls and into a small cave.

But the appeal is more in the overall setting rather than the sight of the falls themselves. The area around them has been turned into a pleasant public park, with plenty of trees and brightly colored flowers, cafés, and a restaurant. Edessa itself is a popular summer resort town on the edge of an escarpment, overlooking the broad Macedonian plain.

### Byzantine Museum

- ✉ White Tower, waterfront
- ☎ 231/086-8570
- 🕐 Closed Mon. morning

### Archaeological Museum

- ✉ Manoli Andronikos/ Leoforos Stratou
- ☎ 231/083-0538
- 🕐 Closed Mon. morning
- 💲 $$

### Folklife & Ethnological Museum

- ✉ Vasilissis Olggas 68
- ☎ 231/083-0591 or 231/081-2343
- 🕐 Closed Thurs.
- 💲 $

### Museum of the Macedonian Struggle

- ✉ Proxenou Koromila 23
- ☎ 231/022-9778
- 🕐 Closed Sat.

by the Former Yugoslav Republic of Macedonia naturally caused great concern throughout Greece, and especially here in what they have always regarded as the true Macedonia. A visit to this gripping museum explains the Greek case, with dramatic displays on the struggle for Greek control of this region, including weapons used by freedom fighters and vivid dioramas.

## Churches

Thessaloniki has many fine churches. **Agia Sofia** is a downtown landmark, built in the eighth century. It is easily distinguished, as it resembles Agia Sofia in Istanbul, and this building, too, was used as a mosque from 1585 to 1912. Note the

base of a minaret that remains in one corner of the church, and see also the frescoes and mosaics that have, remarkably, survived from the ninth and tenth centuries.

Thessaloniki can also proudly boast the largest church in all of Greece, which is dedicated to the city's patron saint, **Agios Dimitrios.** A comparatively modern building, having been rebuilt in 1917 after a horrific fire that devastated the city, it stands on the site where St. Dimitrios was murdered by the Romans in A.D. 305 for refusing to renounce his faith. The crypt where this happened still exists, a haunting place beneath the main altar. The feast day of St. Dimitrios is October 26,

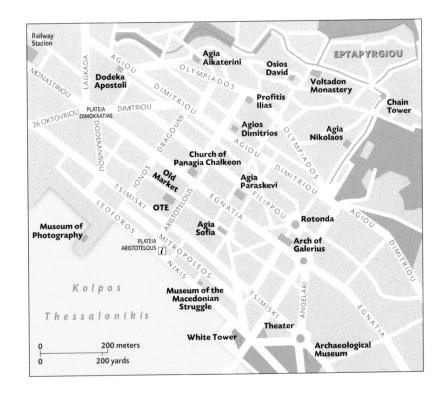

Railway
Station

LAGKADA

AGIOU

MONASTIRIOU

Dodeka
Apostoli

26 OKTOVRIOU

PLATEIA
DIMOKRATIAS    DIMITRIOU

DIMITRIOU

DODEKANISOU

Agia
Aikaterini

OLYMPIADOS

DRAGOUMI

Profitis
Ilias

Agios
Dimitrios

Church of
Panagia Chalkeon

AGIOU

Osios
David

Voltadon
Monastery

EPTAPYRGIOU

Chain
Tower

Agia
Nikolaos

OLYMPIADOS

DIMITRIOU

Agia
Paraskevi

FILIPPOU

AGIOU

DIMITRIOU

IONOS

TSIMISKI

LEOFOROS

Old
Market

OTE

Museum of
Photography

ARISTOTELOUS

PLATEIA
ARISTOTELOUS 🛈

Agia
Sofia

MITROPOLEOS

NIKIS

EGNATIA

Rotonda

Arch of
Galerius

K o l p o s

T h e s s a l o n i k i s

Museum of the
Macedonian
Struggle

TSIMISKI

ANGELAKI

Theater

White Tower

Archaeological
Museum

EGNATIA

0        200 meters
0        200 yards

Hail a taxi and ask to go to Ano Poli, the photogenic neighborhood with preserved traditional Balkan-style architecture.

—DIMITRA KESSENIDES
*National Geographic contributor*

when there are processions and festivities in the city.

For a contrast to the largest church in Greece, visit the tiny fifth-century chapel of **Osios David** in the backstreets of the Upper Town. Its claim to fame is behind its altar. There you find the finest mosaic in Thessaloniki, "The Vision of Ezekiel." Even those with no interest in churches or mosaics will appreciate the incomparable beauty of this work, the way it has retained its colors, and the fact that, unusually, it depicts a beardless Christ. Although the church is kept locked because of the mosaic, there is usually a caretaker on site to open the doors for you.

## Chain Tower

While in the Upper Town check out the Chain Tower, for great views over the city. It formed part of the (incomplete) Byzantine city walls visible in various places in this district, one area of which is known as Eptapyrgiou—"seven towers."

Walk straight down toward the seafront from here to pass close by the house where the first president of the modern Turkish state, Mustafa Kemal Ataturk

(1881–1938), was born. Inside is a small museum dedicated to the life of this extraordinary man, and the rest of the house is kept as it was when Ataturk's family lived there. If you wish to see inside, go first to the adjacent Turkish consulate to obtain permission. With the fragile state of relations in the past between Greece and Turkey, and the fact that the Greeks hold Ataturk responsible for the exchange of populations that shamed Greece in 1923, Turkish officials have to be careful who they admit to the house, as it has been threatened on many occasions. Have your passport on you as proof of identification. ∎

**A heroic pose for Alexander the Great**

# Chalkidiki

Most people think of Chalkidiki as the three peninsulas that dangle like fingers in the Aegean Sea, but there is a fourth part of the area as well, northern Chalkidiki. This hilly, wooded region is a world away from the bustling beach resorts on the two westernmost peninsulas, and much less visited.

A fisherman in the harbor of Nea Skioni, Kassandra, sorts his nets.

The easternmost peninsula is the serene Mount Athos, known throughout the world as the place where no female—human or animal (except the Virgin Mary)—is allowed to set foot (see pp. 186–187).

However, the western peninsula, **Kassandra,** is where you'll find packed beaches and plenty of females. This is the place to head for if you want a lazy day in the sun followed by a lively time at night. In the northwest of the area the beach towns run into each other and eventually merge into the suburbs of Thessaloniki.

Situated at the narrow top of the peninsula, the town of **Nea Moudaniais** is the gateway to Kassandra, and most people head on through without stopping. The town is less attractive than resorts farther south, but it has all the facilities you might want. It is a departure point for boats to the Sporades islands and the Pilion peninsula. You can drive around Kassandra in a very short time to get a feel of the place. There are resorts on both the east and west sides of the peninsula, all fairly similar, although those on the east coast have good views across to the next peninsula, Sithonia.

**Sithonia** is quieter and more attractive, with more of the green hills that are also typical of northern Chalkidiki. The resorts are comparatively low-key and spread out, and again the east coast has the advantage of views—across to Mount Athos. For a boat trip to see the monasteries of Mount

Athos (see pp. 188–189), go to Ouranopolis at the top of the Athos peninsula, or pick one up from Ormos Panagias, the main town on the east coast of Sithonia.

The better beaches are toward the southern tip of Sithonia, at small resorts such as Toroni and Aretes. If you want all the comforts of a planned vacation complex, head for **Porto Carras,** the largest such complex in Greece, spreading out behind a 6-mile (10 km) stretch of beach.

**Northern Chalkidiki** has plenty to see, including beautiful wooded hills and hill villages hardly touched by tourism. A major attraction is the cave near Petralona, sometimes called the **Petralona Cave** but more correctly known as the Kokkines Petres, or Red Stones

Cave. It was here that Greece's oldest archaeological find was discovered in 1960, a Neanderthal skull thought to be around 700,000 years old. The historical interest of the cave is illustrated by reconstructed prehistoric scenes, which are very effective in their natural setting.

A charming road winds through some of the best scenery in northern Chalkidiki. It passes through the large village of **Arnaia,** worth a stop to admire some of its attractive old houses and inspect the distinctive local carpets and crafts that are for sale. Farther on is **Stagira,** the birthplace of the philosopher Aristotle (384–322 B.C.), commemorated with a marble statue on the edge of the village. ■

**Chalkidiki**
🅰 Map p. 168

**Petralona Cave**
🅰 Map p. 168
✉ 34 miles (55 km) southeast of Thessaloniki
💲 $

---

# EXPERIENCE: Shopping in Greece

Different areas of Greece specialize in particular crafts. If you are keen on ceramics, then the best examples are available in Rhodes, Sifnos, and Skiros, though you will find good work for sale almost anywhere in the country.

For jewelry the place to go is Ioanina in Epiros, the traditional center of the silverworkers of Greece. Rhodes and Athens are both good for gold, but prices there tend to be higher. Quality leatherwork is widely available throughout Greece, but the finest examples are available on Crete, and in particular the town of Hania.

Wooden carvings and embroidery are especially good in Metsovo, and quality embroidery is also to be found in the Ionian islands, especially Kefalonia and Zakinthos. Crete has long been a center for embroidery and weaving, traditional

practices since Minoan times, and you can pick up some fine examples in the larger towns and villages on the Lasithi Plateau.

You can buy handmade rugs all over Greece, made by weavers using traditional looms, materials, and techniques. Traditional handwoven wool rugs called flokati are produced particularly in the northern mountains and in Thrace.

Many shops sell sponges in the Dodecanese, and almost all tourist shops will have at least a few on display. There will be several different types to choose from. In order to know what you're buying, bear in mind that there are several things to look for in a good sponge: Naturally colored brown sponges are stronger than artificially colored yellow ones, smaller holes make better sponges, and cut sponges do not last as long as whole sponges.

# Mount Athos

Mount Athos (Agion Oros) means "holy mountain." A visit to this special area requires a permit and some advance planning, but anyone can take a boat trip around the peninsula to take a look at the monasteries that dot the landscape. Some of these are in spectacular clifftop settings, which make you wonder how they were ever built.

Just a few pilgrims are permitted to join the monks of Mount Athos in their austere lifestyle.

**Mount Athos**
Map p. 169

Toward the southern end of the peninsula is the imposing sight of Mount Athos itself, which at 6,668 feet (2,033 m) is the highest point in Chalkidiki.

St. Athanasius founded the first monastery, the Great Lavra Monastery, on Athos in A.D. 963. At that time the place was already regarded as a holy site and had been attracting hermits who sought a contemplative life. That first monastery was set on a rocky outcrop at the very southeastern end of the peninsula, about as far away from civilization as possible. It was followed by the building of other monasteries in the 10th and

11th centuries, until at one time there were 40 active monasteries with as many as a thousand monks in each one.

The population today is nothing like that, with fewer than 2,000 monks living in the 20 monasteries that are still inhabited. However, numbers have increased in recent years as younger people have turned to the monastic life, influenced by the arrival of the new millennium and also as a reaction against rising hedonism.

The Monks' Republic, as it is often called, is an unusual private entity, with its own laws, within the state of Greece.

Famously, no woman is allowed to set foot on the peninsula since 1060, when Emperor Constantine Monomachus of Byzantium (modern Istanbul) issued an edict banning all women from visiting Athos, which was reserved for the Virgin Mary alone. Even female animals are banned. The unique status of Athos was confirmed by a government decree in 1926 that created a Theocratic Republic on Athos, making it independent and self-governing, but still a part of the Greek state. There have been suggestions that this should change, but at the moment Athos still goes its own way.

If you are male and wish to visit Athos, rather than merely observe it from a boat, there is a strict procedure to follow (see Mount Athos's Monastic Life below). It's easy to make a boat trip to the peninsula (see pp. 188–189), and the monasteries in their peaceful settings, but such boats are not allowed to tie up on the shore, so as not to disturb the monks. Arranging to stay on Mount Athos is a little trickier and requires some planning, but it intentionally keeps the number of visitors down.

If you do get to Athos, you will see the strict regime under which the monks live. Services begin about 3 or 4 a.m. The monks are called to prayer by the banging of a piece of wood known as a *simandro,* which is suspended near the entrance to the church. Only two meals a day are allowed, and there are many fast days when only one limited meal is served. When not praying, the monks spend their day at work in the fields or maintaining the monasteries. ∎

## EXPERIENCE: Mount Athos's Monastic Life

For a uniquely Greek experience, stay in the monasteries with the monks of Mount Athos. In order to control the numbers and give the monks the peace they desire, only 10 permits a day are granted to people who are not of the Greek Orthodox faith, and 120 per day to those who are.

Obtaining a permit is not easy. You first need a letter of recommendation from the Greek consul in your own country, showing that you have a good educational, religious, or cultural reason for wanting to visit. Then you must send or take your letter to the Holy Executive of Holy Mount Athos *(Pilgrims' Bureau, Egnatia 109, Thessaloniki 54635, tel 231/025-2578, e-mail: pilgrimsbureau @c-lab.gr),* which issues the permits.

No boat will take you to the island without such a permit. You can apply up to five months ahead of your intended visit, but because of the restrictions there is no guarantee you will get a permit for the exact period you wish to stay, so you have to be flexible.

Permits are inexpensive (€30 at the time of writing) and good for four days (three nights) on Mount Athos, and include your accommodation and meals. However, you will also need to reserve your accommodation at some, but not all, monasteries, if there are particular ones you wish to visit. While you are on Athos, it may also be possible to extend your permit by an extra two nights, if you have a particular reason for wanting to stay longer.

# A Boat Trip Around Mount Athos

Few people get the chance to set foot on Mount Athos (Agion Oros). Most have to content themselves with a boat trip along the coast, taking in the sight of the magnificent monasteries in their clifftop settings, against the backdrop of Mount Athos itself.

The shoreline at Ouranopolis is overshadowed by the Byzantine Phosphori Tower.

Some trips take visitors around the whole peninsula, to see the monasteries on the eastern side as well, but the majority of boats leave from **Ouranopolis ❶** on the northwest of the peninsula and limit themselves to the more spectacular western side of Mount Athos. Ouranopolis itself is not an especially attractive place to be based—most visitors stay in Chalkidiki or Thessaloniki—but you may wish to spend one night there in order to take one of the earlier boat trips.

Boats are not permitted to venture closer than 550 yards (500 m) to the shore, so take a pair of binoculars and, if you want to get close-up photographs, a telephoto lens for

### NOT TO BE MISSED:
**Dochiariou • Agiou Pandeleimonos • Simonopetra • Agiou Dionisiou**

your camera. If you only have a pocket camera, don't leave it behind: You may get some wonderful photos of the dolphins that sometimes swim alongside the boats and leap teasingly out of the water. The boat trips take at least four hours, and although some food and drink is sold on board, the choice is limited so you may wish to bring your own picnic lunch. The boats provide a commentary in Greek, English, and German, but the public-address systems on some boats are poor. The accompanying map will help you identify the main monasteries.

The first monasteries you pass are inland: **Zografou** is the most northerly and, shortly afterward, Kastamonitou. The former was founded in the 10th century but, like many monasteries, was rebuilt in the 18th and 19th centuries. Today it is home to a small community of Bulgarian monks. **Kastamonitou** dates from the 11th century and is also still inhabited.

The first monasteries of which you get good views are down on the coast. **Dochiariou ❷** comes into sight first, a cluster of attractive buildings on a hill behind a jetty. This working monastery was founded in the tenth century, and, in addition to some original frescoes in its churches, claims to have a piece of the True Cross. Farther along the coast is **Xenofondos ❸**, founded in the tenth century by St. Xenofondos, and very much a working monastery—it even has a sawmill. Like many monasteries, however, it has been damaged over the years by fires and now reflects a mixture of periods and styles.

The next coastal monastery is the hugely impressive **Agiou Pandeleimonos ④**, dating back to the 12th century, with additions built by Russian monks in the 19th century. Inside you can glimpse the onion domes of churches standing above the red-roofed buildings. Farther on is the port of **Dafni ⑤**, where pilgrims come ashore and where a small population exists to service the practical needs of the monks and their visitors. Inland from here is the monastery of **Xeropotamou,** another one that has suffered fire damage and been rebuilt in various styles.

One of the most impressive sights is **Simonopetra ⑥**, on top of a rocky ridge, founded in the 14th century. So too was **Grigoriou,** also on a clifftop if not quite as spectacular, and then **Agiou Dionisiou,** with its pink and white balconies, is perched 260 feet (80 m) above the sea. **Agiou Pavlou ⑦** is even higher, nestling below Mount Athos itself. At this point most boats turn around and head back for Ouranopolis, leaving the monks to their contemplative existence, shared by just a select few pilgrims.

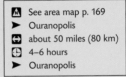

| | |
|---|---|
| ▲ | See area map p. 169 |
| ► | Ouranopolis |
| ↔ | about 50 miles (80 km) |
| ⏱ | 4–6 hours |
| ► | Ouranopolis |

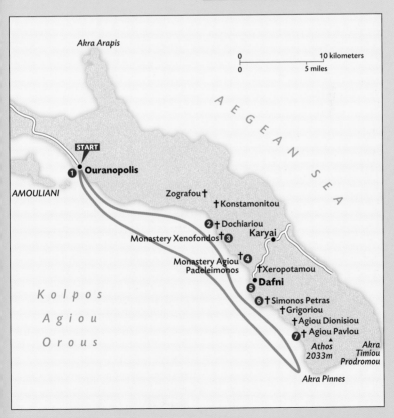

# Nestos Valley

The Nestos River starts its journey high in the Rhodope Mountains (shared with Bulgaria), then runs for 80 miles (130 km) through Greece before dividing and flowing into the Aegean Sea. Its main course marks the administrative boundary between Macedonia and Thrace, and the area is influenced by a variety of cultures.

The lush green Nestos Valley

**Nestos Valley**
⚠ Map p. 169

**Stavroupolis**
⚠ Map p. 169

To the west is modern Greece, to the east lies Turkey, and to the north, central Europe, with its flamboyant tales of gypsies and vampires. The Nestos River Delta is a vital wetland site for the north of Greece, teeming with plants, reptiles, and amphibians, and around 250 species of birds.

Head inland for a wonderful drive through the valley, following the course of the river between Xanthi (in Thrace) and Drama (in Macedonia). This is a remarkable part of Greece, influenced by nearby Turkey and Bulgaria. Few visitors explore this region, but those who do are assured of a warm welcome and a special experience. Be careful if you are driv-

ing in winter as the road can be cut off in severe weather. Warning signs are posted at either end of the valley if this is the case. Make sure you have a full tank, too, as there are few gas stations.

The road winds through thick beech forests and below the mountain tops, which are covered in snow for several months of the year. There are several small, idyllic villages, where you should stop and walk around, to get a glimpse of mountain life in this remote part of Greece, light-years from Athens. At **Stavroupolis** you can fill up both yourself and your car, but there are no accommodations. **Xanthi** (see pp. 194–195) is by far the best base if you plan to spend time here. ■

# Philippi

The impressive remains of the once thriving town of Philippi, 9 miles (15 km) northwest of Kavala, straddle the main Kavala–Drama road. The site was named after King Philip II of Macedonia, the father of Alexander the Great (see p. 30), after he captured it from the Thracians in 356 B.C. However, the remains you now see date mostly from the Roman period.

The most famous part of the site is the remnants of the **prison.** St. Paul was held here when he arrived on his first visit to Europe in A.D. 49.

In ancient times the town was most notable for the Battle of Philippi, fought in 42 B.C. Brutus and Cassius, the murderers of Julius Caesar, killed themselves here when confronted with certain defeat by the pursuing forces of Mark Antony and Octavian.

There is a sizable **theater** on the site, dating from the time of Philip II. It was rebuilt during the Roman era for use as an amphitheater. On this side of the road—part of the Via Egnatia that links Rome with Istanbul—is also the site **museum,** although if time is limited it can be skipped as the main attractions are actually still in place.

On the opposite side of the road are the bulk of the town's remains, including two contrasting features. One is the impressive foundation of a huge church known as **Basilica B,** and the other is the remains of the **public latrine,** equally impressive for the state of preservation of its 50 marble seats! Nearby are the ruins of the Roman baths, built in A.D. 250 but destroyed soon after in a fire. ■

**Philippi**

△ Map p. 169
☎ 251/051-6470
🕐 Closed Mon.
⑤ $

---

## EXPERIENCE: Bound for Bulgaria

Bulgaria, the former Soviet-bloc state just across the Rhodope Mountains, has experienced a renaissance since the fall of communism. If you have the time, take a few days to explore this fascinating country.

There are several ways you can travel to Bulgaria from Greece. The train presents perhaps the best and easiest of the options. Rail Europe *(www.raileurope.com)* offers a Balkan Flexipass—an international train pass that allows you between 5 and 15 days of travel within a month throughout the entire Balkan region. The train ride north from Greece through the mountains is spectacular.

You can also make your way to Bulgaria by bus: Check out the options available at *www.eurolines.com.* Customs procedures at the border are fairly lax.

Nationals from the United States, Canada, and the European Union do not need a visa to stay in the country for fewer than 90 days. However, you will need to register with the police if you are not a resident of the EU. Your travel office or hotel will probably be able to take care of this for you, but it's best to make sure, as failure to do so results in a fine of 2,000 leva ($1,500).

Within Bulgaria, buses offer the best means of getting around. They cost a little more than the train, but the extra cash is worth the faster and more comfortable trip. A good bus site in English is *www.etapgroup.com/grup/en.*

# From Kavala to Alexandroupoli

The port of Kavala is recognizably Greek and, with its harbor, fortress, and seafront restaurants, could be in almost any part of the country. East of here, however, the mood changes, and in towns such as Xanthi and Komotini you realize you are nearing the frontier. By the time you reach Alexandroupoli, you know without being told that this is the last major town before the Turkish border.

Looking over modern Kavala from the ancient citadel

### Kavala
 Map p. 169

**Visitor Information**

✉ Plateia
   Eleftherias

☎ 251/023-1011

## Kavala

This very lively port is a gateway to the islands of the northern Aegean and northern Dodecanese. A popular resort with good beaches either side of the center, it has interesting museums illustrating the historical and cultural interest of the town and surrounding area. Your first impression may not be favorable, as Kavala is big and busy, but it is well worth spending a few days exploring.

Kavala has been a port since ancient times, and was founded as long ago as the sixth century B.C. by emigrants from the island of Paros. St. Paul first set foot on European soil here in A.D. 49 before traveling to Philippi (see p. 191). The town has been fought over throughout history. At different times it was occupied by the Franks, Turks, Venetians, Normans, and others, including the Bulgarians during both World War I and World War II.

**INSIDER TIP:**

The Imaret complex overlooking the harbor was formerly the mosque-school built by Mehmet Ali Pasha of Egypt, born in Kavala. It has been beautifully restored and turned into a luxury hotel.

—DIMITRA KESSENIDES
*National Geographic writer*

The Turkish occupation, from 1371 to 1912, had the biggest impact. Among Turkish legacies is the town's **aqueduct,** which dates not from the Romans as you might expect, but from the 16th century. A **citadel** dominates the eastern end of the harbor. Its imposing walls, built in the 10th and 16th centuries, make an impressive sight when floodlit at night. Inside the walls is the area of town known as Panagia. This is a terrific place in which to get lost, with its meandering streets and its 18th- and 19th-century houses. Among these is the **birthplace of Mehmet Ali** (1769–1849), who became the Pasha of Egypt. The house can be identified by the nearby bronze statue of Ali on horseback. You can visit the house, although the door is not always open. Simply knock and wait for the custodian to show you around the garden and rather grand rooms, including a harem.

The most notable building, known as the **Imaret,** overlooks the harbor on the right-hand side of one of the main streets as you enter the citadel area. This is the largest Islamic building in Europe, and was founded by Mehmet Ali. It originally housed theological students and provided them with inexpensive meals. After standing derelict for many years, it has been refurbished as a restaurant, where the meals cost more than they used to but the setting overlooking the harbor is still superb. If you merely want to take a look around the interior, there is also a simpler bar set around the courtyard.

The **harbor** at Kavala is a busy place, with hints of the Eastern bazaar in the market area just behind it. You can be sure of good fresh fish in the many restaurants that line the front, although if you want something more unusual and Turkish-influenced, head into the Panagia area at night.

At the far side of the harbor, the excellent **Archaeological Museum** has finds from several classical sites nearby, including Philippi (see p. 191). Some of the best exhibits are from Avdira (see pp. 195–196), including an exquisite dolphin mosaic and a huge sarcophagus, unusual in that its paint has survived. The site of Amphipolis, west of the town, is also represented, notably by some fine laurel wreaths made of pure gold in the third century B.C., looking far too delicate to have survived for more than 2,000 years. There are also extensive collections of ceramics, jewelry, coins, statues, and many other items.

The **Folk and Modern Art Museum,** also known as the Municipal Museum, is a superior example of its kind, not dealing just with the past but also finding

**Archaeological Museum**
- ✉ Erythrou Stavrou 17
- ☎ 251/022-2335
- 🕐 Closed Mon.
- 💲 $

**Folk and Modern Art Museum**
- ✉ Filippou 4
- ☎ 251/022-2706
- 🕐 Closed Sun.

**Imaret**
- ✉ 6 Th. Poulidou St.
- **www. lux-hotels .com/gr/imaret/**

**Xanthi**
⚑ Map p. 169

space for displays of more modern Greek art. Among the highlights are several sculptures by an artist from the island of Thassos, Polygnotos Vagis (1894–1965). In other rooms there are the usual displays of traditional folk costumes, as well as household and agricultural items, but the collection is very eclectic and well worth an hour or two of browsing time.

## Xanthi

Xanthi has an undeniable fascination that will make you want to stay for longer than the usual quick look around. You may even decide to use it as a base. It has a distinctly Eastern feel to it, which combines with youthful energy provided by the large numbers of students at the local University of Thrace. Xanthi is a town of bars, bistros, and galleries. The liveliest spot is the main square, which is attractive and modern, with fountains in the middle and restaurants and cafés surrounding it.

Xanthi is home to one of the best **markets** in the region, and if you are here on a Saturday morning you will see the town invaded by a colorful mix of Greeks, Turks, gypsies, and Pomaks, all here for the bazaar. The Pomaks are a highly localized indigenous group—Muslims with Slav rather than Greek origins. There are about 40,000 of them, most living to the north of Xanthi, and their language is a mix of Bulgarian, Greek, and Turkish. The Greeks do not treat the Pomaks favorably. They are required to have travel permits, and visitors need a permit (not easily obtained) to go to one of their villages. The Pomak language is also under threat as the Greeks discourage the people from using it, for instance putting sizable obstacles in the way of the Pomaks who would like to have their own language newspaper.

Xanthi became rich on the proceeds of the large tobacco plantations you will see as you travel through Thrace. Tobacco

## EXPERIENCE: Xanthi Carnival

One reason why many visitors travel to Xanthi is for its annual carnival, which begins near the end of February. Held every year since 1966, the Xanthi Carnival is a Thracian folk festival that draws locals and tourists alike.

During the two weeks of the festival, the streets around the old town become a place of fun and frivolity, packed with revelers young and old. What the Xanthi carnival lacks in size, it makes up in intensity. Musicians and performers entertain throughout the entire festival. But the climax is the carnival parade, in which

nearly everyone in the town marches through the cobblestoned streets decked out in some sort of costume. While the older townsfolk and children come in traditional Thracian garb, students and other youths organize themselves into various carnival clubs whose members dress up in a whole range of outfits—from American football players to red bulls to contemporary video-game characters.

If you plan to visit Xanthi during the festival, book accommodations several months in advance. For more information, visit *www.carnival-of-xanthi.gr.*

**Students enjoying the fun at the Xanthi carnival**

merchants' mansions, most of them built in the 19th century, are concentrated in the old town, a jumble of narrow streets and alleys. One such mansion now houses the town's **Folk Museum,** with displays on the tobacco industry as well as local costumes and jewelry. It is also a chance to see inside one of the mansions, restored to its former glory.

## Avdira

Modern Avdira is a small farming village several miles from the coast. It also lends its name to the nearest beach, which attracts many Greek vacationers in the summer, but few foreign visitors as it is somewhat out of the way. Nearby is Lake Vistonis; the marshlands around it are an important area for wildlife, especially wading birds and rare birds of prey, such as the sea eagle. Observation towers help interested bird-watchers get the best views.

Near the beach of Avdira is the site of **ancient Avdira,** from which many of the best finds have been taken for display in the Archaeological Museums in Komotini and Kavala. The site is pretty overgrown and requires dedication to get the best from it. It stands on a small headland, surrounded by the remains of the acropolis walls. You can see a few remnants of a theater as well as a Roman bathhouse. The foundations of some Roman houses are close by, and the entrance gate to the city is also identifiable, flanked by two towers.

The city was founded in about 656 B.C. by refugees from Klazomenae in Asia Minor, and refounded in about 500 B.C. by more refugees from Persia. It grew into an important member of the Delian League (a fifth-century B.C. confederation of Greek states against the Persian threat), and was known to be a fair-size city until at least the ninth century A.D. At that time it was still the site of a bishopric. Excavations, which did not begin until 1950, unearthed some valuable items, including in

### Folk Museum
- ✉ Antika 7, Xanthi
- ☎ 254/102-5421
- 🕐 Open daily 11 a.m.–1 p.m., & some evenings (call to check)
- 💲 $

### Avdira
- 🗺 Map p. 169

**Komotini**

⚑  Map p. 169

**Visitor Information**

✉  Ap Souzou 14

☎  253/107-0996

**Archaeological Museum**

✉  Symeonidi 4, Komotini

☎  253/102-2411

one place 2,000 small votive vases.

While the site is not especially attractive or spectacular, for that very reason it does not get crowded and you may well be able to wander over the extensive remains by yourself—an evocative experience, and somehow just as rewarding as exploring more significant sites in the company of hundreds of other visitors.

The building of the lighthouse in 1880 marked a general rise in Alexandroupoli's fortunes.

**Museum of Folk Life and History**

✉  Agios Yeoryios 13, Komotini

🕐  Closed Sun.

## Komotini

Komotini, like Xanthi (see pp. 194–195), reveals a fascinating mix of influences, and is even more Turkish than its nearby Bulgarian neighbor. It lies only about 60 miles (100 km) from the Turkish border to the east, and even closer—14 miles (22 km)—to Bulgaria on the north.

Both those countries contribute their color and customs to the Greek melting pot that is eastern Thrace.

The Turkish influence is most immediately seen in the minarets and domed roofs of mosques around the town—14 of them still in use today. Komotini was part of Turkey until as recently as 1920, when the borders were changed. It had been in the Ottoman Empire since 1363. Little wonder that it feels as much Turkish as Greek, although it would not be tactful to express that view to the local people until you know where their affinities lie. Greek-Turkish relations are a touchy subject for discussion, and about half the population are of Turkish origin, with a number of Pomaks living here, too (see p. 195).

Komotini was founded in the fourth century A.D., and its early history is well documented in the **Archaeological Museum.** This museum has some of the great finds from the nearby sites at Avdira (see pp. 195–196) and Maroneia (see p. 202). Beautiful gold jewelry recovered from graves, as well as examples of painted sarcophagi, gravestones, statues, and ceramics, and an extensive coin display reside in its collection.

Another museum of note is the delightfully old-fashioned and jumbled **Museum of Folk Life and History,** which spreads through the rooms of an 18th-century mansion. A turn around the museum provides many rewards—a good selection of traditional folk costumes, domestic items, and especially embroidery, for which the area is noted.

In keeping with the Turkish influence, Komotini has a lively **bazaar,** with the Eastern tradition of similar shops being clustered together, so that you will find, for example, a row of shoe stores all in line. You can find everything here from valuable antiques to the day's fish catch, as well as the region's best tobacco leaves.

## Alexandroupoli

Although dismissed by some as mainly a military base, Alexandroupoli, at the eastern end of the coast of Thrace, is actually very pleasant, with a long promenade and a long stretch of sandy beach. It is very much a family resort town, and the beach has lots of facilities for children, as well as waterski-ing, parasailing, and other water sports for adults. Beyond the promenade is the old part of town, a warren of narrow streets offering a delightful mix of workshops, junk shops, food stores, souvenir shops, bars, and good restaurants and cafés.

In the evening the promenade fills with Greek families doing their evening *volta,* the customary pa-rade up and down prior to eating and drinking. It's a pleasing sight: Grandparents walk hand-in-hand with their little grandchildren, and groups of teenagers take the chance to eye each other.

The town's most notable sight is also on the promenade. The lighthouse was built in 1880, and its illumination at night adds to the atmosphere. Alexandroupoli is a port as well, with ferries to the northeast Aegean islands and as far south as Rhodes and Kos in the Dodecanese. It is also the region's closest town to the Turkish border (hence the military presence), and has railroad links with Istanbul in Turkey, Sofia in Bulgaria, and Athens via Thessaloniki.

Despite these links the town is not as multicultural as Komotini or Xanthi. It expanded only in 1878 during the Russo-Turkish war, when the Russians turned what had been an insignificant fishing village into a purpose-built modern city. It was known then by its 15th-century Turkish name of Dedeagac. It acquired its modern name in 1919 for the then Greek king, Alexandros. While Alexan-droupoli is still a military base, and you will certainly see soldiers in the streets, it is much more attractive than that designation implies. ∎

**Alexandroupoli**
🗺 Map p. 169
**Visitor Information**
✉ Tourist Police
☎ 255/103-7411

### Turkish Influence

With borders in this part of the world being little more than sugges-tions, cultural overlap is understandable. In the early 1980s, a Turkish art historian documented 3,370 instances of Turk-ish architecture within Greece. Due to geographic proximity, most occur in the eastern part of the country; look for pattern-based design and domed mosques. There are 2,336 mosques in Greece ; their domes add an organic element to the facade and, inside, by eliminating internal corners, create the illusion of space.

# Birds of Greece

Like the vacationing visitors, birds flock to Greece. It's the ideal stopover for migrants crossing the eastern Mediterranean, particularly those flying on their way from central and eastern Europe to the warmer climes of North Africa.

The huge untidy nests of storks are seen on roofs and chimneys of northern and eastern Greece.

**Crete,** ideally placed between Greece and North Africa, attracts many such migrants, and has particularly good opportunities for bird-watching in spring and fall. A microcosm of the best of the mainland, it offers a variety of habitats for avian visitors, including marshy wetlands in the south that appeal to stilts and other waders, salt pans to the east favored by avocets, and open plateau that is attractive to birds such as the colorful hoopoe.

## Breeding Grounds

Several locations in Greece are vital breeding places, including for some seriously endangered species. For example, the **Prespa lakes** near Albania are one of the few remaining breeding grounds in Europe for the Dalmatian pelican, a bird regarded as vulnerable by the International Council for Bird Preservation. There are fewer than a thousand pairs worldwide, and around one-fifth of these nest in the Prespa lakes area. This is the only breeding place in Greece for the more common white pelican. Other important species breeding there include the pygmy cormorant (also vulnerable), the goosander, and magnificent birds of prey such as the golden eagle, short-toed eagle, and booted eagle.

## Wintering Spots

The politically sensitive area of the **Evros River Delta,** close to the Turkish border, is a haven for thousands of wintering ducks and geese. Over 75 percent of Greece's 408 bird species have been seen in the Evros Delta. These include pygmy cormorants, common cormorants, white pelicans, herons, egrets, storks, and any number of waders, plus sea eagles.

The best place to see birds of prey is north of the Evros Delta, in the **Dadia Forest.** An incredible 36 of Europe's 39 species of raptors have been spotted here, and 26 of those species are known to live and nest in the pine forests of the Evros Mountains. They include the griffon vulture, Egyptian vulture, golden eagle, and Levant sparrowhawk, as well as sea eagles, and one of the rarest in Europe, the black vulture.

On the western coast of mainland Greece, the wetlands around **Messolongi** are among the most important ecological sites in Greece. Rivers such as the Acheloös and Evinos, flowing from the mountains, have created a vast series of lagoons, mudflats, marshes, and reed beds. Almost 300 species have been observed here; in winter there are vast numbers of coots (an estimated 30,000) and ducks (20,000). Messolongi is a vital stopping-off point for the slender-billed

**The goshawk is one of Greece's most common birds of prey.**

curlew (endangered in Russia) on its migratory journey to its winter home in North Africa.

## Asian Species

The islands of the eastern Aegean are of interest to birders. Species more common in Asia occur here. For example, Kruper's nuthatch has made its way to the island of **Lesvos** (see p. 236) and around the mountain village of **Ayiassos**. The Gulf of Kalloni is a well-known haven for migrants, notably waterbirds such as ducks, stilts, and avocets. The rare Eleanora's falcon is a common visitor to these islands; the sight of one is unforgettable.

---

## **EXPERIENCE:** Off-the-Beaten-Path in Macedonia

Cormorants, Old World flycatchers, and coots are some of the birds you may spot on an organized excursion into Macedonia, which opens up a whole new perspective on nature viewing. Many fascinating places in Thrace and eastern Macedonia, are are off the beaten track for most visitors.

One company, Trekking Hellas (*Rethymnou 10, Athens 106 82, tel 210/331-0323, fax 210/323-4548, www.trekking.gr, €1,950 per person for party of 3, less for bigger parties*) offers a weeklong jeep safari into eastern Macedonia from Thessaloniki to Lake Kirkini (Limni

Kerkinis) and the surrounding wetlands area, a protected national park near the border of Greece and Bulgaria. A canoe trip on the lake allows a quieter approach to see some of the wildlife here, which includes many endangered species. Nearby is the unusual sight for Greece of a herd of wild water buffalo.

There are also visits to waterfalls and caves, and an opportunity to go rafting on the Aggitis River. The final day is spent in the protected Fraktos Forest, one of the few places in Greece where bears still roam. Seeing one is another matter, but it's not unknown to happen.

# Evros Delta & Dadia Forest Reserve

The eastern extremity of Greece includes two regions that are among the best wildlife sites in the country: the Evros Delta and the Dadia Forest. The Evros River rises in Bulgaria, and for much of its length marks the border between Greece and Turkey. For this reason the delta is politically sensitive as well as ecologically sensitive, and the Greek authorities take an interest in anyone visiting the area.

Few visitors discover Greece's tranquil yet vital wetlands.

Don't be surprised if, when wandering around with binoculars and notebooks, you are approached and asked to produce ID. Until the late 1990s a permit was needed to visit certain parts, but this no longer applies.

The town of **Loutros Traianopolis,** on the edge of the delta, has a choice of simple accommodations. From here you can go on foot, as there are numerous paths that lead into the delta area, but be careful with directions as it is easy to get lost.

The region has some poisonous snakes and, while you are unlikely to be bitten, it is sensible to exercise caution. Species include the nose-horned viper, sand boa, cat snake, grass snake, dice snake, and leopard snake. There are plenty of other reptiles, including several species of tortoise, turtle, and lizard. Amphibians are abundant, too, such as the warty newt, yellow-bellied toad, marsh frog, and fire salamander.

The rarest mammal to look for is the (now misnamed) common otter. Wolves, jackals, and polecats also inhabit the area.

There are some magnificent sights to enjoy, and if you are lucky you might be treated to the spectacle of a sea eagle or an osprey hunting—diving to pluck fish out of the water. During the mild Greek winter, vast numbers of wildfowl can be seen here.

Head northeast from the delta to the small town of **Feres,** a good base for exploring the area to the north of here, the 80,300-acre (32,500 ha) **Dadia Forest Reserve.** Set in the Evros Valley and overshadowed by the Evros Mountains, this is another scenically splendid area of Greece, visited chiefly by those with an interest in its wide-ranging wildlife.

The **forest information center** is reached from the village of Likofos, and has good information about the flora and fauna of the reserve, especially its rare birds of prey (see p. 199). You can get advice on exploring the reserve on foot or with an organized tour that goes into areas where other vehicles are banned.

The two main paths are well marked. One leads to the highest point in the reserve, at 2,034 feet (620 m), and the other to a hide that looks out over the Mavrorema Canyon. This is a great place to watch for birds of prey, as they soar on the thermals that rise up from the canyon.

In addition to eagles and vultures, species to look for include the lanner falcon, black kite, goshawk, Levant sparrowhawk, and honey buzzard. You may be lucky enough to see a black stork, but these are increasingly rare, and only a few remain in the forest.

You can stay in the reserve at the pleasant hostel next to the information center, but reserve a place ahead at migration times in spring and fall. There is a café nearby, and more eating options and stores in the village of **Dadia,** about half a mile (1 km) away. ■

**Dadia Forest Reserve Information Center**
- Map p. 169
- ☎ 255/403-2209

## EXPERIENCE: Stay at the Dadia Forest Reserve

It's often very easy when traveling to stay in your comfort zone, and always book yourself into reliable hotels. In Greece this is even easier, as there is a good network of inexpensive and simple hotels that provide the basic needs for anyone traveling on a budget. Sometimes it pays to be more adventurous, though.

In one of Greece's most magnificent wildlife areas, the Dadia Forest, the Ecotourism Center, across from the visitor center, offers 20 ensuite rooms, with heating and telephones, which are much more comfortable than the usual type of basic accommodation you often find in out-of-the-way places. They are also very inexpensive, and the price includes breakfast. There is also a café

and restaurant, and all-inclusive options if you prefer.

The biggest advantage, though, is that it puts you right in the reserve. The optimal viewing times for the birds of prey, for which the reserve is best known (36 of the 39 European species are found here), is in the early morning and again in the evening, so there's no better way to see them than to spend the night. You will also find yourself in the company of enthusiastic Greek naturalists, and will have an experience that goes beyond a normal vacation.

For more information, contact the **Dadia Ecotourism Center** *(Dadia, 684 00 Soufli, tel 255/403-2263, fax 255/403-2463, www.ecoclub.com/dadia, single rooms €30 per night, doubles €43).*

# More Places to Visit in Macedonia & Thrace

## Florina

The mountain town of Florina is 25 miles (40 km) east of the Prespa lakes. It makes an acceptable base for a few nights' stay if you want to explore the northern Pindos Mountains and some of the smaller lakes nearby.

Florina is very close to the border with the Former Yugoslav Republic of Macedonia, giving it something of a frontier feel. One of its main attractions is the old part of the town, which is filled with picturesque Turkish houses and neoclassical mansions. There is also a good small **Archaeological Museum** (Closed Sat.–Mon., $), and a range of hotels and restaurants.

🄰 Map p. 168  🚂 Train from Thessaloniki

## Maroneia

Ancient Maroneia is another of those delightfully remote Greek historical sites that are worth visiting for the journey there and the setting as much as for the remains. The road goes through the cotton and tobacco fields of Thrace, past farms and woodland, and through modern Maroneia, a tiny rural community where your journey is likely to be delayed by tractors on the road, or animals, or both.

A sign to Agios Haralambos directs you down a rough track along the coast, where you soon find the overgrown ruins of **ancient Maroneia.** The star attraction is a small theater, like a toy version of the great theaters at Epidavros and Athens (see p. 108 & p. 61), which has been renovated and is used for modern performances and concerts. There are also the remains of what was a sanctuary probably dedicated to Dionysos, the party-going god of wine, inebriation, and jollity known to the Romans as Bacchus. Dionysos was the father of Maron, the founder of the city of Maroneia.

The ancient city was vastly different from the ruins that you see today. It flourished from the eighth century B.C. right up to about A.D. 1400. Its walls were 6 miles (10 km) in overall length, which gives an idea of the scale of the city, by far the most important in this area.

Continue on to **Agios Haralambos** to find an appealing little harbor with a hotel, a few tavernas, and a scattering of houses, with small-scale tourist development.

🄰 Map p. 169

## Saitista

Like Kastoria, 44 miles (70 km) to the north, Saitista was also once an important fur trading center. The business is now only a fraction of what it once was, but you will still see furs for sale in some of the town's stores.

Here, too, are the 18th-century mansions of the wealthy, with their ornate interiors, some of which can be visited. Most are well maintained and still lived in by families, while a few have fallen into ruin.

The main town church of **Agia Paraskevi** has frescoes dating from the 17th-century that are well worth seeing.

🄰 Map p. 168

---

### Greek Yogurt

Greece is known for its distinctive, thick, and creamy yogurt, a key ingredient in tzatziki, savory dishes, and many desserts. Several differences set Greek yogurt apart from that found in the United States. For one, Greek yogurt is traditionally made with ewe's milk. (Mass commercial makers, however, have started to shift toward the use of cow's milk.) The milk has a higher fat content than U.S. yogurt (5–9 percent compared to 3.5). The active culture content is also much higher in the Greek variety. In addition, the Greeks strain the yogurt, to remove the whey, giving the yogurt a cheesy texture. Whatever the minor differences, yogurt is a cornerstone of the Greek diet, and rightfully so.

Greece's second largest island after Crete, separated from the mainland by just a narrow channel

# Evia

Gorgon head from Eretria

# Evia

The Greeks know all about Evia's beauty, but relatively few visitors get to appreciate it. This is partly because guidebooks often overlook it. Athough Evia is an island,
it is connected to the mainland by a bridge. Books about the Greek islands, therefore, frequently treat it as part of the mailand, and books about the mainland leave
it out because it's an island.

This is a great advantage if you want to
spend time in a part of Greece that is not
overrun by visitors. While only a couple of
hours drive from Athens, Evia's large size
means that the people who do go there
tend to be well dispersed.

Evia is the second largest island in Greece
after Crete. Like Crete, it has a distinctive
feel to it, as if set slightly apart from the
rest of Greece. Some parts have been influenced by Albania, and others by Turkey. It
has few really good sandy beaches, and for
this reason is overlooked by vacationers who
prefer to sunbathe in the more southerly
Greek islands.

Like Crete, Evia is a long, thin, mountainous

island. It measures 109 miles (175 km) from
one end to the other, and its highest point,
Mount Dirfys, is 5,737 feet (1,749 m) above sea
level. It is extremely fertile, filled with woods,
orchards, olive groves, and vineyards. The best
retsina in Greece comes from here, they say.
There is good grazing land, too, and in fact

## NOT TO BE MISSED:

the original Greek name of the island (still frequently used) is Euboea, which translates as "rich in cattle." There are rugged cliffs around the coast, as well as beaches and charming, untouched fishing villages.

For such a large island, Evia is not rich in classical sites. However, one that is widely known and should be on everyone's itinerary is ancient Eretria. Despite the lack of important sites, there are vast numbers of minor ones, including many Frankish and Byzantine fortresses.

According to mythology, Evia became an island when the god Poseidon created the channel separating it from the mainland with a blow from his trident. It then became his favorite island, and he lived in an underwater palace there. A list of later residents has almost everyone who ever invaded Greece, including Macedonians, Romans, Franks, Byzantines, Venetians, and, of course, Turks, who handed the island back to Greece in 1830.

All these varied historical cultures have left some kind of mark on Evia, but today the impact of foreign visitors is much less than on most of the other Greek islands. If you plan to spend some time here, make sure you have a Greek phrase book with you, especially if you're hoping to visit the lovely villages of the interior—other languages are not widely spoken here. ■

Area of map detail

# Halkida

The industrial port of Halkida (or Chalkis) is the capital of Evia, and your first sight of the island if you have driven across from the mainland. The Evvoikos Channel is at its narrowest here—a mere 130 feet (40 m) across. The channel is renowned for its inexplicable currents: It is still not understood how they can sometimes change direction more than a dozen times a day, and on other days change only once.

The venerable mosque in the Kastro quarter shows signs of wear and tear over the centuries.

**Halkida**

🗺 Map p. 204

**Visitor Information**

✉ Tourist Police

☎ 222/107-7777

According to legend, the philosopher Aristotle was so frustrated at his inability to understand the phenomenon that he threw himself into the waters and died. Aristotle did die in Halkida in 322 B.C., but whether in this fashion is another matter.

Halkida is very much a working island capital, with lots of industry, including a cement works, and a large population. Its attractions include a lively Turkish quarter, but the town should not be taken as a reflection of the island as a whole.

The Evvoikos Channel has been bridged since 411 B.C. (the present bridge dates from the 1960s), and the town was an independent city-state until it was conquered by Athens in 506 B.C. Like the rest of the island, Halkida was later ruled by Macedonians, Turks, Franks, and Venetians.

The name Halkida is thought to derive from the Greek word for copper, *halkos,* as this mineral was one of the island's major early sources of wealth. The town once controlled and gave its name to the Chalkidiki peninsula (also spelled Halkidiki in Greek, see p. 184), and it had several Italian colonies too.

**INSIDER TIP:**

When driving two-lane highways that have a shoulder, and somebody comes from behind, try to move to the shoulder and allow them to pass.

—MIKE GERRARD
*National Geographic author*

For many years, Halkida vied with Eretria (see pp. 210–211) for control of Evia—especially the fertile Lelantine Plain, which feeds much of the island. It was not until the seventh century B.C. that Halkida finally proved its superiority and developed as Evia's capital.

Today, although at first glance not immediately appealing, Halkida is still worth a day or two of your time for its museums, old town, and waterfront areas. The main **waterfront** is to the left as you cross the bridge; here you will find restaurants, cafés, *ouzeries,* and hotels. It makes a good place to sit over a coffee or a full meal, gazing over the channel to the mainland. Athenians will drive out for the evening to eat here, a distance of 55 miles (88 km). Here, too, is the market, where island produce is brought in by the farmers to be sold. It is busy most days, especially Saturday mornings—the worst time of the week to drive through Halkida or across the bridge connecting the capital with the mainland.

Head for the quarter known as **Kastro,** turning inland and to the right away from the bridge, to find much quieter streets. Many of the old houses here testify to the Turkish and Venetian legacies of the town. A community of Muslims from Thrace, much farther to the east, brings an unusual touch of the Orient to this part of town, augmented by an imposing 15th-century mosque and a Turkish aqueduct that used to bring water from Mount Dirfys some 16 miles (25 km) to the northeast.

Christianity is represented by the somewhat bizarre and dominating church of **Agia Paraskevi** (not far from the bridge), originally constructed in the 13th century. In the 14th century the Crusaders converted its exterior into a Gothic cathedral, complete with rose window, but the interior is a mixture of all of the island's historical influences. Note the ornate wooden pulpit and ceiling.

Halkida's **Folk Museum,** just by Agia Paraskevi, has the usual collection of folk costumes and rural artifacts.

The town's **Archaeological Museum** is better. In the modern part of Halkida, it has excellent sculptures from the Temple of Apollo at ancient Eretria, as well as items from some of the island's lesser-known sites. The building that houses the collection is almost one hundred years old and has some ancient artifacts to show. Ceramic items and figurines from the third century B.C. were found in the cemetery and historic town of Manika, north of Halkida. There is little to see at the site itself, but excavations continue. Other historic sites on the island represented in the museum include Agios Stephanos and Tries Kamares. ∎

**Folk Museum**
- ✉ Skalkota 4
- ☎ 222/102-1817
- ◷ Closed Mon.– Tues., Thurs., & Sat.

**Archaeological Museum**
- ✉ Venizelou 13
- ☎ 222/107-6131
- ◷ Closed Mon.
- 💲 $

# Drive: Exploring Northern Evia

This drive takes you from the busy town and port of Halkida, out along the coast road, and up into the mountains for a glimpse of life in the rugged and beautiful north of the island.

Assuming that you enter **Halkida** ❶ (see pp. 206–207) from the mainland across the bridge, stay on the main road through the town center, turning left onto Route 44 and then right onto Route 77, marked for Mandoudion. Outside the main town most road signs are written only in Greek, so you need to have a copy of the Greek alphabet with you to help you make sense of the Greek place-names. You will also need patience.

The road north out of Halkida takes you through some salt marshes and along the coast, with great views across to the mainland. After about 7.5 miles (12 km) look for the right fork on a local road marked for Psachna, which you reach in just over a mile (2 km). **Psachna** ❷ is an attractive market town, worth a brief stop to admire the 13th-century frescoes in the main church.

From Psachna, follow the signs for Prokopion, which takes you back to Route 77. Prokopion is 19 miles (30 km) farther. The road to it is a marvelous drive, passing through olive groves, and then into pine forests as the landscape becomes more mountainous.

There are now even more spectacular views back to the mainland, as well as vistas over Evia itself, showing how green this island is—especially in the spring and early summer. For a time the road runs alongside a river, through the deep, narrow, and lushly wooded ravine of the **Kleisoura Valley,** with walnut, plane, and poplar trees. Continue along this road to Prokopion.

**Prokopion** ❸ (see p. 212) is an essential stop along the route. It is a settlement that grew up after the arrival of Greek refugees forced out of Turkey during the population exchanges in 1923. Its church of **Agios Ioannis**

---

**NOT TO BE MISSED:**

**Halkida • Psachna • Prokopion Mandoudion • Limni**

---

o Rosos (St. John the Russian) contains the mummified body of that saint, brought from Turkey. Prokopion is also the home of the **Kandili Center,** a base for specialist arts vacations. This is set around the once-feudal estate of Englishman Edward Noel, a relative of Lord Byron, and takes its name from the mountain to the south. It is worth visiting just to see the handsome old mansion and the beautiful grounds.

From Prokopion continue on Route 77 for 5 miles (8 km), following the signs for Limni and Mandoudion. **Mandoudion** ❹ is a beautiful village of whitewashed houses, about half a mile (1 km) off to the right of the main road. Don't hesitate to make the slight detour to stop here for a while and relax in the pretty main square.

Go back to Route 77 and turn right, following the signs for Strofylia and Limni. The road takes you through more agricultural land, past rows of vines bent under the weight of the grapes in the fall. In Strofylia the road forks. Follow the left fork, which passes through a few more hill villages before dropping down toward the pretty coastal village of **Limni** ❺ (see p. 213). A good seafood lunch or supper awaits you here. Make time, if you can, for the walk to the spectacular **Moni Galataki.** There are no formal opening hours, but anyone arriving in the morning or early afternoon will be welcome to look around, if he or she is respectably dressed.

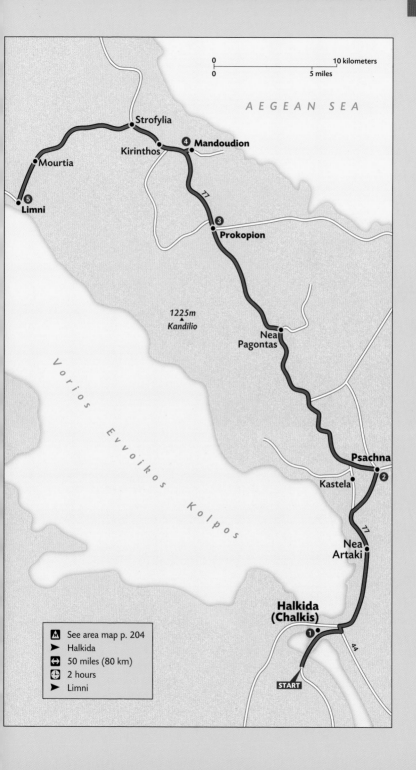

# Around Evia

Beyond the main town, the large and beguiling island of Evia awaits the curious traveler. From ancient sites to modern beach resorts, from lowlands to mountains, this is an island with something for everyone.

Cut off from the rest of Evia by mountains, Karystos sits on a curving bay.

**Eretria**

🏔 Map p. 204

**Archaeological Museum**

✉ Eretria

☎ 222/906-2206

💲 $

## Eretria

Ancient **Eretria** is the most important historical site on Evia. At one time the city rivaled Halkida for dominance of the island, before Halkida took power in the seventh century B.C. Eretria itself was finally destroyed in 87 B.C.

Unfortunately for the archaeologists, modern Eretria has grown up on top of the ruins of the ancient city, instead of on a nearby site as often happened. There is still much to enjoy here, both ancient and modern, though the best artifacts from the site are in the Archaeological Museum in Halkida (see p. 207).

Displays in Eretria's own **Archaeological Museum** include a fearsome Gorgon's head, retrieved from a villa of the fourth century B.C. Nearby is the **House of Mosaics,** a restoration of a fourth-century house with well-preserved floor mosaics; the key is held at the museum. A cluster of other remains in this northwest corner of the town includes the **theater,** which is particularly interesting for a passageway under the stage. This led to the place from where the deus ex machina (providential interruption) could pop up. An unexpected event brought about by the sudden appearance of the gods, who control human fate, was a favorite theatrical device often used to resolve a Greek drama. There are also the remains of a gymnasium and a palace.

Above the theater a short walk leads to the acropolis, with some remnants of its walls and towers, and good views northwest over the Lelantine Plain, the fertile ground that was desired by both Eretria and Halkida in ancient times.

In the center of town, look for the foundations of the **Temple of Apollo** and the site of the agora. The modern town of Eretria now sprawls along the coast as one of the island's main resorts but is not the most interesting place to stay on Evia. Far nicer resorts beckon the traveler.

## Karystos

Almost at the southern tip of Evia, Karystos is an attractive town of mainly modern origin, having been built up only after the War of Independence (1821–1829). Otto, the first king of modern Greece, liked the site so much that he modestly renamed the town after himself, Othonoupolis. He made it the new capital of Greece, inviting a Bavarian architect to create a grand town plan of long, wide streets lined with mansions. But not long after this first stage was completed, Otto was gone. Karystos reclaimed its name and kept the streets. Today it is one of the destination points for the ferries from Rafina (see p. 95) on the mainland, making it busy—especially during the summer—but in a lively, appealing way.

Dominating the town, the **Castello Rosso** is a massive medieval fortress that looks over modern Karystos from the site of the ancient acropolis. Nothing much remains inside the fortress, which gets its name from its ruddy-colored walls, but it gives good views back down over the town and farther inland to Mount Ochi.

## Kymi

Kymi lies halfway along Evia's northern coast, a town set among vineyards and orchards. The **Folk Museum** is outstanding, with a fascinating collection of old photographs showing life in the last century in this quiet, rural place. The town's sleepy nature and remote location belie its rich past, evident from

**INSIDER TIP:**

**If you're interested in a romantic and rustic holiday, the smaller islands are the way to go. They offer a more intimate environment, while still allowing you to enjoy your own Greek adventure.**

—WILLIAM BARR
*National Geographic contributor*

the fine 19th-century mansions that line the streets. These houses were built on wealth from a combination of local silk production and international maritime trade.

Kymi also has an interesting church dedicated to the **Panagia**

**Karystos**
⬛ Map p. 205

**Kymi**
⬛ Map p. 205

**Folk Museum**
✉ Kymi
☎ 222/902-2011
💲 $

**Steni Dirfyos**
⚠ Map p. 204

**Prokopion**
⚠ Map p. 204

**Koimisis** that contains a rare seventh-century icon of the Madonna and Child. North of the town is the dramatically situated clifftop monastery of **Moni Sotira,** built in the 17th century and still inhabited today by a small number of nuns. Men are not admitted.

### Steni Dirfyos

Thanks to its location at the foot of Evia's highest point, **Mount Dirfys,** the mountain village of

Steni Dirfyos has developed into a thriving tourist town. The peak gives wonderful views over the island, out to the Aegean, and back toward the Greek mainland. It is relatively accessible, provided you are in reasonably good shape and are used to hiking. Take the four-hour walk to the summit for a good day out and enjoy a picnic lunch at the top.

You will need a map. The walk begins at the end of the main road that runs through Steni Dirfyos, which peters out into a parking lot after about 2 miles (3 km). Follow the trail and look for the turning to the left that is clearly marked "Fountain of Liri Refuge." From the refuge another trail, marked with dabs of red paint on rocks, leads straight up to the summit.

### Prokopion

Prokopion is another mountain village, overlooked by the highest point in the north of the island, Mount Kandilio (4,087 feet/1,246 m). The drive on pages 208–209 passes through Prokopion, where it is well worth taking a break.

Many pilgrims stop to visit the church of **Agios Ioannis o Rosos,** which contains the remains of St. John the Russian. A Ukrainian, he served in the tsar's army, was captured and enslaved by the Turks, and then killed by the Turks in the town of Prokopion in central Turkey. With the exchange of populations in 1923, his devoted followers brought his bones to Greece. They named their new settlement Prokopion

---

## EXPERIENCE:
## Learn to Scuba Dive & Explore the Greek Seas

There are antiquities in the seas of Greece as well as on the land, and for this reason the laws governing scuba diving are quite strict. You can only go diving in certain places, so if you want to organize something while you are in Greece, you must do it with a reputable group. The Greek National Tourist Organization *(www .visitgreece.gr)* can provide you with details of where scuba diving is permissible and the names of accredited diving schools.

Don't be put off by the regulations, however. They are there for a purpose: to protect the antiquities that shipwrecks have scattered on the seabeds, and as long as you know and obey the rules, the crystal-clear waters of Greece make for some marvelous diving. If you haven't dived before, they also make a good place to learn, and you can do this through the **Aegean Dive Centre in Athens** *(Zamanou 53, Glyfada, 16674 Athens, tel 210/894-5409, www.adc .gr).* Not only can the center provide a list of permitted dive sites off the coast near Athens, but it can also organize courses, diving trips, and night dives, for beginners as well as more experienced divers.

and built a church to house the relics. You may see Russian Orthodox visitors here, too; in 1962 St. John was also canonized by the Russian Orthodox faith.

## Loutra Gialtra & Loutra Aidipsou

There is a pleasant surprise at the remote northwestern end of Evia, where you find a beautiful wide bay surrounded by wooded slopes. Spa resorts sit on either side of the curve. The smaller spa, **Loutra Gialtra,** is a pretty harbor town with an old windmill and a decent beach, and with access to even better beaches toward the extreme northwestern tip of the island.

Across the bay, **Loutra Aidipsou** is the largest spa town in Greece and renowned for its sulfur springs—a reputation that brings visitors flocking here every summer at the prospect of being made young and beautiful. It is not the best time of year to turn up without making reservations. However, the influx of summer visitors means that the town has ample accommodations (many hotels have their own hot springs and spa centers) at other times of year. Then you can enjoy the town's excellent beach and the picturesque charm of a working fishing harbor, with the prospect of day trips to the Sporades (see pp. 224–227).

## Limni

By contrast, Limni, 28 miles (45 km) down the coast from Loutra Aidipsou, is a peaceful fishing village. It is just starting to wake up to the tourist trade.

It lacks the good beaches of Loutra Gialtra, Loutra Aidipsou, and some other Evia resorts, and so for the moment remains a low-key traditional village of whitewashed, red-tiled houses, with boats bobbing in the harbor, some grand 19th-century houses, and a relaxing waterfront with cafés and tavernas. See it while you can.

More energetic visitors make the 5-mile (8 km) walk all the way to the Byzantine monastery of **Moni Galataki.** This is the oldest

**Built by Venetians, Castello Rosso overlooks Karystos's waterfront.**

monastery on Evia, with remains going back to the 13th century, although most buildings date from the 16th. Frescoes in the church, also from the 16th century, have survived in vivid detail, including a Last Judgment guaranteed to frighten anyone onto the path of righteousness. The monastery, deserted for many years, was reinstated as a convent in the 1940s. It is still inhabited by nuns today and can be visited. ∎

**Loutra Gialtra**
Map p. 204

**Loutra Aidipsou**
Map p. 204

**Limni**
Map p. 204

# More Places to Visit on Evia

## Akra Artemision

On the northern coast of Evia is the attractive headland of Artemision. Several sandy beaches nearby are very popular with local people in summer. Above the curving bay sits the pretty village of **Agriovotanon.** It was off the cape here in 1928 that local fishermen found a statue of Poseidon, now one of the star exhibits in the National Archaeological Museum in Athens (see pp. 82–85). Poseidon, the god of the sea, is said to have lived on Evia.

🅰 Map p. 204  🚌 Bus from Halkida

## Mount Ochi

At 4,587 feet (1,398 m), Mount Ochi is the highest point in the south of Evia. It is surrounded by quaint little villages, both inland on its slopes and on the surrounding coasts. The hill village of **Mili** overlooks Karystos near the Castello Rosso (see p. 211) and is the starting point for those wishing to climb the mountain. However, this is a serious four-hour hike, and you will need to be healthy and have a good map or guide.

The exceptional views from the top include one of Evia's so-called **dragon houses**—so named because it was thought that only dragons could have transported the massive stones to the high locations where the buildings are found. (In reality, it is likely that slaves were used to shift the huge rocks.) No one knows their purpose for sure, but it is thought they may have been miniature temples for the worship of Poseidon in the sixth century B.C.

🅰 Map p. 205

## Ochthonia

The hill village of Ochthonia is a bewitching place, with a more prosperous past indicated by neoclassical mansions and ruined towers, and by the remains of the Frankish castle above the village. Down on the coast below, three long stretches of white sandy beach are too remote to attract big crowds, so they are good places to aim for if you like to sunbathe in seclusion.

🅰 Map p. 205  🚌 Bus from Halkida

## Styra

On Evia's west coast, the busy port of Nea Styra (New Styra) is linked by ferry to Rafina on the mainland. It has developed into a small summer resort especially popular with Athenians, who can reach it very easily. It has a wonderful long sandy beach, which is packed in midsummer. At other times of the year Nea Styra makes a convenient base for a few days.

Climb inland for 3 miles (5 km) and you reach the hill village of Styra itself, a quiet place noted for its mysterious **"dragon houses"** (see Mount Ochi, left), just outside the town.

🅰 Map p. 205  🚌 Bus from Halkida

---

### Gyro

As far as nourishment goes, there is nothing more Greek than the gyro (except maybe olive oil). The gyro—from the Greek *gyros,* to turn—is found in every fast-food joint in the country. With a preparation that is mouthwatering to some and brow-furrowing to others—a slowly turning spike, layers of dripping meat (lamb, beef, or chicken, plus layers of fat for good measure), and the electric razor that shaves off portions—the great taste is only as good as the sum of its parts. The meat comes served on a fried piece of pita with onions, tomatoes, *tzatziki* sauce, and regional accoutrements such as chili or garlic sauce. In fact, much of your gyro's size, cost, and ingredients depend on where you're ordering it.

Uninhabited specks of land, mass-market tourist destinations, and everything in between to seduce the curious traveler

# Aegean Islands

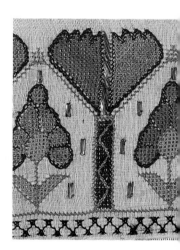

Embroidery from Skiros

# Aegean Islands

**The rich diversity of the Aegean islands draws many travelers back year after year. No matter how many islands you explore, another one always awaits just over the horizon. Other visitors prefer to return to the same island again and again, the islanders welcoming them back like the return of migrating swallows.**

Plan carefully to select the island or islands that best suit you. If your preference is for a relaxing stay and an authentic Greek island experience, avoid tourist traps like Rhodes and Kos, or disco-centered party islands such as Mikonos and Ios. On the other hand, if you like a choice of eating places and want to meet other travelers, don't go to a small island out of season. It can be almost dead, with hotels and restaurants all closed, their owners returned to Athens for the winter.

Time permitting, go to one of the groups of islands, such as the Cyclades or the Dodecanese. Travel around, experiencing their tremendous variety before settling on the island that fulfills your needs. It is usually easy to travel between islands from spring to fall; the exception is the more widely scattered northeastern Aegean islands.

The Saronic islands make for safe and easy traveling, conveniently close to Athens. However, in summer and on weekends they are busy with fun-seeking Athenians, and they have all been discovered by overseas tour groups and cruise ships.

The Sporades, farther north, are greener and more cosmopolitan. Skiathos has crowds and beaches, Alonissos is quieter, and Skopelos is somewhere in between—as it is geographically. In the northern and eastern Aegean, larger islands such as Lesvos and Hios encompass both vacation resorts and unspoiled villages, while Samothraki is harder to get to and remains one of the least developed islands. The Dodecanese and the Cyclades, with their whitewashed houses, offer the best-known images of the Greek islands. Somewhere within those large groups is likely to be everyone's island dream. ■

VORIES SPORADES (NORTHERN SPORADES)

Giou Pelagos

Alonissos

Skiathos    Skopelos

CENTRAL GREECE, THESSALY, & EPIROS
p. 137

EVIA
p. 203

AROUND ATHENS
p. 89

★ ATHINA (ATHENS

Salamina

PELOPONNISOS
p. 103

Egina

Poros

Idra

SARONIC ISLANDS

Spetses

Athens

Area of map detail

MACEDONIA & THRACE
*p. 167*

nos
nou •Thassos
•Limenaria
*Thassos*

*Samothraki*

*Limnos*
Myrina •

A E G E A N

ri

*Agios*
*Efstratios*

Mithymna •
Eresos •
Agiasos •
*Lesvos* • Mitilini

*Skiros*

S E A

*Psara*
*Oinousa*
*Hios*  Hios •

*Andros*

T
U
R
K
E
Y

*Ikaria*

*Samos*  Samos •

Kea
*Gyaros*
*Tinos*
*Mikonos*

*Fournoi*

*Agathonisi*

*Kithnos*
*Siros*
*Rinia*  *Dilos*
*Patmos*
*Arkoi*
*Lipsoi*

K I K L A D E S
( C Y C L A D E S )
*Leros*

*Serifos*  *Paros*
*Andiparos*
*Naxos*

*Sifnos*
*Kalimnos*
*Pserimos*

molos

*Kos*

D
O
D
E
K
A
N
I
S
S
A
(DODECANESE)

*Sikinos*  *Ios*
*Amorgos*
*Astipalea*
*Nissiros*
*Symi*

*Milos*
*Folegandros*
*Tilos*
Rodos
(Rhodes) •

*Anafi*
*Syrna*
*Halki*

*Thira*
*(Santorini)*
Lindos •

Se a
*Rodos*
*(Rhodes)*

0                    100 kilometers
0              60 miles

*Saria*

*Crete*  *Karpathos*

of

*Kassos*

# Argo-Saronic Islands

Lying in the Saronic Gulf just off the coast of Argolid, this archipelago is easily accessible to Athens—and, therefore, inundated with locals wishing to escape the summer heat. Nevertheless, each island retains its individual identity—from stylish and charming to rustic and green. Good ferry connections make it possible to visit all of them in the course of a few days.

A donkey waits patiently by a caïque for its next load at Idra's harbor.

Egina, the biggest of the Saronic islands, has residents who commute to Athens. The reverse happens on weekends, when hordes of Athenians descend here for a break. It has some great mansions and one of the best temples in Greece. Like all of these islands it is best seen in spring or fall, without the summer crowd. Egina and the

other islands in this group are a regular stop for cruise ships on their way to and from Athens. Combined with weekend visitors, the summer tourists make it a hive of social activity.

Poros, farther south, appeals to walkers with its gently rolling terrain. Nightlife is lively in the summertime. The proximity of the adjacent Peloponnese mainland is a bonus, allowing easy access for exploration of the Argolid (a car ferry crosses the connecting strait every 20 minutes in summer).

Idra was discovered in the 1950s by bohemian artists and became a very fashionable hangout, which it has remained to this day. Idra is too rugged to be spoiled, and it retains a chic charm around the harbor area, which contrasts with the rocky interior and the remote monasteries scattered around the coastline.

The farthest island from Athens, Spetses, has some grand architecture. Its pine groves, even having suffered from fires, make it the greenest island in the group. It attracts mainly wealthy Athenians and more upscale travelers.

These islands are an hour or two away from Athens by Flying Dolphin (hydrofoil) and can be used as a place to stay while commuting to Athens to see the sites, if you don't want to stay in the city itself. In fact, the Argo-Saronic islands are the ideal group for the newcomer to Greece to try some island-hopping. They are close enough to get from one to another quite easily, and yet all are distinctively different.

Island-hopping is great for those who don't like a fixed itinerary and prefer the freedom to travel from one island to the next as the mood takes them, staying longer in the places that really appeal.

Provided you are not traveling in August or at Easter, finding accommodations is not usually a problem.

**Egina**
🅰 Map p. 219
**Visitor Information**
✉ Tourist Police,
   Leonardou Lada,
   Egina town
☎ 229/702-2100

**Temple of Aphea**
✉ Egina
☎ 229/703-2398
🕐 Closed Mon.
💲 $

## Egina

Egina means "pigeon island," a name given it by early Phoenician settlers. Today Egina is an elegant spot, even when busy with vacationing Athenians out for the weekend. Behind the crowds are fine 19th-century mansions testifying to a prosperous past as a trading port. During Greece's classical period Egina town was a major rival to Athens. It was also the first town in Europe to issue its own silver coins, minting a currency that was later adopted throughout Greece. In 1828 the town was briefly the capital of Greece—hard to believe if you compare it with Athens today. Nowadays the island's economy is based on pistachio nuts and tourism.

Egina town has a wealth of churches and other historical buildings to explore. The remnants of the ancient town scatter across the acropolis on a low hill near the beach. The distinguishing feature of the acropolis is a still standing column from the Temple of Apollo.

The island is famous, however, for the magnificent **Temple of Aphea,** standing about 7.5 miles (12 km) east of Egina town. It is easily accessed by bus or car and close enough to walk to from the beach resort of Agia Marina. The temple is an excellent example of Doric architecture, built on a hill known to have been a place of religious worship since at least the 13th century B.C. The remaining temple was built around 490 B.C., making it 60 years older than the Parthenon. Like the Parthenon, its pediment sculptures are no longer in place. Even without them, the temple is well worth seeing.

## Temple of Aphea

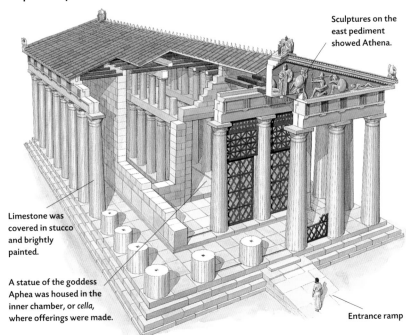

Sculptures on the east pediment showed Athena.

Limestone was covered in stucco and brightly painted.

A statue of the goddess Aphea was housed in the inner chamber, or *cella*, where offerings were made.

Entrance ramp

## Poros

Poros is almost a part of the Peloponnese, separated from the mainland by a channel just 380 yards (350 m) wide at its narrowest point. The channel gives the island its name (poros means "passage"), and small boats chug back and forth taking people between Poros and the mainland town of Galatas, from where you can catch buses to Epidavros and Nafplio.

Poros offers two islands for the price of one. **Sferia,** on which Poros town stands, is separated from the much larger Kalavria by a small road. **Poros town** is a popular destination for cruise ships, weekending Athenians, and Europeans, despite a lack of good beaches. The town is attractive, with its picturesque mix of white and pastel-colored houses on the hillside above the harbor. The waterfront is filled with bars and restaurants promising an entertaining night out.

For a quieter time, walk or cycle along the single main road that loops around the main island, **Kalavria.** This leads past the abandoned 18th-century monastery, **Moni Zoödochou Pigis.** Higher up on this wooded, hilly island are the scant remains of the **Temple of Poseidon,** dating from the sixth century B.C. It is free and open to anyone who makes the small effort to get there.

When you have fully explored Poros, take the short and inexpensive boat ride to tiny **Galatas.** Turn left from the quiet harbor and walk until you reach the lemon groves of Limonodassos. There are tens of thousands of

**Sailing yachts berthed in the picturesque harbor of Poros town**

lemon trees here, and it's wonderful to stroll up the gentle hills, through the groves, taking in the scent of citrus on the breeze.

## Idra

Idra (or Hydra) is a small, rocky, and quite barren but nonetheless fascinating island. The main town clusters around the harbor, and while it is attractive, its popularity can mean severe overcrowding and shortage of accommodations in summer. It is also expensive, by island standards. The waterfront, lined with chic boutiques and art galleries, shows a much more sophisticated face than most other Greek islands.

Idra became fashionable in a bohemian way in the 1950s and early 1960s, when painters and poets—including Canadian songwriter Leonard Cohen—made their homes here.

Like other Saronic islands, Idra has some fine 18th- and 19th-century mansions, funded by the wealth created by the island's

**Poros**

⬛ Map p. 219

**Visitor Information**

✉ Tourist Police, waterfront

☎ 229/802-2256

**Idra**

⬛ Map p. 219

**Visitor Information**

✉ Tourist Police, Odos Votsi

☎ 229/805-2205

## Spetses

Map p. 219

astonishing fleet of merchant ships. Looking at the tiny harbor today, it is hard to believe that the island owned some 150 ships that traded across the Atlantic with North America. It is also hard to believe that a population of 40,000 people once lived here, when today there are barely 3,000.

Idra is not an island for sun worshippers, as there is only one sandy beach and that is attached to the Miramare Hotel, just over a mile (2 km) from Idra town. There are a number of pebble beaches scattered around the island, which is big enough to enable you to escape the crowded harbor during the day by walking along the coastal paths or taking the roads inland.

## Spetses

Spetses, like Idra, became rich through shipbuilding and maritime trade in the 18th and 19th centuries. The grand houses from this period can still be seen in **Spetses town.** Many are now weekend retreats and vacation homes for wealthy Athenians. Spetses has become fashionable, and while it is more sophisticated than boisterous little Poros, it lacks the artistic chic of Idra.

The islanders are proud of their maritime heritage and in particular of their most famous daughter, Laskarina Bouboulina (1771–1825), whose statue graces the harbor. Bouboulina became an admiral in the navy and was prominent in fighting the Turks during

**A jumble of little boats shelter around the jetty in Idra's harbor.**

## EXPERIENCE: Island Nightlife

For those interested in experiencing the islands between dusk and dawn, the following hot spots are worth noting.

**Egina:** The influx of Athenians into Egina town keeps prices high around the harbor, so venture down one of the side streets. The trendy clubs are One for the Road (*Afeas 3, tel 229/702-2340*), Yes! (*Dimokratias, tel 229/702-8306*), and **Perdiotika** (*Afaias 38, tel 029/723-443*). The bar/bistro Avli (*Pan Irioti 17, tel 229/702-6438*) is much calmer.

**Poros:** The island is quieter than Egina, but Poros town offers numerous tavernas as well as the Orion (*tel 694/414-8422*), a

mainstay, and Poseidonio (*tel 229/802-2361*), the island's premier club.

**Idra:** Though touted as an escape from the modern rush, Idra still has a throbbing nightlife, especially in the summer. The young flock to Spelia Beach Café and Bar (*tel 229/805-4160*) and Nautilus Bar (*tel 229/805-4166*), while those fond of tradition go to the Douskos Taverna Xeri Elia (*tel 229/805-2886*).

**Spetses:** Along the waterfront, the Balconi Wine Bar (*tel 229/807-2594*) is a great choice, but don't miss Bar Spetsa (*tel 229/807-4131*), a unique, homegrown bar with more character than ouzo.

---

the War of Independence in the 1820s. Her coffin and bones are displayed in the **Chatzi-Giannis Mexis Museum** (*Spetses town, tel 229/807-2994, closed Mon.*), which takes its name from the former owners of the late 18th-century mansion and has displays on local history, especially the War of Independence. Close to the harbor is **Bouboulina's House** (*near Plateia Ntapia, tel 229/807-2416, closed Oct.–April*), also now a museum in her memory. The house is still owned by descendants of Bouboulina. Admission is by way of a guided tour every half hour in season, in Greek and English.

A more recent resident was British novelist John Fowles (born 1926), whose 1966 novel *The Magus*, later filmed, became a cult classic. Fowles turned Spetses into the fictional island of Phraxos. Fowles taught at Anaryiros College, on the edge of Spetses town, and used this as a location.

There are no major historical remains around the island, but

there are good beaches, like the one at Agii Anargiri, and quiet villages, making Spetses a rewarding island to explore. Its original name, Pityoussa, referred to its pine forests, and these still scent the air in the heat of summer.

**INSIDER TIP:**

The peak flowering time for the native flora in the lowlands of southern Greece and the islands, including Crete, is April.

—NICHOLAS TURLAND
*National Geographic field scientist*

You can get around on foot or by renting a bike or motorbike. For a long time cars were banned from here. Now local residents are allowed to bring cars onto Spetses, although cars are still prohibited downtown. This makes Spetses town one of the more pleasant capitals in the Greek islands. ■

# Sporades

This small group of four main islands gets its name from the Greek for "scattered." They have all been opened up to tourism in varying degrees, in roughly inverse proportion to their size. The smallest, Skiathos, is by far the busiest and has the best beaches, while the largest, Skiros, retains much more of its traditional Greek ambience.

Peaceful Mourtia beach beckons from a quiet corner of Alonissos.

The islands were once extensions of the Pilion peninsula (see pp. 150–151), and like that part of the mainland are green with thick pinewoods. The lushness means that mosquitoes can be more of a problem here than in the drier islands farther south in the Aegean, so come prepared.

Mere mosquitoes can't keep the crowds from rushing to Skiathos in the height of summer, so visit in the spring or fall if you want its superb beaches to yourself. Another option is to take the ferry to the neighboring island of Skopelos to the east, which is scenically much more dramatic, making it a good base for walkers. Its beautiful beaches are almost as good as those on Skiathos.

Alonissos, the next Sporadic isle to the east, is long and thin, and has few roads. It was left behind in the tourist boom, although many foreigners, notably from Germany, bought property here either to live in cheaply or to start up tiny businesses. Alonissos has many small islets around it, home to Europe's rarest mammal, the Mediterranean monk seal. In 1992 the Greek government created the country's first national marine park here to protect the seals and bring ecotourism to Alonissos.

On Skiros, old customs and costumes survive, helped by the fact that it is remote from the other islands and harder to reach from the mainland.

## Skiathos

If you want to see rampant tourist development at its best, or worst (depending on your tastes), then visit Skiathos in the height of summer when its wonderful beaches become a

**INSIDER TIP:**

**The best beaches are almost always at the end of dirt roads or apparent dead-end tracks. You have to be prepared to explore.**

—EVA VALSAMI-JONES
*National Geographic field scientist*

veritable mecca for sun worshippers. The south and east coasts are filled with endless lines of villas, hotels, souvenir shops, bars, and restaurants, so that one area merges into the next, depriving them of individuality.

As with many popular destinations, only a narrow strip of land near the beach is affected. The interior of Skiathos is beautifully wooded and rugged, with wonderful opportunities for walking.

Monasteries carry on their peaceful existence here as they have done for centuries. The 18th-century **monastery of Evangelistria** is just an hour's walk north of Skiathos town. Take the airport road and look for the left turn that directs you to this magnificently located and peaceful set of buildings. For other walks,

**Skiathos**

Map p. 225

**Visitor Information**

✉ Tourist Police

☎ 242/702-3172

**Skiros**
⚑ Map p. 225
**Visitor Information**
✉ Tourist Police
☎ 222/209-1274

**Archaeological Museum**
✉ Plateia Brooke, Skiros
☎ 222/209-1327
🕐 Closed Mon.
💲 $

**Alonissos**
⚑ Map p. 225

check the local bookstores for the recommended-walks booklets.

Most of the island's population lives in **Skiathos town,** with its twin harbors and twin existence. One harbor is for pleasure boats and visitors, the other for the fishermen. Enter the backstreets and you could be in any Greek town, but get into the shopping areas or down onto the waterfront and you could be in a tourist town almost anywhere in the world. Even the medieval fortress known as the **Bourtzi,** which separates the two harbors, is now occupied by a restaurant.

The town looks best from the sea, and more discerning travelers make sure they are quickly out

### Goat Dance

Some distance from the other islands in this group, Skiros has maintained its individuality and character. A notable example of this is the Skiros Goat Dance, a tradition descended from pagan festivities, which still takes place during the island's pre-Lenten carnival. Masked revelers roam the streets of Skiros town, and the principal figure is the rather alarming *geros,* or old man, wearing a goatskin mask and with goat bells strapped to his back. Another unique sight on Skiros is its tiny wild horses, some of which have been tamed. During festivities on August 15, local children race them near Magazia beach, outside Skiros town.

there, heading for one of the other islands. There are daily outings from the harbor to Skopelos and Alonissos.

## Skiros

**Skiros town** would look more at home in the Dodecanese or the Cyclades, with its jumble of white houses at the foot of the slopes topped by a Venetian fortress. Little remains of the fortress, which was built on the site of the original acropolis. It is accessed via a tunnel and offers great views down over the town.

Different aspects of the island's history are told in the town's museums: the **Archaeological Museum** and **Municipal Museum** (*Megalou Stratou, tel 222/209-1327, closed Nov.–March*), and the **Faltauïts Museum** (*Palaiopyrgos, tel 222/209-1232, closed Nov.–March*), a folk-art museum in a grand mansion.

Near Treis Boukes, the deepwater harbor at the southern end of Skiros, is the simple grave of British war poet Rupert Brooke (1887–1915). He died of septicemia on a hospital ship that was bound for Gallipoli during World War I. He is best remembered for his prophetic and patriotic lines: "If I should die, think only this of me: that there's some corner of a foreign field that is forever England."

## Alonissos

A hilly wooded island, Alonissos is not the most attractive of the Sporades groups—the upside being less tourist development. It suffered extensive earthquake damage to its main town, Patitiri, in 1965. Before that, in 1950, a disease destroyed its vineyards and grapefruit orchards.

The creation of an offshore **national marine park** in 1992 has contributed to an upturn in the island's fortunes. It was established to protect the rare and endangered Mediterranean monk seal. Fewer than 800 of these creatures survive worldwide, and about 30 breed on the tiny islands around Alonissos. Fishing is banned in certain areas, as local fishermen used to regard the seals as rivals for diminishing fish stocks. If anyone offers to take you to see the seals, refuse—monk seals are very shy creatures and easily disturbed. Other wildlife takes advantage of the marine park, from migrant birds to dolphins.

The park has created new tourism for Alonissos through the attention it has brought to the island and surrounding waters. Yachts visit in much larger numbers than before, as many of the islands outside the protected area offer good harbors, isolated beaches, and excellent swimming.

Alonissos itself consists mainly of the little port of **Patitiri,** the attractive restored old town of **Palaia Alonissos** high above it, and a few other traditional villages scattered around. None are very developed, and all make ideal getaways for travelers who want to avoid the trappings of tourism.

## Skopelos

Possessing one of the most beautiful ports in Greece at Skopelos town, Skopelos is densely vegetated, with pine forests sweeping down to secluded coves. Fruit and nut orchards fill its interior, source of the island's famous plums and almonds.

Before moving on from Skopelos town, take a look at some of its 123 churches, including that of **Agios Athanasios,** built in the 9th century and boasting

Tradition is important in Skiros; older men may still be seen wearing the old-style baggy pants.

16th-century frescoes. This church lies within the sturdy walls of the **Venetian fortress,** which stands above the harbor on the site of a temple to Athena.

Outside Skopelos town there is only one main road, but many paths lead to other resorts and villages. A good walk climbs up through olive groves to the island's highest point, **Mount Delphi** (2,230 feet/680 m).

In the hills east of the town are five monasteries and convents, three of them open to visitors. The nuns at **Evangelistria** sell their own handicrafts in a small gift shop, while the monastery of **Metamorphosis,** closed in 1980, has reopened after restoration by the monks. The convent of **Pro-dromos** looks across the Aegean to Alonissos. ■

**Skopelos**

⬛ Map p. 225

**Visitor Information**

✉ Waterfront

☎ 242/402-3220

# Northeastern Aegean Islands

The several islands, large and small, in this corner of the Aegean form no particular group, geographically or politically, so they are invariably lumped together. Because they are widely scattered and, in some cases, difficult to get to, they are among the least visited.

A sandy bay on Thassos epitomizes the beauty of the Greek islands.

That is not to say that they are all untouched by tourism—parts of Thassos, Samos, and Lesvos are as busy as anywhere else in the Mediterranean in high summer—but if you go to tiny Samothraki or to Limnos, for example, you are likely to be welcomed as that rare creature, a foreign visitor.

Lesvos is Greece's third largest island and offers variety and plenty to explore, even though you can drive across it in a leisurely few hours. Hios and Samos are also sizable islands, if you want a place to stay for several days. All three are linked by ferries to Turkey. Samothraki, connected to the mainland (Alexandroupoli) by summer hydrofoil, is notoriously difficult to visit, as it has no natural harbor and the regular ferries cannot always come in to dock during stormy weather. That's something to bear in mind if you have to catch a flight from Athens!

There are several even smaller islands in this area, such as Ikaria near Samos, named after the legendary youth Icarus, who flew too close to the sun. Oinousa

MACEDONIA & THRACE
p. 167

Ormos Prinou
Thassos
Potamia
Limenaria ▲ 1142m
Potos
**Thassos**

Kamariotisa
*Samothraki*
Samothraki

| 0 | | 60 kilometers |
| 0 | 30 miles | |

*Limnos*

Plaka
Myrina • Moudros
◇ **Poliochni**

TURKEY

*Agios Efstratios*

Mithymna
Kalloni
Sigri • Mistegna
Eresos
Skala Kalonis
Skala Eresou  Polichnitos  Mitilini
Agiasos
*Lesvos*

and Psara, off Hios, both have just one village and plenty of empty beaches if you want a real getaway-from-it-all island.

The islands share a proximity to Turkey, so there is a noticeable defensive military presence, and it is not unusual to hear the roar of jets overhead as they patrol the edge of Greek airspace. Despite this closeness, there are fewer signs here of Turkish domination than elsewhere. This is because Turkey's western coast was home to many Greek settlers, before the exchange of populations in 1923.

Melanios
*Psara*  Kardamyla  *Oinousa*
**Nea Moni** ◇
*Hios*  • Hios
Mesta
Olympi  Pyrgion

*Samos*
Neon Karlovasion
• Samos
**Heraion** ◇ Pithagoria
Evdilos
*Ikaria*  Agios Kirykos  *Fournoi*

**Thassos**

 Map p. 229

**Visitor Information**

✉ Tourist Police, waterfront

☎ 259/302-3111

## Thassos

Attracted by Thassos's pine-covered mountains, beaches, and ancient remains, Greek vacationers have flocked here for years. Hikers love the remote north coast. In more recent times, overseas travelers have discovered its charms, thanks to the convenience of the Thessaloniki airport. Most visitors stay in and around Thassos town, the island's modern capital, and make day trips from there.

Confusingly, **Thassos town** is also known as Limin, Limenas, or just Thassos, something you need to know if traveling by bus or ferry. To add to the confusion, the island's second town, on the southern side of Thassos, is called Limenaria. Regular ferries link Thassos with the Macedonian port at Kavala—though most ferries actually dock at the port of Ormos Prinou, 7 miles (11 km) west of Thassos town.

Out of high season Thassos town is a pleasant place to stay, with added interest provided by the Roman remains scattered about. Because it is close to the mainland (only 7.5 miles/12 km), Thassos was inhabited as long ago as the Stone Age. As a known source of gold, silver, and white marble, it was fought over in ancient times. It was a wealthy port during the Roman occupation.

The most extensive area of surviving Roman buildings is the **agora.** It is fenced off and not officially open, but if the gate is unlocked no one minds if you wander through and take a look. With a little imagination and a good map, available locally, you can make out the remains of shops and the foundations of temples and other public buildings. The ruins of a temple to Athena Poliouchou (meaning "patroness of the city") from the early part of the fifth century B.C.

**Situated close to the mainland, Thassos is a popular getaway.**

are located just below the site of the **acropolis,** and on the far side of this is one of the gates in the original city wall, the **Gate of Parmenon.** This still has its immense lintel and takes its name from that of the mason who made the gate. It is worth taking a walk up to the remains of the **theater,** not so much for the ruined building itself but for its breathtaking views over the Aegean.

The other main sight is the **fortress,** dating mainly from the 13th–15th centuries but incorporating stonework from a temple to Apollo that stood on the site. The best of the finds are on display in a newly revamped **Archaeological Museum** in Thassos town.

**Around Thassos:** Thassos has a hilly interior. Unfortunately, many of its pine forests were wiped out in extensive forest fires in the 1990s. A coastal road goes all the way around this almost circular island, and you can do the whole journey easily in one day, whether with your own transportation or on the local bus service. This makes it easy to sample different resorts over the course of a few days. Several roads branch inland from the coastal road, going into the hills to the remoter villages and monasteries of the interior.

**Limenaria,** on the south coast, is an appealing town that manages to combine vacation resort and business center. It has attractive old mansions but no good beach. However, the best beaches are on the south coast, and one of them is at **Potos,** 2 miles (3 km) east of

## Swimming Safely

Swimming in Greece is mostly safe and pleasant—though you need to be aware of some hazards. You can find sea urchins almost anywhere, but locals tend to know where they are and so the areas can easily be avoided. Sea urchins usually congregate around rocks. If you tread on one, seek medical help. Less predictable are jellyfish, and swarms of these do turn up from time to time in the warm waters of the Aegean. Fortunately they usually disappear again fairly quickly. Stings are painful but not life-threatening, and over-the-counter remedies can be bought. There are also stingrays, poisonous eels, and poisonous fish in Greek waters—fortunately they aren't too abundant.

### Archaeological Museum

- ✉ Next to Roman agora, Thassos town
- ☎ 259/302-2180
- 🕐 Closed Mon.
- 💲 $

Limenaria. It is the island's second busiest resort.

If it is peace you seek, then head for the interior of Thassos. Many of the coastal resorts have a village inland, where the inhabitants used to find refuge from pirate raids. Most of these villages have simple rooms to rent and a handful of tavernas. **Potamia** is one of the biggest, and you can begin the climb to the island's highest point, **Mount Ipsarion,** at 3,746 feet (1,142 m). This is a tough hike of three and a half hours, and a guide or a good map (available locally) is essential.

Inland from Potos is the

Limnos's craggy interior gives way to a sandy beach at Aktamarina.

**Limnos**

🅜 Map p. 229

**Visitor information**

✉ Town Hall

☎ 225/402-2996

**Lesvos**

🅜 Map p. 229

**Visitor Information**

✉ Aristarchou 6, 811 00 Mitilini

☎ 225/104-2511 or 225/104-2513

🕐 Closed Sat.–Sun.

pleasing old village of **Theologos** —founded in the 16th century by refugees from Constantinople (modern Istanbul)—which was the island's capital for a time.

## Limnos

Limnos produces top quality retsina and other wines. The vineyards are in the western, more volcanic half of the island. Limnos is almost cut in two by the deep gouge of Moudros Bay, one of the biggest and most beautifully situated harbors in the Aegean. For this reason, and because of the island's closeness to Turkey, there are several military bases, and the sound of jet fighters is not uncommon.

In contrast to the rocky west, the east is mostly low-lying and agricultural, apart from some areas of marshland. There are good beaches around the coast, but few visitor facilities. The main town is **Myrina,** on the west coast, the ferry port that links Limnos with other islands and the mainland.

Myrina is pleasantly situated, with an attractive waterfront, a couple of nice beaches close by, and a picturesque fishing port. The ruins of its **Byzantine castle,** on the site where the original acropolis stood, offer awesome views over the town and the entire west coast. The old part of town has cobbled streets and grand Ottoman houses; the **Archaeological Museum** (*Romaikos Gialos, Myrina, tel 254/102-2990, closed Mon., $*) does its best with limited displays. Several ancient sites dot the island, including the fortified town of Poliochni (dating from 3000 B.C.), the once important city of Ifaistia, and the sanctuary site of Kabireio. A great deal of work remains to be done on these sites.

## Lesvos

By far the largest of the islands in the northeast Aegean, Lesvos is better known to English speakers as Lesbos, from which we get the word *lesbian*. The seventh-century B.C. poet Sappho (see p. 234) was born here, in Eresos, making her a Lesbian—that is, simply, a native of Lesbos. The island is more familiar to Greek people as a popular vacation destination and as the source of some of the best ouzo in the country.

The sheer size of the island makes for plenty of variety, from the busy port and capital of Mitilini to quiet mountain villages, and from bustling beach resorts to good bird-watching sites around Skala Kalonis. Lesvos has been a vacation paradise since Roman times. It has two high points: Mount Olimpos at 3,173 feet (967 m) in the south part of the island, and Mount Lepetimnos at exactly the same height in the north. Naturally there is rivalry between the local communities, each one maintaining that its mountain is actually higher.

The name of the main town, **Mitilini,** is also sometimes used for the island itself, a common Greek practice that can confuse visitors when boarding or disembarking from ferries. It is a big and busy port of mostly modern buildings, but worth a day's exploration before moving on to more appealing towns and villages around the island.

Mitilini has a **fortress** (Kastro, Ermou 201, tel 225/102-7970, closed Mon., $), almost mandatory for harbors in these parts. The sprawling ruins here date mainly from the 14th century although the original castle on the site was founded in the sixth century by Emperor Justinian (527–565). It's a good place to wander, to see the views, and to escape the noise of town for a while.

Other escapes include three museums. The **Byzantine Museum** (Agios Therapon, tel 225/102-8916, closed Sun. & Oct.–May, $) has a good collection of icons ranging from the 13th to the 18th centuries, but is probably mostly of interest to the specialist.

The **Archaeological Museum** (Argyris Eftaliotis, tel 225/102-8032, closed Mon., $) is housed in one of the town's many belle epoque mansions. It has stunning Roman and Greek mosaics, and a wealth of prehistoric finds from the site of Thermi, just to the north.

(continued on p. 236)

## Theophilos Museum

- ✉ Mikras Asias, Varia
- ☎ 225/104-1644
- 🕐 Closed Mon.
- 💲 $

---

## Greek–Turkish Relations

To describe relations between the Greeks and the Turks as turbulent would be the understatement of the last few thousand years. It is still a touchy subject, and probably best avoided unless you are very close friends with someone and can talk to them freely. In recent years relations have improved somewhat between Greeks and their neighbors to the east, as there has been a slight easing of the tension over the divided island of Cyprus, but that can change at any minute. Suffice it to say that the Greeks are very patriotic, and many have an aversion to all things Turkish, so any sympathy toward the Turkish point of view will probably not go down well.

# Great Greek Poets

For such a small nation, Greece has produced an astonishing number of exceptional poets, including in modern times two winners of the Nobel Prize for literature. Names known in most countries around the world include those of Homer, Sappho, and C. P. Cavafy.

Left: Homer (Mattia Preti), believed to have been blind, told his epic tales in verse. Right: Sappho is commemorated on her native island, Lesvos.

Homer (see pp. 326–327) can justifiably be regarded as the father of poetry. Nevertheless, he is far from being the only Greek figure of importance, ancient or modern, in the world of verse.

Consider the female poet Sappho (circa 610–580 B.C.), whose very name has entered the English language in the term *sapphic* to describe lesbian love. The word *lesbian* itself comes from the fact that Sappho was born on the island of Lesvos in the northern Aegean. In fact there is no concrete evidence that Sappho was herself a lesbian, and much to indicate the opposite. She is said to have been a lover of the male poet Alcaeus (circa 620–580 B.C.), to have married and had a child by another man, and to have committed suicide by throwing herself

off a clifftop on the island of Lefkada because of unrequited love for a boatman. The belief in her lesbianism came from another poet, Anacreon (circa 582–485 B.C.), who claimed that Sappho was sexually attracted to the women to whom she taught poetry.

Of the poetry itself only fragments survive from the nine books that Sappho wrote, but she was highly regarded long after her death. The philosopher Plato (circa 428–347 B.C.) described her as the tenth Muse.

## Modern Poets

Of modern Greek poets, one of the greatest is Constantine Cavafy (1863–1933). Although he was born and spent most of his life in Alexandria, Egypt, Cavafy was a Greek and incorporated many Greek myths and historical incidents in his work. This included such poems as "Ithaca," "Returning from Greece," and "In Sparta," but he published comparatively little during his lifetime.

Poet and diplomat George Seferis (1900–1971) was an admirer of Cavafy. In 1963 he became the first Greek poet to win the Nobel Prize for literature. Although no Greek writer can ignore the country's long and rich history, Seferis wrote more about what it was to be a modern Greek and about the question of alienation. He himself was born in Smyrna (now Turkish Izmyr) when it belonged to Greece. He studied in Athens and at the Sorbonne in Paris, and in addition to his own work undertook the challenging task of translating T. S. Eliot's *Waste Land* into Greek.

In 1979 Odysseus Elytis (1911–1996) became the second Greek poet to be awarded the Nobel Prize. Elytis was born in Crete and, like Seferis before him, was educated in Athens and Paris. He fought against the Italians when they invaded Greece during World War II and wrote powerfully and poignantly about the experience, continuing the tradition of war poetry that goes back to the unknown Greek poets who originally told the tale of the Trojan Wars. Elytis began writing poetry in 1929, at which time he was still a regular visitor to the Greek islands, where he would return every summer. His poems from the 1930s celebrate the islands but make references to the long shadow of the war to come. Fifty years later, when well into his 70s, he was still as prolific as ever. His popularity in Greece increased when some of his poems were set to music by composer Mikis Theodorakis.

# EXPERIENCE: Poetry in Motion

Because the lives of the ancient Greek poets and dramatists are shrouded in as much apocrypha as their original works, a trip based on their biographies would disappoint.

A better idea is to visit the places that Homer, Sappho, and Euripides wrote about. Even if such locales are bound only to their texts by a thin, meandering line of myth and hearsay, it is a moving experience indeed to visit what Alfred Lord Tennyson called the "ringing plains of windy Troy."

Spend a day wandering **Eressos** on the island of **Lesvos**, Sappho's birthplace. The town and adjacent beach are located in the southwestern part of the island, about 55 miles (90 km) from Mytilini. This region of the island is known equally for its unsurpassed ouzo and for the legions of women who come looking to be inspired by the poetess's spirit.

Or travel to the ruins of ancient **Corinth** to see where Euripides' Medea, spurned by her husband, Jason, killed King Creon, the king's daughter Glauce (Jason's intended new bride), and her own two sons to spite Jason.

Fans of Homer can board the small cruise ship *Corinthian II* for its "Journey of Odysseus" tour, which retraces the path of the hero's long journey home. The cruise, at 11 days, is a tad shorter than the eventful decade that Odysseus took to make it from Troy to Penelope's open arms. The tour begins in **Athens** then proceeds to **Troy,** to the barren island of **Dilos,** on to **Pilos,** where King Nestor once resided, and then Calypso's island on Malta. After that, the *Corinthian II* stops in Trapani, Sicily, where the fearsome man-eating Laestrygonians lived, and on to Naples, home of the Cyclops Polyphemus. After a stop at Helios, the ship ventures on to Ithaca before returning to Athens.

For more information about the "Journey of Odysseus" tour, call 800/314-8602 (U.S.), as the cruise regularly changes hands between tour providers.

**Hios**

Map pp. 229 & 237

**Visitor Information**

Kanari 18, Hios town

227/104-4389

The most interesting museum of all is about 2 miles (3 km) south of the center of town, in Varia. This was the home of the primitive Greek artist Theophilos Hadzimichalis (1873–1934), who was born in Mitilini. His vivid paintings, full of life and the Greek spirit (see p. 44), are displayed in the **Theophilos Museum.**

**Around Lesvos:** The main attraction in the south is the pretty hill town of **Agiasos,** with ancient houses, cobbled streets, and the 12th-century Church of

On Lesvos labyrinthine streets wind up from Mithymna's harbor to its castle-crowned hill.

the Panagia Vrefokratoussa, a place of pilgrimage for an icon reputedly painted by St. Luke.

In the western part of Lesvos, **Eresos** is a place of pilgrimage for lovers of the poetry—or just the reputation—of Sappho, and the glorious beach at Skala Eresos is one of the best on the island. Farther west still is the charming fishing port of **Sigri,** which remains unaffected by the comparatively small number of visitors

who venture there each year.

**Skala Kalonis,** on the Gulf of Kalonis in the center of the island, is a busy resort at the height of summer. But each spring sees the arrival of other visitors: Thousands of migrating birds, attracted to the surrounding salt flats and pursued by hundreds of bird-watchers. Storks and waders are particularly prominent, while sardines and anchovies feature both in the diet of the birds and on local menus.

No one should visit Lesvos without seeing the town of **Mithymna,** (also known widely as Molyvos) on the north coast. Its red-roofed houses cluster around a Genoese castle, and its cobbled streets are in many places completely shaded with vines, while below is a picturesque harbor. South of Mithymna is the expanding coastal village of **Petra,** noted for its flaming sunsets.

The harbor just along the coast at **Skala Sikaminias** is even prettier. Featuring a lovely chapel perched on some rocks at the end of a jetty and dedicated to the Virgin Gorgona (a mermaid), it seems designed with the picture postcard in mind.

## Hios

Despite the obvious attractions of its green, fertile valleys and the hilly north of the island— Mount Pellinaion Oros is 4,255 feet tall (1,297 m)—Hios is surprisingly free of visitors. This makes it an ideal island for those who want a more adventurous trip, where they can see authentic Greek life and where they will be welcomed with true Greek hospitality. The latter can come

Akra
Kampi
Agia Gala
Melanios
Kambia
Pambaria
1297m
Pelinao
Marmaro
Kardamyla
Volissos
Kipouries
Pitou
Sidirounda
Langada
Nea
Moni
799m
Marathovounos
Ormos
Elintas
Anavatos
H i o s
Karies
Vrodados
Dafonas
Hios
Lithio
Akra
Mesta
Pasa-Limani
Elata
Thimiana
Mesta
Tholopotami
Olympi
Kallimasia
Armolia
Pyrgion
Kalamoti
Nenita
Komi
Emporio
Oinousa
Oinousa

0          10 kilometers
0      5 miles

as a surprise, for Greek people like to look after their guests in a generous manner.

The sizable island of Hios, 29 miles (47 km) from north to south, is known as the Mastic Island because it owes much of its prosperity to the resin produced from the native mastic trees. This versatile sticky substance was once much in demand as a base for paints, varnish, cosmetics, and medicine, and is still used today for chewing gum and as a liqueur. Hios has a wealth of lemon and orange groves and once had a flourishing sea trade, so it is not surprising that there are some splendid mansions in Hios town, although sadly most were lost in a devastating earthquake in 1881.

One of the island's attractions is a cluster of **"mastic villages"** in the south, about 20 villages that were the focus of the mastic trade. They are unique in Greece, with houses compacted into tiny spaces, surrounded by an outer circle of houses that acted as a defensive wall in case of pirate attack. When the Genoese ruled it in the Middle Ages, Hios was

## EXPERIENCE: Go Fishing with a Local Fisherman

Fishing is a way of life, literally, for many Greek families. It has been for thousands of years, and if tourists ever stopped coming to the country, no doubt the fishermen would just go back to feeding their families and their neighbors, rather than also providing fresh fish for the local restaurants.

All that most people see of the fisherman's life is that he spends part of the day sitting in the harbor mending his nets, which are usually a bright yellow color and appear in many of our most picturesque vacation photos. But the fisherman's life is much more than sitting by his boat in the sunshine, lazily checking his nets for holes. He has usually spent

the night fishing, and it isn't always the romantic experience it might sound. It can be dangerous, and tedious, and in recent years when fish stock have fallen frustrating.

To find out the truth about the fisherman's life, just find one that looks friendly and perhaps speaks a little English, and ask if you can go fishing with him one night. Most fishermen will be perfectly happy to oblige, glad of a little company, as many of them do go out to sea on their own. They may like the solitude of it all, but an occasional change is always welcome. After the experience, you may never complain again about the seemingly high price of fish in restaurants.

---

### Justiniana Museum

- Plateia Frourio, Hios town
- 227/102-2819
- Closed Mon.
- $

### Byzantine Museum

- Plateia Vounakiou, Hios town
- 227/102-6866
- Closed Mon.

### Monastery of Nea Moni

- Hios
- Map p. 237
- 227/107-9370

### Samos

- Map pp. 217 & 229

considered the most prosperous island in the Mediterranean and a natural target for pirates. **Pyrgion** is known for its black-and-white patterned houses, **Olympi** retains its original central defensive tower, and **Mesta,** the best of the villages, still has the outer defensive towers that existed at the corners of each village.

In contrast to these little villages, **Hios town** has 25,000 inhabitants and is the kind of bustling port typical of a Greek island capital. Its dominant feature is the **fortress,** with parts dating back to the Byzantine era, but extensively renovated and expanded when the Genoese took Hios in 1261. Within its walls are a Turkish mosque and cemetery, the remains of a bathhouse, and centuries-old houses. At the castle entrance is the **Justiniana Museum,** with a wide collection of religious art including icons,

frescoes, mosaics, and wood carvings. Hios town also has the **Byzantine Museum,** which is just as much an archaeological museum, and the **Philip Argenti Museum** (*Odos Korai 2, closed Sun., $*), a folk arts and crafts museum, which also has portraits of members of the prominent local Argenti family.

The island's prime attraction, one that should not be missed, is the 11th-century **monastery of Nea Moni,** beautifully located in a rural retreat 9 miles (15 km) west of the capital. It is noted throughout Greece for its outstanding original 11th-century mosaics, which rival those at Osiou Louka near Delphi (see pp. 142–143).

## Samos

One of the most sublime islands in the Aegean, Samos is fertile and green, with rolling hills and valleys of vineyards and olive groves—all this, and fantastic beaches too. Little wonder that it has been admired through the centuries—even Antony and Cleopatra are known to have relaxed together on Samos—and it is a very popular vacation destination today.

A visit in high summer will mean that many hotel rooms are reserved by travel companies. However, when the spring flowers bloom, and again in the fall when the vines are heavy with grapes, Samos is a dream destination. Its vines provide a dessert wine as sweet as honey, exported around the world. Look for a Samos Grand Cru or Samos Anthemis from the Samos Co-op vineyards.

**Samos town,** also known as Vathi, is the capital, and its gleaming white houses spread out between a swath of green hills and a beautiful horseshoe-shaped harbor. In the upper town, the maze of narrow, shaded, cobbled lanes is a world away from the bustle of the port below (the area where you will want to be at nighttime).

Samos has a long and fascinating history, having been inhabited since about 3000 B.C. Much of the story is told in the world-class **Archaeological Museum** (*Kapetan Gymnasiarchou Katevani, tel 227/302-7469, closed Mon., $*). This has one of the best collections of votive offerings in Greece, thanks to the popularity of the Heraion Sanctuary, where the goddess Hera was worshipped. The museum's other star feature is a 16-foot (5 m) kouros (archaic marble statue of a youth) from the sixth century B.C.

**Heraion** is 14 miles (22 km) to the southwest of Vathi. The first

temple on the site, built in the eighth century B.C., was replaced by another in the sixth century B.C., but this was soon destroyed in an earthquake. Work began on a replacement, which, though never completed, was nevertheless much used. The site is confusing, even after extensive archaeological work, but it fills in part of the picture of ancient Samos.

Nearby **Pithagoria,** the original capital built in the sixth century B.C., is now a fashionable tourist town. Its attractions include the remains of some Roman baths

## Heraion

☎ 227/309-5259
🕐 Closed Mon.
💲 $

**Tomatoes strung up like rosary beads dry in the sunshine on Hios.**

and the startling Efpalinion Tunnel, an aqueduct almost two-thirds of a mile (1 km) long, dating from 539–524 B.C. Pithagoria was named after the philosopher and mathematician Pythagoras, born here in about 580 B.C. Little is known for certain about his life, but his advanced ideas, not only about mathematics but also about music and the harmony of the universe, live on. ■

# Cyclades

**If you see a photograph illustrating the Greek islands, there is a strong chance it was taken on one of the Cyclades (Kiklades). It will show an ink-blue sky, a jumble of dazzlingly white houses set higgledy-piggledy against a hillside, and, somewhere, a blue-domed church. In many people's minds, this is the archetypal picture of a Greek island.**

On these particular islands, you'll also find red poppies growing from bare white rock, the aroma of wild herbs filling the air, and idyllic beaches gleaming in the sun. To top it off, lively nightlife, bountiful shops, fine restaurants, and bustling bars fill picturesque town streets, making the Cyclades the epitome of summer fun.

The name Cyclades comes from *kyklos,* a circle, and a glance at the map indicates that the islands circle the sacred isle of Dilos. In historic terms, the Cyclades are probably the most significant group of all the Greek islands. Over the period 3000–1000 B.C. the so-called Cycladic civilization flourished here, producing extraordinary works of art thathave had a lasting impact on the world. Incidentally, it is the only Greek civilization to have a museum entirely dedicated to it: the Museum of Cycladic Art in Athens.

The administrative capital and commercial center of the Cyclades is Siros. It is less concerned with by tourism than you might expect, given its status.

Naxos, the largest island, along with its neighbor Paros, is more precisely in the geographical center of the group than is Dilos. Despite being at the hub of the transportation network in the Cyclades and their quiet beauty, neither Naxos nor Paros has been too spoiled by tourism. Unfortunately, the same cannot be said of nearby Ios and Mikonos, which almost sink under the weight of incoming fun seekers during the summer. But it is easy to get away from noise and people if you wish, as there are

24 inhabited islands in the Cyclades, some with very small populations, and island-hopping by ferry is relatively straightforward.

Most travelers visiting only one island in the group choose to stop off at the extraordinary Santorini, whose rugged volcanic crater and black sand beaches give a contrasting but equally potent picture of the Cyclades.

## Andros

**Map pp. 240–241**

**Visitor Information**

Gavrion, Andros town

228/202-2300

# Andros

Andros is the most northerly of the Cyclades and second largest of the group. Its ease of access from Rafina on the mainland has made it popular with Athenians seeking a second home and with other Greeks as a vacation

Despite Moni Panachrantou's large size, only a few monks live there today.

### Archaeological Museum

Plateia Kairi, Andros town

228/202-3664

Closed Mon.

$

### Museum of Modern Art

Plateia Kairi, Andros town

228/202-2444

Closed Tues.

$$

getaway. Tourists arriving at Athens's international airport will find Rafina the closest port for visiting the Cyclades.

Extending more than 21 miles (34 km) from one end to the other, the island is large enough to absorb plenty of visitors. Andros is mountainous: **Mount Petalo** (3,261 feet/994 m) in the center divides the island into two distinct halves—the north rugged and barren, the south fertile and green. The Ionians settled here in about 1000 B.C., and Andros has seen Romans, Venetians, and Turks come and go over the centuries.

**Andros town** (or Chora), with its many elegant neoclassical mansions, shows the influence of the

wealthy Athenians who have lived here over the past 200 years. The town has a prosperous air, its main street pedestrianized with marble slabs. Andros has been particularly rich in archaeological finds, many of which are displayed in the fine **Archaeological Museum.** The best exhibit is a second-century B.C. marble copy of an original bronze statue, the Hermes of Andros. The excellent **Museum of Modern Art,** a rarity in these islands, is housed in two buildings and features work by Picasso and Braque on permanent display, with changing exhibitions of contemporary art and a delightful sculpture garden.

Don't miss the **monastery of Moni Panachrantou** in the mountains south of Andros town. It was founded in A.D. 961 and is still immaculately maintained.

# Tinos

Only a tiny stretch of water separates Andros from **Tinos,** a miniature version of its neighbor—roughly the same shape and with a mountainous spine down the middle. Like Andros, Tinos was settled by the Ionians, then inhabited by Romans, Venetians, and Turks; its landscape is dotted with the same type of Venetian dovecotes you see on Andros.

**Tinos town** lacks the wealth of Andros town and is more typical of a Cycladic island capital, with a busy little port and narrow streets zigzagging among blindingly whitewashed buildings. Its **Archaeological Museum** is surprisingly interesting. The island's principal site is the remains of the fourth-century B.C. **Sanctuary of**

**With about 8,500 inhabitants, Tinos boasts some of the finest food in Greece, plus quiet beaches, over 50 whitewashed villages, and about 600 decorative dovecotes, a legacy of the game-loving Venetians.**

—RACHEL HOWARD
*National Geographic writer*

**Poseidon and Amphitrite,** 2.5 miles (4 km) northwest of town.

To all Greeks, Tinos is known for just one thing: the **Church of the Panagia Evangelistria** (the Annunciation). On August 15—the Feast of the Assumption of the Virgin, a national holiday in Greece—Tinos is packed with pilgrims who come to pray to a miraculous icon. Many of them crawl up the main street that leads to the church to prostrate themselves before the Virgin; the street is lined with stalls and stores selling candles, icons, and votive offerings. The icon is carried through the streets in a solemn procession, an event repeated on March 25, when the Feast of the Annunciation and Independence Day are celebrated.

The pilgrimage dates from 1822, when a nun at the convent of Moni Kechrovouniou, in the hills above Tinos town, had visions of the Virgin Mary. The Virgin told her where an icon lay buried. When the nun's directions were later followed, an icon depicting the Annunciation of the Archangel Gabriel was found, having lain buried for 850 years. The icon was still in good condition. It is believed to have healing powers, so Tinos has become a Greek Orthodox equivalent of the holy shrine at Lourdes, in France. If you want to be on Tinos on either

**Tinos**

Map p. 241

**Visitor Information**

Tourist Police, Plateia L. Sochou 5, Tinos town

228/302-3670

**Archaeological Museum**

Megalochori, Tinos town

228/302-9603

Closed Mon.

---

# EXPERIENCE: Study Marble Sculpting on Tinos

As well as being one of the holiest places in Greece, Tinos in the Cyclades is renowned for the quality of its marble. It was highly prized by the ancient Greeks, whose finest sculptors all wanted to work in marble from Tinos. The craft of sculpting has continued down through the years, and the island still quarries marble and has several marble workshops.

It's possible to arrange a day with one of the sculptors through the **Dellatolas Marble Sculpture School** (*www.tinosmarble.com*) on Tinos or through the company **Trekking Hellas** (*www.trekking.gr*) in Athens. If you're based in Athens it's a three-day trip for one five-hour day at the workshop, although you can arrange to stay longer. On the first day, you travel to the port of Rafina outside Athens, from where it's a two-hour ride on a fast ferry to Tinos.

At the workshop on day two, you learn not only how to carve marble but also about the geology of Tinos marble, how it's formed and how it's quarried, and why it's of such good quality. Then you will be introduced to the tools used by carvers, and given the chance to make your own small carving on marble from Tinos, including hand-lettering.

## Siros

 Map p. 241

**Visitor Information**

✉ Cyclades
Islands H.Q.,
Dodekanissou
10, 841 00

☎ 228/102-2375
or 228/108-
6725

March 25 or August 15, plan well
in advance, as ferries and accommodations are always reserved
well ahead.

## Siros

Despite being a fairly barren and
rocky place, Siros is the administrative center of the Cyclades. It
owes its status to a good natural
harbor at **Ermoupoli,** once the
main port for all of Greece. As
recently as the 19th century
it was still the most powerful
port in the eastern Aegean, and
as a result there are many fine
mansions here. Ermoupoli is
the best-preserved neoclassical
town in the country by some accounts and, with a population of
13,000, is the largest settlement
in the Cyclades.

Although important, Siros is
not overwhelmed by tourism.
Its role as the administrative and
cultural center for the Cyclades
means that, unlike some of the
smaller islands, it prospers with-

out needing to cultivate visitors.
Nevertheless, tourists do come
in increasing numbers, drawn
by the island's small resorts,
little fishing villages, and enough
good beaches to keep everyone
happy. Some of these, such as the
ones at Armeos and Delfini, are
secluded enough to have become
nudist beaches.

Siros, probably first inhabited by the Phoenicians, was an
important center for the Cycladic
civilization by 2800 B.C. Later it
became part of the Roman
Empire like the rest of Greece.
When the Romans left, the island
was abandoned until the 13th
century, when it was taken by the
Venetians. They founded the town
of **Ano Siros,** on one of the two
hilltops that now join up as Ermoupoli (the other is Vrondado).
Because of its Venetian pedigree,
Ano Siros was unusual in Greece
in being a Roman Catholic town
long before Vrondado was established as an Orthodox community.

**The blue-tiled dome of Agios Nikolaos overlooks Ermoupoli's commercial harbor.**

Below and between Ano Siros and Vrondado is the lower town, with a grand marble-floored main square, **Plateia Miaouli,** as its central focus. The whole area around here has been designated a national historical landmark,

and so has protected status. Fine mansions and shaded cafés line the square, which has an amazing marble bandstand in the center. At one end of the square, the grand town hall of 1876 was designed by the German architect Ernst Ziller, who designed several of Athens's fine neoclassical buildings, including the Presidential Palace.

Alongside the town hall is Siros's small **Archaeological Museum,** worth a quick visit. The nearby **Apollo Theater** was built in 1864 as the first opera house in Greece—based on Teatro alla La Scala in Milan. Following years of neglect it was restored

in the 1990s to something of its former glory. Close by the 19th-century church of **Agios Nikolaos** has a stunningly grand marble iconostasis (a screen with doors and tiers of icons, found in Eastern churches); outside is the world's first monument to an unknown soldier, erected in the late 19th century. There are many other churches worth seeking out in Ermoupoli, notably the Byzantine church of the Anastasi at the top of the Vrondado hill, and the baroque Cathedral of St. George crowning Ano Siros.

Most of the island's population lives in villages in the southern half of Siros, easily reached by car or by local bus. On the west coast are the two most popular resorts, Kini and Galissas. Located on a scenic bay, **Kini** is still very much a fishing village alongside its development as a resort. Its main advantage for the sun-seeking vacationer is that it is just a short walk from here to the best and biggest beach on Siros, Delfini. The sandy beach is popular with nude sunbathers.

A couple of miles south, **Galissas** is at the head of a long bay and has a good beach nearby, at Armeos. It also has the only two campgrounds on the island, which in the summer attract crowds of youngsters who can turn Galissas into the liveliest spot on Siros.

In the northern part of the island the roads peter out into dirt roads leading to villages such as Chalandriani and Syringa, where few visitors are seen—which should result in a warm welcome for the more adventurous travelers who explore this area.

---

## The Naked Truth

Nude sunbathing is illegal in Greece except on its few designated nude beaches. Filaki Beach on Crete is one, Banana Beach on Skiathos another (posted signs will warn the unwary). In practice nudity is tolerated in remote beaches or out-of-the-way places. Generally, common sense prevails. Don't bare your body in busy places, on family beaches, or within sight of tavernas. Topless sunbathing is not illegal but should likewise be done with discretion.

---

### Archaeological Museum

- ✉ Plateia Miaouli, Ermoupoli
- ☎ 228/108-8487
- 🕐 Closed Mon.
- 💲 $

## Mikonos

**Mikonos**
⚠ Map p. 241
**Visitor Information**
✉ Waterfront,
   Mikonos town
☎ 228/902-2482

**Folklore Museum**
✉ Waterfront
☎ 228/902-5591
🕐 Closed
   Oct.–April

# Mikonos

Mikonos was renowned in the 1980s and 1990s as the gay center of the Aegean. Today, however, gay people are a small percentage of the partygoers who flock here during July and August. Visitors in spring and fall can enjoy the island without the all-night revelries.

The interior of the island is small, rocky, and barren, and won't occupy you for long. Mikonos owes much of its popularity to its plentiful golden sandy beaches. The two main resorts are Ornos and Platys Gialos. The resorts have become the focus for the tourist trade, with plenty of lively, glamorous clubs and bars.

**Mikonos town** is one of the most attractive capitals in the Cyclades. It is easy to get lost in the maze of winding backstreets between the brilliant white houses that lead you sometimes to quiet churches with their distinctive blue domes, sometimes simply to deadends. If you are exploring the island from a cruise-ship base, allow plenty of time to get back to the boat. You might like to buy a town map from one of the many stores and kiosks.

The town has other attractions, which means that it warrants at least a day's visit even if you don't want to linger for the nightlife. The **Folklore Museum** is one of the best of its kind in the whole of Greece: Mikonos has always been a cultured and independent island, and its local arts and crafts have flourished. The **Archaeological Museum** *(Waterfront, tel 228/902-2325, closed Mon.)* has a good range of interesting finds, including many from the nearby sacred island of Dilos (which is reached from Mikonos).

In addition, the town has a **Maritime Museum** *(Enoplon Dynameon, tel 228/902-2700, closed Oct.–April),* with artifacts representing the Aegean's maritime history; and a good **Municipal Art Gallery** *(Matogianni, tel 228/902-2615, closed Oct.–April).* The fortress dates from the 15th to 17th centuries. Below this is the buzzing area known as **Little Venice,** the artists' quarter. It is named for its waterfront buildings with their elegant iron balconies, many of which are cocktail bars.

**The backstreets of Mikonos town are extremely photogenic.**

## Dilos

This parched, uninhabited holy island lies about a mile and a half (2 km) southwest of Mikonos. It can only be visited during the day; no one is permitted to stay overnight. This is in order to protect one of the most priceless archaeological sites in Greece. Ionians arrived here about 1000 B.C., although it was probably first inhabited more than a thousand years earlier by migrants from Asia Minor.

The Ionians made Dilos their religious capital and dedicated it to the god Apollo. They began an annual festival of arts and sports in honor of Apollo, and by 700 B.C. Dilos was a major pilgrimage center. It became a successful port but fell into decline after the Romans left, a hideaway for pirates but otherwise cut off from the world.

Dilos's precious ruins spread over a large area. Its most famous sight is the **Lion Terrace,** overlooking and protecting the **Sacred Lake** that was said to have witnessed the birth of Apollo. Originally there were nine lions, made of marble from nearby Naxos in the seventh century B.C., but only five have survived. The originals are in the site's museum, leaving replicas to guard the now dry lake.

Other highlights include a **theater** from 300 B.C., beautiful **mosaics** in houses such as the House of the Dolphins and the House of Dionysos, and the **Sanctuary of Apollo,** with the remains of three temples alongside one another.

It is a site that merits as much time as you can give it. Boats for Dilos leave Mikonos in the early morning and return in the early afternoon. The site closes at 3 p.m. There is a small café on the island with limited choices, so take supplies with you—especially water.

## Naxos

The lush island of Naxos, its green valleys filled with endless olive groves and orchards, is the largest and one of the most fertile islands of the Cyclades. It is mountainous—Mount Zas in the south rises to 3,280 feet (1,001 m)—and has excellent

### Dilos

- 🗺 Map p. 241
- ☎ 228/902-2259
- 🕐 Closed Mon.
- 💲 $$

### Naxos

- 🗺 Map pp. 241 & 249

**Visitor Information**

- ✉ Waterfront, Naxos town
- ☎ 228/502-5201

---

### EXPERIENCE:
## The Simple Pleasures of Naxos

Green tourism is a fast-growing industry on the verdant island of Naxos. Because the island is large and can support itself with farming, many of the sites open to visitors are rural. Olives are big business here: There are more than 400,000 olive trees on Naxos, many of which are in the Tragaia. Begin at the bus stop Damalas on the Naxos–Chalki road and walk through the groves. If you're looking for something with a little more kick to it than olives, you can visit the original Vallindras distillery (tel 228/503-1220) in Khalki (est. 1896) to see how Kitron, a local liqueur, is made from the leaves of the citron tree. And if the water is tempting, try scuba diving with Blue Fin Divers (Agios Prokopios, tel 228/504-2629, www.bluefindivers.gr). The dive company was opened in 2006, immediately following the lifting of a government ban on commercial diving. Explore a shipwreck, a plane crash, or just the natural environment.

Naxos town's Portara Gateway frames a perfect sunset.

### Archaeological Museum

✉ Palace of Sanoudo, Naxos town

☎ 228/502-4150

🕐 Closed Mon.

💲 $

cultural and architectural mark on the island.

**Naxos town** is a bustling port and a lively town, with bars and busy restaurants around the harbor, and in the area leading up to the high-walled **Venetian** *kastro* (fortress). In the district below, known as Bourgos, is the impressive 18th-century **Cathedral of Zoödochou Pigis,** built using stone from older churches and an even older temple.

One of the oldest and most impressive sights in Naxos town is the **Portara Gateway,** on the islet of Palatia in the harbor, which is connected to the main isle by a road. This huge gateway was intended to be the entrance to a

**INSIDER TIP:**

For an out-of-this-world archaeological experience visit the Portara (remains of an ancient gate) on the island of Naxos. The views at sunset alone are worth the journey.

—EVA VALSAMI-JONES
*National Geographic field scientist*

beaches, many of which are deserted. Despite these attractions, the island has not been overrun with tourist development, although the recent opening of an airport may change that.

Naxos became one of the main centers of the Cycladic civilization when it started to flourish around 2800 B.C. and was one of the first islands to use marble for sculpture and architecture. Naxian marble was used for some of the finest kouros statues, including several in the National Archaeological Museum in Athens (see pp. 82–85), and for the Lion Terrace on Dilos (see p. 247). In more recent times, Naxos was conquered by the Venetians and later the Turks, both of whom left their

Temple of Apollo, begun in 530 B.C. but never completed. Today it is frequently used as a symbol for the town and the island, and gives visitors arriving by ferry a dramatic greeting.

The fascinating **Archaeological Museum** houses an extensive collection of local artifacts, which naturally includes a good number of the graceful carvings made during the Cycladic civilization. The museum is also of interest for the building that houses it, a palace built in 1627 that later became the French School. One of its pupils was Cretan novelist Nikos Kazantzakis (see p. 283).

Naxos is large enough to reward a long stay, allowing time to explore its natural charms. These include the **Livadi Valley,** where the best Naxian marble was mined, and the **Melanes Valley,** which has some of the distinctive Venetian watchtowers. The **Tragaia Valley,** with wonderful mountain villages and excellent walking country, is at its best in spring when the flowers and blossoms are out, and again in the early fall when the fruit trees offer their bounty. **Halkio** is one of the most appealing villages, with attractive old churches. But if you want to stay and use it as a base for walking, there are no accommodations and so you will have to take potluck in getting a room in somebody's house—which can be a wonderful way to experience Greek hospitality.

Of the resorts, **Apollonas** in the northeast is one of the most popular, not least for its choice of excellent fish restaurants. In the ancient marble quarries on a hillside outside the village is an unfinished statue, thought to represent the god Apollo, which has been lying there since being abandoned about 600 B.C. It is more than 30 feet (10 m) long and an imposing sight.

For good beaches head for **Ormos Avraam** on the north coast or **Moutsouna** in the east. Don't forget to pick up some local woven goods, embroideries, honey, and cheese before you move on.

## Paros

Paros, the third largest of the Cyclades islands, is even more famous for its marble than Naxos. As the raw material desired by all the finest sculptors and architects, it was transported throughout Greece in classical times. The second-century B.C. Venus de Milo (see p. 250) is made from Parian marble, as is the celebrated Winged Victory of Samothraki (circa 200 B.C.), both prime exhibits in the Louvre, in Paris.

As a result of this natural bounty, and the island's

### Paros
Map p. 241

**Visitor Information**
Tourist Police, Plateia Mando Mavroyenous, Paroikia
228/402-1673

Akra Stavros
Apollonas
778m
Mirisis
Ormos Amitis
Koronis
Lionas
997m
Koronos
Agios Thaleleos
Egara
Naxos
Kinidaros
Kourounochori
Melanes
869m
Ano Potamia
Moni
Moutsouna
Galanado
Apeirathos
Agia Anna
Kaloxilos
Vivlos
Halkio
Filotion
Kato Sangri
Danakos
Ano Sangri
Tragaia
1001m
Zas
Mikri Vigla
N a x o s
Kastraki
523m
Ormos Kildos
Pirgaki
Ormos Agiasos
Agiasos
Ormos Kaladou
Akra Katomeri
0      8 kilometers
0      4 miles

## Archaeological Museum

- ✉ Paroikia
- ☎ 228/402-1231
- 🕐 Closed Mon.
- 💲 $

## Milos

- ▲ Map p. 240

**Visitor information**

- ✉ Waterfront, Adamas
- ☎ 228/702-2445

## Christian Catacombs

- ✉ Trypiti, Paros
- ☎ 228/702-1625
- 🕐 Closed Mon.

abundant fertility, Paros has always been prosperous and has had no need to court tourism to the extent of some of its neighbors. It has retained its Greek customs and culture much more than, say, Mikonos or Ios.

This is not to say that the island does not get busy, especially at the height of the summer when the strong winds that blow across it attract windsurfers from all over the world. The port of **Naoussa** has become a chic place to eat, drink, and shop. From here, catch water taxis to the island's best beaches, located in the north, around Lageri.

**Paros town,** or Paroikia, in a sheltered harbor on the west coast, is a focal point for ferry services around the Cyclades. It has all the activity, bars, and restaurants

you might expect. Away from the waterfront, typical Cycladic houses, with their flower-hung courtyards, line picturesque streets.

The Byzantine **Cathedral of the Panagia Ekatondapiliani,** dating from the tenth century, exemplifies the use of local marble. Next to it, the **Archaeological Museum** displays further work in Parian marble, plus a unique fragment from the Parian Chronicle. Carved on marble, it records the history of Greece from the 16th century b.c.

## Milos

Marble from Paros was used to carve one of the most famous figures in the world, the beautiful Venus de Milo—a statue of Venus found on the island of Milos. It came to light on April 8, 1820, when a local farmer uncovered a cave in one of his fields. Inside was half of the statue. The other half was soon found, and the whole statue was purchased as a gift for Louis XVIII of France (r. 1795–1824), subsequently ending up in the Louvre.

A plaque marks the spot where the first half of the statue was found, close to the **Christian Catacombs,** in Trypiti. The catacombs are the only example of their kind in Greece, believed to contain up to 8,000 bodies in the 291 tombs that have been discovered.

**Trypiti** is almost a suburb of Paros's main town, Plaka, although to talk of suburbs is misleading; the entire island has a population of less than 5,000. This figure is boosted in summer by visitors, although not yet in great numbers.

---

## EXPERIENCE: Surfing the Cycladic Winds Around Paros

Swathed in the Meltemi, the warm Cycladic wind, Paros is one of the best places on Earth to windsurf. Because of this, the Professional Windsurfing Association has chosen Paros's New Golden Beach to host the World Championship repeatedly since 1993. If walking along the beach when the championship is being held in August, don't count on seeing much water through the multicolored sails.

To try your hand at windsurfing, visit **Sunwind Surf Club** at Golden Beach (tel 228/404-2900, www.sunwind.gr) for windsurfing rentals and lessons. Another reputable provider is **Paros Surf Club** (tel 228/404-3264, www.parosurf.gr). Prices are reasonable at both places, and lessons are recommended. It's harder than it looks.

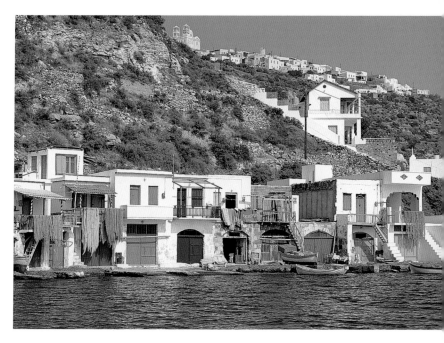

**Like Santorini, the island of Milos is the shell of an old volcanic crater.**

**Plaka** stands on what is thought to be the original acropolis, dating back to 1100–800 B.C. The **Folklore Museum** tells the island's more recent history, with fascinating old photographs alongside the local folk costumes and crafts.

There is an **Archaeological Museum,** too, where a copy of the famous Venus greets visitors in the entrance hall. Displays include remains from the island's most significant site, that of ancient Fylakopi. This is toward the north of the island, but much has been lost to the sea. Two of the most exquisite finds from the site are in the National Archaeological Museum in Athens (see pp. 82–85): the famous fourth-century B.C. statue of Poseidon and a kouros—a statue of a young man—from the sixth century B.C.

## Ios

If one of the Cyclades can be described as an island of contrasts, it is tiny Ios. The permanent population of fewer than 2,000 is outnumbered many times over in the summer by young visitors attracted by its nightlife and golden beaches.

If you stay in **Ios town** in August there won't be time for a peaceful night's sleep, as the bars and discos thump away into the early hours. However, that is not your first impression of this achingly beautiful little Cycladic town with immaculate whitewashed houses, blue-domed churches, and, above the town, 12 windmills. There used to be several more windmills, and not all are in pristine condition, but they still look pretty even if they no longer

**Folklore Museum**

✉ Plaka, Paros
☎ 228/702-1292
🕐 Closed Mon.
💲 $

**Archaeological Museum**

✉ Main square, Plaka, Paros
☎ 228/702-1620
🕐 Closed Mon.
💲 $

**Ios**

🗺 Map p. 241

**Visitor Information**

✉ Ano Chora, Ios town
☎ 228/109-1505

## Amorgos

🗺 Map p. 241

**Visitor Information**

✉ Quay, Katapola

☎ 228/507-1210

function. Here, too, at the top of the town is what remains of the Venetian fortress built in 1400.

Ios is said to be the last resting place of Homer (see pp. 326–327). Some say that Homer's mother was from Ios and that the great poet came back here

---

### Greek Coffee Guide

Greek coffee is what in other countries is called Turkish coffee. It's strong, like espresso, and served in its own small cup, with a glass of water. It comes in three main ways, so you should learn to order it *glyko* (sweet), *metrio* (medium), or *pikro* (without sugar). Even if you normally don't take sugar, you might welcome a metrio. If you want a larger cup of regular coffee, ask for an American coffee or Nescafé (synonymous in Greece with instant coffee). It is not usually very good. Real filtered coffee is harder to find. Greeks prefer a frappé, a long, cold coffee, with or without milk or sugar.

---

to die. Others say that he simply happened to pass away on board a ship while traveling to Athens. His grave is at **Plakotos,** a small town in the hilly north of the island (only the rock on which the tomb was supposedly built remains). Every year on May 15—a much better time to visit than midsummer—the Homer Festival takes place. This includes a proces-

sion in which the people of Ios carry a flame from the port where Homer died to the place where he is buried, a pilgrimage of 6 miles (10 km).

The island is said to be home to some 400 chapels, along with its many superb sandy beaches— some deserted and some packed with young bodies recovering from their nights on the town. For a quieter time head for the beaches at Psathi or Kalamos, or walk on the quiet roads inland to visit the monasteries of Kalamos or Mount Pyrgos.

## Amorgos

The rugged mountain scenery of Amorgos sets it apart from most of the other islands in the Cyclades, and the lack of accessible beaches means that it has not succumbed to mass tourism. Instead it attracts visitors who want to enjoy the Greek way of life, finding that a better mode of relaxing than simply lying in the sun.

Amorgos is a long, thin island, and the mountains are such a dominant feature of the landscape that it was not until the 1990s that a decent road was built, making for easier connections between the northeast and the southwest. Until then, it was just as quick, and often more comfortable, to make the journey by boat.

Amorgos's challenging scenery has been no barrier to cultural development. The island was settled as long ago as 3300 B.C. and was one of the most influential centers of the Cycladic civilization, with three important cities: Minoa, Arkesini, and Egiali. The Romans used it later as a place of exile before it fell, like nearby islands, under the Venetians and then the Turks. During the regime of the colonels (see p. 38) it was again used as an island of exile for political prisoners, but it received a boost to its image and its tourism figures when it featured in the 1988 movie *The Big Blue,* by French director Luc Besson (born 1959).

The main town is **Amorgos town,** or Chora, a wonderful example of a Cycladic town, with whitewashed houses gathered below a 13th-century Venetian castle, several windmills, and more than 40 churches and chapels. Don't miss **Agios Fanourios,** the smallest chapel in Greece, with room for just three people inside.

**Katapola** is the main port and is a typically lively Greek town, although made up in effect of three separate small villages. You'll find plenty of fine hotels and restaurants, and all the facilities you might need. If you are looking for good beaches there are better elsewhere, such as at **Ormos Aigialis** in the north, which has the island's only real sandy beach but remains small and unspoiled.

## Santorini

Santorini (Thira) is dramatic and unique, formed from the remains of a volcanic crater. Ferries sail into the flooded crater to reach the port of Skala Thiras. High above perches the town of Thira. It's a very steep hike up the zigzag path from the port to the town, but there are always plenty of waiting donkeys for rent to help you on your way,

and now there's a cable car too.

The name by which the island is more commonly known in Greece, **Thira** is also the capital. Devastated by an earthquake in 1956, it was rebuilt and now welcomes vast numbers of tourists. The season lasts longer here than elsewhere, as cruise boats and ferries bring visitors on one-day trips in spring and fall as well, when other islands are much quieter.

There are some quiet spots on Santorini, too, such as the village of **Oia,** which is dramatically perched on the rim of the caldera at the northern end of the island. At the other extremity is **Akrotiri,** the remarkably well-

**Santorini**

◩ Map p. 241

**Visitor Information**

✉ Tourist Office, Thira

☎ 228/602-5490

**Akrotiri**

◩ Santorini map p. 241

🕐 Closed Sun.–Mon.

💲 $$

The remarkable monastery of Panagia Hozoviotissa, founded in 1088, is built into the cliffs below Amorgos town.

The stark white and blue of a church mellow in the setting sun

## Archaeological Museum

✉ Thira town, Santorini

☎ 228/602-2217

🕐 Closed Mon.

💲 $

preserved remains of a Minoan city devastated in the massive volcanic eruption of 1625 B.C. that also destroyed the old island, creating the present one. The great cataclysm may also have unleashed a tidal wave in the Aegean and the eastern Mediterranean that may have been the possible cause of the destruction of the Minoan civilization on Crete.

The **Archaeological Museum** in Thira has on display finds from Akrotiri, and a new museum is currently being constructed opposite the bus station as a place to house the island's famous frescoes, which were until recently in the possession of the National Archaeological Museum in Athens. On the east coast, the remains of **Arkhea Thira** (Ancient Thira) overlook the sea.

Santorini produces surprisingly good wine. At first glance you might think that the island was too windy, too hot, and too dry, but the *assurtiko* grape flourishes here nonetheless. The oldest vines are thought to be almost 200 years old, and they are deliberately cultivated to grow low to the ground, hunkered down to protect themselves from the wind. Fields of what at first look like basket trees are actually vines

covered by cane baskets. The white wines made on Santorini range from dry to sweet and are stronger in alcohol than the average table wine.

Tucked in and around Santorini's caldera are several tiny islands, accessible by boat trip from Thira. The largest, **Thirasia,** was part of the main island until an earthquake in 236 B.C. caused it to split away. Like Santorini, it has a fertile volcanic soil. **Manolas** is the island's harbor, with eating places and some rooms to rent. The second largest island, **Nea Kameni,** only appeared in 1720 and is uninhabited as it still erupts, most recently in 1950. ■

**Ancient Thira**

🅰 Santorini map p. 241

🕐 Closed Mon.

## Windmills

Strong seasonal winds buffet the Cyclades, providing an obvious and plentiful supply of free energy; thus was born the beautiful Cycladic windmill. Although the islands were blessed with wind their soils were not (and still aren't) fertile enough to support grain production. As such the grain came from the mainland, and the windmill owners ground the grain in exchange for 10 percent of the flour.

During World War II, the millers secretly did their grinding at night in order to supply the occupied Greeks with food. Alas, the vitality in war and peace that these mills once embodied has now softened. Most now only star in the iconic picture-postcards of Greek islands and in the photograph memories of tourists, their beauty most often captured against a sunset.

It's worth pointing out that **Mikonos** has some of the loveliest windmills in the Cyclades. Sitting atop a bluff above the town of Mikonos, within reach of the

harbor where grain ships used to dock, a cluster of whitewashed windmills stand out against the bright blue Aegean sky.

Architecturally, the Cycladic windmills are simple structures. They are built in a fixed position (as opposed to the ones that have the capacity to rotate at the top) because the direction of the wind rarely changes. The main structure is a white, ascetic cylinder with a thatched roof, and the blades are thin rays of wood that recall the hands of a clock. Today, the windmills fall somewhere between disrepair, having long ago lost their sail, and a new life as a converted home or bed and breakfast.

The handsome stone windmill on **Milos** is a memorable way to spend a vacation. The lodging is located in the hilltop village of Trypiti, and rates are reasonable *(tel 22870 22147, www .marketoswindmill.gr)*. There are many other great windmill-hotels throughout the islands, as they have now become beacons for tourists.

# Dodecanese

Dodecanese (Dodekanissa) means "12 islands," although, given the Greek genius for improvisation, there are actually 14 major islands, three minor ones that are inhabited, and dozens more that are uninhabited. As they are the most southerly group of islands, they are very popular with visitors because of their hot summer climate.

Working windmills on Karpathos grind flour that is then baked in stone ovens under the hillside.

Of course, spring is the best time to visit if you want to see greenery and wildflowers. During the long hot summers there can be water shortages. By fall the islands can appear quite barren.

For the most part the islands hug the Turkish coastline, with Kastellorizo lying less than 2 miles (3 km) off Turkey. Kastellorizo has a population of fewer than 300. By contrast, the biggest island, Rhodes, is home to a permanent population of 100,000, and many more in summer as it is also the most developed for tourism. The much smaller island of Kos is close behind.

In between there are islands like Tilos and Halki, where tourism has arrived but on a modest, manageable level, and where visitors are still met with friendliness.

The group also includes Patmos, where St. John is said to have had the vision described in the New Testament's Book of Revelation, and little Nissiros, a volcanic island whose sulfurous crater today bubbles quietly. Two hours by ferry from Rhodes, Symi is one of the gems of the Aegean, with a port almost too perfect to be true—as anyone will know who has ever sailed into it at dusk with the harbor lights twinkling.

Despite their proximity to Turkey, the Dodecanese show no more Turkish influence than other island groups. They have

A stag and a doe stand sentry over Mandraki harbor, Rhodes town.

## Rhodes

⚿ Map pp. 257 & 261

**Visitor Information**

✉ Plateia Raminis, Rhodes town

☎ 224/102-3255

✉ Makariou, Rhodes town

☎ 224/102-3655

**Palace of the Grand Masters**

✉ Odos Ippoton, Rhodes town

☎ 224/102-3359

$ $$

an Italian ambience: Occupied by the Italians during World War II, they were returned to Greece by a treaty signed only in 1948. Since then, the Dodecanese have welcomed tourists, needing the boost to their economies once provided by shipbuilding, fishing, and sponge fishing.

## Rhodes

Rhodes (Rodos) is the largest of the Dodecanese and also their capital. Much of the coast on the northern end of the island is given over solidly to tourism, as one town has merged into the next resulting in one long stretch of hotels, tavernas, and souvenir shops. This part of the island has great beaches, so it's the perfect place to be if you simply want to lie in the sun all day and then have a good time at night in the bars and discos. But the island is big enough to provide alternative attractions.

**Rhodes town** is a mixture of the very old and the very new. The medieval walled Old Town, often compared to Jerusalem, is one of the jewels of the Aegean and was designated a World Heritage site in 1988. Many cruise ships use the harbor, giving their passengers a few hours ashore to explore the Old Town—and to experience the high quality shopping in the New Town.

The Old Town dates back to the arrival of the Knights of St. John in 1306, although a town has existed on the spot since 408 B.C. and the island has been historically significant since at least the fifth century B.C. However, it was the medieval Knights of St. John who stamped their lasting identity on the place by building the Old Town, which they ruled until 1519. The imposing fortress at the top of the hill known as the **Palace of the Grand Masters** and the cobbled **Street of the Knights (Odos Ippoton)** are unrivaled in the Dodecanese for their splendor and beauty. Heavily restored over the centuries, the latter is lined with Inns of the Order of the Knights of St. John. The inns were meeting places for different nationalities—hence the Inn of Italy, the Inn of England, and so on. That the Old Town has also turned into a tourist bazaar is inevitable, but only the few main streets have been affected. If you venture into the backstreets you see authentic life still going on as it does in any close-knit Greek community.

Near the main entrance to the Old Town is the **Archaeological Museum,** a place of historical interest in itself as it is within the former hospital of the Grand Knights, built between 1440 and 1481. Rhodes is rich in archaeological discoveries, and there are examples here from its main sites, including Kamiros, Ialyssos, and Lindos. Its star exhibit is the Aphrodite of Rhodes, a sensuous first-century B.C. carving in marble.

Other museums of note within the Old Town's thick walls include the **Byzantine Museum,** set in a 13th-century church that became the Mosque of Enderum during the Turkish occupation. The **Decorative Arts Museum** has a fine collection of works that are unique to the island, with decorative tiles from Lindos, and a reconstructed house showing traditional raised sleeping platforms and the local style of courtyard patterned with black and white pebbles.

In the center of the New Town, the **Nea Agora** market building is of interest, just across the main street from the harbor. It is small

### Archaeological Museum

- ✉ Plateia Mouselou, Rhodes town
- ☎ 224/102-7657
- 🕐 Closed Mon.
- 💲 $$

### Byzantine Museum

- ✉ Apellou, Rhodes town
- 🕐 Closed Mon.
- 💲 $

### Decorative Arts Museum

- ✉ Plateia Argyrokastrou, Rhodes town
- ☎ 224/102-1954
- 🕐 Closed Mon.
- 💲 $

---

# EXPERIENCE: Touring Greek Vineyards

The last 10 to 20 years have seen a revolution in Greek winemaking. A new generation of winemakers, more widely traveled than their predecessors, have been able to sample and learn about the best wines around the world. They have brought back to Greece the latest techniques and are determined to make wines that are as good as those of other Mediterranean countries by applying what they have learned in France, Spain, and Italy to Greece's unique grape varieties.

Although there are some areas of the country where attempts have been made to create an organized wine trail, the general approach is more typically Greek: very casual. Plenty of winemakers open their vineyards to the public for visits, but not many of them have proper facilities, such as tasting rooms, which you would

expect in places like Bordeaux and Napa Valley. But it is this very approach that makes a tour of Greek wineries so enjoyable. You take potluck. If the vineyard is busy, your visit may be brief. If it's a quiet spell, however, and the proprietor is welcoming, you'll get the kind of personal tour and tasting that you would never get anywhere else.

This does mean you need to do a little research first—luckily, you'll find several websites devoted to Greek wine. The one at *http://greekwinemakers.com* has a vast amount of information about all the vineyards in the major wine-growing areas—Macedonia, Thessaly, Thrace, Epirus, the Peloponnosis, central Greece, the Aegean islands, and the Ionian islands. Other helpful websites include *www.greekwine.gr, www.thegreekwine.com,* and *www.allaboutgreekwine.com.*

**Lindos**
◭ Map p. 261

**Acropolis**
✉ Lindos
☎ 224/403-1258
⊕ Closed Mon. in winter & Mon. morning in summer
💲 $$

**Petaloudes**
◭ Map p. 261

but invariably lively, with simple but good cafés and restaurants.

**Lindos:** South of Rhodes town, on the eastern side of the island, the resorts at first merge one into another. Eventually the towns regain their distinct identities, and no town is more distinctive than Lindos. It is a popular spot with an excellent beach, yet the backstreets of whitewashed houses manage to retain their beauty. Above the town and the beach, the impressive acropolis stands on a huge outcrop of rock.

Lindos has been inhabited since about 3000 B.C., and the remains on the **acropolis,** which towers 380 feet (116 m) high, date back to the fourth century B.C. with the **Temple of Lindian Athena.** This was one of the most sacred temples in ancient Greece, and even Alexander the Great made a pilgrimage here. Just a few of its columns remain, but it is still a fabulous sight. The 13th-century church of Agios Ioannis also stands on the acropolis site. The battlements surrounding the acropolis rock were added in the 13th century by the Knights of Rhodes.

The village of **Lindos** looks almost impossibly beautiful as you approach, and its charm is maintained by the banning of traffic from the streets—a ban that is not difficult to enforce as vehicles are unable to get around the majority of these narrow lanes. Inevitably there are souvenir shops and sometimes far too many people, but at other times you can explore the quiet alleys and admire the mansions. Most of these were built by sea captains who became

**INSIDER TIP:**

Go by small boat beyond the edge of the map to wonderful Kastellorizo, close to the Turkish coast, and visit its blue grotto to see the color welling from the water. Relax at its harbor and dine at one of the harborside restaurants.

—JAY PASACHOFF
*National Geographic field scientist*

incredibly wealthy between the 15th and 18th centuries.

On the far side of the acropolis from Lindos's own beach is **St. Paul's Bay,** where the apostle arrived in A.D. 43 to bring Christianity to the island. A small white chapel is dedicated to St. Paul. In sharp contrast nearby, there is a beach much favored by nudists.

**Around Rhodes:** The most popular destination on the western side of Rhodes lies at the end of a side road off the main coastal road, just past the airport. The side road leads to **Petaloudes,** which has been renamed Butterfly Valley—a misnomer, but Moth Valley just doesn't have the same ring. Between June and September millions of Jersey tiger moths live here, attracted by the unusual storax trees. Their resin smells like vanilla and is used in the manufacture of frankincense. Unfortunately, the tour guides who lead busloads of tourists up here daily in summer encourage visitors to clap their hands to make the moths fly into the air. This thoughtless practice has led to a serious decline in moth numbers over the last few years.

Farther west is the fascinating site of **ancient Camirus.** It is one of the best-preserved examples of a classical Greek city and has been compared to Pompeii in its significance. Many of the remains date back to the sixth century B.C., including a cistern that supplied water for 400 families and the Temple of Athena. Camirus was destroyed in an earthquake in 142 B.C. and lay undiscovered until 1859. Local farmers reported finding a few graves, after which excavations took place in earnest and revealed the remains of an entire city.

South of Camirus is **Embonas,** where top wine producers open cellars for tastings (Mon.–Sat.).

**Monolithos** is the main village in the southwest corner of Rhodes, and it is easy to see how it acquired its name. The area is dominated by a huge monolith of rock that towers 774 feet (236 m) above the surrounding woods and drops almost sheer to the sea. At the top of the rock is a 15th-century castle built by Grand Master d'Aubusson, and within its walls are two 15th-century chapels, both with original frescoes. It is a demanding and precarious

(continued on p. 264)

**Ancient Camirus**

- Map p. 261
- ☎ 224/104-0037
- 🕐 Closed Mon.

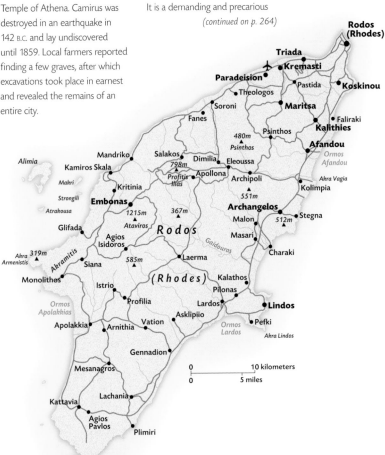

# A Walk Through Rhodes's Old Town

The Old Town of Rhodes may be a World Heritage site, but many visitors see only the few main streets lined with souvenir shops that are no different from anywhere else in Greece. Yet there are many fine monuments and quiet backstreets, not to mention the stunning fortifications of the Old Town. The following short walk leads you to them.

Begin at either side of the entrance to **Mandraki harbor ❶**, the channel where it is said (probably erroneously) that one of the seven wonders of the ancient world, the Colossus of Rhodes statue, once stood.

**NOT TO BE MISSED:**

**Eleftherias Gate • Street of the Knights • Palace of the Grand Masters • Town walls**

Impressive gateways pierce the ancient walls of Rhodes town, built about 1330.

Walk along the harborfront with the town on your right and the walls of the Old Town ahead of you. Cross the busy street at the first traffic lights and carry on walking in the same direction, under trees and past kiosks, to reach the **Eleftherias Gate ❷**. The name means "liberty" to commemorate the Greek independence from Turkish rule. Pass through the imposing walls, which date back to 1330 and in places are 40 feet (12 m) thick.

Walk straight ahead along Apellou, passing on your left the remains of the Temple of Aphrodite and on your right the **Decorative Arts Museum** and, opposite it, the **Byzantine Museum** (see p 259). After the Decorative Arts Museum, turn right onto Odos Ippoton, otherwise known as the **Street of the Knights ❸**. Built in the 14th century, the cobblestoned street is lined on either side with the Inns of the Knights of St. John, once used as eating clubs and temporary residences for visiting dignitaries. Architectural details on each facade reflect its respective country. On your right as you walk up the street are the Inns of Italy and France, and on the left is the Inn of Spain. The inns today house offices and foreign embassies.

At the top of the street on your right is the entrance to the **Palace of the Grand Masters**

**INSIDER TIP:**

## Walk through the walled capital, with its museums, shops, and Holocaust memorial.

—JAY PASACHOFF
*National Geographic field scientist*

❹, from where the 19 grand masters of the Order of the Knights of St. John ran the affairs of the order. The 14th-century palace was destroyed in an accidental explosion in 1856. What you see now is a faithful reconstruction carried out by the Italian rulers of Rhodes in the 1930s as a summer home for dictator Benito Mussolini (1883–1945), who never actually stayed there. It is well worth visiting for the wonderful central courtyard and the fine mosaic floors.

Carry on past the palace to the end of Odos Ippoton and turn left along Orfeos, past the souvenir shops, cafés, and restaurants. Where the road swings to the left look for the 1523 Mosque of Suleiman, opposite the Turkish Library. Turn right after the library, down Ippodamou. At the far end, follow the road left and at the first intersection turn right. This takes you outside the **town walls.** Go through the **Agiou Athanasiou Gate ❺,** turn left along the main road, and take the next left back into the Old Town through the Koskinou, or **Gate of St. John ❻.** Turn left at the first T-junction and follow Pithagora to **Plateia Ippokratous,** where there are several excellent cafés.

▲ See area map p. 257
► Mandraki harbor
↔ 1.2 miles (2 km)
⏱ 1 hour
► Plateia Ippokratous

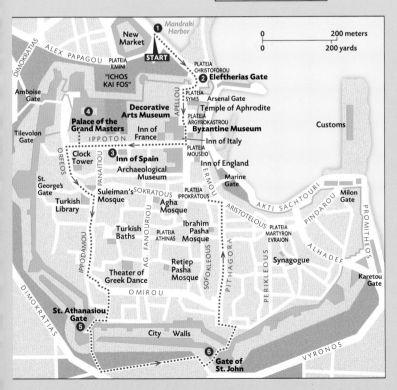

**Patmos**

Map p. 256

**Visitor Information**

Dimou, Skala, Patmos town

224/703-1666

walk to the top, but this does not deter large numbers of people from coming, particularly to watch the sunset over the sea.

## Patmos

St. John the Divine arrived on Patmos in A.D. 95, and it was here that he had the vision described in the Book of Revelation, which he then dictated to a disciple. The vision took place in the Holy Cave of the Apocalypse, which can be visited inside the church of Agia Anna, founded in 1090, two years after the founding of the Monastery of the Apocalypse. It is the presence of the monastery and the Holy Cave that has kept Patmos a place of religious significance, one of the most important in the Greek Orthodox Church. As a result the island, while welcoming tourists, has retained much of its original charm and spiritual peace.

Patmos is a beautiful island, with excellent beaches, a scattering of hill villages, and great mountain scenery to attract avid walkers. The highest point, at the southern end of the island, is Mount Prasino, which is 2,543 feet (775 m) above sea level, plunging steeply to the Aegean Sea. To its west, at **Psili Ammos,** is the best beach on Patmos, a fine stretch of sand backed by dunes, with the mountains as a backdrop.

**Patmos town** is divided into two parts. Below is the harbor, or **Skala,** with an attractive waterfront that is much more chic than many such places. It is a steep but spectacular walk up to the high part of town, the **Chora,** which has lots of impressive old mansions as well as about 40 churches, chapels, and monasteries. The **Monastery of St. John** *(tel 224/703-1234)* is the most

---

## EXPERIENCE: Making Pottery on Patmos

Although raku pottery is a Japanese style, first developed more than 400 years ago, Greece has its own great ceramic tradition, and many of its modern practitioners look to other styles from around the world for inspiration. The ancient Greeks themselves were influenced by the artistic work of both the Roman and Egyptian civilizations, and learned new ways of doing things as well as teaching others something of their own methods.

The raku style is a simple style, deliberately chosen to avoid any hints of luxury, and so has gained a following in the Greek islands, where simplicity is a way of life. The raku workshops on Patmos are at the home of local potters Nikos and Ritsa

Eliou. They show students how to make pots, plates, cups, and even statues in the traditional raku manner. After a first firing–application of heat–the glazes are chosen and the colors and decorations decided upon. The final firing ceremony takes place on the beach in the evening, around a bonfire, with food and wine.

The raku firing only takes an hour or two, compared with up to 16 hours for some other forms of pottery, and because of the low temperatures used, and the fact that the object is plunged into cold water when the firing is finished, raku pottery develops cracks in the glaze that are considered part of the design. For more details, visit **AegeanScapes** at *www.aegeanscapes.com.*

famous of these. Built in 1088 with fortified walls to resist attack by pirates, it is still a working monastery—only certain parts are open to visitors.

The **Monastery of the Apocalypse** (tel 224/703-1234) lies between Skala and Chora. Here you can see frescoes and icons, as well as the Holy Cave, and the fissure in the rock from where it is believed that God's voice spoke to St. John.

## Kalimnos

Known throughout Greece as the island of the sponge fishermen, Kalimnos has struggled to survive. Blight destroyed the best sponge fields, others were overfished, and some (such as Libya's) became off-limits for political reasons. Kalimnos diversified into shipping and tourism, but a few of the old sponge-fishing fleets still set sail for a few months in late spring and early summer.

There is no doubt when you are in **Pothia**—also known as Kalimnos town—that you are in a sponge-fishing center. Souvenir shops have sponges by the hundred, and retailers will offer to show you how to tell the best sponges, which they naturally all sell. At **Astor Sponge Workshop** they will demonstrate the entire process, showing how sponges are turned from black, odorous objects into clean and pleasant ones that you are happy to share your bathtub with.

Away from the busy harbor, the backstreets of Pothia remain authentically Greek, and life goes on pretty much as it has for cen-

turies. Seek out the 19th-century cathedral of **Agios Christos,** with its distinctive silver dome, and visit the **Archaeological Museum,** which is actually more of a general island museum.

---

### Sponge Fishing

Ancient vase paintings show that the Greeks have been sponge fishermen for several thousand years. The islands of Kalimnos and Symi are the two best known centers.

Local sponge fields no longer provide the rich harvests they once did, having been badly affected by disease. The introduction of synthetic sponges, inferior to the real thing but much cheaper, has continued the demise of the industry. If you buy sponges, remember that the best quality sponges are darker (i.e., unbleached), with the greatest concentration of holes; those with fewer holes tend to fall apart.

---

The main vacation spots are on the northwest coast, at **Mirties** and **Masouri,** which have nice beaches. You can also catch boats from there to the island of **Telendos,** where there are quieter beaches and a few places to eat and to stay. East of Pothia, **Vathi** is and often called the Fjord of Kalimnos. A deep inlet of the Aegean, which leads into a lush valley with several beautiful traditional villages, it is one of the island's most attractive spots.

### Kalimnos
▲ Map p. 256

**Visitor Information**
✉ Plateia Charalampous, Pothia
☎ 224/302-9301

**Astor Sponge Workshop**
✉ Off Plateia Eleftherias, Pothia

**Archaeological Museum**
✉ Near Plateia Kyprou, Pothia
☎ 224/306-1500
🕐 Closed Mon.
💲 $

A hillside taverna on Zia offers fabulous views.

## Kos

**Map** pp. 257 & 267

**Visitor Information**

✉ Vassileos Yeoryiou 3, Kos town

☎ 224/202-4460

### Castle of the Knights

✉ Plateia Platanou, Kos town

🕐 Closed Mon.

$ $

### Archaeological Museum

✉ Plateia Eleftherias, Kos town

☎ 224/202-8326

🕐 Closed Mon.

$ $

## Kos

After Rhodes, Kos is the second largest island of the Dodecanese; it is also the second busiest when it comes to mass market tourism. Because of its size—almost 28 miles (45 km) from end to end—Kos still has places to escape the crowds. At the height of the summer season you need to be careful in choosing where to go.

The island is one of the more fertile in the Dodecanese, with bountiful orchards, olive groves, and vineyards. It is not particularly mountainous, although Mount Dikaios in the southeast does reach 2,779 feet (847 m) in height. Kos has a number of excellent beaches and dozens of lively bars. **Kos town** is an enjoyable mix of ancient culture and modern hedonism.

Hippocrates (460–357 B.C.), the father of modern medicine, was born on Kos. A plane tree that

he is said to have planted and to have taught under stands in Plateia Platanou in Kos town. In fact the tree is almost 2,000 years too young for that to be true. Close by is the town's dominant feature, the **Castle of the Knights,** which dates back to the days when the medieval Knights of St. John ruled the island. It was built over several centuries, mostly from the 14th to the 16th, and incorporates marble taken from the island's principal archaeological site, the Asclepio (see opposite).

Kos is rich in both Greek and Roman remains, and the town's **Archaeological Museum** has a good collection of the best of them, including a marble statue of Hippocrates that has been dated to the fourth century B.C., when he may still have been alive. Kos town also has the splendid remains of the **Casa Romana** (*Grigoriou, Kos town*), a grand Roman villa restored in the 1930s that has wonderful mosaics, painted walls, and, within the site, part of a Roman road. The **Roman Agora** survives nearby as part of the ancient agora site with several layers of history, including the Temple of Herakles from the third century B.C.

Two and a half miles (4 km) north of Kos town, in a seductive hillside setting, is the **Asclepio,** built in the fourth century B.C. It is the ancient Greek equivalent of a health club and dedicated to Asklepios, the god of healing.

**INSIDER TIP:**

**Don't bother with bottled wine in the countryside: Ask for *dopio krasi*, village wine—pale red, sherrylike, and potent.**

—CHRISTOPHER SOMMERVILLE
*National Geographic writer*

Gymnasia such as this were scattered throughout Greece, and the fine remains here include baths and several temples.

Kos's biggest beach resort is at **Kardamaina,** along the south coast, a onetime fishing village that has been transformed beyond recognition into a rendezvous for young people drawn here by bars and discos that mar its long stretches of beautiful sandy beach. The island's best beaches lie farther west and include the white-sand Paradise Beach. Many of these beaches are somewhat remote from the resorts, but that doesn't prevent them from getting busy as large numbers arrive by water taxi. For a more peaceful experience, visit the villages on the slopes of Mount Dikaios, known as the **Asfendiou Villages,** although even here the peace is shattered by the arrival of

**Asclepio**

🅰 Map p. 267
☎ 224/202-8763
🕐 Closed Mon.
💲 $

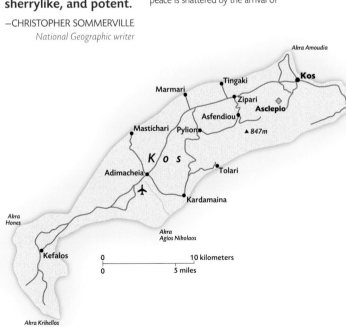

**Astipalea**

⚠ Map p. 256

regular tour buses. Take a walk in the woods until the tourists have disappeared, then experience the villages as they really are.

## Astipalea

Shaped like a butterfly, the island of Astipalea is the most westerly of the Dodecanese. With a tumble of whitewashed houses on the slopes below its Venetian castle and with a string of windmills silhouetted against the sky, it could just as easily be one of the Cycladic islands. Astipalea is hilly and has lots of good beaches, its peculiar shape giving it much more coastline than other islands of similar size. The main town is busy in summer, but there are still numerous quiet retreats to be found.

The original **town of Astipalea** was built on top of the hill, where the castle now stands on the site of the former acropolis. The castle followed in the 13th century and is remarkably preserved, with two 14th-century churches incorporated into the walls, houses also built into the walls for protection, an art collection, and stunning sea views.

The ruins of a Byzantine castle stand on the west coast at **Agios Ioannis,** which has an excellent beach and—a rarity in the Greek islands—a waterfall. Also on this western "wing" is the main resort, **Livadia.** Even it has far fewer visitors than comparable resorts on more popular islands. It is easily reached on foot from Chora, and if you wish to cast your clothes to the wind, carry on a little farther to Tzanaki, where there is an unofficial nudist beach.

Heading east from Astipalea town, the road crosses the narrow neck that links the two halves of the island, with the sea visible on both sides. Just beyond is this

## EXPERIENCE: Stay with a Family

Although some people get nervous about traveling with no accommodation booked, it's always been common in the Greek islands, and people never get left high and dry. If you're looking for a novel experience, you should try it. Just be sure to avoid the absolute busiest times, which are August (especially near August 15) and around Easter.

Ferries arriving in the islands, especially the smaller ones, are usually met by locals hoping to get you to stay with them. It can seem a bit daunting at first, but the people are usually genuine, and will often have photos of the properties, and testimonials from previous guests, to show you. Some of the places may be small hotels or guesthouses, but often

you'll be met by people offering you a room to rent in their home. Sometimes to make a little extra cash in the summer, a spare bedroom may be given over for the use of guests.

Staying with a Greek family is sure to be an experience of one kind or another—and usually overwhelmingly positive. Most Greeks are enormously kind and welcoming, and although you might not get the privacy and comfort that a hotel room provides, you will probably be made a real member of the family for a while, be included in meals and outings, and be invited to any special celebrations that are going on—and there usually is something going on most of the time in Greece.

region's main resort, **Analipsi** (or Maltezana). Relatively quiet, it is increasing in size and popularity. At the very northern tip of the eastern "wing" are the caves of **Drakospilia,** accessible only by boat and not yet a recognized tourist attraction.

## Symi

If you arrive on Symi via ferry from Rhodes, as most people do, it is hard to imagine that this tiny place, with just one main town and a few scattered villages, once had a population that was greater than that of Rhodes. In its prime, from the 17th to the 19th centuries when the island prospered thanks to sponge fishing and shipbuilding, there were as many as 30,000 people living here, often in conditions of some splendor. Today the population is less than one-tenth that figure, but it is boosted by the arrival of summer visitors.

Plenty of sponges are for sale along the harbor in **Symi town.** The last remnants of the shipbuilding trade are seen around the corner from the main harbor, on the road that leads to the tiny, rocky town beach. For a glimpse of how wealthy the island must have been, take the steep walk up the 357 steps of the Kallistrata, from the harbor part of the town, known as **Gialos,** to the upper town, or **Chora.** On either side of the street are examples of the neoclassical mansions that graced the town. Regretably, many are now decayed beyond repair, but others are being restored thanks to the pros-

perity that tourism has brought to Symi.

Villages and beaches are scattered around the island. The **monastery of Moni Taxiarchis Michail Panormitis** *(opens to greet ferries and other organized visits)* is in Panormitis Bay, in the far south. Most sightseeing boats from Rhodes bring visitors to the monastery first, and some ferry services stop at the cluster of houses here. It is not a particularly old monastery, dating back only to the 18th century, with many

**Symi**

Map p. 257

**Looking down on Symi town's beautiful old harbor of Gialos from the upper town**

On Karpathos, the village of Olimpos, isolated for so long, retains many of its old ways.

## Karpathos

 Map p. 257

later additions. There is a small museum and a church, and most notably an icon of the archangel Michael, the patron saint of Symi and of mariners. Many a Greek sailor has made a pilgrimage here, to thank St. Michael for a safe passage at sea.

### Karpathos

The third largest of the Dodecanese islands, Karpathos remains one of the most traditional despite recent increases in tour-

ism following the opening of its own (domestic) airport. Before that, visitors faced a long ferry ride from Rhodes, but what greeted them was a dramatic and rugged island with a high mountain range running down its spine. The highest point is the 3,674-foot (1,120 m) Mount Kalimni, almost dead center on this long, thin island.

The capital, **Karpathos town** (also known as Pigadia), is in the south at one end of a long, sheltered bay with a 2-mile (3 km) sweep of sand. It has a delightfully old-fashioned fishing harbor, where the fishermen still mend their nets, not yet having surrendered their places to fashionable yachts. This is naturally the best place to go for the freshest fish, straight from the sea.

The essential trip on Karpathos is to one of the unspoiled mountain villages, the best example being **Olimpos** in the far north of the island. The village was founded in 1420 and for most of its existence remained virtually cut off from the rest of the island. The only way to get there was to sail to the nearest landing at the coastal village of Diafani, then make a long, steep haul up to Olimpos at some 2,000 feet (600 m), its houses clustered along a mountain ridge. Because the village was so remote, its traditions remained for the most part untouched by the modern age. Even today you will see many women, and some men, still wearing traditional costumes. You can visit Olimpos on a day trip from Karpathos town.

There are more mountain villages closer to the town, each with its own attractions. **Menetes** is also high in the mountains, if not quite as high as Olimpos at only 1,150 feet (350 m) above sea level. Several of its streets are covered with vines, making it a wonderful place to visit in the fall when the grapes are heavy and ready for picking.

**Aperi,** in the hills north of Karpathos town, is also well worth a visit. It was the island capital until 1896 and is said to be the wealthiest village in all of Greece per capita. Many villagers have made their fortune in the United States and then returned. One family who stayed was that of TV and movie star Telly Savalas (1924–1994). ∎

## Kastellorizo

Kastellorizo is a delightful anomaly, as its official name is Megisti. This means "the biggest," but the island is actually the smallest of the main Dodecanese. Its name derives from the fact that it is the biggest of the handful of islands that cluster here in a small group. The other curious point is that Kastellorizo is 75 miles (118 km) from its closest Greek neighbor, Rhodes, yet it is tucked just 1.5 miles (2.5 km) off the coastline of Turkey.

The island remained a remote little outpost, largely forgotten by the Greeks and undiscovered by foreign vacationers until 1987, when its new airport brought it more into contact with the outside world. Even so, its present population of just 300 does not compare with the 15,000 or so who lived here a century ago. In those times the closest Turkish towns were still Greek, and Kastellorizo had a flourishing shipping trade. Its prowess was due in no small part to the magnificent harbor of the capital, Kastellorizo town, said to be the finest natural harbor in the eastern Mediterranean.

Today the island is still a peaceful backwater, and even at the height of summer you'll see few visitors around. There are no beaches, accommodations are basic, and restaurants are pricier than you might expect.

# More Islands to Visit in the Dodecanese

## Halki

Not far from Rhodes, little Halki has seen a renaissance in its fortunes recently, thanks to sensitive tourism development. The island badly needed a boost after the decline of sponge fishing. You will find plenty of English-speaking tourists here, with restaurants catering for local people and tourists alike. In summer, make reservations in advance if you want to be sure of a room in one of the island's many hotels.

 Map p. 257

## Nissiros

This volcanic island is the one to choose if you want to get away from it all. It makes a popular one-day visit from Kos, although it does have a few hotels of its own. The volcanic crater is the island's particular attraction, with its bubbling sulfurous vents and its heat captured by the surrounding rim. More conventional delights are to be found in the small port of **Mandraki,** with its maze of narrow whitewashed streets.

 Map p. 257

## Pserimos

Little more than a speck in the sea, with one small town and about a hundred inhabitants, Pserimos is swamped by visitors in midsummer, who come across on daily visits from nearby Kos and Kalimnos. After the tourists depart, the village and its pretty beach return to normal, with just a handful of visitors left to enjoy its peaceful charm, simple accommodations, and friendly tavernas.

 Map p. 257

## Tilos

Tilos is the perfect escape if you like your pleasures simple. Its remoteness—a two-hour hydrofoil journey from the nearest port at Rhodes—has discouraged large-scale development. Once there, however, you are made very welcome, and local people will soon be greeting you in the street.

The port and main town is **Livadia,** with some accommodations and several very good eating places. There is a small pebble beach, and plenty of paths lead to coves along the coast. A bus links Livadia with the island's other village, **Megalo Horio** (Big Town), which is set below the ruins of a Venetian castle and is, despite its ambitious name, even sleepier than Livadia.

 Map p. 257

**A girl in traditional dress for Easter celebrations, Olimpos, Karpathos**

More a country than an island, with patriotic citizens who will proudly announce that they are Cretans first, Greeks second

# Crete

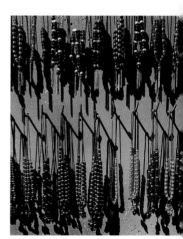

**Worry beads**

# Crete

**Crete (Kriti) is the largest island in Greece and the fifth largest in the Mediterranean (after Sicily, Sardinia, Cyprus, and Corsica). It is a long, thin island, 155 miles (250 km) from one end to the other, yet at its narrowest only 7.5 miles (12 km) wide.**

Within its shores are high mountain ranges, the longest gorge in Europe, hundreds of excellent beaches, and one of Greece's most significant ancient sites: Knossos.

Knossos is only one of countless historical sites on Crete, although the island will satisfy the sun worshipper just as much as the historian, the archaeologist, the plant lover, and the photographer. Long stretches of the north coast have been developed for tourism in a way that makes them indistinguishable from other beach meccas all over the world, but the rugged southern coast limits access and therefore further development. In the interior, the

mountain villages remain much as they have been for the last few centuries, and it is here that you will encounter the most generous hospitality. Crete is, after all, the island of Zorba the Greek and his creator, novelist Nikos Kazantzakis. Zorba brilliantly sums up the proud, fiery, life-loving side of the Cretan character.

Crete is fiery in its climate, too. The little offshore island of Gavdos is the most southerly

Area of map detail

point in Europe, and Crete is actually farther south than some places in North Africa, including Tunis and Algiers. Temperatures in midsummer can reach over 100°F (38°C), making the spring and fall better times to visit if you don't like the heat. However, if a summer visit is unavoidable, there are always the cooler mountains to escape to, and you can follow the Greek custom of having an afternoon siesta, thus staying out of the sun in the hottest part of the day. Crete has very little rainfall from late May through mid-September, but it's wetter in the winter, when temperatures remain pleasantly warm.

Crete leaves an indelible impression, no matter what time of year. Hania is one of the most charming towns anywhere in the Aegean, with its backdrop of the White Mountains. First impressions of the capital, Iraklio—a big and noisy city by Greek island standards—are seldom favorable, but even here the Cretan charm can work its magic as you get beneath the skin of the city. Travel elsewhere and you will still find that it is the soul of Crete that gets to you. ■

## NOT TO BE MISSED:

# Iraklio

**Greece's fifth largest city has plenty to offer. As with Athens, you have to take time to get acquainted with it. Iraklio suffered significant bomb damage during World War II and now has many unappealing concrete buildings and a chaotic road system. But it also has great character and a treasure house of an archaeological museum containing some of the world's most renowned antiquities.**

Iraklio has been settled since Neolithic times, and it flourished as the harbor for the Minoan center at Knossos (see pp. 280–283), 3 miles (5 km) to the south. The Venetians conquered it in the 13th century and made it their capital for the Aegean, building a fort to protect the harbor. The **fort** that stands there today was built in the 16th century after the first was destroyed in an earthquake, and it played an important role in the city's history. It was the focal point when the Turks beset the city in 1648, a siege that lasted until 1669, when the Venetians surrendered the island to the Turks. Thirty thousand Cretan and Venetian residents of the city lost their lives, as did 118,000 Turks, which gives an idea of the ferocity with which the city was defended.

On the southern side of the harbor is another Venetian structure, the **Arsenal,** constructed in the 16th century as the place where the shipping fleet for the Aegean was both built and repaired. Iraklio's magnificent **city walls** are from the same period. They run for 2 miles (3 km) around the old part of the town, passing several impressive gates, such as the Porta Kornarou, where the walls are 60 feet (18 m) high and 130 feet (40 m) thick. By the Martinengo Bastion, at the southernmost corner of the walls lies the grave of Nikos

Iraklio's squat Rocco al Mare fortress is also known as the Koules.

Kazantzakis (see p. 278), who asked to be buried here.

## Archaeological Museum

The Archaeological Museum is one of Iraklio's undoubted highlights. Rich finds have been made all over this large and historically important island, and most of them have ended up on display here. The result is an immense, outstanding collection that warrants plenty of your time, maybe even two short visits instead of one longer one.

In October 2006 renovations were started on the museum; these are expected to continue until 2010. During this time exhibits may be open to a limited number of people. Be prepared to wait in long lines, especially if cruise ships are docked.

Among the 400 or so treasured artifacts on display during the renovations are the Lily Prince from the queen's apartment—belonging in the Hall of Frescos. Other frescos from Knossos, which date from 1600-1400 B.C., such as the "Bull Leaping", "La Parisienne", the "Saffron Gatherers" and the "Blue Bird" are also on view. Neolithic tools, pottery from prepalatial and early palatial times, jewelery and vases as well as the Phaistos Disc can also be seen during the renovations. Hope that the Town Mosaic is on display; it goes back to the old palace period (2000–1700 B.C.).

The museum is close to **Plateia Eleftherias** (Liberty

### Iraklio

🅐 Map p. 275

**Visitor Information**

✉ Crete Island H.Q.
☎ 281/022-8225

### Archaeological Museum

✉ Plateia Eleftherias
☎ 281/022-6092
🕐 Closed for renovation, call for more information
💲 $$

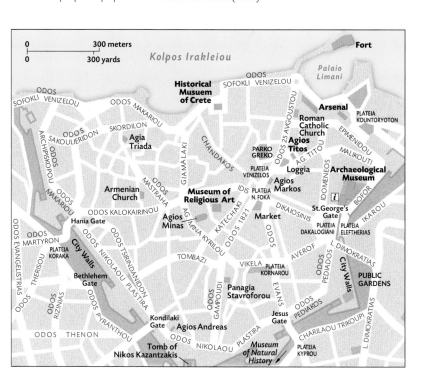

Square), very much the heart of Iraklio. A busy traffic hub day or night, it is pedestrianized and tree-shaded in the center. The square comes alive in the evenings, when the bars and restaurants open and half the city seems to congregate here for the evening *volta* (communal stroll).

It is only a short walk from Plateia Eleftherias to the city's other main square, **Plateia Venizelos,** also known unofficially as Fountain Square. The fountain in question was originally built in the 17th century by Venetian governor Francesco Morosini and has recently been restored to its full glory.

There's a Turkish fountain on nearby Plateia Kallergon, where you will also find the 17th-century

## Nikos Kazantzakis (1883–1957)

If there is one fictional figure who typifies most people's idea of the exuberant, emotional Greek character it is Zorba, portrayed by Anthony Quinn in the 1964 movie *Zorba the Greek*. The character was created in the novel of the same name by Nikos Kazantzakis, the greatest modern Greek novelist. Born in Iraklio, he traveled widely in Europe, Africa, and Asia before starting to write. Best known for novels such as *Christ Recrucified* and *The Greek Passion* (both 1948), he also wrote essays, poetry, and plays. Martin Scorsese's 1988 movie of his novel *The Last Temptation of Christ* proved controversial in its attempt to depict the human nature of Jesus Christ. The tomb of Kazantzakis can be visited in Iraklio (see map p. 277).

The 1964 film *Zorba the Greek* brought Kazantzakis's work to world attention.

## INSIDER TIP:

At Iraklio's Archaeo-
logical Museum, seek
out the exquisite
Minoan frescoes from
Knossos, above all "La
Parisienne" and "The
Prince of the Lilies."
You'll obtain a tangible
glimpse into ancient
palace life.

—BARBARA A. NOE
*National Geographic editor*

**Loggia.** Originally a meeting place for the Cretan nobility, this building has been lovingly restored and now serves as the city hall. If you need a respite from the traffic-filled streets, just off this square is **El Greco Park,** which also offers some welcome shade in the heat of the day.

Behind the Loggia is the church of **Agios Titos.** Built in the tenth century and dedicated to the island's patron saint, St. Titos, who brought Christianity to Crete, it was reconstructed in 1878. It contains the saint's relics and is therefore a holy place to Cretans, to be treated with respect.

## Historical Museum

From Plateia Venizelos, Chandakos leads toward the waterfront and, just to the right, the Historical Museum of Crete. Smaller than the Archaeological Museum, it nevertheless gives a good picture of Cretan life through the ages. There are examples of art from the Venetian period, as well as an interesting collection of Byzantine art. The highlight is the only painting by El Greco (1541–1614) displayed on the island where he was born. The "Monastery of St. Catherine on Mount Sinai" (also referred to as "The Landscape of the Gods-trodden Mount Sinai" and "View of Mount Sinai and the Monastery of St. Catherine") warrants its own room and a reverential display; it is a powerful work painted about 1570.

No museum on the history of Crete could ignore the events of World War II, and in particular the bloody Battle of Crete (see p. 301). The Historical Museum tells the full story of the suffering on the island in sometimes shocking detail, illustrated with photos from the period. Another glimpse of Cretan life is given in a reconstructed study of Nikos Kazantzakis, indicating the esteem in which he is held on his native island.

Iraklio has other museums worth seeing if time allows. The **Museum of Religious Art** is appropriately situated next to the city's 19th-century cathedral of Agios Minas and contains an extensive collection of Byzantine icons and frescoes and fine examples of religious manuscripts. The building itself is a 16th-century church built by the Venetians in honor of St. Catherine and was originally a monastery and center for art and learning. El Greco studied here. The **Museum of Natural History** has displays on the flora and fauna not only of Crete—which is incredibly well blessed in this respect—but of the whole Aegean. ∎

### Historical Museum

- ✉ Lysimachou Kalokairinou 7
- ☎ 281/028-8708
- 🕐 Closed Sun.
- 💲 $

### Museum of Religious Art

- ✉ Plateia Agias Aikaterinis
- 🕐 Closed Sat.–Sun.
- 💲 $

### Museum of Natural History

- ✉ Neoria
- ☎ 281/039-3276
- 🕐 Closed Sat.
- 💲 $

# Knossos

The remains of the vast Royal Minoan Palace at Knossos, 3 miles (5 km) south of Iraklio, are the major tourist attraction on Crete. You should plan to spend at least two hours here if you hope to see much of the palace and surrounding town. If you are visiting in summer, take a bottle of water as it can be very hot and dry.

The reconstructed Lustral Bath was for bathing in company—many individual clay baths were found.

**Knossos**

- 🅰 Map p. 275
- ✉ 3 miles (5 km) S of Iraklio
- ☎ 281/023-1940
- 💲 $$

Summer is a very busy time here, so you are advised to arrive at the very start of the day or in the early evening (in summer the site remains open until sunset). It is well worth purchasing the guidebook. Consider being shown around by an official guide—the fee will depend on the length of the tour and the number of people on it.

The remains you see today at Knossos are far from being the earliest on the site, which was first settled in Neolithic times, about 6000 B.C. The first palace here has been dated to 2000 B.C. This was destroyed in an earthquake in about 1700 B.C. The most recent palace was built after that earthquake and survived until 1380 B.C., when it too was destroyed, this time by fire. This palace was built on a vast scale, with some 1,300 rooms, and in its heyday, at the height of the Minoan civilization, it is estimated that there would have been 12,000 people living here, with four times as many in the immediate surroundings. The site is extensive, covering 185 acres (75 hectares) in all, but only a part of it is open to the public.

One of the best-known legends of ancient Greece originated here, that of the labyrinth and its monstrous guardian, the Minotaur. After the wife of King Minos of Knossos gave birth to a beast that had the head of a bull on the body of a man, the king imprisoned the Minotaur (the name means "bull of Minos") in a labyrinth beneath his palace and fed it with human sacrifices. Theseus, with the help of Minos' daughter, Ariadne, tracked down and slew the formidable Minotaur and, in so doing, liberated Athens from an oppressive bondage.

It was thought that King Minos was just a legend, too, until British archaeologist Sir Arthur Evans (see pp. 284–285) found the Minoan Palace at Knossos. In fact the word *labyrinth* derives from *labrys,* which is a double-headed ax, a Minoan symbol seen throughout the palace. Bulls and bull symbols figure largely, too.

Buildings scattered over the site today are reconstructions by Evans. His use of modern materials is still the subject of controversy, but it is fascinating to see some of the palace rooms brought to life. When you enter the site you pass a **bust** of Evans, and behind this are three large pits, probably used for storing grain. As you progress you will see on the right one of the famous symbols of Knossos, the **Horns of Consecration.** It has been restored and represents the horns of the sacred bull that would originally have stood at the very top of the palace. Left of the main path, almost opposite the Horns, are steps leading to the **piano nobile,** the upper floor, which has the remains of some shrines and good views over much of the site.

In this area, look for the **Throne Room.** When Evans discovered it, the room was in a state of turmoil, leading him to speculate that some significant final event had occurred here, such as an earthquake, coinciding with the destruction of the palace. In one room is a copy of the original throne, maybe the oldest

## EXPERIENCE: Exploring Crete on Horseback

If you're looking for an out-of-time way to explore the sights of Crete—something different from the tour bus experience—then hit the trails, specifically, the horse trails. Several stables offer such trips. On the beach of Karteros, near Knossos, the **Karteros Equestrian Center** (tel 281/038-0244) provides many horseback programs, ranging from an hour to several days in length and from walks along the beach to exploring Minoan archaeological sites. Farther away, the **Odysseia Stables** (tel 289/705-1080, www.horseriding.gr), in the village of Avdou, offers the Lassithi Trek, a six-day, 100-mile (160 km) ride along the Dikti Mountain Range to the Libyan Sea. The trek costs €900.

in the world, and all around it is a wonderful restored fresco showing griffins, sacred Minoan symbols.

There are many more frescoes around the site, replicas of originals that have been removed for safekeeping in the Archaeological Museum in Iraklio (see p. 277). The priest-king fresco, which is just beyond the Horns of Consecration, is a highlight. Also known as the Lily Prince, it is a delicate depiction of a figure in a crown made of lilies and feathers.

In the center of the site is a large, open central courtyard, where the sport of bull leaping took place. Sportsmen would face charging bulls head-on and leap over them by grasping their horns and performing a somersault. Beyond this area are the main parts of the palace, including the royal apartments. The Queen's Hall is decorated with a replica of the famous, vivid dolphin fresco. ■

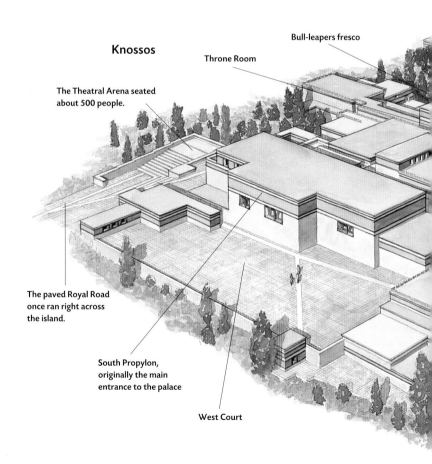

## Knossos

Bull-leapers fresco

Throne Room

The Theatral Arena seated about 500 people.

The paved Royal Road once ran right across the island.

South Propylon, originally the main entrance to the palace

West Court

Stylized frescoes, including that of the water-carriers, have been copied on the site and restored, showing bold use of color, pattern, and design.

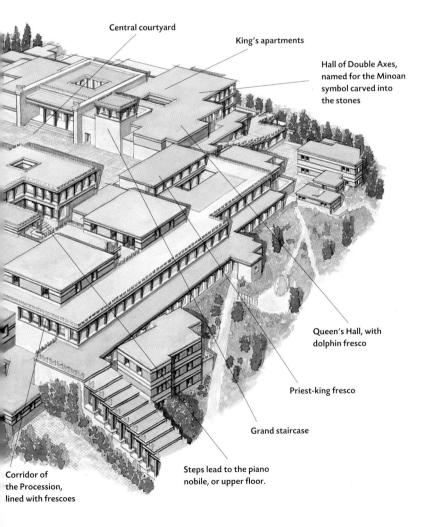

Central courtyard

King's apartments

Hall of Double Axes, named for the Minoan symbol carved into the stones

Queen's Hall, with dolphin fresco

Priest-king fresco

Grand staircase

Corridor of the Procession, lined with frescoes

Steps lead to the piano nobile, or upper floor.

# Arthur Evans

The British archaeologist Sir Arthur John Evans (1851–1941) is the man who brought Knossos to the attention of the world. He was born in Hertfordshire, England, then educated at the famous public school Harrow before going to Brasenose College at Oxford University. He later attended the University of Göttingen, in Germany, and became the curator of the Ashmolean Museum in Oxford, a position he was offered at the age of 33 and held for 24 years.

Evans at Knossos, by Sir William Blake Richmond (1842–1921), with the water-carriers fresco behind

It was while he was working at the Ashmolean Museum that Evans developed an interest in the coins and seals of ancient Greece, and in particular the strange, indecipherable script that appeared on those of Crete. He first visited the island in 1894 in order to learn more and devoted much of the rest of his life to unearthing its secrets.

By 1899 Evans had begun excavations at Knossos, where he quickly unearthed a Bronze Age city and a royal palace that he named Minos after the legendary Cretan king and son of the god Zeus—the plan of the palace appeared to him to be something of a labyrinth. The civilization he dubbed Minoan. Although he completed the bulk of the important excavations in the first few years of the 20th century, Evans continued work on the site until 1935, by which time he was 84 years old.

The most controversial aspect of his work is the reconstruction and painting of the royal palace, which he undertook in order to give some idea of its appearance some 3,500 years ago. To some scholars this was sacrilege, while to others it was a bold attempt to bring the palace back to life, conveying some of its grandeur to the general public. Anyone who has seen the Stoa of Attalos at the Ancient Agora in Athens, splendidly reconstructed by the American School of Archaeology, will have some sympathy with this view.

Another important discovery made by Evans at the site was 3,000 clay tablets covered with two distinct types of indecipherable writing. One of these was referred to as Linear A, which is regarded as the language of the Minoans and has still not been fully deciphered to this day. The other was called Linear B, and this was also a mystery until 1952, when it was shown to be an early form of Greek, dating back to about 1500–1400 B.C. This was an important step in understanding the development of the ancient Greeks, as it showed they had a written script much earlier than had previously been thought.

It is thought that one reason Evans found so much material on the site still intact was because the grounds of the palace were taboo to such an extent that looters would not go near them. One theory suggests that the famous bull-leaping scenes were not a macho demonstration of skill but rather a prelude to some brutal sacrificial rites that involved young children and virgins of both sexes. This theory proposes that the palace was then destroyed, not by natural forces such as a tidal wave, but by its own guards, repelled by the debauchery of their rulers. Subsequently, the sense of evil here kept people away for ever.

Such theories did not meet with Evans's approval. He felt very possessive about Crete and invariably dismissed any theories put forward that did not coincide with his own. Evans himself worked on books in which he attempted to decipher the two scripts, but he is mostly remembered as the man who discovered the Minoan Palace of Knossos.

Not as well known is the fact that he was a war correspondent in the Balkans in his early days, and that in the 1880s he researched

The delightful bull-leapers fresco indicates the purpose of the palace's large central courtyard.

and wrote a book that would sadly be just as relevant a century later: It was about the plight of the Slavs and Albanians in the regions of Bosnia and Herzegovina, at that time struggling for their independence from Turkey.

Arthur Evans was created a Knight of the British Empire in 1911 and died in 1941 at the age of 90.

# Kastelli Pediados

Kastelli Pediados—not to be confused with Kastelli Kissamos in western Crete—is the principal village in an area known as Pediada, to the southeast of Iraklio. There are basic accommodations and tavernas, and you will be warmly greeted if you do stray here, but most visitors pass through on their way to the area's main attractions, the Lasithi Plateau and Dikteon Andron (see opposite).

Distillation of the fiery Cretan spirit called *raki* is still a home-based industry in Pediada.

**Kastelli Pediados**
Map p. 275

There are some beautiful unspoiled villages in the region, where people make their living from the soil, as they have for thousands of years. The landscape is dotted with ancient churches, such as the one dedicated to Isodia Theotokon near Sklaverochori, which dates from the 15th century and has some original murals inside. **Agios Pandeleimon,** near the village of Pigi, is mainly 13th century but contains fragments from a 10th-century basilica in the structure.

East of Kastelli the road climbs toward **Mount Dikti,** 7,045 feet (2,148 m) high, taking you first to the villages and windmills of the **Lasithi Plateau.** This fertile and much photographed place,

hemmed around by mountains, contains a reputed 10,000 windmills. These simple, elegant, white-sailed structures were once used to pump water to the fields, but most are now electrified or purely for decoration.

The plateau has several other sites worth visiting, including the **Cave of Trapeza.** Take a flashlight to explore the oldest inhabited site yet discovered on Crete, with tombs dated from 7000 B.C. Nearby is the small site of **Karphi,** where Minoan culture and religion were still alive in 1000 B.C., hundreds of years after the civilization had vanished elsewhere. Most visitors then go on to visit the area's biggest attraction, Dikteon Andron. ■

# Dikteon Andron

The origins of Dikteon Andron (Dikteon cave), in legend at least, go back even further than the Neolithic remains found at the nearby Cave of Trapeza. It was here that the goddess Rhea gave birth to Zeus. His father, Kronos, had been told that he would one day lose his throne to a son and was so fearful of the prophecy that he ate all his children the moment they were born. Rhea hid Zeus in Dikteon Andron and tricked Zeus into eating a stone instead.

Zeus did indeed go on to become father to all the other gods (see pp. 172–173). However, there is a suggestion that the Zeus who was born here was not the same Zeus who later resided on Mount Olympus but was rather a Cretan Zeus, worshipped as a fertility god who died and was reborn each year.

If you have never visited a cave before, you will be amazed by the enormity of this one and by the extraordinary shapes of the stalactites and stalagmites. Even if this is not your first cave, you will not be disappointed. Take a flashlight and wear rubber-soled shoes or boots. A guide is available, but it is easy enough to explore on your own.

To reach the cave you must stop in the village of Psychro and follow the sign up a pleasant track that weaves through oak woods; it takes about 15 minutes on foot. Donkeys are available to rent for those who find the going difficult. Be careful on entering the cave, as the steps down are awkward and can be slippery—your flashlight is for these as much as for viewing the rock formations. As with many sites in Greece, viewing is best done early or late to avoid the crowds. Long lines can form during the day in summer.

The **main chamber** is 230 feet (70 m) deep, and impressive; several smaller chambers lead off it. At the bottom is a small pool, and it is in the chamber off to the left of this that Zeus—whichever Zeus it was—is said to have been born. ■

**Dikteon Andron**

- Map p. 275
- Psychro
- $

## Donkey Pride

Sure, you can explore Dikteon Andron on foot, but why not enlist the steady, stubborn gait of a donkey? The locals are happy to oblige, and chances are the donkey will better handle the steep descent.

Long a beast of burden on Crete—they've been here since the Neolithic period—donkeys have become somewhat a point of pride for Cretans. Smarter and tougher than horses, donkeys can easily go where automobiles can't. Once you see some of the roads in Crete, you'll understand the Cretan preference for the sure-footed, albeit sometimes recalcitrant, donkey. So rent one—but only if you don't mind being led by it.

# Malia

Malia is a very lively resort—a great place for the young at heart. At the same time it has one of Crete's most evocative and least visited Minoan sites, with the remains of a palace. It is also one of the best coastal spots on Crete for seeing migrating birds in the spring and fall.

**Summer crowds on Malia beach—rise early to stake out a good spot.**

**Malia**
🅰 Map p. 275

**Minoan Palace**
✉ 2 miles (3 km) E of Malia
☎ 289/703-1597
🕐 Closed Mon.
💲 $

The summer wildlife is found in the center of town, where you can enjoy music in the bars and discos until the early hours. During the day, the glorious long, sandy beach is the place for sun worshippers, but it does get very crowded. While you may have to search for a spot on the main beach, there is another excellent beach near the **Minoan site** that is often empty because so few people make the short 2-mile (3 km) journey to visit it.

French archaeologists have been working on the site for some time, but visitors can wander over much of the site. Information boards have been placed to help you make sense of it all. There is also a burial site known as

Chrysolakkos. Treasures found in the tombs are held in the Archaeological Museum in Iraklio.

The main area to see is the former **palace,** which was built in 1900 B.C., destroyed in 1700 B.C., rebuilt, and then destroyed again in about 1450 B.C. in the cataclysmic annihilation of the Minoan civilization on Crete. The central courtyard is a focal point from which to try to understand the sumptuous buildings that would have surrounded you. The remains of storage areas and pits, as well as a huge administration block, indicate that the palace was as well populated and well stocked with provisions as any large modern town. ■

## Greeks at Sea

Since ancient times, Greece has always been one of the greatest and most accomplished maritime nations in the world. With about 2,000 islands and 8,547 miles (13,676 km) of coastline, it has had to be. It's no wonder great great shipping dynasties have grown here. So to go sailing in Greece is to go to the most natural place in the world for it. Opportunities abound to try your own hand at it while you are here.

# Elounda

Like Malia, Elounda is a mix of ancient and modern. It has a long and rich history, but today it is mainly known as an upmarket beach destination. Greece's most luxurious hotels are clustered on the coastline toward Agios Nikolaos, along a road leading from a pretty little fishing harbor.

Elounda is on the site of the ancient Greco-Roman town of **Olous.** If you look from the bridge joining Elounda and the Spinalonga peninsula, you can make out the remains just beneath the surface of the water. Olous had one of the most important harbors in eastern Crete, and there are at least two remaining temples. It is thought that the city was destroyed in the second century B.C., when immense land movements caused several areas of eastern Crete to sink below the waves, while parts of western Crete rose.

On either side of the bridge are the remnants of Venetian salt pans. It was the Venetians who developed Elounda as a port in 1579. On the sheltering peninsula, which is a good place to escape the crowds, there is a church that was once part of ancient Olous and still has some of its original frescoes. From here, if the light is right, you can make out parts of the old harbor beneath the waves.

**Spinalonga island,** offshore, helps protect the bay and is where the Venetians built their defensive fortress. This was such an effective stronghold that it was the last place on Crete to surrender to the Turks, in 1715, some 40 years later than most of the rest of Crete. From 1903 to 1957 the island was renowned throughout Greece as a leper colony, where a thriving town built up. The ruins can still be seen. It is a haunting spot, filled with the ghosts of those who lived out their lives in enforced isolation on the island. ■

**Elounda**
🔼 Map p. 275

The most popular tavernas in Elounda cluster around the harbor.

# Agios Nikolaos

The port of Agios Nikolaos—a major administrative, cultural, and communications center—is one of the most developed tourist areas in Crete and, indeed, in all of Greece. The city, beautifully situated on the Gulf of Mirabello, boasts not one but two harbors: a lovely fishing harbor and, right in the town, an inner harbor that is really a lake. Edged with open-air cafés, it's said the lake is where the goddess Athena used to take her bath.

Agios Nikolaos's picturesque inner harbor, the "bath of Athena"

**Agios Nikolaos**

🗺 Map p. 275

**Visitor Information**

✉ Marina

☎ 284/102-2357

All these attractions, and many more in and around the town, turn it into one of the busiest places on Crete in the middle of summer.

Agios Nikolaos was a thriving place in ancient times, serving as the port for the city-state of Lato, inland from here. It remained a port under the Venetians, who

called it Agios Nikolaos after a church of the same name built in the 10th and 11th centuries. The Venetians also named the gulf Mirabello (Italian for "beautiful view"). The town declined under the Turks, who destroyed its Genoese fortress, but in the late 19th century it began to thrive again as a popular destination for

**INSIDER TIP:**

If you need a snack between Agios Nikolaos and Sitia, stop at the traditional Cretan bakery in Kavousi; ask for Marcella and she will give you a fresh *kalitsouni* (sweet cheese pie).

—DONALD HAGGIS
*National Geographic field scientist*

travelers. Agios Nikolaos is still an important port, and you will find fishermen drying their nets in the harbor, and ferry boats coming in regularly from the Dodecanese, the Cyclades, and Pireas.

The **harbor** is lined with bars, stores, cafés, and tavernas, which make full use of their setting by charging prices that are expensive by Greek standards. If you want better food and a more Cretan atmosphere, forgo the setting and follow your nose into the port's backstreets.

On the south side of town you will find a small beach and a marina, home to some pricier restaurants. Near the bus station at the western end of the marina stands the church of the **Panagia Vrefotrofou,** which dates from the 12th century—another Cretan example of the ancient and modern standing side by side.

The pool that acts as the inner harbor, **Lake Voulismeni,** is known as the Bottomless Lake because of its very steeply sloping sides, and it is indeed deep for its size, although it isn't bottomless.

The depth has been measured at 210 feet (64 m). The lake is linked to the outer harbor by a channel built between 1867 and 1871. Overlooking the channel is the town's **Folk Museum,** well worth seeing for its Cretan costumes, and the distinctive crafts and folk art of the island.

Agios Nikolaos has an excellent and modern **Archaeological Museum,** slightly away from downtown to the northwest. The museum has a good display of artifacts from several Minoan sites. One notable exhibit is the Goddess of Myrtos vase in Room II, found at Mochlos just outside Gournia (see p. 292). This vessel is made of clay and dates from the early Minoan period. It was probably used for fertility purposes; the neck and head are clearly phallic, while the body of the vessel shows two breasts.

The most unusual—if unsettling—exhibit is a skull thought to be that of an athlete. It was found intact, complete with the golden laurel wreath traditionally given for victories in athletics, and a silver coin to pay the dead man's fare to the ferryman for the journey across the River Styx to the underworld. The skull was found near the town and can be dated by the coin to the first century A.D. Its survival is remarkable.

The beaches around Agios Nikolaos are not especially good, but this does not prevent them from getting overcrowded in the summer. You can find better beaches at Elounda (see p. 289) and at **Ammoudara** and **Almyros** on the road toward Sitia. ■

**Folk Museum**

- ✉ Palaiologou 2
- ☎ 284/102-5093
- 🕐 Closed Sat., Mon., & Oct.–April
- 💲 $

**Archaeological Museum**

- ✉ Palaiologou 68
- ☎ 284/102-4943
- 🕐 Closed Mon.
- 💲 $

# Gournia

A mere 12 miles (19 km) south and east of the clamor of modern Agios Nikolaos is a magical place—one of the best preserved of all the Minoan towns on Crete. Gournia is also a site that reminds us of what can happen to even the busiest of communities over long periods of time. Ancient Gournia, a flourishing town in Minoan times, was first inhabited about 5,000 years ago.

The small Minoan town of Gournia was first excavated in 1904.

**Gournia**
- Map p. 275
- 284/209-3028
- Closed Mon.
- $

It now stands deserted on a small hill overlooking the beautiful Gulf of Mirabello. Few visitors take the trouble to make the slight detour off the busy road between Agios Nikolaos and Sitia, but it is worth it.

Gournia centers around the remains of a palace that, at only one-tenth its size, was significantly less important than Knossos. Yet it is that small scale, and the preservation of the ruins, that brings the town to life in the imagination. Here you see a maze of streets, lined with the foundations of simple one-roomed houses—very like the jumble of backstreets you will find in the older Cretan towns today. The paving of the main street survives, so you are stepping on the very same place that the

ancient Cretans walked around 1550 to 1450 B.C.

Most of the remains date from that era. Like other Minoan sites on Crete, Gournia was destroyed in a fire caused by the cataclysmic event—probably an earthquake—that wiped out the Minoans around 1450 B.C. You can still see the steps that lead up to the palace entrance and alongside them a massive stone slab where animals were probably tethered prior to their sacrifice. Or it may simply have been a butcher's block.

Gournia was a busy commercial center, with evidence of pottery, carpentry, metalworking, fishing, and weaving. Once again, the similarities with modern Cretan communities are evident. ∎

**INSIDER TIP:**

**At Gournia, don't just poke around the fenced-in area of the site, but walk down to the beach, where Minoan ship sheds are still visible, marking the original Bronze Age harbor works for the town.**

—DONALD HAGGIS
*National Geographic field scientist*

# Sitia & Ierapetra

Despite being the capital of the eastern province of Crete, Sitia is off the main tourist trail and so makes a good base for anyone who wants to have a taste of the real Crete. Taste is the word, as the food here is authentically hearty and Cretan. Ierapetra is the chief south-coast settlement in eastern Crete and boasts of being the most southerly city in Europe.

## Sitia

Here the principal crop is not tourists but raisins. Every August Sitia hosts the Raisin Festival, a lively occasion with music, dancing, and all the Cretan wine you can drink. There is plenty to see and do in Sitia at other times, too, including the 13th-century **Venetian fortress**, partly restored as an open-air theater. A small **Folklore Museum** has examples of regional crafts. In the excellent **Archaeological Museum** (*Piskokefalou 3, tel 284/302-3917, closed Mon., $*) look for the Minoan kouros

statue made of ivory; it shows the damage inflicted by the fire that wiped out Minoan settlements in 1450 B.C.

## Ierapetra

This was first a Dorian settlement, a gateway for trade with the Middle East. Today the trade is in tourism. Outside town are long beaches, backed by equally long stretches of hotels, villas, and tavernas. In town are a small **Archaeological Museum** (*Adrianou Koustoula, tel 284/202-8721, closed Mon., $*) and the remains of a 13th-century **fortress**. ∎

### Sitia
⬛ Map p. 275
**Visitor Information**
✉ Waterfront
☎ 284/302-8300

**Folklore Museum**
✉ Kapetan Sifi 33
🕐 Closed Nov.–March
💲 $

**Ierapetra**
⬛ Map p. 275

---

## EXPERIENCE: Greece at Easter

Easter is the biggest feast in the Greek religious calendar, and it is celebrated widely and enthusiastically. Everyone joins in on this feast, for several days, and it's a very special time for visitors to be in Greece. It celebrates not just the Resurrection of Christ but also the coming of a new year, as Easter indicates the arrival of summer. It's also a time for families to get together, so be prepared for transport to be busy.

If you're planning an Easter a visit, make sure to check the dates first. The Orthodox Easter can occur a few weeks to either side of the Western Easter. In nearly every town things begin on about the Thursday before Easter, when it's essential to visit the churches to see them being decorated with flowers in

readiness for the services. On Friday evening the richly decorated funeral bier symbolically carrying Christ's body is paraded through the streets, with the priest leading the way and people processing behind. Others stand in their windows and doorways to watch. It can be a moving experience to join the procession, and to feel yourself swept up in the faith of the Greeks.

Events climax at midnight on Saturday, the moment when the priest announces to the people that "Christ is Risen" and everyone lights their candles from those next to them, to walk home through the streets. Sunday is celebrated with a big lunch, often outdoors, and it's common for visitors to be invited to share in the joy of the day.

# Phaestus

The Palace of Phaestus in south-central Crete was second only to Knossos in size and importance, but outshone—and still outshines—it in terms of location. Phaestus stands spectacularly on a plateau overlooking the wide and fertile Messara Plain. To the north you can see the slopes that rise to their peak in Mount Psiloreitis, more popularly known as Mount Ida, at 8,058 feet (2,456 m), the highest point on Crete. It is an incomparable setting.

A curve on the shallow steps of Phaestus enables rainwater to run off quickly—one example of the palace's extensive and sophisticated drainage system.

**Phaestus**
- Map p. 274
- 289/209-1315
- $$

The history of Phaestus is the history of many other Minoan sites. The first palace was built here in about 1900 B.C. but destroyed by the same earthquake that devastated the island and its cities in 1700 B.C. A second palace was quickly constructed, only to be wiped out along with the Minoans in 1450 B.C. At Phaestus, however, some remains of the first palace still survive. They were found by Italian archaeologist Federico Halbherr,

who undertook the first major exploration of Phaestus in 1900.

The layout of the site is similar to that of Knossos, but little attempt has been made at reconstruction. At Phaestus the remains have merely been uncovered and cleaned up, with small amounts of reconstruction here and there, for example where walls were known to have collapsed.

The hillside on which Phaestus was built has been incorporated into the construction as the **Grand Staircase** of the palace, 45 feet (13 m) wide and consisting of 12 steps that have been partly carved out of the ground. The steps use the common Greek architectural trick of being slightly curved, in this case marginally higher in the center than at either end, which makes them look straight and emphasizes their grandeur.

At the top of the Grand Staircase is the west entrance to the second palace, and over to the right is the equally grand **Central Courtyard,** a common feature of these great Minoan palaces. The colonnades that lined two sides of the courtyard have gone, but the view from the north side toward Mount Psiloreitis is as impressive today as it was 4,000 years ago. To the palace dwellers, the view was of particular significance because the Kamares cave, a sacred place to the Minoans, was visible high on the mountainside. Certain rooms in the palace also enjoyed a view of Kamares.

To the north of the courtyard is the entrance to the royal apartments, and you can still see the remains of the sentry boxes where the guards stood watch on either side. As you walk down the corridor note the drainage channel beneath your feet: This passageway was open to the elements. Beyond it are the **Royal Apartments,** which have been fenced off because they are among the most important areas of the site. They contain separate chambers for the king and queen, the remains of a swimming pool, and even the remnants of a lavatory. Beyond here and

to your right is what was the **Archives Room,** which is where the Phaestus Disk was found (see below).

When visiting Phaestus, don't fail to make a small detour 2 miles (3 km) to the east to see the ruins of **Agia Triada,** a villa or palace built about 1600 B.C., perhaps as a summer residence for the royal family or for a wealthy resident of Phaestus. It has some superb frescoes, and many important finds were made here that are now on display in the Archaeological Museum in Iraklio (see p. 277). Historians believe that the

villa or palace originally stood much closer to the sea, which has retreated over the centuries. A sloping ramp in front of the villa may have led down to a small private harbor. ∎

### Agia Triada

🄰 Map p. 274

☎ 289/209-1360

💲 $

---

## Phaestus Disk

**It was in 1903 that the Phaestus Disk was discovered. The code encrypted in this baked clay disk, 6 inches (16 cm) in diameter and dating from 1700–1600 B.C., has yet to be cracked. Both sides are inscribed with pictorial symbols, much like Egyptian hieroglyphics, including people, animals, ships, and flowers, all radiating from the center. The disk may have some religious significance, possibly containing the words to a prayer. See for yourself at Iraklio's Archaeological Museum (see pp. 277-279).**

# Samaria Gorge Walk

One of the greatest experiences on Crete is to walk the Samaria Gorge (Farangi Samarias), the longest gorge in Europe. In fact, if visitor numbers are a guide, it is the island's second most popular attraction: Almost half a million people walk its length every year, a number exceeded only by visitors to Knossos.

Early in the season the wildflowers are at their best in the gorge. However, the river is still unpredictable, and the path may be closed at short notice, so check ahead.

**NOT TO BE MISSED:**

View from Omalos • The xyloskalon Samaria • Sidiroportes

most of the way it is perfectly achievable by the reasonably fit, plodding walker. Wear hiking boots and take a plentiful supply of food and some water—although you can replenish your water at fountains along the route.

The walk begins from a large, signed parking lot south of the village of **Omalos ❶**, where you can reserve accommodations. In this way you can beat the crowds by making an early

**INSIDER TIP:**

If you're in the White Mountains, you can hike or drive up to the Greek Mountaineering Club's Kallergi mountain refuge and be surrounded by the best views of the dramatic Samaria Gorge and the high summits.

—NICHOLAS TURLAND
*National Geographic field scientist*

At the height of summer thousands of people walk the gorge every day. If you can time your visit for late spring or early fall, there is a greater chance that you will be able to appreciate the grandeur and solitude. But even if you have to walk in the company of many others, it is still well worth doing.

The walk is about 11 miles (17 km) in total, and most people do it in five to seven hours. It is a demanding hike, but as you are descending

start. The gorge opens at 6 a.m. Keep your ticket, as it will be needed later.

From the parking lot head straight down the marked **xyloskalon ❷**, which means "wooden stairway." It is, in fact, a steep zigzag path cut out of the rock but with wooden rails for support and protection. This is one of the most spectacular parts of the walk, dropping by

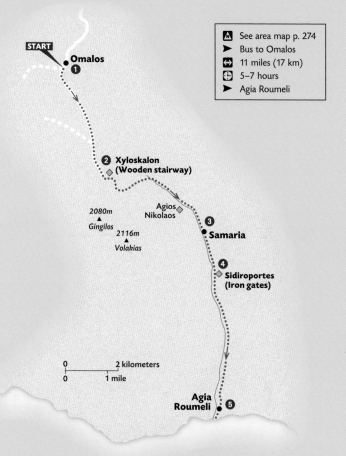

START
**Omalos** ❶

❷ **Xyloskalon (Wooden stairway)**

2080m ▲ **Gingilos**

2116m ▲ **Volakias**

**Agios Nikolaos**

❸ **Samaria**

❹ **Sidiroportes (Iron gates)**

**Agia Roumeli** ❺

🅝 See area map p. 274
► Bus to Omalos
⬌ 11 miles (17 km)
🕔 5–7 hours
► Agia Roumeli

0                    2 kilometers
0            1 mile

almost 2,300 feet (700 m) in just 2 miles (3 km). At the bottom is the tiny chapel of **Agios Nikolaos.** There are also benches if you want a rest after the challenging descent.

The path from here widens and levels out for a time and crosses back and forth over the stream that runs down the gorge. In winter and early spring, this can turn into a torrent, which is why the gorge is closed until May. In summer the stream turns into a pleasant and cooling trickle. About 4 miles (6.5 km) into the gorge, to the left, you pass the abandoned village of **Samaria** ❸, whose inhabitants left when the gorge was designated a national park in 1962.

Entering the most dramatic section of the walk, the gorge narrows until it is a mere 10 feet (3 m) wide at the so-called **Iron Gates, Sidiroportes** ❹, with the walls towering 1,000 feet (300 m) above. Then the walls widen out again, and you enter a broader valley with another abandoned village, Agia Roumeli, where safety procedures require you to hand in your ticket to show you have left the gorge.

Twenty minutes farther on is the modern village of **Agia Roumeli** ❺ and the sea—cool and welcoming for your tired feet. There are rooms here, or boats can take you to other coastal villages (principally Chora Sfakion; see p. 299) from where you can return to Rethimno or Hania by bus. Connecting buses run throughout the afternoon in summer but can get very crowded.

# Palaiochora & the South Coast

Crete's south coast is a series of jagged indents where mountains and gorges plunge dramatically to the sea. It would take a colossal feat of engineering to link the resorts by a coastal road, and as a result there is much less development here than in the north. However, in the height of summer the towns do get crowded.

Agia Galini on the south coast of Crete is a bustling resort town.

**Agia Galini**
🗺 Map p. 274

**Amari Valley**
🗺 Map p. 274

The resort of **Agia Galini,** west of Phaestus, is a case in point. The archetypal Greek coastal settlement, it was once a small, quiet fishing village. Now it is a large, busy tourist town. An old part survives, in charming contrast to the rest of the town, and the area around the harbor has a row of lively tavernas.

A popular drive from here leads inland to the **Amari Valley,** in the shadow of Mount Psiloreitis (Mount Ida). This is the heart of Crete, where some men still wear the traditional costume of baggy black pants and high mountain boots. It's an area of rural villages, fertile valleys, and dramatic gorges.

West of here, the Kourtaliotiko Gorge leads down to the coastal monastery of **Moni Piso Preveli.** It dates from the 17th–19th centuries. You can visit, but it is still a working monastery, so dress respectfully (see Dress to Visit below).

In the resort of **Plakias** farther along the coast, a 1.2-mile (2 km) strip of sandy beach attracts sunbathers galore, and more beaches are accessible along the coast. Plakias sits at the end of another scenic ravine, the Kotsyfou Gorge. The next major town west, Chora Sfakion, is close to the **Imbros Gorge,** almost as impressive as the Samaria Gorge and less visited.

Rising from a rare stretch of coastal plain between Plakias and Sfakion are the remains of the Venetian fortress of **Frangokastelo,** built in 1371, whose walls survive in almost perfect condition. Little remains of the interior, but its atmospheric setting by the sea and the view from outside make a visit well worthwhile. It was built partly to protect this rugged coast from pirates, but also to keep the local population in order. The residents of the next town along the coast, Chora Sfakion, had a particular reputation for troublesome independence.

**Chora Sfakion** is the preferred base for those who want to enjoy some of Crete's finest scenery and see something of its traditional way of life. The town's location, hemmed in to the west by a steep mountain range—meant that for many years access was almost entirely by sea. Today the road across the island snakes down in a dramatic series of hairpin bends. Modern life has impinged less on the town than elsewhere. It is busy and popular with visitors, but local residents have held on to their history and traditions much more strongly. Those traditions include tribal feuding, but also immense hospitality to the outside visitor. Here again, some of the older men still wear traditional costume.

Tourism reached the westernmost resort of **Palaiochora** many years ago, and although it remained relatively quiet for a long time, recently it has boomed as a tourist resort. The town has two fine beaches on either side of a headland topped by the remains of a Venetian fortress and excellent conditions for windsurfing and other water sports. It is a good base for those who like to mix relaxation with exploration. ∎

**Chora Sfakion**
Map p. 274

**Palaiochora**
Map p. 274

## Dress to Visit a Monastery

You will probably visit a monastery at some stage of your visit to Greece, and respectful dress and behavior is called for. Although monasteries are used to foreign visitors, and in summer can be overrun with them, it is still important to dress properly. Women should avoid bare shoulders and skimpy shorts, although it's common to see Greek men in shorts touring monasteries. Some places are more tolerant than others, but you won't know till you get there, so be sure to have a cover-up option with you. In some places you might be turned away, though most will have a robe of some kind that you can don for the visit.

# West Coast

The west coast is a very special part of Crete that has not yet been modernized. There are some busy resorts, of course, but there are even more unspoiled villages where the men while away their time in the cafés as they have done for centuries. The beaches are wonderful and comparatively isolated.

**Elafonisos**

🗺 Map p. 274

**Kastelli Kissamos**

🗺 Map p. 274

About 8 miles (13 km) north-west of Palaiochora is the stunning beach at **Elafonisos,** with its pink-white sand and deep-blue water under an azure sky. Summer temperatures remind you that North Africa is only 190 miles (306 km) away. The sea is very shallow, and it's possible to wade out to the nearest of the little offshore islands, where another idyllic beach awaits. While the main beach gets busy, development is limited. Access to the beach is along a windy road, discouraging some lazy car users.

Inland and overlooked by the 3,878-foot (1,182 m) peak of

Agios Dikaios is the main town of this region, **Elos.** The area is known as **Kastanokhoria,** "chestnut villages," after the main local crop, celebrated with a big Chestnut Festival in late October.

The hair-raising coast road takes you through citrus orchards and olive groves, with hills on one side and the wine-dark Aegean on the other. The main town at the northern end of the west coast is **Kastelli Kissamos,** a place that goes about its own business, not worrying too much about visitors but welcoming them all the same. Sit in the peaceful main square in the evening, enjoy a coffee or an ouzo, and people-watch. ∎

## EXPERIENCE: Cretan Culture

Tourism can be very beneficial to local communities, by bringing income to them and helping to keep small towns and villages alive. Thoughtful travelers might seek out these opportunities, as a way to put something back into the communities that provide them with such wonderful and memorable experiences.

One such enterprising community is the village of Vamos in northwest Crete, a few miles inland from the popular beach resorts of Almerida and Kalives. The latter were themselves once fishing villages, now given over to tourism; while they are still charming little resorts, there is no doubt that life in Almerida and Kalives has changed in significant ways. Some villagers in Vamos decided to preserve their

traditions by showing them to foreign visitors and making them part of the travel experience.

They began by renovating some old cottages, restoring them to provide modern comforts in a traditional village house setting. In addition to being able to stay in one of these beautiful cottages, visitors to Vamos have the opportunity to learn about Cretan culture in a number of ways. These include dancing classes, cookery lessons, and the chance to join in the grape or olive harvest at the right time of year, including treading the grapes. For further details, contact Vamos Apokoronou *(Chania, Crete, 73008 Greece, tel 282/502-3251, fax 282/502-3100, www .vamossa.gr).*

# Maleme

**The Battle of Crete, which raged for ten days in May 1941, was a momentous event in Cretan history. To learn something of the grim truth of this disastrous episode and its aftermath, a visit to the main site of the battle at Maleme, on the coast west of Hania, now the site of the German War Cemetery, is essential.**

German War Cemetery graves are tended with care, despite memories of the German occupation.

The Allied airfield at Maleme was the target of German paratroopers who invaded the island in 1941, after Greece had fallen to the German forces. The Allies, for whom Crete had been a vital naval base, retreated across the island and were mostly evacuated by sea from the south coast. It was an extraordinary operation that involved the help of many local people, who put their own lives in danger. Fierce fighting by the Cretan resistance continued until 1945.

The **German War Cemetery** is laid out on the crown of what was known as Hill 107. A small building near the entrance acts as the information center; with a map showing how the battle progressed. The hill is covered with rows of graves. The German losses were 6,580 men, many of them shot by snipers as they parachuted down. Today in the spring the lower slopes are strewn with wildflowers, bringing serenity to this turbulent spot.

From the top of the hill you can look down on the Maleme airstrip, the vital piece of land that was the focus for the attack and which had to be seized at all costs. The airstrip is still in military use.

For a fuller picture, go on to the smaller **Commonwealth War Cemetery,** at the end of the Akrotiri peninsula north of Hania. This is the burial place of 1,522 of the 2,000 Allied dead from the Battle of Crete—Britons, Australians, and New Zealanders who died alongside the Cretan men, women, and children fighting to defend their island. ■

**Maleme**

🗺 Map p. 274

# Hania

The main city in western Crete, Hania is one of the most appealing towns on the island (also written as Chania, Khania, or Kania). Its perfect setting, lively harbor, historical remains, busy market, interesting museums, and nearby beaches make it the ideal spot. It retains its unique charm and character no matter how many visitors pack into the streets.

The deceptively space-age Mosque of the Janissaries stands out on Hania's busy waterfront.

**Hania**

⬛ Map p. 274

**Visitor Information**

✉ Akti Tombnzi

☎ 282/102-0369

Big enough to have all the facilities of a city, Hania is nevertheless on a human scale, a place you quickly find your way around, where you soon start to feel at home.

The setting undoubtedly helps. To the north are the sparkling blue waters of the Sea of Crete, while to the south is the Lefka Ori range of mountains, and the White Mountains, the backbone of this end of the island. If you choose your waterfront café carefully, you may be able to see snow-topped mountains and azure seas at the same time. There is no better

place for a breakfast of Greek yogurt with local honey and fresh fruit—or for lunch, or maybe for a romantic dinner as the sun begins to set.

Parts of the **waterfront** are lined with tall mansions, creating an effect not unlike that of Venice. Of course the Venetians are just one of several groups of people who have made their impact on this beautiful place. It was an important Minoan city, but one that is relatively unknown, as the modern city has been added layer after layer on top of the Minoan remains. The site of

Kydonia (as the Minoan city was called) is being excavated within the city boundaries, but it will be some time before it is open to the public.

The best finds from Kydonia are on display in Hania's **Archaeological Museum,** which is also rich in artifacts from other sites in western Crete. It has a fine pottery collection and several superb sculptures and mosaics. The building itself is of interest, although the outside belies the interior. It was once the Venetian Church of San Francesco and later converted into a mosque by the Turks. You can see the remnants of a minaret and a fountain in a pretty little courtyard.

Turkish influence is evident elsewhere, such as the **Mosque of the Janissaries,** right on the harbor. It dates from 1645 and is the oldest surviving Ottoman building on Crete. It was damaged in World War II, then restored, and for many years made an unmissable tourist information center; after renovation, however, it lies empty.

The bulk of the harbor reflects Hania's Venetian era, especially in the restored **Firkas** fortress. It's an interesting place to wander around, with good views of the harbor. One of its towers contains the **Naval Museum,** with a collection of model ships and accounts of sea battles in the waters off the coast. Even if you are not a naval enthusiast, it is worth a visit to see an incredibly detailed scale model of Hania as it was in the 17th century, town as well as harbor, including the Venetian Arsenale, or boatyards, which can

still be seen on the harbor. The Naval Museum also contains one of the most vivid accounts of the Battle of Crete that you will see anywhere on the island.

Hania's Historical Museum, tucked away in the southeastern corner of the city, is well worth walking out to. You may want to stop on the way at the bustling **Central Market,** a huge hall offering souvenirs as well as the usual array of fresh fish, meat, vegetables, and delicious cheeses.

The **Historical Museum** is located in what was obviously once an elegant town house, at

**INSIDER TIP:**

**The scenic Omalos plateau is a great excursion from Hania; the entrance from the road is called Neratzoporta. On the way up you will see a picture-perfect village called Lokki. Stop and take a photo!**

—ARTEMIS LAMPATHAKIS
*National Geographic retiree*

a time when this area was one of Hania's more fashionable districts during the late 19th and early 20th centuries. Among the collected memorabilia of local worthies are some gems, including excellent information on the Cretan resistance movement during World War II and the earlier struggle for independence from the Turks. ■

**Archaeological Museum**
- ✉ Chalidon 21
- ☎ 282/109-0334
- ⏱ Closed Mon.
- 💲 $

**Naval Museum**
- ✉ Akti Kountourioti
- ☎ 282/102-6437
- 💲 $

**Historical Museum**
- ✉ Sfakianaki 20
- ⏱ Closed Sat.–Sun.

# Rethimno

With a population of some 25,000, Rethimno (sometimes written Rethymnon or Rethimnon) is Crete's third largest city. It feels, however, more like a scaled-down, more touristy version of Hania, complete with a similar harbor, architecture with clear Venetian and Turkish influences, and a strong traditional culture.

Cafés and fish restaurants crowd around the inner harbor.

**Rethimno**
⚑ Map p. 274
**Visitor Information**
✉ E. Venizelou, Paralia
☎ 283/102-9148

**Fortetsa**
✉ Katechaki
☎ 283/102-8101
💲 $

**Archaeological Museum**
✉ Cheimaras
☎ 283/105-4668
🕐 Closed Mon.
💲 $

The Greco-Roman town of Rithymna preceded modern Rethimno, and the site is known to have been occupied since Minoan times. There are no palatial remains but many from the Greco-Roman period, when Rethimno was already a busy trading center and port. During the 16th century the city boomed under Venetian rule, acquiring a reputation for art and scholarship that it retains to this day.

The town's dominant feature is the **Fortetsa,** a Venetian fortress. It was built in the 1570s to defend against pirate attack as well as to keep one prescient eye on the Turks' increasing power. The strength of the fortress, however, was short-lived: The Turks conquered it in 1645 after a siege that lasted 23 days.

The Fortetsa is said to be the biggest Venetian fortress ever built and is still in quite good condition. Inside are the remains of some administrative buildings, a barracks, cisterns, the church of St. Catherine, and the Sultan Ibrahim Mosque. It is even big enough to contain a small theater, used for performances in summer. The views from the huge ramparts over coast and town alone are worth the visit.

Opposite the entrance to the Fortetsa is the former prison, which now houses the **Archaeological Museum.** The conversion has been well done and the displays are arranged in rooms around a light, central atrium. Although the city itself is not rich in Minoan remains, the surrounding area certainly is, and the museum has an excellent collection of them, including a fascinating and large selection of painted burial chests known as *larnakes*. There is a good range of statuary, especially from the Greco-Roman period.

To the south of the Archaeological Museum lies the old part of the town, with numerous structures of historical interest that seem far removed from the jostle of foreign visitors in the harbor tavernas and on the town beaches. Life in the old town centers around the **Rimondi Fountain,** which stands at one end of a busy main street surrounded by cafés and stores. The fountain was built in 1629 by the Venetian governor (he was jealous of the Morosini Fountain in Iraklio, so they say), with waterspouts in the shape of the lions' heads that are emblematic of Venice. About 50 yards (46 m) to the south is an even older building, the 16th-century **loggia,** built by the Venetians as a marketplace. The former home of the Archaeological Museum, it is now the museum shop.

Southeast of the loggia is the little **Venetian harbor,** able to take only smaller boats and the local fishing fleet; the bigger inter-island and Pireas ferries are forced to moor outside. It's here that the fishermen can be found mending their nets and in the mornings selling their catch from the night before. The 16th-century lighthouse here is another notable Venetian legacy. By night the scene is transformed, as all the world comes to the harbor to see and be seen, and to eat and drink the night away.

Some 14 miles (23 km) southeast of Rethimno, in a spectacular setting at the head of a gorge and surrounded by groves of fruit trees, stands the 16th-century monastery of **Moni Arkadiou,** a must on any itinerary. In 1866 the invading Turks attacked villagers hiding out here; the Cretans lit a store of gun powder, and the ensuing explosion killed all but one little girl. The ornate, double-naved church is the most impressive feature. ■

**Moni Arkadiou**
- Map p. 274
- 283/108-3076 or 283/108-3116
- $

---

# EXPERIENCE: Teach English to Children on Crete

The island of Crete is a very special part of Greece, with a long and proud culture. One way to gain a better insight into this is to get to know local people and to gain their respect by helping contribute something to their community. Instead of going to Greece to learn Greek for yourself, another option is to go there to teach English to local people.

There are plenty of chances to go to Athens to teach English to students or to business people, but more interesting opportunities exist. With **Elderhostel** (*11 Avenue de Lafayette, Boston, MA 02111, tel 800/454-5768, www.elderhostel.org*) you can go to Amoudara, just west of Iraklio, to teach English to children. You'll work with local teachers in the classroom, facilitating conversation lessons. The two-week schedule allows plenty of time to also explore the island's highlights, including the Palace at Knossos and the Samaria Gorge. Also built into the programs, which begin in late March, is the chance to attend community events, meet with local community leaders, and generally get a deeper understanding of life in Crete today than the average vacation will provide.

Accommodation is in a three-star, family-run hotel, close to the sea but surrounded by vineyards. Meals are also included, and you do not need to have had any previous teaching experience, as coaching will be given. Prices start from $2,900 per person.

# More Places to Visit on Crete

Crete's rugged southern coast, near Chora Sfakion

## Archanes

The Minoan site of Archanes lies at the twin villages of Kato and Archanes, south of Knossos, in a green region of olive groves and vineyards, source of much of Crete's wine. On the site of the Temple of Anemospilia, in what was evidently a large town, the remains of four bodies were found in 1979. Their position has led to speculation that the Minoans were carrying out a human sacrifice when the temple was destroyed in an earthquake. Today the scene is much more peaceful.
Map p. 275

## Gavdos

The remote island of Gavdos, reachable by boat from Palaiochora or Chora Sfakion, has the distinction of being the most southerly point in Europe. It has few other distinctions, although the handful of people who still live here claim that this was the island of Calypso, described in Homer's *Odyssey.*

The capital, such as it is, is **Kastri,** and there are rooms and a taverna in the tiny resort of **Korfos,** with pretty beaches around the island. But if you're planning any kind of a visit, check ahead for both accommodations and return ferries. Out of season, even the two ferries per week are not kept up.
Map p. 274

## Limenas Hersonisou

One of Crete's major summer resorts, Limenas Hersonisou's streets are filled with bars and discos, and in summer there's little evidence of the original fishing village. A Roman fountain with delightful mosaic decoration, from the second or third century A.D., remains on the waterfront. But it's the culture of the popular **Aqua Splash Water Park** (*$$$*) that dominates.
Map p. 275 **Tourist Police** ☎ 289/ 702-1000

## Theriso Gorge

If your fitness does not allow you to walk the Samaria Gorge (see pp. 296–297), then drive through this gorge, south of Hania, for spectacular scenery. Vehicles on the snaking road are dwarfed by the sheer cliffs.

## Zakros

The fourth largest Minoan palace is the Palace of Zakros, at the remote eastern end of Crete and usually free of visitors. It was an important trading port for the eastern Mediterranean, and while the palace itself has not survived well, surrounding houses and other buildings are better preserved.
Map p. 275 ☎ 284/306-1204
🕐 Closed Mon.

Strong European influences and the closest of the Greek islands—culturally and physically—to Italy and the rest of Western Europe

# Corfu & the Ionian Islands

Zakinthos cliffs and arches

# Corfu & the Ionian Islands

**Located just a short boat ride across the Ionian Sea from Italy, Corfu (Kerkira) and the other Ionian islands have been popular vacation destinations since Roman times. Visitor numbers today are higher, especially in resorts such as Kavos and Sidari, which have opened the floodgates to mass tourism aimed at young people who want to party all night.**

Gaïos, on Paxi, has its own little tree-covered offshore island.

This aspect of the islands is generally restricted to a handful of resorts, leaving the rest of the region in comparative peace.

There is plenty to enjoy. Anyone who has visited the dry, hot Aegean islands will be astonished at how green the Ionians are, with vast stretches of olive groves, vineyards, and citrus orchards. This of course indicates that they receive more rain than the Aegean islands. But when winter departs, spring here is glorious and recommended to anyone who loves walking amid carpets of wildflowers and searching out the many species of orchid that grow here.

Sample some of the local food specialties, including *sofrito,* which is a flavorful veal dish, and *bourdetto,* a spicy fish dish. Kefalonia's golden honey is excellent, as are its quince preserves and almond pralines. Wines from Theotaki and

Liapaditiko come recommended as well.

The Ionian islands encompass enormous variety. Visit Corfu town, and you will find how much more cosmopolitan it is than other island capitals due to the influence of the French, Venetians, and British who have all ruled here since the 11th century.

Yet an hour or so south is the tiny island of Paxi, with just three small towns and a cluster of little inland communities. It's the smallest of the main Ionian islands, but some say the best olive oil in Greece is made here.

South again from Paxi is even smaller Andipaxi, with just a handful of inhabitants, some rooms and villas to rent, and guaranteed tranquillity. Ithaca is another tiny but famous island, the legendary home of Odysseus. The other main Ionian islands—Lefkada, Kefalonia,

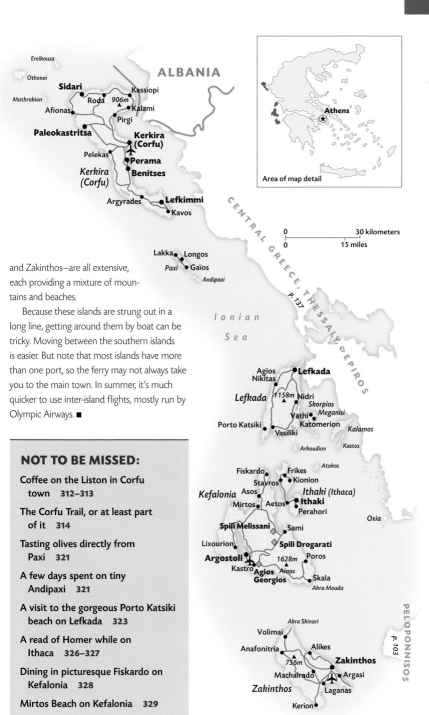

and Zakinthos—are all extensive, each providing a mixture of mountains and beaches.

Because these islands are strung out in a long line, getting around them by boat can be tricky. Moving between the southern islands is easier. But note that most islands have more than one port, so the ferry may not always take you to the main town. In summer, it's much quicker to use inter-island flights, mostly run by Olympic Airways. ∎

## NOT TO BE MISSED:

**Coffee on the Liston in Corfu town  312–313**

**The Corfu Trail, or at least part of it  314**

**Tasting olives directly from Paxi  321**

**A few days spent on tiny Andipaxi  321**

**A visit to the gorgeous Porto Katsiki beach on Lefkada  323**

**A read of Homer while on Ithaca  326–327**

**Dining in picturesque Fiskardo on Kefalonia  328**

**Mirtos Beach on Kefalonia  329**

# Corfu

The most northerly of the Ionian islands, Corfu (Kerkira) is the closest to both Italy in the west and Albania in the east, and it has been touched over the years by several other foreign cultures. As a result it has acquired a certain sophistication and an offbeat charm. It is the only place in Greece where the game of cricket is played, a legacy from the days of British influence (1814–1908).

**Corfu (Kerkira)**

🅰 Map pp. 309 & 311

The Greek name for the island is Kerkira, which is something to remember if you are heading there by ferry or bus. (There are buses to Corfu town from

With their balconies and arches, the narrow backstreets of Corfu town are reminiscent of Venice.

Athens and even from as far as Thessaloniki in Macedonia. The Greek bus network doesn't let a little water stand in its way—the bus goes onto the ferry and continues its journey on the other side.)

The name Kerkira derives from Corcyra, who was the daughter of the river god Asopos. The great sea god Poseidon fell in love with her and brought her to this island, which he then named after her. Their son Phaeax went on to found the Phaeacian race (the Phaeacians were kind hosts to Odysseus on his ill-fated journey home following the Greek victory at Troy; see pp. 326–327). The name Corfu is an Italian version of the ancient Greek word *koryphai*, meaning "the hills," referring not to the mountainous north of the island, but rather to the two elevated spots in Corfu town where the Old and New Fortresses were founded.

There is evidence of human habitation 40,000 years ago in the area of modern Corfu town, at a time when the island was joined to the mainland. The island's fertility, size, and natural beauty all contributed to its development, and by the time of the Persian Wars (520–448 B.C.) it was so powerful that only Athens sent a larger naval fleet to the Greek

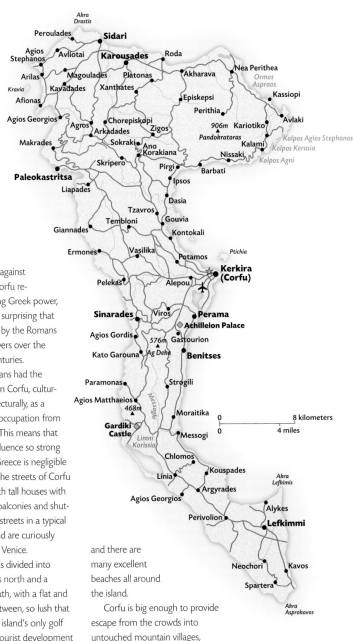

forces massed against the Persians. Corfu remained a strong Greek power, and it is hardly surprising that it was coveted by the Romans and other powers over the succeeding centuries.

The Venetians had the most impact on Corfu, culturally and architecturally, as a result of their occupation from 1386 to 1797. This means that the Turkish influence so strong elsewhere in Greece is negligible here. Instead, the streets of Corfu town, lined with tall houses with wrought-iron balconies and shutters, resemble streets in a typical Italian town and are curiously reminiscent of Venice.

The island is divided into a mountainous north and a lower-lying south, with a flat and fertile plain between, so lush that it provides the island's only golf course. Most tourist development is in the northeast of the island, spreading north from Corfu town,

and there are many excellent beaches all around the island.

Corfu is big enough to provide escape from the crowds into untouched mountain villages, as the drive described on pages 316–317 shows.

**Palaio Frourio**

✉ The Esplanade, Corfu town

💲 $

# Corfu Town

Nowhere is the pan-European background of the Ionian Islands more evident than in beguiling Corfu town. It may have Greek tavernas in the backstreets and may celebrate Easter even more exuberantly than the rest of Greece (try to catch the breaking of the crockery on the morning of Holy Sunday), but it also shows very strong influences from Britain, France, and Italy in its architecture. Residents of Corfu town proudly regard themselves as more sophisticated than people from other Greek island capitals.

This cosmopolitan mix is most evident in the very center of town, around the **Esplanade.** This combination of park and town square centers on a very English-looking cricket field, once a Venetian firing range. At the far end, on a promontory sticking out into the Ionian Sea, stands the Venetian **Palaio Frourio (Old Fortress),** completed in 1559 on a site believed to have been fortified since the seventh century A.D.

At the north end of the cricket field stands the **Palace of St. Michael and St. George,** constructed between 1819 and 1824 as the residence of the British High Commissioner. It was renovated in the 1950s and now contains administrative buildings, a library, the tourist office, and, in one wing, the **Museum of Asiatic Art** *(tel 266/103-0443, closed Mon.).* This collection, unique in Greece, was built up from 10,000 items amassed by Grigorios Manos (1850–1929), a Greek diplomat from Corfu who traveled extensively in the Orient.

At the western end is the **Liston,** a row of cafés and stores that could only be French. It was built by a Frenchman in 1807 at

**The chapel at Viahema along the coast**

the request of Napoleon, who wanted its colonnades to echo the famous rue de Rivoli in Paris. The cafés along the Liston are where everyone comes to socialize. Your coffee will cost more here than

INSIDER TIP:

**Perfect hammock reading for understanding the isles?** *My Family & Other Animals,* **the story of Gerald Durrell's childhood on the Greek island of Corfu; and the sumptuously illustrated** *The Greek Islands,* **by his brother Lawrence Durrell.**

—CHRISTOPHER BAKER
*National Geographic author*

anywhere else in Corfu, but it's *the* place to be.

At the southern side is a park with a magnificent fountain and, nearby, the **Enosis Monument (Unification Monument).** This monument celebrates the occasion in 1864 when the Ionian islands were at last united with the rest of Greece after their final period of British rule.

### Around Corfu Town:

There are numerous sites and museums about Corfu town that you should see. Stay for at least a few days if you can. The star attraction alone at the **Archaeological Museum** *(Odos Vraila 5, tel 266/103-0680, closed Mon.,*

*$$)* is worth the visit: a fearsome Gorgon frieze made in the sixth century B.C. for the Temple of Artemis in the southern suburbs of Corfu town.

The enjoyable **Paper Money Museum** *(Ionian Bank, Plateia Iroon Kypriakou, tel 266/104-1552, closed Sun.)* tells the fascinating story of how banknotes are made and shows how Corfu's currency has reflected political changes. Exhibits include notes issued in German and Italian currency during World War II.

The **Byzantine Museum** *(tel 266/103-8313, closed Mon.),* in the church of the Panagia Antivouniotissa, has a small and stylishly displayed collection of icons, some dating back to the 15th century. Look for examples of work by the so-called Cretan school, from the days when Cretan artists would visit Corfu on their way to study with the masters in Venice.

Don't miss the **church** dedicated to the island's patron saint, Agios Spyridon. His mummified body is contained in a silver casket inside, and four times a year this is carried through the streets to celebrate the occasions when the saint is believed to have come to the rescue of islanders during battles and plagues. Religious fervor combines with partying, and these are marvelous times to be in Corfu town: Palm Sunday, Easter Saturday, August 11, and the first Sunday in November.

### Northern Corfu

The northern half of Corfu is by far the most dramatically diverse part of the island—although if you drive north out of Corfu

**Kalami**
Map p. 311

**Mount Pandokratoras**
Map p. 311

town along the main coast road, the first few miles give no indication of the historical and geographical riches in store.

The first resorts you come to—**Gouvia, Dasia, Ipsos, and Pirgi**—offer wonderful beaches and plenty of water-sports facilities. Popular with families, they have lost any sense of individuality. It is not until the road approaches the lower slopes of **Mount Pandokratoras** that you start to see signs of true charm in villages like **Nissaki** and, later, **Kalami.**

Kalami's claim to fame is the White House (no presidents here, though), just behind the beach, where British novelist Lawrence Durrell (1912–1990) lived while writing his book about Corfu, *Prospero's Cell.* He was visited here by his friend, American writer Henry Miller (1891–1980). Miller's *Colossus of Maroussi* includes his

visit to Corfu and remains one of the most vivid books ever written about Greece.

Corfu's prettiest bays, including Agni, Agios Stephanos, and Kerasia, are wonderful spots to enjoy a fish lunch, enhanced by the backdrop of towering **Mount Pandokratoras.** The mountain rises so steeply that its highest point, at 2,972 feet (906 m), is only 2 miles (3 km) from the coast. The mountain's bulk perfectly fits the translation of its name: the Almighty. Visible from almost everywhere, it dominates northern Corfu. You can drive all the way to the top of Mount Pandokratoras if you don't mind some rough road toward the end, but the best approach is on foot from the village of Old Perithia. The mountain is crisscrossed with paths, including the **Corfu Trail** (see Walk below), which runs the

## EXPERIENCE: Walk the Corfu Trail

There is good hiking to be had throughout Corfu, but the delightful Corfu Trail is the only long-distance footpath. It opened in 2001 and runs from the northern tip to the southern tip, a distance of about 137 miles (220 km). Experts say that walking from south to north is the best way to tackle the trail.

The Corfu Trail was the brainchild of an Englishwoman resident on Corfu, Hilary Whitton Paipeti. Part of her purpose in creating and maintaining it was to help bring visitors and income to some of the Corfu mountain villages, which were starting to die out as people moved down to the coast to work in the lucrative tourist trade. Paipeti encouraged people to open their houses to visitors for over-

night stays, which not only brings a boost to the local economy but provides the visitors with some wonderful experiences of Corfiot hospitality.

The best time to do the walk is from May to June, when Corfu is very green, and again in September and October, once the midsummer heat has passed. Paipeti has written a guide to the trail, or you can make arrangements through a travel agent in Corfu town, who will book accommodation for you and arrange luggage transfers each day, leaving you to carry just your day pack. For more information, contact **Aperghi Travel** (*tel 266/104-8713, www.travelling.gr/aperghi, e-mail: aperghi@travelling.gr*).

length of the island. The flowers, especially in spring, are spectacular. At the top await a small monastery and seemingly endless views over the island and across the sea to remote Albania.

The interior of northern Corfu has lots of mountain villages worth exploring, and the drive on pages 316–317 takes in some of the best. Apart from the occasional bus passing through on a scenic drive, the villagers live in a world hardly affected by the thousands of tourists on the nearby beaches.

The northern coastline has its own variety, and even within one of its busiest resorts—**Kassiopi**, in the east—it combines bustle with friendliness, in a picturesque setting around a small harbor, with a wooded headland at either end. Fishermen and water-sports enthusiasts both enjoy the seas. Emperor Nero is said to have visited a temple of Jupiter here, but this no longer exists.

## West Coast

The main resort in the west is **Sidari,** offering a good range of shops, bars, and restaurants. It is known to have had one of the first Neolithic settlements on Corfu, dating back to 7000 B.C. Some unusual rock formations are its main attraction. Wind and rain have weathered the sandstone into surreal swirls, most famously in the gap between two rocks known romantically as the Canal d'Amour. One story says that any couple swimming through the channel will stay together forever.

**Paleokastritsa** is the second major west-coast resort. So strong

Boats anchor in a rock-strewn cove near Paleokastritsa.

was its appeal to one British High Commissioner, Sir Frederick Adam (commissioner 1824–1831), that he had the road built to make access easier for him from Corfu town. It is easy to see the attraction. Green, wooded headlands stand over a deep blue sea, while a road zigzags down to a cluster of coves and sandy beaches, from where tourist boats ride out to visit hidden grottoes. With the 17th-century monastery of **Moni Theotokou** and the ruins of a 13th-century Byzantine fortress both close at hand, it would be pretty hard to design a more perfect vacation spot.

## Southern Corfu

The southern half of Corfu, from the capital down, is much less mountainous than the north but a lot more varied in its landscape.

**Kassiopi**
Map p. 311

**Sidari**
Map p. 311

**Paleokastritsa**
Map p. 311

# Drive: The Two Faces of Corfu

The marriage between traditional Greece and modern tourism affects every Greek island to some degree. Visitors who never stray from the beaches and the bars have no idea what life is like for the average Greek person. To drive through northern Corfu is to see both sides of the picture, from busy resorts to quiet mountain villages, as you take in some of the most breathtaking scenery on the island.

Sandstone eroded by the waves at Sidari

Leave **Corfu town** ① (see pp. 312–313) on the main coastal road (No. 24) going north, following the signs for the first two resorts, Kontokali and Gouvia. (In Corfu, road signs are in both Roman and Greek alphabets.)

In Gouvia the road divides. Take the left fork marked for Paleokastritsa, which takes you around the lower slopes of Mount Pandokratoras and through a delightful wooded valley. Pass through the village of **Sgombou,** and just over a mile (about 2 km) beyond here the road divides again. Take the right turn, towards Sidari.

The road now climbs to the **Troumbetas Pass** ②, one of the prettiest spots on the island, with some of the most dramatic views. All of the fertile Ropa Plain in the center of the island spreads out below to the left. At the pass, take the right turn for Roda and Sidari. The road now winds and descends through the villages on the western side of Mount Pandokratoras, places where rural life goes on

## NOT TO BE MISSED:
**Troumbetas Pass • Sidari • Avliotai • Kavadades**

as it has for centuries: Chorepiskopi, Valanio, Kiprianades, Xanthates, Platonas, and Sfakera. Stop in some of these places to walk around and get a feel for life in rural Corfu.

After Sfakera, continue toward the sea and the coastal road. When you reach it, turn left toward Karousades and Sidari. **Sidari** ③ (see p. 315) is the busiest resort on this part of the coast. You will find plenty of action on the waterfront, worth a stop to grab some lunch or just to admire the unusual rock formations. Continue on the main coastal road, and stop at a lookout at **Avliotai** ④ on the northwest corner of Corfu. There are three offshore islands here (Erikoussa, Othoni, and Mathraki), barely inhabited but with accommodations for a real get-away-from-it-all experience. Boats leave regularly from Sidari and other coastal towns.

Continue on through Arilas and, after about another mile (1.5 km), look for the left turn to Sidari. You are starting to complete a circle that will eventually return you to the Troumbetas

Pass. At **Kavadades ⑤,** leave the car and look for signs to the Viewpoint. This is a great view over the wooded mountains.

In Kavadades take the right turn toward Armenades. When you get there, turn right again through Dafni, then Agros, and back to the Troumbetas Pass. From here, return the way you first came, following the signs for Corfu town.

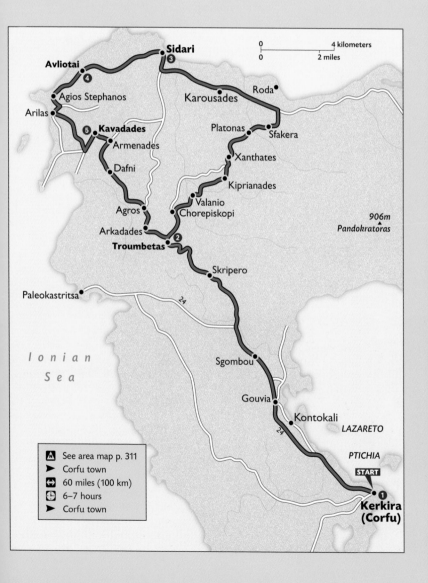

## Achilleion Palace
🅰 Map p. 311
☎ 266/105-6210
💲 $

## Benitses
🅰 Map p. 311

## Petrakis *Dolphin* Ferry
✉ Port of Corfu
💲 $$$ (Must clear customs on both sides)

## Hotel Kaonia
✉ Rr. 1. Maji, Saranda, Albania
☎ 355/852-2608

For visitors interested in architecture, the first stopping-off point south of Corfu town is the **Achilleion Palace.** "A monstrous building," according to British writer Lawrence Durrell, who spent part of his youth on Corfu with his naturalist brother Gerald. It has to be said that this building is not to everyone's taste with its mishmash of styles. But it cannot be denied that it is unique.

The Achilleion was built in 1890–1891 for Empress Elizabeth of Austria (1837–1898), wife of Emperor Franz Joseph (1830–1916). Elizabeth used her new palace as a retreat from the difficulties she was experiencing at the Habsburg court, not least the unfaithfulness of her husband. Another woe had been the suicide at Mayerling of her second son, Archduke Rudolph.

Elizabeth commissioned a design from an Italian architect that reflected her admiration for

**INSIDER TIP:**

Take the 9 a.m. *Dolphin* ferry from Corfu to Saranda, Albania; spend the night at Hotel Kaonia on the water. From there, visit the nearby islands at Ksamil for beautiful beaches or the untouched Butrinti ruins.

—BRIDGET ENGLISH
*National Geographic contributor*

Achilles, hero of the Trojan Wars. The palace is named after him, and he features prominently in statues and paintings throughout the house and gardens.

The gardens are absolutely beautiful, taking advantage of the climate to produce a riot of color, with terraces leading down to extensive breathtaking views along the coast. Some of the original furniture remains inside the house, although after the assassination of Elizabeth in 1898 the palace lay empty for nine years, until it was bought by Kaiser Wilhelm II (1859–1941). Today the Achilleion survives as a bustling tourist attraction, with a casino open in the summer.

Nothing could be further from the rarefied atmosphere of the Achilleion than the tourist resort of **Benitses,** a few miles down the coast. For those looking for a piece of the action, this is the place. In midsummer little remains of its origins as a fishing village, as it fills up with tourists. However, if you visit in the spring or fall

**Marble statuary adds feminine grace to the exuberant gardens of the Achilleion Palace.**

you may get a glimpse of the way things used to be. There are some Roman remains here, including part of an old bathhouse, but it's hardly worth breaking a journey to find them.

Beyond Benitses the resorts are more spread out, and you can enjoy driving down the coastal road, with the Ionian Sea on your left and green hills dotted with villas on your right. The bustle builds up again as you approach the twin you are sure to find some quiet stretches to yourself if you are prepared to walk to them. The relative peace attracts wildlife, which also appreciates the abundance of fresh water (rare on Corfu) that the lagoon provides. Look for ibises and egrets, along with waders such as stilts, sandpipers, and avocets. Rare Jersey orchids flower here in the spring. Snakes and lizards inhabit the nearby dunes, while the ditches, creeks, and

**Korissia Lagoon**
Map p. 311

**Gardiki Castle**
Map p. 311

---

## The Ouzo Effect

Regardless of bias, most Greeks will admit that the best ouzo comes from the island of Lesvos. But that doesn't preclude the other regions from competing.

Besides crystal blue sea water and olive oil, ouzo is the most famous liquid in Greece. So why not enjoy? Ouzo is an apéritif, similar to sambuca, pastis, or absinthe. In earlier times, it was prepared by fermenting of grape skins that were then distilled with anise and fennel seeds, though today it is more likely made from pure alcohol derived from grapes and infused with essential oils. It is served chilled or mixed with water but never on ice, as ice changes the chemistry and taste. There are many cocktail recipes—all are avoided by purists. For a guilty science experiment, add water to a shot of ouzo. The two clear liquids will combine to form a hazy cloud. This was coined "the ouzo effect" by scientists at Johns Hopkins University. If only Chemistry 101 was this fun.

The drink is often central to social gatherings, but it is usually served with meze, tapas style plates designed to provide a flavorful barrier against the effects of the alcohol. When the ouzo-to-meze ratio is correct, nobody will become too full or drunk, just at ease. And if you're far enough out of the tourist epicenters, many of these mezes are free.

---

resorts of Moraitika and Messogi, now more or less merged into one.

Just south of here on the western coast is one of the most interesting areas in the south, the **Korissia Lagoon (Limni Korissia).** The lagoon stretches for about 3 miles (5 km), cut off from the Ionian Sea by equally long expanses of beaches and sand dunes. The beaches and dunes are far from undiscovered, but they are so big compared with the number of people who venture here that pools around the lagoon provide habitats for frogs and turtles.

North of the lagoon is **Gardiki Castle,** built in the 13th century by Michail Angelos Komninos II, the Byzantine despot of Epiros. Komninos was also responsible for the Angelokastro, the ruined fortress near Paleokastritsa on the northwest coast. The walls and some of the towers of Gardiki still stand. The oldest human remains on Corfu were found near here, dated to 40,000 B.C. ∎

# Paxi & Andipaxi

Paxi, also known as Paxos or Paxoi, is a contrast to its bigger and busier neighbor to the north. A speck of an island 7 miles (11 km) south of Corfu, Paxi has just three main villages and is small enough—only 5 miles (8 km) long and 2 miles (3 km) wide—to be walked across in a single day using the network of paths that traverse the numerous olive groves. Just as Paxi lies like a speck south of Corfu, Andipaxi is an even tinier dot south of Paxi.

The Venetians first exploited the potential for olive cultivation on Paxi.

**Paxi**

⛰ Map p. 309

## Paxi

The visitors attracted to Paxi are those who prefer somewhere quieter, more laid-back, and more directly in touch with its traditions than hectic Corfu. Paxi's symbol is the trident, which is a nod toward one story of how it came into existence: The god of the sea, Poseidon, needing a place to hide his lover Amphitrite, created Paxi by striking the sea with his trident.

Gods notwithstanding, Paxi is thought to have been uninhabited until mainland settlers arrived in the sixth century A.D. Even now there are fewer than 3,000 people here, spread among the three main harbor villages and a scattering of rural settlements inland.

Only limited accommodations are available, most reserved for the summer months by British and German tour companies, who have taken to Paxi in a big way. The Paxiots have taken to them, too, welcoming the prosperity that small-scale tourism has brought.

Paxi may be simple, but it is not inexpensive. Much of the produce has to be imported from

Corfu, and the well-to-do on their visiting yachts have created a demand for more sophisticated food. Each of the three harbor towns, all delightfully pretty, can provide food of far better quality than you might expect.

The main settlement is **Gaïos,** a beautiful village huddled around a small harbor and a Venetian town square. Its charm is enhanced by two tiny islands in the bay. The remains of a Venetian fortress crown pine-covered Agios Nikolaos, while Panagia has a

church of the same name. Boats from the harborfront will take you over to the islands for a closer look. There is only one hotel in Gaïos, but there are many apartments and villas to rent. Except in the height of the tourist season, finding somewhere to stay should not be hard.

North of Gaïos the island's solitary main road heads inland through quiet hill villages—well worth walking to—and then back down to the next main coastal settlement, **Longos** (or Loggos). This is equally charming, with a harbor that looks designed with picture postcards in mind, a small town beach, good walks in the vicinity (brochures are available in local stores), and several of the best restaurants on the island. There are more good walks either along the coast to quiet coves or by climbing the steep steps from the harbor to the whitewashed hamlet of Dendiatika.

At the far north of the island is the delightful **Lakka,** with a large harbor surrounded by tree-covered hills, several stores and more fine restaurants, two town beaches, and more beaches along the coast offering sunbathing, swimming, and water sports.

## Andipaxi

Only a handful of people live on the island, where there are no stores and only a few beachside tavernas. In summer the island is inundated with day visitors from Corfu and Paxi, although the beaches are inferior. You can easily escape the crowds by going for a walk among the ubiquitous olive groves. ∎

**Andipaxi**

Map p. 309

### Olives & Olive Oil

The Greeks consume more olive oil than anyone else in the world: about 48 pints (23 l) per person per year. That amounts to an awful lot of olives—but then Greece produces an awful lot of the fruit. Its output is around 225,000 tons per annum, making it the world's third highest producer, after Spain and Italy.

Olive cultivation goes back at least 5,000 years on Corfu, where almost four million trees cover 30 percent of the island. The islanders harvest the fruits in an unusual manner for Greece, simply letting them fall to the ground when they are ready, rather than beating on the branches as is done elsewhere. Together with Kalamata in the Peloponnisos, Paxi is said to produce the finest olive oil in all of Greece.

# Lefkada

Lefkada (also referred to as Lefkas) is only barely an island—it was joined to the mainland until the Corinthians created a 65-foot-wide (20 m) canal in the sixth century B.C. to ease the passage of ships down the western coast of Greece. The channel still exists, with an artery and a bridge that is raised on the hour to let boats through (occasionally holding up traffic to and from the island).

**Lefkada**
Map p. 309

Lefkada makes a good base to explore the mainland by car and visit other islands in the southern Ionian group. Regular ferries sail to Ithaca and Kefalonia, with connections to Zakinthos.

Peaceful shrine in the old village of Agios Nikitas

The main point of entry is the capital, **Lefkada town,** closest point to the mainland.

It is an attractive setting, with a lagoon and low-lying mountains nearby. The town was almost flattened in 1953 by a major earthquake, and hurried rebuilding has not produced a pretty result. The waterfront is pleasant, however.

The busy main street, **Odos Dorpfeld,** is named after German archaeologist Wilhelm Dorpfeld (1853–1940). Something has been learned of Lefkada's history through his excavations, and he is regarded with great respect by locals. Settlers came here as long ago as 8000 B.C., and some Mycenaean remains have also been discovered. Dorpfeld worked with Schliemann (see pp. 112–113) at Mycenae, and just as Schliemann was determined to prove that Agamemnon lived there, Dorpfeld believed that Lefkada rather than Ithaca was the home of Odysseus, though he found no evidence.

Some of the artifacts found by Dorpfeld are on display in the small **Archaeological Museum** in Lefkada town. The little jumble of the **Folklore Museum** is more interesting, with scale models of some of the digs that Dorpfeld carried out, as well as photographs showing what the town looked like before the 1953 earthquake.

Dorpfeld is buried outside a church on a peaceful headland, at the far side of the lovely bay from the resort town of **Nidri.** This is the harbor for ferries to Meganisi, and to Ithaca and Kefalonia, but unless you like busy beaches and noisy nightlife, Nidri is a place to pass through. **Meganisi,** a small and tranquil island with rooms to rent and one pleasant hotel, can be visited on a one-day stop.

**Vasiliki,** in the south, is not as big as Nidri but still commercial, popular with the young because of its excellent windsurfing.

The best beaches are on the west coast. **Porto Katsiki** is stunning, with unbelievably blue waters and soft sand. Inevitably, it is also one of the busiest beaches, overcrowded in high summer. North of Katsiki, back toward Lefkada town, is one of the most unspoiled resorts on the island, tiny **Agios Nikitas.** Its beach is not especially good, but it has some lovely old houses and is still very much a Greek village first and vacation resort second. ∎

### Archaeological Museum

- ✉ Cultural Centre, Sikelianou & Svoronou Sts., Lefkada town
- ☎ 264/502-1635
- 🕐 Closed Mon.

### Folklore Museum

- ✉ Stefanitsi 2, Lefkada town
- ☎ 264/503-3443
- 🕐 Closed Sun.–Mon.
- 💲 $

---

# EXPERIENCE: Learning to Sail

Given the amount of water encompassing Greece, it's no wonder sailing is one of its national pastimes—making it a supreme place to learn or improve your skills.

On a typical "learn to sail" vacation, novices work toward earning a Crew Certificate, which teaches you what different members of the crew do to sail the yacht and will be of benefit to anyone seeking work on a yacht. More confident sailors (aged 16 and above) can aim to achieve a Skipper Certificate, which proves that you can skipper a yacht in a safe and seamanlike manner in nontidal waters during daylight hours. Guests can frequently either live onboard, to really prepare them for a life at sea, or can have shore-based accommodation while they learn the ropes—quite literally, as knot-tying and the use of ropes are among the skills needed.

Those living onboard also quickly discover one of the attractions of sailing, as they tie up in a new harbor every evening and go ashore to dine. It's easy to imagine the life the mariners of old must have had, learning to navigate and arriving in a new destination.

The would-be mariner can also choose to do two-day program, while the rest of the group stays ashore and has a regular Greek island holiday. The yachts leave harbor at about 9:30 a.m., and lunch is taken in another port or eaten on board, before the boats return in time to re-unite the group for the evening. There's plenty of opportunity, too, with either accommodation option, to enjoy swimming, diving, and other ways of making the most of the wine-dark seas of Greece.

For more information on such a vacation, contact **Sunvil Sailing** (*Upper Hose, Old Isleworth, Middlesex TW7 7BJ, England, tel (440) 208/568-4499, www.sunvilsailing. co.uk*). Greek companies offering learn to sail vacations include the **Athens Institute of Sailing** (*Alimos Marina, Athens, www.sailingcoursesingreece.com*) and **Odyssey Sailing Greece** (*Antonopoulou 158 D, Volos, 382 21 Magnisia, Greece, tel 242/103-6676, www.odysseysailing.gr*). U.S. companies include **Real Adventures, Cedora, Inc.** (*50 Franklin St., Ste. 403, Boston, MA 02110, tel 617/338-1020*) and **Meander Adventures** (*P.O. Box 4168, Park City, UT 84060, tel 435/649-6015, www.greece-travel-turkey-travel.com*).

# Ithaca

Let the *Odyssey* be your guidebook, and you will recognize Ithaca (Ithaki) from Homer's description: narrow and rocky, with a heavily indented coastline. The symbolic Ithaca—the notion of a homeland to which we all want to return—is recalled by a sign in the port reminding visitors that "Every traveler is a citizen of Ithaca." If you harbor such thoughts yourself, you'll find that arriving at Ithaca is like arriving at no other island.

A blue-domed church gives a splash of color to the sun-baked hills of Ithaca.

**Ithaca**

 Map p. 309

On approach it looks forbidding and barren, with high rocky hills, hauntingly shrouded in mist at certain times of the year. Ferries arrive in several different places. Those on the Lefkada–Kefalonia route call at Frikes in the north, while those from Kefalonia or the mainland port of Astakos call either at Piso Aetos Bay in the shadow of Mount Etos or at the deeply indented bay with the main town, Ithaca.

To arrive at **Ithaca town** is itself something special, as the boat sails into the picturesque fjordlike harbor, past the remains of two French fortresses built in 1805 to guard the harbor entrance. There are mountains on either side, and the ferry passes the pretty little island of **Lazaretto,** covered in trees. Lazaretto was made into a quarantine station by the Venetians in 1668, used as a prison from 1864 onward, and

INSIDER TIP:

Take a day off from touring archaeological sites and go to a quiet island like Ithaca and rent a Vespa. Spend the day driving around the island, taking in the scenery and beautiful Greek sunshine.

—WILLIAM BARR
*National Geographic contributor*

today contains only a small chapel. At the far end of the horseshoe bay is the welcoming sight of the tiny main town.

Although ferries dock daily, each arrival is still an event, with people waiting to greet friends and family, or offering rooms to visitors. There are a handful of hotels, some pensions, and plenty of eating places, notably around the harbor.

Despite Ithaca's rich history in legend, few remains have been discovered to shed light on whether there was actually a palace here belonging to Odysseus. But the locals insist that this was the case, and they may well be right. The island certainly trades well on its Homeric connections, and several sites have been linked with episodes in the *Odyssey*. A local map is available that guides you to some of these, and they are pleasant places to visit in their own right, with or without a legendary link. Two miles (3 km) from Ithaca is the **Cave of the Nymphs,** where Odysseus is supposed to have concealed treasure,

and it is about 7 miles (11 km) to the **Fountain of Arethusa.**

In Ithaca town (also called Vathi), a small **Archaeological Museum** has a few Mycenaean finds. Next door is the **Library,** which collects editions of Homer, including a rare Japanese edition from 1600. There is also a charming little **Folklore Museum,** with displays on local life. The other place of note in the town is the **Church of the Taxiarchos,** containing an icon of the Crucifixion said to have been painted by the young El Greco.

On the south end of the island, the only other settlement of any size is the village of **Perahori,** which stands nearly 1,000 feet (300 m) above sea level on a fertile plain that contains most of the island's vineyards. From here a rough trail leads around the slopes of Mount Nerovouno (1,811 feet/552 m) to the handsomely set 17th-century **Monastery of the Taxiarchos.** Destroyed in the earthquake of 1953, its church was later rebuilt.

The second largest town on the island is in the north. **Stavros** is a lively market town in the hills, with a statue of Odysseus and, on the edge of the town, a small **Archaeological Museum** with local finds, including part of a terra-cotta mask on which the word *Odysseus* can be seen. It was found at nearby Pelikatas Hill, where there are the remains of a building, the closest anyone has come to establishing a possible location for the Palace of Odysseus. Down the hill from Stavros is the small resort and ferry port of **Frikes,** great for windsurfing. ∎

**Archaeological Museum**
- ✉ Kallinikou, Ithaca town
- ☎ 267/403-2200
- 🕐 Closed Mon.

**Folklore Museum**
- ✉ Ithaca town
- 🕐 Closed Sun.–Mon.
- 💲 $

**Stavros**
- 🅜 Map p. 309

**Archaeological Museum**
- ✉ Stavros
- 🕐 Closed Mon.

# Homer & the *Odyssey*

**Little is known about the ancient Greek poet Homer, except that he may have been blind. We don't know where he was born, although Ithaca is one of several places that claim him as a son. Another is the island of Hios, where he is remembered in legend as a blind beggar poet. We don't even know when he lived, except that it was some time around the seventh century B.C.**

Was Homer even the author of the two works with which he is credited, the *Iliad* and the *Odyssey*? As with the works of Shakespeare, it is sometimes hard to believe that one mind could have come up with such a rich and creative body of work. For some time it was thought that Homer might have been two different writers collaborating on the works, although the latest linguistic analysis suggest that both of them are indeed the work of one author.

The poems are based on a mix of history and myth, blended with the art of a supreme storyteller. In Homer's day, a poet was literally a teller of stories, for the great epics were related orally, not written down. The author had to be an actor, too—with a phenomenal memory.

The *Iliad* is set at the end of the Trojan Wars, which took place (if they happened at all) probably three centuries before Homer was born. There is no absolute proof of the existence of Troy, although it may have been established at Truva in Turkey, where archaeologist Heinrich Schliemann began excavating in 1870. He certainly believed that he had found the site of Troy, although Schliemann was always more noted for enthusiasm than accuracy. Research at Truva continues today.

The *Odyssey* is again an intriguing mix of legend, history, and heroism, leaving scholars guessing as to what is truth and what is fiction. The book follows the story of Odysseus, King of Ithaca, who after fighting in the Trojan Wars sets off on his voyage home, a journey so eventful as to make a Tom Cruise movie look tame.

Odysseus' journey from the western coast of Turkey to the Ionian islands takes ten years

---

## EXPERIENCE: Visiting Homer's Tomb

Ios has recently been a hot spot for young partiers. It is thus quite the juxtaposition that the island, now known for risqué encounters and murderous hangovers, is reputed to be the final resting place of Homer, one of the few constants of Western civilization. To get to Homer's tomb, you can rent a motorcycle or ATV from either the port or Hora. A car isn't recommended, as much of the island isn't accessible by road. **Jacobs Rent a Car & Motorbike** *(Port of Ios, tel 228/609-1047, www.jacobs-ios.gr)* is reputable. Travel north to the valley of Pano Kambos. After 3 miles (4.5 km), there will be a road that

turns left. Take that, and then go right toward Plakoto beach, where you'll find the tomb. Little more than a heap of jagged rocks, there is no physical evidence that Homer's remains lay beneath the sun-bleached gravel, yet no other place in Greece claims to harbor his bones. The tomb represents one of the most touching and apparent qualities of the Greek people—faith in the past. For a nation that has surrendered the torch of civilization during centuries of foreign occupation and strife, sometimes the only constants are the sky, the sea, and crumbled stones that might contain meaning.

as a result of angering Poseidon, the sea god. Early in the voyage, Odysseus' ship encounters the Cyclops Polyphemus, a one-eyed giant who imprisons Odysseus and his men in a cave. To escape, Odysseus gets the Cyclops drunk and blinds him, but unfortunately Polyphemus is the son of Poseidon, so ....

Needless to say, when Odysseus does eventually make it home, after encounters with Sirens and whirlpools, shipwrecks and lotus-eaters, his adventures are still not over, for he must prove his identity to his faithful wife, Penelope (and confirm it with his old dog), and seize back power from those who have taken advantage of his absence and moved in. This he does after a tumultuous battle leads to a reunion in the best traditions of storytelling.

**Carved relief to the glory of Homer**

# Kefalonia

Although Corfu is the best known of the Ionian islands, their administrative center, Kefalonia, is by far the largest at 301 square miles (781 sq km). The island encompasses a wide variety of landscapes and features, from picture-perfect beaches often used in Greek tourism advertising campaigns to mountains, castles, and remote monasteries. This was the setting for Louis de Bernière's novel *Captain Corelli's Mandolin* (1994).

Fishing boats rest at the end of the day's work.

**Kefalonia**
🅰 Map p. 309
**Visitor Information**
✉ Waterfront next to Port Authority, 281 00 Argostoli
☎ 267/102-2248

**Historical and Folklore Museum**
✉ Ilia Zervou 12, Argostoli
☎ 267/102-8835
🕐 Closed Sun. & Nov.–April
💲 $

Sadly, large parts of the island, including the capital, Argostoli, were badly affected by the 1953 earthquake, and few old houses remain. The one town that did survive, in the far north, was **Fiskardo.** Its 18th-century mansions in bright colors, grouped around the harbor, show how beautiful the island was before the natural disaster. Fiskardo has been turned into a fashionable resort, expensive by local standards, but it is a memorable place to stay, with a lively atmosphere and good restaurants.

To find out what life was like at the time of the earthquake, visit Argostoli's **Historical and Folklore Museum.** It has displays about the quake, as well as collections of furniture, costumes, historical documents, paintings, and re-created rooms. The capital also has an **Archaeological Museum** *(Rokku Vergoti, tel 267/102-8300, closed Mon., $$)* with a room on the island's Mycenaean finds.

**Argostoli** itself is a pleasant town with a busy port area and a good market. There are waterfront tavernas and a lovely view across the bay. The bay is crossed on the Drapanos Bridge, a flimsy-looking structure that nevertheless survived the earthquake. It was built in 1813 to provide access to the island's second town, Sami.

The road to the port of Sami on the east coast passes the *Spili Drogarati,* **Drogarati Cave,** where steep steps lead down to one huge chamber, so big and acoustically perfect that concerts are held inside it in the summer.

The *Spili Melissani,* **Melissani Cave,** to the north of Sami is the site of an underground saltwater lake, illuminated by shafts of natural light where the roof of the cavern has fallen. The name translates as "purple cave," but it is usually a deep blue. Boats take visitors for a closer look at this haunting place, once a sanctuary to Pan.

A sanctuary to Aenios Zeus once crowned **Mount Ainos,** highest point on the island (5,340 feet/1,628 m). You can drive to the top, where the views are impressive, but the latter part of the road is rough, and you may have to walk from here. The area is covered in the indigenous fir tree *Abies cephalonensis,* and the region is one of Greece's national parks.

Northwest of the mountain is **Kastro,** former capital of Kefalonia. It grew up around the 16th-century Venetian **fortress of Agios Georgios,** which affords panoramic views. All of the overgrown interior is worth exploring.

The beach at **Mirtos,** on the west coast, is one of the most photographed in the Ionian. There are many other gorgeous beaches, and while tourism is concentrated around **Lassi** and the south-coast resorts, the rest of this large island rewards those who are adventurous and look a bit farther afield. ■

**Drogarati Cave**
- 🅰 Map p. 309
- 🕐 Closed winter
- 💲 $$

**Melissani Cave**
- 🅰 Map p. 309
- 🕐 Closed winter
- 💲 $$

**Agios Georgios Fortress**
- ✉ Kastro village
- 🕐 Closed Mon.
- 💲 $

---

## EXPERIENCE: Help Protect Kefalonia's Sea Turtles

A concerted effort, led by the Katelios Group, is being made to protect the wildlife of Kefalonia, both on land and in the sea. Of particular concern is the endangered loggerhead sea turtle, *Caretta caretta,* which nests on the sandy beaches of the island.

To help with their work, the Katelios Group needs volunteers during the summer season. Work starts in about May, just before the turtles come ashore to lay their eggs in the sand, and continues until October, when the eggs hatch and the baby turtles attempt to make their way safely to the sea. Volunteers must pay (approximately $185), cover their own costs, and commit themselves to the project for one month, during which time they work for seven to eight hours a day, six days a week.

The volunteers help monitor the nests, keep the beaches free of debris, and educate the public about the turtles and their requirements. Some beaches the turtles choose appeal to vacationers, with lots of nice, soft sand; others can be remote and difficult to get to, and some volunteers prefer to stay semipermanently on these quieter beaches, frequently with just the turtles for company. It is undoubtedly worthwhile work, helping to preserve the wildlife of Kefalonia and gaining a deeper understanding of its ecology. For more information, contact the **Katelios Group** (Katelios, 28086 Kefalonia, Greece, tel 267/108-1161, www.kateliosgroup.org).

# Zakinthos

South of Kefalonia and connected to it by ferry, Zakinthos (also called Zante) is a popular island. Along with gorgeous sandy beaches and an interesting capital, the island possesses one unique asset: It is the principal nesting site in the Mediterranean of *Caretta caretta*, otherwise known as the green loggerhead turtle.

With dramatic cliffs and clear blue water, Wreck Beach is a popular stop on island tours.

**Zakinthos**
🅰 Map p. 309
**Visitor information**
✉ Tourist Police, Zakinthos town
☎ 269/502-4482

Turtles have nested in **Laganas Bay** for thousands of years, but following the advent of tourism in the 1960s, they had competition for the lovely soft, golden sand in which they lay their eggs. Although the turtles came ashore at night to lay their eggs, during the day nests were being disturbed and eggs destroyed by the spikes on beach umbrellas. At nighttime the lights and music of increasing numbers of bars and discos disturbed and disoriented the animals. They also had the misfortune to nest on prime development land.

Thankfully, the authorities took steps to protect the turtles to some extent, with stretches of the 8.5-mile (14 km) beach fenced off from visitors. Local people have also realized that the turtles are a tourist attraction, even if hardly anyone ever sees them—buying the T-shirt is enough for most visitors. Laganas Bay is a gorgeous stretch of beach, but Laganas itself is a loud and tacky tourist town.

The island's capital, **Zakinthos town,** was almost wiped out in the 1953 earthquake but has been rebuilt in a mostly successful attempt to re-create the original style. It has a pretty waterfront, with lots of little fishing boats alongside the large inter-island ferries. Behind the waterfront are

## National Anthem

**The poet Dionysios Solomos was born on Zakinthos, and inside the town's museum to his memory is a piece of wood from a tree in the nearby hillside park of Strani. Beneath that tree in May 1823, he composed "Ode to Freedom." Part of the poem, set to music, became the Greek national anthem, "Hymn to Freedom."**

**Solomos was the first poet to compose in the vernacular rather than classical Greek. It was his belief that poetry should be available for everyone to read, not just the elite few. Now every Greek throughout the world knows at least one of his works.**

some attractive shopping streets, colonnaded to provide protection from sun in summer and rain in winter. They show the influence of the Venetians, who ruled here from 1484 until 1797 and who

referred to the island as *fiore di Levante,* "the flower of the East."

One building that did survive the earthquake (locals believe it was divine intervention) was the grand **cathedral** of 1925, dedicated to the island's patron saint, Agios Dionysios (1547–1622). Interestingly, the church and chapel at the 16th-century monastery of **Moni tis Panagias tis Anafonitrias,** where St. Dionysios was the abbot for the last years of his life, also survived the earthquake. The monastery is on the northwest end of the island and is a popular inclusion in organized tours around Zakinthos.

The saint's bones are contained in a silver coffin in the cathedral in Zakinthos town, and his vestments are kept in the chapel of **Agios Nikolaos sto Molo,** at the far end of the harbor on Plateia Solomou. This fishermen's chapel was destroyed in the earthquake but lovingly rebuilt stone by stone, and given a new interior.

The square is named for the island's other famous son, the poet Dionysios Solomos (1798–1857; see National Anthem left), who like so many boys here was given the name of the local saint. A **museum** to his memory stands next to his mausoleum. It has some of his personal effects, as well as photographs of the pre-earthquake town. The **Byzantine Museum** here is more interesting than many, for Zakinthos was one of the centers of the Ionian school of painting in the 17th and 18th centuries. The revolutionary, very realistic treatment of the saints by painters of the school is still striking today. ■

### Solomos Museum
✉ Plateia Agiou Markou, Zakinthos town
☎ 269/504-8982
💲 $

### Byzantine Museum
✉ Plateia Solomou, Zakynthos town
☎ 269/504-2714
🕐 Closed Mon.
💲 $

# More Places to Visit in the Ionian Islands

**Local transportation in Meganisi**

Off of the major Ionian islands there are smaller islands, where fewer visitors venture. Some offer accommodations, while others are accessible only by day. Whatever the options, you should see these out-of-the-way places if time allows.

## Off Corfu

Corfu has a group of five small islands off its northwest coast, known as the Diapontia islands. Only three of these are inhabited, and while you might find basic rooms to rent if you wanted to escape the crowds for a few days, you could also take an organized boat trip to some of the islands from a resort such as Sidari or Agios Stefanos.

**Ereikousa** is the most popular destination, and this island has one good hotel and some excellent beaches. Many boat trips from Corfu just stop at Ereikousa, leaving people to enjoy themselves on the beach for a few hours and providing a tasty barbecue lunch.

**Othonoi** has some dramatic scenery inland and is the perfect choice if you want to spend your time walking. There are simple rooms to rent and a handful of tavernas.

**Mathrakion,** with only a few dozen inhabitants and a few rooms to rent, is the best

of the three for both magnificent beaches and good walks. The beach is about 2 miles (3 km) long and occasionally busy with visitors from Corfu, but if you venture into the island's wooded and hilly center you will see no one, not even local people.

Map p. 309

## Off Lefkada

Lefkada has several offshore islands, not all of which can be visited. The most famous of them is Skorpios, owned by the Onassis family. Aristotle Onassis (1906–1975) is buried here. It is off-limits when the family is in residence, otherwise just the beach can be visited.

You can also visit **Meganisi,** the biggest island, a short ferry ride from Nidri. Meganisi has a beautiful little harbor town, **Vathi,** where few visitors stay although some make the trip for a few days' visit over from Lefkada. It's a delightfully undeveloped place, little more than a village. A few minutes' walk up the winding, wooded road above Vathi brings you to **Katomerion.** This is the main village and the only one with a hotel, a pleasant and peaceful place to escape the crowds. You can easily explore Meganisi on foot. The deserted coves are little treasures.

Map p. 309

# Travelwise

**Getting about—in style**

# TRAVELWISE

## PLANNING YOUR TRIP

### When to Go

Greece is a year-round destination, so if you can only travel in midsummer or midwinter, you'll still enjoy your visit. However, August is best avoided, not only because it is the peak vacation month, when space is limited in hotel rooms and on beaches, but also because temperatures can soar to well over 100°F (38°C), and Athens in particular can be very uncomfortable. In midwinter there may be rain and temperatures below 50°F (10°C), but equally you may get clear blue skies and temperatures of 20°F (-6°C)—and no crowds outside the honey pots of Athens, Delphi, and Olympia.

The best time to visit is in the spring and the fall, when the weather is comfortably warm, there is little rain, and, since there are fewer vacationers, the naturally hospitable locals have time to talk to visitors. In the springtime wildflowers will be blooming and the landscape lush. If you wish to visit mountainous regions, late May onward is when the snow starts to melt and paths become passable again.

An especially good time to visit is during Easter week, when there are many celebrations: Easter is the most important festival in the Greek calendar. However, it only occasionally coincides with the dates of Western Christian Easter as it is determined by a different system, so check the dates.

### What to Take

Greece is a casual country and in only a handful of more formal restaurants would men need a jacket and tie in the evening. If you're traveling in summer, casual dress such as shorts and T-shirts are all you will need during the day, plus a swimsuit as one is never far from a beach, and light cotton clothing for the evenings. It remains warm enough to eat outdoors until late at night during the summer, and even in spring and fall you would probably need to add only a sweater or light jacket. In summer it rarely rains in most of the Greek islands, and if it does it will be in the form of a short, sudden shower. Rain is more common in the Ionian islands and in the mountainous areas of northern Greece, where a raincoat will be essential. In winter a warm coat or jacket and a sweater is advisable.

Mosquitoes occur in many places, especially in the greener Ionian and Sporades islands and on the mainland. They can be a minor nuisance almost anywhere and at any time of year, so carry plenty of repellent. This can be purchased locally, along with the effective plug-in mosquito-repellent devices that are now available.

Most medical supplies will be available unless you are traveling to a remote part of the country or an island where there is very little tourism. Pharmacies are usually well stocked and the staff knowledgeable, with good English. Make sure you have an ample supply of sunscreen—cooling breezes can be deceptive, and the Greek sun is fierce.

Take film for your camera with you. Color-print film is available everywhere, but it is expensive and may not be fresh. It could have been sitting in the sun for several weeks and have deteriorated in quality.

Color-slide film is slightly more difficult to find, as are digital memory cards, so stock up before leaving home.

### Insurance

You are advised to take out full travel and medical insurance for a visit to Greece. Public medical care is pretty basic, and while there is plenty of private medical treatment available, it is costly. Pharmacists or doctors' offices will deal adequately with minor injuries, but major ones could prove costly.

### Books about Greece

There are numerous books about Greece, ancient and modern, which would enrich a visit here.

Homer's *Odyssey* is a splendid adventure tale, while *The Histories* by Herodotus and the *Guide to Greece* by Pausanaias will add background to visits to many of the classical sites. *The Greek Myths*, by Robert Graves, will illuminate the often complex world of Greek mythology, and A. R. Burn's *History of Greece* is a good all-around introduction to the world of the ancient Greeks.

*Modern Greece: A Short History*, by C. M. Woodhouse, is a good way of bringing yourself up to date. The best of the 20th-century travelers' tales about Greece are those by Lawrence Durrell (*Prospero's Cell, Reflections on a Marine Venus*), his brother Gerald Durrell (*My Family and Other Animals*), Patrick Leigh Fermor (*Roumeli, Mani*), Henry Miller (*The Colossus of Maroussi*), and Patricia Storace (*Dinner with Persephone*).

For the Greek perspective read any of the novels by Nikos Kazantzakis, particularly his most famous, *Zorba the Greek*. The poems of C. P. Cavafy, Odysseus Elytis, and Nobel

Prize–winning George Seferis are also recommended. Other modern Greek novels available in translation include Eugenia Fakinou's *Astradeni*, the story of a teenage girl who moves to Athens, and Dido Sotiriou's best seller, *Farewell Anatolia*.

## How to Get to Greece
### By Air
Greece's main international airport, Eleftherios Venizelos, is about 20 miles (33 km) east of downtown Athens. The national airline, Olympic Airways *(tel 210/926-9111, www.olympic-airways.gr)*, has scheduled flights from major cities all over the world.

Direct flights to Greece from the U.S.A. include two a week from New York on Olympic Airways, while Delta has flights from New York to Athens. Other flights from major cities such as Chicago, Washington, D.C., Los Angeles, San Francisco, and Seattle are either through gateway cities in the U.S. or via European connections such as London (on British Airways, United, and others) or Amsterdam (on KLM).

From Athens there are numerous connecting flights to Greek airports on the mainland and throughout the islands. Olympic Airways has had a virtual monopoly of the internal services, but several new carriers now offer a wider service to major routes such as Crete and Rhodes.

### By Sea
There are several ferry services to Greece from Italy, notably from Bari, Brindisi, Ancona, Trieste, and Venice. Other services go from Croatia, including Dubrovnik. A high-season journey between Italy and Greece costs from around $70 one-way for a foot passenger, up to around $150 for a car. Since

agents in Greece normally only represent one ferry line, it is best not to consult them for general advice.

### By Rail
Greek trains are cheaper than buses but also tend to be slower. If you are planning a long stay in Europe, it is worth considering crossing the continent by train. The route goes through France, Switzerland, or Italy, and the journey takes about three days (you could stop off on the way). You can then cross by ferry from Italy to Patra in the Peloponnisos and continue on to Athens.

## Entry Formalities
### Passports & Visas
A valid passport is required for all visitors to Greece, entitling them to stay for up to 90 days. Visas are required for a visit of over 90 days.

### Drugs & Narcotics
Customs inspections are usually fairly informal affairs, but for anyone caught carrying drugs the penalties are severe. If you have prescription medicine, make sure to bring the prescription with you, both as a precaution at customs and in case you lose or use up your supplies. One anomaly is that codeine, which is widely available around the world as a painkiller, is illegal in Greece. You will not necessarily get into serious trouble for having it, but it may be confiscated.

### Pets
Pets must have a valid health and rabies inoculation certificate, and it must have been issued between six days and six months before arrival for cats, and between six days and twelve months for other animals.

## Money
There is no limit to the amount of foreign currency and traveler's checks that you can take into Greece.

# GETTING AROUND
## Traveling from Athens Airport
### By Public Transportation
You can get from the new International Airport to Athens's city center (20 miles/33 km) by public transportation. Six express buses operate 24 hours a day. The cost is minimal and journey time between 70 and 90 minutes. Buy your ticket from the driver. The new metro link is even quicker.

### By Taxi
Do not take a taxi from solicitors inside the airport terminal building, but go outside and join the official line at the taxi rank. Check that the meter is switched on. If the meter is not working, you should know that the fare from the airport is approximately 20 euros for a 45-minute journey to downtown. Heavy traffic can slow that considerably. There is usually an additional charge for items of baggage. If you feel you are being overcharged, call the Tourist Police on 171.

## Traveling in Athens
### By Subway
Athens has several Metro (subway) lines, the main one (Line 1) running from Kifissia in the north to Pireas in the south, with useful central stops at Omonoia and Monastiraki. A southeast–northwest line (Line 2) links Omonoia with Syntagma, and will eventually reach Glyfada on the coast. Line 3 starts in Aegalio (western suburbs), connects Monistiraki and Syntagma, and links downtown with the airport. The subway is divided into zones, and you pay according to how

many zones you cross. Buy your ticket at the station and then time-stamp it in the machine as you enter the platforms. The service is very cheap and trains are frequent, but you should check destination boards as not all trains run the full length of each line. Lines 2 and 3 are wonderfully modern. While Line 1 shows its not inconsiderable age, its stations are slowly being renovated.

## By Bus
The Athens bus network is extensive and cheap. That said, buses are invariably very crowded, hot in summer, and prone to cancellation. You will need geographical knowledge of the city and sometimes of the Greek alphabet to read the destinations if you plan to use buses. Within the center, walking is usually the best option. If you do take a bus, note that tickets are bought in advance from kiosks near the major bus stops or from some stores. Stamp your ticket in a machine when you enter the bus.

## By Train
The aboveground train network in central Athens is of little practical use to the visitor. The mainline stations serve the distant suburbs and the rest of Greece.

## By Taxi
Taxis are a convenient way of getting around and are very cheap, provided you have some idea of what the fares should be. The cars are yellow, and you simply wave them down in the street, although there are also several official taxi ranks. The bottom of Syntagma Square is a good place to pick up a taxi. They are not supposed to stop there other than to drop off passengers, but drivers usually take the opportunity to pick up a fare.

Athenian taxis are shared, and the driver is entitled to pick up other passengers, and most will attempt to fill their vehicles; each person pays the fare on the meter. This arrangement counteracts a severe taxi shortage and boosts drivers' incomes without putting up individual fares. You will see Athenians standing in the street shouting their destination to passing taxis, in case they are headed in that direction.

# Traveling Around the Country
## By air
Greece has a good internal flight network, though most flights are to and from Athens, with a few connecting with Thessaloniki. It can frequently be more convenient to fly into Athens and out again, as a way of getting around the country. Single fares are around 80 euros. Flights quickly get full during the summer months, so make advance reservations.

## By Ferry/Boat
Greece has an excellent ferry service, as you might expect from one of the world's great maritime nations, although it can be somewhat erratic. There are numerous rival ferry companies, and schedules change constantly (an up-to-date schedule can be obtained from the Greek National Tourist Organization). Boats may be canceled or delayed because of the weather conditions, so if you have a flight to catch allow an extra day in case of problems.

For travel between islands, or between the mainland and the islands, there are usually several choices. You will need to ask around to find out what these are, as travel agents often operate on behalf of one ferry line only. In addition to the slow and cheap regular ferries,

there is a rapidly increasing network of hydrofoil services, which are much quicker but naturally much more expensive. If you get seasick, then you may feel the additional expense is worth it.

You will also find many small boats operating between neighboring islands or running excursion trips in the summer. Even if you don't want the full excursion these can sometimes be more convenient options than the larger commercial ferry services, and an individual running his own boat will be open to bargaining. Commercial fares are fixed, and tickets can be bought from a travel agent, sometimes from a table set up on the quayside or on the boat itself when it docks.

## By Train
Because of its mountainous landscape and long tradition of traveling by sea, Greece has not developed an extensive railroad network. Trains are limited to the mainland, and whole areas of western Greece and the southeastern Peloponnisos are not served at all. There are two mainline stations in Athens, one serving the Peloponnisos, the other the more direct line to Thessaloniki and on through Macedonia and Thrace into Bulgaria and Turkey.

## By Bus
Greece has an excellent and extensive bus system, which is by far the most popular form of transportation for the Greeks themselves. There are few towns that do not have a busy bus station, and it can even be the simplest way of reaching some of the islands. For example, the Ionian islands have regular bus services to and from Athens, with the cost of the ferry included in the price.

Most rural areas are well served by buses, and the easiest way of traveling around many islands is by bus. On smaller islands buses will frequently meet an incoming ferry, to take passengers from the harbor to the main town. Rural bus journeys can be quite an experience, with passengers transporting all kinds of baggage and drivers carrying and delivering parcels for people and sometimes diverting from the route to do a favor for a friend. In addition to specific stops, most drivers will drop people off and pick them up anywhere that is convenient, so feel free to wave a bus down wherever you happen to be.

Tickets for the main intertown services (usually in reasonably comfortable air-conditioned buses) need to be bought in advance at the bus station; on local routes you may have to buy your ticket in a store near the main stop or on the bus itself. Schedules might be displayed on telegraph poles, placed in store windows, or pinned to walls, and may or may not be up-to-date and accurate. It is always best to check.

## By Car

The general standard of driving in Greece is not good. Some drivers regard the middle of the road as their rightful place to be, which is disconcerting when coming around a blind bend. That said, provided you take care, driving in Greece can be enjoyable since it opens up areas of the mainland and the larger islands, such as Rhodes, Crete, and Corfu, which are not easily accessible to tour groups.

## Car Rental

Renting a car in Greece is straightforward and a great pleasure, although expensive. All the major names, such as Avis and Hertz, have offices throughout the country, at airports, in major towns and cities, and on the larger islands. The established inter-national names are usually more reliable. Some of the smaller firms run their fleets throughout the year, giving minimal attention to servicing, in order to keep costs down. However, if you travel at a quiet time of year, you are more likely to be able to negotiate a better deal with an independent company than with one of the international chains, whose prices are fixed.

An ordinary national driver's license is all you need, and car rental agreements automatically include third-party insurance, which is a legal requirement. It would be wise to add personal accident insurance as accident rates here are among the highest in Europe. You must be at least 21 years of age, or 25 years for more powerful cars. There is a wide range of automobiles available. A credit card can be used as a deposit.

## Roads & Road Signs

The standard of Greek roads is improving all the time, thanks to generous grants from the European Union. There are few roads of a standard comparable to expressways, but the average is a reasonable standard. Tolls apply on the expressways—but these are not expressways as you know them. Four lanes can become two without warning, and you may well encounter slow-moving farm vehicles. In rural areas a smooth-surfaced road can suddenly become a dirt track, with herds of animals a common hazard.

Road signs are not good and a decent map is essential. A knowledge of the Greek alphabet is also vital: Main roads are usually marked in both Greek and Roman letters, but on side roads you may find signs in Greek only.

## Regulations & Rules of the Road

In Greece driving is on the right, but in practice many drivers use the center of the road, especially when going around a corner, so be careful. Note that if a driver flashes his headlights at you, it is a warning that he is going ahead. Speed limits are 31 mph (50 kph) in built-up areas, 49 mph (80 kph) outside built-up areas, and 62 mph (100 kph) on divided highways.

Seat belts must be worn where fitted, and drivers can be fined for not carrying a warning triangle, fire extinguisher, and first-aid kit.

Drunk driving (DWI) is a serious offense in Greece. One glass of wine or beer is probably enough to create a misdemeanor, and if you drink much more than that you will be committing a criminal offense leading to a possible prison sentence. Drivers should therefore observe complete abstinence.

## Fuel

Unleaded gasoline is now available everywhere, at least in the busier places. In remoter areas gas stations may be few and far between, so try to keep your tank full or check where there are gas stations. In smaller towns and villages stations will be family enterprises, so they may close on a Sunday, or you may find yourself being served by a small boy or girl who speaks no English. Many smaller stations don't accept credit cards, so be sure always to have some cash with you.

## Parking

Parking in Greece is straight-forward, with only major cities having zones for which you need to buy a parking permit. Otherwise it is obvious that you either can or cannot park somewhere. If you do need a permit, there will be a notice in Greek and English on the street telling you where to obtain one (usually in a earby store).

### Accident & Breakdown

In the event of an accident, for roadside assistance dial 10400, the call-out number for ELPA (the main Greek recovery service, like the AAA). If you have a rented car you should have been given this or another emergency number to dial (see p. 342). It is an offense to drive away if you have been involved in an accident, which must be reported to the police. Do not sign any document that is written only in Greek.

Rental companies will tell you what to do in case of breakdown. They usually belong to one of the Greek equivalents of the AAA (ELPA, Hellas Service, or Express Service) and will give you the contact phone number in case of problems.

### By Motorbike or Moped

Mopeds and motorbikes are usually available to rent in tourist centers and can be an excellent and economical way of getting around. Before taking to the road, be sure to check that the vehicle is in a safe condition. Although not mandatory, helmets are recommended. Be aware that accidents are common with inexperienced drivers.

### Hitchhiking

Hitching a short ride with a local is usually no problem as people are used to it. Hitching can be a good way to meet locals and try out your Greek. Longer rides might be less easy.

## PRACTICAL ADVICE

### Communications

#### Post Offices

Post offices can be found practically everywhere in Greece. Even the smallest island has one, although it may also double as a bank or may be open only part-time. Major post offices, known as *tachydromeia,* are generally open Monday to Friday from 7:30 a.m. to 2 p.m., although some may stay open later on one night a week. Some also open on Saturdays until about noon. In larger post offices there will be separate lines for different services, so make sure you join the right one. Parcels have to be sealed in front of the post office clerk, which is why you will see people standing in line with scissors and scotch tape. If you only want postage stamps, look for the sign saying *grammatosima.*

Post offices no longer act as money exchanges due to the proliferation of ATMs and the credit card culture.

### Mailboxes

Mailboxes are yellow and usually small, so they are not always easy to spot at first. If you are visiting more isolated islands or remote places on the mainland, then you may well get home before your vacation postcards arrive. Otherwise, airmail letters to North America and elsewhere outside Europe take around 1 to 2 weeks (up to a week to European countries). Postcards can take even longer. Sometimes you will encounter separate boxes for domestic and international mail, and there are also red boxes, which are for express mail only.

### Telephones

There are numerous options for making phone calls in Greece, aside from in a hotel room where charges are excessive. Local calls are cheap, but long-distance and international calls are very expensive.

You will see public pay phones all over the country, not just on the street but also at train and bus stations, by harbors, in hotel receptions, and at offices of OTE (the Greek national telephone company). Pay phones are increasingly taking phone cards, which are widely available, including from the little kiosks on every street corner. If you don't wish to buy a card, use the OTE office where the call will be metered and you can pay in cash or by credit card. Alternatively, do what many locals do, which is to use the phone that almost all street kiosks have, and pay in cash according to the meter. OTE offices can be found in most places, large or small, and are generally open from early in the morning until late in the evening, Monday to Saturday.

### Conversions

Greece uses the metric system, so road signs are in kilometers, gas is sold in liters, and stores sell in grams and kilos.

1.61 kilometers = 1 mile
100 kilometers = about 62 miles
1 meter = 3.28 feet or 39.37 inches
1,000 meters = about 3,300 feet
1 liter = 0.264 U.S. gallons
10 liters = a little more than 2.5 gallons
1 kilogram = 2.20 pounds
2 kilograms = nearly 4.5 pounds

Weather reports are given in Celsius. The freezing point is 0°C. For an approximate conversion from Fahrenheit to Celsius, subtract 30 and divide by 2. To convert approximately from Celsius to Fahrenheit, multiply by 2 and then add 30.

0°C = 32°F
10°C = 50°F
20°C = 68°F
30°C = 86°F
100°C = 212°F

## Women's Clothing

| U.S. | 6 | 8 | 10 | 12 | 14 | 16 |
|------|---|---|----|----|----|----|
| Greece | 36 | 38 | 40 | 42 | 44 | 46 |

## Men's Clothing

| U.S. | 36 | 38 | 40 | 42 | 44 | 46 |
|------|----|----|----|----|----|----|
| Greece | 46 | 48 | 50 | 52 | 54 | 56 |

## Women's Shoes

| U.S. | 6 | 6½ | 7 | 7½ | 8 | 8½ |
|------|---|----|---|----|---|----|
| Greece | 36 | 38 | 39 | 39 | 40 | 41 |

## Men's shoes

| U.S. | 8 | 8½ | 9½ | 10½ | 11½ | 12 |
|------|---|----|----|-----|-----|----|
| Greece | 41 | 42 | 43 | 44 | 45 | 46 |

## Electricity

The electricity supply is 220 volts/50 Hz AC. North American appliances will need a transformer. The Greek electrical socket is a simple one with two round pins and occasionally three where devices need to be earthed. If you forget to take an adapter with you, it should be possible to buy one in most vacation areas in supermarkets or electrical stores.

## Etiquette & Local Customs

Greece is an informal country in many ways, yet good manners and courtesy are an essential part of everyday living. Most Greeks are very polite and exceptionally hospitable to strangers. They appreciate any attempts to speak their difficult language, and you should try to master at least the basic courtesy words. As in several languages, it is the custom when someone says *efharisto* (thank you) to reply with *parakalo* (please, meaning "think nothing of it").

When Greeks meet they go through various formalities, such as asking about a person's family and health, and they take their time about this. Don't try to hurry them if you are waiting to be served. In Greece patience is not a virtue, it is a way of life. As with the French custom of always saying *bonjour*, you should first greet a Greek person politely with *kali mera* (good day) before starting the conversation.

Greece is a macho society, and in more rural areas you will seldom see Greek women sitting in male domains such as bars and cafés. Foreign women are allowed to break the rules and will never be made to feel uncomfortable. In return, they should dress modestly in public. In tourist areas it is increasingly common to see both men and women walking around in flimsy attire, but this is emphatically not approved of, simply tolerated. If you wish to respect your Greek hosts, you should dress discreetly. This applies particularly when visiting churches and monasteries, where you may not be admitted if you are wearing shorts and have bare arms, although some places are more open-minded about this than others. You will occasionally see Greek men and women wearing respectable shorts when visiting churches if there is no service taking place.

Topless sunbathing is quite widespread but not appreciated on busy beaches in town centers. Nude sunbathing is officially restricted to a small number of designated nudist beaches, but provided you are sensible about it and do not offend anyone, you can usually find quiet coves and beaches where you can sunbathe naked if you wish.

## Internet Information

www.greektravel.com/index
.html

Excellent and comprehensive site with numerous links, from Greek enthusiast Matt Barrett

harpy.uccs.edu/greek/

Covers the art of the Aegean, Mycenaeans, and Tiryns

www.athensguide.com/
www.ametro.gr

For up-to-date information on the expanding Athens Metro

www.gogreece.com/

Guide to Greece and the islands

www.kypros.org/cgi-bin/
lexicon/

Greek-English online dictionary

www.greekhotel.com/
home.htm

Guide to Greek hotels and tour operators

www.hellasguide.gr/

General Greek guide

www.culture.gr/home/
welcome.html

Hellenic Ministry of Culture

In addition, there are countless websites devoted to individual islands, districts, or towns, examples being:

www.psirri.gr/english/

A guide to the newly fashionable Psirri district in Athens

www.symi-island.gr/

A guide to the island of Simi

## Liquor Laws

Greece has no restricting liquor laws. Alcohol is freely available in restaurants, bars, cafés, supermarkets, and other stores.

## Media

**Newspapers:** American newspapers are likely to be available in Athens the day after publication. Most major European newspapers are available on the evening of the day of publication. Try the kiosks around Syntagma Square. Foreign newspapers are also sold in major centers such as Thessaloniki and Rhodes town, and in summer in the main tourist destinations, but will probably appear a day or so late. In Athens there are several English-language publications to keep you abreast of world events from a Greek perspective. One of the longest standing is the *Athens News* (weekly, every Friday).

**Television:** Greece has three government-controlled television channels, ET 1, NET, and ET 3. ET 1 broadcasts some foreign TV programs and movies with Greek subtitles. More recent movies tend to be dubbed into Greek. ET 3 has news summaries in English (check papers for timings), and most large hotels have cable or satellite TV picking up CNN and other English-language programs. There are numerous other channels, many of them regional and available by cable or satellite.

**Radio:** Greek airwaves are full of stations—national, international, and local—and Greek music is never far away. The two state channels are known as ERT 1 and ERT 2; ERT 1 is divided into three programs on different frequencies. The BBC World Service can be picked up on shortwave frequencies and The First Program broadcasts a multilingual news service in English, French, German, and Arabic (728 KHz). English-only news bulletins are broadcast daily on ERT 2 (98 KHz).

The BBC World Service can be picked up on shortwave (MHz) frequencies with news broadcasts on the hour and a range of English-language programs. In Athens try 88.7. In the Athens area the American Forces Radio Service also broadcasts, on 1484 and 1594 KHz, with news on the hour.

## Money Matters
The Greek unit of currency is the euro. There are coins for 1, 2, 5, 10, 20, and 50 cents and 1 and 2 euros, with bills for 5, 10, 20, 50, 100, 200, and 500 euros.

Traveler's checks can be changed at most banks, hotels, and post offices on production of a passport, and in some stores and restaurants in tourist areas,

although generally at a less favorable rate of exchange. Exchange rates are published in daily newspapers.

ATMs are widespread in cities, large towns, and major tourist resorts. Check ahead if traveling to quieter places.

Credit cards are widely accepted in the more expensive hotels, stores, and restaurants in popular areas. Do not assume, however, that you need only travel with "plastic." In Greece it is normal to settle even large transactions in cash. "No checks" is a common sign, even in some mid-range Athens hotels.

## National Holidays
**January 1**   New Year's Day
**January 6**   Epiphany
**March 25**   Independence Day
**February/March**   Shrove Monday (41 days pre-Easter)
**March/April**   Good Friday, Easter Sunday, and the following Monday
**May 1**   Labor Day
**June**   Whitmonday (50 days after Easter)
**August 15**   Assumption of the Virgin
**October 28**   Ochi Day
**December 25/26**   Christmas

On national holidays you will find almost everything closed, including sites, museums, banks, post offices, and some stores and restaurants. However, in tourist areas and major cities, you will have no trouble finding somewhere to eat and to buy provisions. Traveling can be difficult, so check before setting off.

## Opening Times
Banks are generally open from 8 or 8:30 a.m. until 2 p.m. on weekdays only, and post offices from 7:30 a.m.–2 p.m. In larger towns some banks and post offices may open on Saturday mornings.

Stores open from 8 a.m. to 2 p.m., when they close for the afternoon. They generally reopen at about 5, until 8 p.m., but some supermarkets and stores catering for visitors stay open much later. Opening and closing times may vary by an hour or so, but all stores will close for those few afternoon hours. Stores are generally closed on Sundays, except in tourist areas.

It is difficult to be precise about opening hours for museums and ancient sites as the hours change from winter to summer, and at some sites according to the mood of the keeper. Most are almost invariably open year-round, but are closed on Mondays and public holidays, except for major sites such as Delphi, Olympia, the Acropolis, and others in that league. Check locally for exact times.

## Photography
Most travelers now carry digital cameras. But if you still carry film, remember: The sun in Greece is strong, and slow film is ideal. Try to photograph ancient sites early in the morning before the crowds arrive and when the light is at its best. The deep blue seas and rustic villages make interesting subjects, and Greek people also like to be photographed, but it is polite to ask first. Never photograph near military bases, and ask permission first in museums and churches. Film is expensive, but major brands of film and camera batteries are widely available in tourist areas.

## Places of Worship
Greece is 97 percent Greek Orthodox, so only in major cities such as Athens and Thessaloniki will you find places of worship for other denominations or faiths. Contact the local visitor information center for details of locations and times of services. Elsewhere in Greece, you will

not generally be able to attend services of your own religion. Visitors are always welcome to attend a Greek Orthodox Sunday morning service (you can stay for just as long or brief a time as you wish), and you should always dress respectfully.

## Rest Rooms
Public lavatories in Greece are few and far between, and those that do exist are probably better avoided. Finding a friendly taverna or bar is the best bet, but standards still vary enormously. It's polite to ask if you can use the facilities, and most places will happily let you.

Greek plumbing is of a small nonstandard size, and pipes easily become blocked if toilet paper is flushed down them. Only in the latest hotels is this an exception, and even here you should check first. Bathrooms have a wastebasket for the disposal of toilet paper and sanitary napkins. It may seem unhygienic but is better than a blocked pipe flooding the room.

## Time Differences
Greek time is seven hours ahead of U.S. and Canada Eastern Standard Time and ten hours ahead of Pacific Standard Time. It is two hours ahead of GMT (Greenwich Mean Time) and eight hours behind Australian New South Wales Time. Greek Summer Time begins on the last Sunday in March at 4 a.m., when clocks go forward an hour, and ends at 4 a.m. on the last Sunday in September, when they go back an hour. Take care if traveling at those times, especially spring, when ferries and flights could be missed. Dial 141 for a recorded time message in Greek.

## Tipping
In Greek restaurants service is included, but it is normal to leave any small change left after paying the bill on the table. If you are very impressed with the service, a tip of 1 euro would not go amiss. A small bill also rewards the wine waiter or the person who clears the table.

In hotels you will seldom be pressured into tipping, but a small gratuity to the porter or barman of 2 euro will be gratefully accepted. For chambermaids, 2 euro per day, left at the end of the stay, would be generous.

For taxi drivers, "keep the change" is the usual practice.

## Visitors with Disabilities
Visitors with disabilities may encounter difficulties in Greece. Hotels, transportation, and other facilities all lag behind the times. Although most Greeks are cheerfully helpful, you should assume nothing and check everything in advance. Things are slowly improving: For instance, most of the new Metro stations in Athens have disabled access. But be aware that visiting ancient sites and museums usually involves climbing steps and stairs and can be difficult if not impossible.

## Visitor Information
### Offices Abroad
The Greek National Tourist Organization (GNTO) has offices in:

**Australia**
37–49 Pitt Street, Sydney NSW 2000
tel 612/9241-1663, fax 612/9235-2174

**Canada**
91 Scollard Street Toronto, Ontario M5R 1G4
tel 416/968-2220 fax 416/968-6533;

1223 Rue de la Montagne, Ste. 101 Montreal, Quebec H3G 1Z2
tel 514/871-1535 fax 514/871-1498

**United Kingdom**
4 Conduit Street London W1R 0DJ
tel 0207/734-5997 fax 0207/287-1369

**United States**
645 Fifth Avenue New York, NY 10022
tel 212/421-5777 fax 212/826-6940

168 North Michigan Avenue Ste. 600, Chicago IL 60601
tel 312/782-1084 fax 312/782-1091

611 West Sixth Street, Ste. 2198, Los Angeles, CA 92668
tel 213/626-6696 fax 213/489-9744

**Mainland Greece**
There are regional information offices in most large towns and cities on the mainland:

**Head office of the GNTO** Tsoha 7, Ambelokipi Athens tel 210/870-7000.

Athens International Airport visitor information center tel 210/353-0445.

**Olympia** Praxitelous Kondili tel 262/402-3100

**Greek Islands**
**Corfu** Look for small kiosks near the Esplanade.
**Crete** Odos Xanthoudidou 1, Iraklio, tel 281/022-8225
**Kos** Vassileos Yeoryiou 3, Kos town, tel 224/202-4460
**Rhodes** Archiepiskopou Makariou & Papagou, 85 100 Rhodes town, tel 224/102-3655
**Samos** 25th March 4, 83100 Samos, tel 227/302-8582

# EMERGENCIES
## Crime & Police
Greece is one of the safest countries in the world, and you are unlikely to experience any problems with crime. Nevertheless, crime is on the increase—mostly petty theft—so keep your money and valuables in a money belt or leave them in the hotel safe. Athens is a city with very few no-go areas, and in tourist districts even late at night you should be safe. Greeks are late-night people, and the streets are often busy until the early morning hours.

Women traveling alone may be subject to the attentions of young Greek men known as *kamaki* (harpoonists). Most will stop if you are persistent in your refusal. If attention turns into harassment, ask the nearest Greek for help: If you do need help, contact the **Tourist Police** *(tel 171)* from any pay phone in Athens. Note outside of Athens you will need to find the local number for the Tourist Police.

## Emergency Telephone Numbers
Emergency calls are free from phone booths.

**Medical emergency:** In Athens dial **166**, or **171** for the Tourist Police. Elsewhere dial **166** for an ambulance *(asthenoforo)*, or **100**, which connects you to the branch of the police known as the *Ekato* (meaning "100"), who deal with fire and medical emergencies.

**Fire** *(fotyá):* **199**

**Road assistance: 10400** (call-out number for ELPA, the main Greek breakdown and recovery service, see p. 338). There are emergency telephones at regular intervals on highways.

## Embassies & Consulates
### Canada
G. Gennadiou 4, Athens
tel 210/725-4011

### United Kingdom
Ploutarchou 1, Athens
tel 210/723-6211

### United States
Vasilissis Sophias 91, Athens
tel 210/721-2951,
e-mail usembassy@pd.state.gov

There are also consulates in Thessaloniki for the United Kingdom *(Aristotelous 21, tel 231/027-8006)* and United States *(Nikis 59, tel 231/024-2905).*

## Lost Property
If you lose anything there is a strong chance it will be waiting for you if you can remember where you lost it; the vast majority of Greeks are scrupulously honest. If you do not know where you lost your property, then report the loss to the hotel management or call the Tourist Police. You will need a police report if you wish to make a claim.

## Health
There are no mandatory inoculations required for visiting Greece, but it is wise to be up-to-date with tetanus and polio injections.

Tap water is chlorinated and is considered safe to drink, but in the dry summer months drinking bottled water (which is inexpensive) may be safer.

## Medical Treatment
Greek pharmacists are highly trained and often multilingual. For minor ailments they can offer advice and a prescription. Look for the red cross sign or ask for the *farmakio*.

There are health centers in most towns, with signs in both Greek and English. Opening hours are usually 8 a.m.–noon only. If anything happens requiring lengthy hospital treatment, you are advised to seek private treatment; it is superior to basic state care (which has to be paid for anyway). Medical insurance is therefore essential. There are doctors in most large villages, and these are well trained and usually speak English. They are familiar with the common ailments that affect visitors and will do their best to help you.

Dental treatment is not available free of charge and should be covered by your private medical insurance. Check with the Tourist Police or at your hotel for the name of the nearest dentist. Have a dental checkup before leaving home.

## Hazards
Sunburn is a common problem. Use sunscreen of as high a factor as your skin needs, and be particularly careful with children's skin. Wear a hat. To prevent dehydration, be sure to drink plenty of fluids (not alcoholic) and take salt with your food.

When you are swimming beware of sea urchins and jellyfish. The former are common in rocky areas, so wear light shoes. If one of the black spines pierces your skin, it must be removed. Ask local people for help, or visit the farmakio. Jellyfish are less common and not all are poisonous, but if you are stung visit the farmakio for a remedy. Ammonia (urine) can be used in an emergency for both stings and urchin spines.

Mosquitoes can be a nuisance in many places, but they are not malarial. There are a few scorpions around, but they are very seldom seen, and the same is the case as far as snakes are concerned. As long as you are careful when you are walking, and if you don't turn over rocks or poke sticks into holes, you will probably never encounter either. Do not touch stray dogs, and if you are bitten seek medical help right away.

# Hotels & Restaurants

The vast majority of accommodations in Greece are relatively inexpensive for the overseas visitor, with the exception of the top 5-star hotels. Standards vary enormously, and while there is a Greek accommodations rating system (see below) it is not a perfect guide. Don't automatically dismiss hotels in the lower categories, as many are spotlessly clean and beautifully located, but may lack some extras such as minibars or satellite television. If traveling in summer, especially in the popular tourist areas, it is vital to make advance reservations as a lot of accommodations are reserved by European travel companies. Outside these areas and outside the high season of July and August, finding somewhere acceptable to stay is rarely a problem.

Eating out is one of the great pleasures in Greece. For much of the year it is warm enough to eat outdoors, and there is a ready supply of fresh fish and meat, which, simply grilled and then eaten at a table right by the water's edge, is a delightful way to spend an evening. The Greeks are also natural hosts, and most restaurants and tavernas have a great atmosphere. As with hotels, appearances can be very deceptive. You are just as likely to find good food in a tiny backstreet family taverna, where the husband waits on tables and his wife cooks in the kitchen, as in some seemingly classy restaurants that cater purely to the tourist trade and serve dishes adapted for it.

## Accommodations

The official government rating system classifies all hotels and other accommodations from A to E, which very roughly corresponds to 5-star down to 1-star in other ratings systems. There is also a Deluxe category. The rating dictates the price, and accommodations are inspected and graded annually. The grading is taken seriously, and all establishments must display in each room an official notice that tells the grade of the hotel, the rate for that room at different periods of the year and for different numbers of occupants, and whether the price includes breakfast or not. If there is no such notice for you

to check then the establishment is breaking the law, but early in the year it is common to find the previous year's notice still displayed, until the new ones are available.

## Checking in

If you are visiting a hotel without a reservation then it is the usual practice in Greece to ask to see the room first, before taking a room. When you check in, you must give them your passport for the hotel's records, and this will normally be returned to you within a day.

Breakfast is sometimes included in the price and sometimes an optional extra. In more expensive hotels, breakfast is normally a generous buffet including juices, fresh fruit, yogurt and honey, cereal, eggs, cheeses, cold meats, and a variety of breads. In more basic places, you may be offered just a few slices of cold toast and coffee. You may find more choice in nearby cafés.

## Checking out

Most hotels will take major credit cards, but don't assume that you will always be able to pay by credit card in every establishment. Some smaller family-owned places will take only one type of card or none at all, requiring checks, or travelers' checks, or even preferring cash.

## Restaurants

There is no rating system for Greek restaurants, and ordinary-looking places can be wonderful, while classy-looking ones can be dreadful. It is best to avoid any place that employs someone to stand outside and tempt you in, a ploy used only to inveigle overseas visitors who will probably never return, not Greek customers. Be cautious, although the rule is not infallible.

Many restaurants in tourist areas do not take reservations, so in some cases you will find no telephone number in the listings below. Most places are expandable; another table will be brought out unless they are absolutely at their maximum capacity, in which case you will be told how long you have to wait for a table. For this reason, the number of restaurant seats is not listed here, as for the vast majority of establishments it simply does not apply.

There are several types of eating establishments in Greece. Restaurants (*estiatorio*) are classier, and tavernas more casual. In a taverna you may well have a paper tablecloth, and in more out-of-the-way places the waiter might even use it to write the bill on at the end of the meal. An *ouzerie* is an old-fashioned bar serving ouzo as well as other drinks and snacks. There are also *psarotavernes,* which specialize in fish, and *psistaries,* which specialize in food cooked on a grill or spit roasted.

## Eating Times

Greeks tend to eat late, like other Mediterranean people. Lunch will not normally be before about 2 p.m., and dinner may begin as late as 9 or 10 p.m. Most restaurants catering to overseas customers open much earlier to suit their different dining habits.

## Parking

Hardly any Greek restaurants have their own parking lots. In Athens and other major cities it would be madness to drive anyway, so take a taxi or walk. In smaller towns and on the islands, there is usually ample parking in streets nearby, and the Greeks take a relaxed attitude to parking. For these reasons, no indication is given in the restaurant listings as to parking availability.

## Credit Cards

Not all restaurants accept credit cards, so never assume that you can use one. Greeks prefer to pay in cash anyway, and as meals are generally inexpensive, paying in cash should not be a problem. Abbreviations used are AmEx (American Express), DC (Diners Club), MC (Mastercard), and V (Visa).

## Facilities for Visitors with Disabilities

Few restaurants have customized facilities for customers with disabilities, as most are long established in old buildings. Despite this, the Greeks are wonderfully helpful, and staff will always lend a helping hand. Simply telephone first, and ask.

## Summer or Winter Closing

A fair number of restaurants, especially in Athens, close for August and sometimes longer in the summer. This is often to escape the summer heat, at a time when many of their Athenian customers leave the city for a break on the islands. Some restaurateurs have island restaurants, which they open up for the summer months, before returning to Athens for the winter. Many island restaurants are therefore closed all winter! Set dates cannot be given here, as they vary year by year according to the whim of the owner, but where possible a rough indication of major closings is given in the listings.

In the following selection, under each location hotels are listed first, grouped according to price and in alphabetical order within each group; they are followed by restaurants, which are similarly listed by price and by alphabetical order.

L = lunch        D = dinner

## ■ ATHENS

As might be expected, there is a greater dining choice in Athens than anywhere else in Greece, with cuisines from all over the world as well as the best of Greek cooking. The Plaka is a popular eating area but has a number of poor places aimed purely at the passing foreign visitor trade, as well as some excellent and authentic Greek establishments. Nearby, the newly fashionable Psirri district (north of Monastiraki Square and to the west of Athinas) has a wide choice of truly Greek dining places, although you will certainly need your phrase book and menu reader.

## HOTELS

### SOMETHING SPECIAL

#### ▥ GRANDE BRETAGNE
**$$$$$**
PLATEIA SYNTAGMATOS

---

**PRICES**

**HOTELS**

An indication of the cost of a double room in the high season is given by **$** signs.

| | |
|---|---|
| **$$$$$** | Over $240 |
| **$$$$** | $160-240 |
| **$$$** | $110-160 |
| **$$** | $70-110 |
| **$** | Under $70 |

**RESTAURANTS**

An indication of the cost of a three-course meal without drinks is given by **$** signs.

| | |
|---|---|
| **$$$$$** | Over $65 |
| **$$$$** | $50-65 |
| **$$$** | $30-50 |
| **$$** | $20-30 |
| **$** | Under $20 |

---

TEL (210) 333 0000
www.grandebretagne.gr
Athens's landmark hotel right on Syntagma Square was built in 1864. It retains much of its old elegance, but inside are marbled interiors, a pool, modern business facilities, skyline city views, and a top restaurant. Illustrious guests have included Sir Winston Churchill, who stayed here in 1944 toward the end of World War II, and guests of King Otto, the first king of Greece, in the days when the nearby Parliament building was the Royal Palace. Top-floor front rooms are in demand, with their spectacular Acropolis views. A magnificent spa has been installed, plus a lavish mosaic-tiled pool and *hamam* area, though treatments are, predictably, expensive.

🛈 341 🚇 Syntagma 🅿 🔄
🏊 ⛱ All major cards

---

🏨 **HILTON**
**$$$$$**
VASILISSIS SOFIAS 46
TEL (210) 728 100
www1.hilton.com

Recently renovated to its former landmark glory, with a fine restaurant and the popular Galaxy bar. Convenient for Syntagma, Benaki Museum, and National Gallery, but not the Plaka.

[i] 453 🚇 Evangelismos [P] 🚭 ❄ 🏊 All major cards

### KING GEORGE PALACE
**$$$$$**

PLATEIA SYNTAGMA

TEL (210) 322 2210

Recently renovated to a sumptuous standard, it now rivals its neighbor the Grande Bretagne as *the* hotel in Athens. It has a fabulous spa, classical and comfortably designed rooms, the Tudor Hall restaurant whose Acropolis view is only matched by the superb food (the chef trained with Alain Ducasse), and yet the staff oozes relaxed friendliness.

[i] 102 🚇 Syntagma 🚭 ❄ 🏊 🏋 All major cards

### ST. GEORGE LYKAVITTOS
**$$$$$**

KLEOMENOUS 2

TEL (210) 729 0711

www.sglycabettus.gr

Very convenient and comfortable luxury hotel in the fashionable Kolonaki district. It has a highly recommended rooftop restaurant with great views of the city at night.

[i] 167 🚇 Syntagma [P] 🚭 ❄ 🏊 All major cards

### ANDROMEDA ATHENS
**$$$$**

TIMOLEONDOS VASSOU 22

TEL (210) 641 5000

www.andromedahotels.gr

Luxury hotel in a quiet street aimed at the business traveler, with computers and fax machines available on request.

[i] 42 🚇 Evangelismos [P] 🚭 ❄ 🏊 All major cards

### ATHENAEUM INTER-CONTINENTAL
**$$$$**

LEOFOROS SYNGROU ANDREA

89–93

TEL (210) 920 6000

www.ichotelsgroup.com /intercontinental/en/gb /home/

Superb hotel from the InterContinental chain, adapted to Greek style with paintings and sculptures by modern Greek artists in the public areas. Range of stores, bars, and restaurants. A short walk to downtown.

[i] 520 [P] 🚭 ❄ 🏊 🏋 🏊 All major cards

### DIVANI CARAVEL
**$$$$**

LEOFOROS VASILEOS ALEXANDROU 2

TEL (210) 720 7000

www.divanis.com

Very classy and modern hotel, much used by business travelers for its wide range of facilities. Short walk or taxi ride to downtown.

[i] 470 🚇 Evangelismos [P] 🚭 ❄ 🏊 All major cards

### DIVANI PALACE ACROPOLIS
**$$$$**

PARTHENONAS 19–23

TEL (210) 922 2945

www.divanis.com

Sitting in the shadow of the Acropolis in a quiet neighborhood, the hotel is convenient to downtown. Bland but large, comfortable rooms.

[i] 253 [P] 🚭 ❄ 🏊 All major cards

### OCHRE AND BROWN
**$$$$**

LEOKORIOU 7

TEL (210) 331 2950

The Psirri neighborhood is now even more fashionable with the opening of this super-chic designer hotel, which offers personal services like free parking (a blessing in central Athens), DVD players, a welcoming champagne drink, and the kind of personal attention that can be provided when there are just

11 rooms.

[i] 11 🚇 Thissio [P] 🚭 ❄ 🏊 All major cards

### PERISCOPE
**$$$$**

HARITOS 22

TEL (210) 729 7200

Yes, there is a periscope as you enter, one of the quirky stylish touches of this intimate boutique hotel in Kolonaki, and every bit as chic as the neighborhood. It gets a lot of business travelers who want both character and hi-tech facilities, and it raised the bar on hotel standards in Athens.

[i] 21 🚇 Evangelismos/ Syntagma 🚭 ❄ 🏊 All major cards

### BABY GRAND
**$$$**

ATHINAS 65

TEL (210) 325 0900

Stylish and fun new hotel with a great restaurant, Meat Me, and the first champagne bar in Athens. Some rooms are decorated by local artists—ask for the Spiderman room.

[i] 76 🚇 Omonia 🚭 ❄ 🏊 🏋 🏊 All major cards

### DORIAN INN
**$$$**

PIREAS 15–17

TEL (210) 523 9782

www.dorianinnhotel.gr

Very classy hotel near Omonia Square, recently improved with the opening of the new subway lines. Centrally located and handy for the National Archaeological Museum. Beautiful, 360-degree views of the Acropolis from the rooftop garden and pool.

[i] 146 🚇 Omonia [P] 🚭 ❄ 🏊 🏊 All major cards

### ELECTRA PALACE
**$$$**

NIKODIMOU 18

TEL (210) 324 1401

---

www.electrahotels.gr
Luxury option right in the
Plaka, with rooftop pool and
Acropolis views. All rooms
have TV, telephone, and minibar. Extremely comfortable,
and within walking distance
of Syntagma and most of the
main sights.
[i] 106 🚇 Syntagma P 😊
😊 🏊 All major cards

### 🏨 HERODION
**$$$**
ROVERTOU GKALLI 4
TEL (210) 923 6832
Classy hotel on the south
side of the Acropolis, away
from the Plaka but with
several highly recommended
restaurants located nearby.
All of the rooms have TV
and telephone. Rooftop
terrace has magnificent views
of the Parthenon.
[i] 90 😊 😊 🏊 All major
cards

### 🏨 HOLIDAY INN
**$$$**
MICHALAKOPOULOU 50
TEL (210) 727 8000
www.hiathens.com
Located slightly away from
downtown in the Ilisia district,
this comfortable business
hotel compensates by having
all the facilities you might
expect from a Holiday Inn,
including a rooftop swim-
ming pool and a choice of
restaurants.
[i] 188 P 😊 😊 🏊 🏊 All
major cards

### 🏨 LEDRA MARRIOTT
**$$$**
SINGROU 115
TEL (210) 930 0000
www.ellada.net/Ledra-
Marriott/
One of the Marriott chain's
superior hotels with light and
spacious rooms plus all the
facilities, close to downtown.
Don't miss its highly rated
Kona Kai restaurant (see
p. 348).

[i] 258 P 😊 😊 🏊 🏊 All
major cards

### 🏨 ROYAL OLYMPIC
**$$$**
ATHANASIOU DIAKOU 28-34
TEL (210) 928 8400
www.royalolympic.com
Conveniently located near
the Acropolis, and looking
out over the ruins of the
Temple of Olympian Zeus
and Hadrian's Arch. The
Olympic looks unimpressive
from the outside, but its facilities are excellent and
the rooms spacious.
[i] 304 🚇 Syntagma P 😊
😊 🏊 All major cards

### 🏨 TITANIA
**$$$**
PANEPISTIMIOU 52
TEL (210) 332 6000
www.titania.gr
Huge hotel with high stan-
dards, close to Omonoia and
within walking distance from
the Plaka and the National
Archaeological Museum. Well-
equipped rooms; roof bar with
view of the Acropolis.
[i] 396 🚇 Omonia P 😊
😊 🏊 All major cards

### 🏨 FRESH
**$$–$$$**
SOFOKLEOUS 26
TEL (210) 524 8511
One of the new breed of
Athens boutique hotels, with
stark design, a relaxing hip
atmosphere, fashionable bar-
restaurant, and fabulous pool
on the ninth floor.
[i] 133 🚇 Omonia P 😊 😊
🏊 📺 🏊 All major cards

### 🏨 ACHILLEAS
**$$**
LEKKA 21
TEL (210) 323 3197
www.achilleashotel.gr
Newly renovated and reasonably priced hotel, very close
to Syntagma. All rooms have
bathrooms and are large,
airy, and clean with balconies
and phones. Don't let the

mundane exterior put you
off—there's a pleasant dining
room on the first floor.
[i] 37 🚇 Syntagma 😊 😊
🏊 All major cards

### 🏨 ACROPOLIS VIEW
**$$**
10 GKALLI AT WEBSTER ST.
TEL (210) 921 7303
E-MAIL AV_HOTEL@OTENET.GR
www.acropolisview.gr
Affordable upscale option on
south side of the Acropolis, in
a quiet spot near Philopappos
Hill, with wonderful views.
Recently renovated rooms are
small but pleasant.
[i] 32 😊 😊 🏊 AmEx,
MC, Visa

### 🏨 ATHENS ACROPOLE
**$$**
PIREAS 1
TEL (210) 523 1111
E-MAIL AHOTEL@OTENET.GR
www.acropole-hotel.gr
This large, moderately priced
hotel close to Omonoia has
been renovated and has clean
rooms, all with telephones. Bar,
restaurant, and lounges.
[i] 167 🚇 Omonia P 😊 😊
🏊 All major cards

## EXARCHION

**$$**

THEMISTOKLEOUS 55

TEL (210) 380 0731

E-MAIL INFO@EXARCHION.COM

www.exarchion.com

Inexpensive option located close to the National Archaeological Museum in the lively student area of Exarchia. Many rooms have a balcony, and there is also a rooftop dining area/bar.

🛈 49 🚇 Omonoia 🔄 ⛄

## LA MIRAGE

**$$**

KOTOPOULI 3

TEL (210) 523 4755

On Omonoia Square but shielded from the noise, all of the rooms have a telephone and a minibar. Good example of a C-class hotel, with restaurant, bar, and lounges. Reasonable rates for those who want to be where it's all happening.

🛈 208 🚇 Omonoia 🅿️ 🔄 ⛄ 🅰️ All major cards

## NEFELI

**$$**

YPERIDOU 16

TEL (210) 322 8044

This is a small, family-run hotel that has many regular visitors. It is inexpensive, friendly, modern, and spotlessly clean, although some of the rooms are small. It is convenient to both the Plaka and downtown.

🛈 18 🚇 Syntagma 🔄 ⛄ 🅰️ AmEx, V

## PHILLIPOS

**$$**

MITSEON 3

TEL (210) 922 3611

E-MAIL PHILIPPOS@HERODION
.GR

www.philipposhotel.gr

Good mid-range option for the Makriyanni district, south of the Acropolis and close to several excellent restaurants. All rooms have telephones and TVs.

🛈 48 🔄 ⛄ 🅰️ All major cards

## PLAKA

**$$**

KAPNIKAREAS 7

TEL (210) 322 2096

E-MAIL PLAKA@TOURHOTEL.GR

www.plakahotel.gr

Slightly pricier Plaka option, but chic, clean, modern, and bright in both the public areas and the rooms. Extremely well located close to Mitropoleos. Some rooms have views of the Acropolis, as does the roof garden.

🛈 67 🚇 Monastiraki 🔄 ⛄ 🅰️ All major cards

## ACROPOLIS HOUSE

**$**

KODROU 6–8

TEL (210) 322 2344

E-MAIL HOTEL@ACROPOLIS
HOUSE.GR

www.acropolishouse.gr

Inexpensive Plaka option in restored mid-19th-century mansion. Well maintained and family-run, it is a great place for those who prefer charm and character to modern conveniences (not all rooms have bathtubs).

🛈 19 🚇 Syntagma 🔄 ⛄ 🅰️ V

## ADONIS

**$**

KODROU 3

TEL (210) 324 9737

E-MAIL INFO@HOTEL-ADONIS
.GR

www.hotel-adonis.gr

Good standard, economical hotel in pedestrianized street right on the edge of the Plaka and not far from Syntagma. Helpful staff; breakfast room/bar with Acropolis views. Has many regular visitors.

🛈 20 🚇 Syntagma 🔄 ⛄

## CAROLINA

**$**

KOLOKOTRONI 55

TEL (210) 324 3551

E-MAIL INFO@HOTELCARO-
LINA.GR

www.hotelcarolina.gr

A budget option that has seen better days but is perfectly acceptable if funds are limited. Some rooms are en suite and most are small, but they are kept clean and it is a convenient central base.

🛈 31 🚇 Monastiraki 🔄 ⛄ 🅰️ AmEx, MC, V

## CECIL HOTEL

**$**

ATHINAS 39

TEL (210) 321 7079

E-MAIL INFO@CECIL.GR

www.cecil.gr

Retro-style interiors with cage elevator. Roof garden has wonderful Acropolis views (plus four rooms). The hotel is run by two friendly brothers.

🛈 40 🚇 Monastiraki 🔄 ⛄ 🅰️ All major cards

## KOUROS

**$**

KODROU 11

TEL (210) 322 7431

Budget option in a street with several small hotels. In an ideal situation—quiet, but a few yards from the heart of the Plaka. No frills here, but rooms are clean and sizable. The hotel was formerly a mansion.

🛈 10 🚇 Syntagma 🔄 ⛄ 🅰️ No credit cards

## MARBLE HOUSE PENSION

**$**

ZINNI 35A

TEL (210) 923 4058

E-MAIL INFO@MARBLEHOUSE.
GR

www.marblehouse.gr

Friendly, inexpensive small hotel in quiet location, a short walk from the southern side of the Acropolis. Half the rooms are en suite, some have vine-covered balconies. Owners extremely helpful.

🛈 16 ⛄ 🅰️ No credit cards

## MUSEUM HOTEL

**$**

BOUBOULINAS 16

TEL (210) 360 5611
E-MAIL INFO@MUSEUM-HOTEL
.GR
**www.museum-hotel.gr**
Behind the National Archaeological Museum but overlooking its gardens. Quiet and well maintained, this is a good affordable option if you want to be in this area. All rooms have a telephone.

🛏 58 🚇 Omonia 🅿 🛗
🚫 AmEx, DC, V

🏨 **ORION**
**$**
EMMANUEL BENAKI 105
TEL (210) 382 7362
**www.orion-dryades.com**
Very cheap but perfectly acceptable if you're traveling on a strict budget and don't mind a long walk to the nearest subway station (Omonoia). In the lively Exarchia district, great for student nightlife and bars.

🛏 23 🚇 Omonia 🛗 🛗
🚫 No credit cards

## Restaurants

🍴 **BOSCHETTO**
**$$$$**
EVANGELISMOS PARK
TEL (210) 721 0893
This delightful Italian restaurant, in Evangelismos Park on the edge of Kolonaki, serves fashionable food and fresh pasta, and uses ingredients popular in both Greece and Italy: squid, spinach, zucchini, cheese.

🕐 Closed Sun., L in winter, & 2 weeks in Aug. 🛗 🚫 All major cards

🍴 **VARDIS**
**$$$$**
DELIGIANNI 66
TEL (210) 623 0650
In the Pentelikon Hotel in Kifissia is this elegant French restaurant serving lobster, filet mignon, a range of other meat dishes, and salads. Pianist plays in the evening. Costly

but good quality.
🚇 Kifissia 🛗 🚫 All major cards

🍴 **GB CORNER**
**$$$**
GRANDE BRETAGNE HOTEL
PLATEIA SYNTAGMATOS
TEL (210) 333 0000
Part of the Grande Bretagne Hotel (see p. 344), this restaurant serves a variety of good Mediterranean cuisine and has a mouth-watering grill section.
🚇 Syntagma 🛗 🚫 All major cards

🍴 **GEROFINIKAS**
**$$$**
PINDAROU 10

TEL (210) 362 2719
Excellent food with a strong Middle Eastern influence. Chic and secluded.
🚇 Syntagma 🕐 Closed national holidays 🛗 🚫 All major cards

🍴 **KIKU**
**$$$**
DIMOKRITOU 12
TEL (210) 364 7033
One of the best, but most expensive, Japanese restaurants in Athens, with sushi and sashimi prepared by Japanese chefs. Located in the Kolonaki district, it caters more to business and diplomatic visitors than to tourists.
🚇 Syntagma 🕐 Closed Sun. L, & midsummer 🛗 🚫 All major cards

🍴 **KONA KAI**
**$$$**
SYNGROU 115
TEL (210) 930 0074
This restaurant in the Ledra Marriott Hotel (see p. 346) specializes in Polynesian food (with decor as exotic as the dishes) but also has a Japanese menu. Very popular, so reservations are advisable.
🕐 Closed L Sun., & mid-Aug. 🛗 🚫 All major cards

🍴 **L'ABREUVOIR**
**$$$**
XENOKRATOUS 51
TEL (210) 722 9106
Upscale French restaurant in Kolonaki, where Pavarotti and other celebrities have dined. Elegant decor and equally elegant food: steaks a specialty. Extensive and expensive wine list.
🚇 Syntagma 🛗 🚫 All major cards

🍴 **MAMACAS**
**$$$**
PERSEPHONIS 41
TEL (210) 346 4984
The food at Mamacas had Athenians trekking out to the unfashionable Gazi district years ago, and the area's transformation is in no small part due to places like this. It serves traditional kitchen favorites like meatballs and stuffed peppers, but like you've never tasted before. It stays open late when the bar becomes a great place to hang out.
🚇 Keramikos 🕐 Closed Mon. 🛗 🚫 All major cards

---

🏨 Hotel  🍴 Restaurant  🛏 No. of Guest Rooms  🅿 Parking  🚇 Metro  🕐 Closed  🛗 Elevator

## 🍴 MELROSE

**$$$**

ZOSIMADOU 16

**TEL (210) 823 1627**

Athens's finest Pacific Rim restaurant, with superb seafood such as salmon, tuna, shrimp, and lobster, in a chic setting with immaculate service.

🚇 Omonia ⏰ Closed L, Sun., & Aug. ❄️ 💳 All major cards

## 🍴 PIL POUL

**$$$**

APOSTOLOU PAVLOU/POULO-POULOU

**TEL (210) 342 3665**

The Thissio and Psirri districts are the places to head for good modern Greek cooking, and this fashionable place also offers views of the Acropolis.

🚇 Thissio ⏰ Closed L & Sun. D ❄️ 💳 All major cards

## 🍴 ORIZONTES (HORIZONS)

**$$$**

LYCAVITTOS HILL, KOLONAKI

**TEL (210) 722 7065**

Upscale dining atop Lykavittos, the highest point above the city. Reached by the funicular on the corner of Ploutarchou and Aristippou (9 a.m.–midnight).

🚇 Syntagma ❄️ 💳 All major cards

## 🍴 HERMION

**$$**

PANDROSSOU 7–15

**TEL (210) 324 6725**

Long-established restaurant just off the flea market, with both indoor seating and attractive courtyard dining area. Excellent service of good quality, moderately priced Greek favorites.

🚇 Monastiraki ❄️ 💳 All major cards

## 🍴 IDEAL

**$$**

PANEPESTIMIOU 46

**TEL (210) 330 3000**

Chic restaurant, with attentive service and an extensive menu, including "drunkard's tidbits" (pork in a tomato sauce with olives, onions, mushrooms, and cheese) or shrimp with feta.

🚇 Omonia ⏰ Closed Sun. ❄️ 💳 All major cards

## 🍴 MEAT ME

**$$**

BABY GRAND HOTEL ATHINAS 65

**TEL (210) 325 0900**

Traditional taverna fare but with a 21st-century atmosphere and style, in this simple, fun, and inexpensive restaurant at the boutique Baby Grand Hotel.

🚇 Omonia ❄️ 💳 All major cards

## 🍴 PALIA TAVERNA

**$$**

MARKOU MOUSOUROU 35

**TEL (210) 701 7135**

Established in the late 19th century, this taverna remains traditional in both its dishes and its atmosphere. There is often music, always good service, indoor and outdoor seating, and a reliable menu.

⏰ Closed L & Sun. ❄️ 💳 All major cards

## 🍴 PRUNIER

**$$**

IPSILANTOU 63

**TEL (210) 722 7379**

This French bistro near the Hilton Hotel offers a romantic setting with typical bistro dishes, such as coq au vin and escargots. Some more exotic choices, too, like quail in oregano and lemon sauce.

🚇 Syntagma ⏰ Closed L & Sun. ❄️ 💳 All major cards

## 🍴 SHOLARHIO

**$$**

TRIPODON 14

**TEL (210) 324 7605**

This wonderfully simple place has no menu. Trays of meze are brought round and you choose what you like the look of, and pay accordingly. The drinks are equally simple. Inexpensive but oozing atmosphere—and the food is tasty.

🚇 Monastiraki ❄️ 💳 All major cards

## 🍴 TO CAFENEIO

**$$**

LOUKIANOU 26

**TEL (210) 722 9056**

Chic but relaxed restaurant in Kolonaki, serving excellent Greek specialties such as spinach pie, baked eggplant with cheese, chicken in lemon sauce, and other dishes to an international clientele.

🚇 Syntagma ⏰ Closed Sun. ❄️ 💳 All major cards

## 🍴 XINOS

**$$**

ANGELOU GERONTA 4

**TEL (210) 322 1065**

On a Plaka backstreet that few tourists find, this place is very popular with Athenians. Superior food, music late in the evening, and charming outdoor garden seating.

🚇 Syntagma ⏰ Closed L, Sat.–Sun., & winter ❄️ 💳 All major cards

## 🍴 BAKALARAKIA

**$**

KYDATHINAION 41

**TEL (210) 322 5084**

Simple Greek food in what claims to be the oldest taverna in Athens, established in 1865. Salt cod in garlic is the specialty that gives this basement place its name.

🚇 Monastiraki ⏰ Closed L midsummer ❄️ 💳 No credit cards

## 🍴 BARBA YANNIS

**$**

EMMANUEL BENAKI 94

**TEL (210) 330 0185**

This great favorite frequently has lines outside the door.

---

🚭 Nonsmoking  ❄️ Air-conditioning  🏊 Indoor Pool  🏊 Outdoor Pool  🏋️ Health Club  💳 Credit Cards

Brisk service, and a limited menu of good hearty Greek dishes. There is often impromptu music.

🚇 Omonia 🕐 Closed Sun. D & Aug. 💳 💳 No credit cards

## SOMETHING SPECIAL

### 🍴 EDEN
$
PLAKA 12
TEL (210) 324 8858
This was the first purely vegetarian restaurant in Athens, and serves food so tasty that meat eaters will not notice its absence. The bread is delicious, baked daily, and your coffee cup will be endlessly refilled.

🚇 Monastiraki 🕐 Closed Tues. 💳 💳 💳 All major cards

### 🍴 FIVE BROTHERS
$
EOLOU 3
TEL (210) 325 0088
Indoor and outdoor seating near the Roman Agora with various fixed-price menu options, generous portions, and good grills and chops. A decent house wine and friendly waiters add to the appeal.

🚇 Monastiraki 💳 💳 All major cards

### 🍴 GURU
$
PLATEIA THEATROU 10, PSIRRI
TEL (210) 324 6530
On the ground floor, a Thai restaurant, known for good food and creative alcoholic concoctions, overlooks a lively bar area. Above, a laid-back, Asian-style mezzanine lounge leads up to a late night music club.

🚇 Monastiraki 💳 💳 All major cards

### 🍴 I SAITA
$
KYDATHINAION 21
Unpretentious basement

taverna, wine from the barrel, murals on the walls, with a standard menu that occasionally offers some delicious surprises, such as pork in a cream of celery sauce.

🚇 Syntagma 🕐 Closed L 💳 💳 No credit cards

### 🍴 KLIMATARIA
$
KLEPSIDRAS 5
TEL (210) 321 1215
Century-old tavern in the backstreets of the Plaka where the food is simple (chops, moussaka, stuffed vine leaves) but well prepared and very good value, and there's live music some nights, too.

🕐 Closed L 💳 No credit cards

### 🍴 KOUKLIS
$
TRIPODON 14
TEL (210) 324 7605
Also known as To Yerani, this *ouzerie* is a well-established favorite, concentrating on hearty mezes (snacks) such as *saganaki* (deep-fried cheese), *taramosalata*, fried fish, and sausages cooked in ouzo. Pleasant dining terrace, too.

🚇 Monastiraki 💳 💳 All major cards

### 🍴 NEON
$
MITROPOLEOS 3
TEL (210) 322 8155
Neon is one of a chain of restaurants worth knowing about if you want somewhere a bit less formal and more cafeteria-style. Inexpensive, clean, lots of seating and an international menu including pastas, steaks, chicken, and a range of simple Greek dishes.

🚇 Syntagma 💳 No credit cards

### 🍴 O PLATANOS
$
DIOGENOUS 4
TEL (210) 322 0666

## PRICES

### HOTELS

An indication of the cost of a double room in the high season is given by $ signs.

| $$$$$ | Over $240 |
|---|---|
| $$$$ | $160-240 |
| $$$ | $110-160 |
| $$ | $70-110 |
| $ | Under $70 |

### RESTAURANTS

An indication of the cost of a three-course meal without drinks is given by $ signs.

| $$$$$ | Over $65 |
|---|---|
| $$$$ | $50-65 |
| $$$ | $30-50 |
| $$ | $20-30 |
| $ | Under $20 |

An Athenian favorite that offers few concessions to tourism. It has one of the best locations in the Plaka, with tables outside in the summer under the plane tree that gives it its name.

🚇 Monastiraki 🕐 Closed Sun. 💳 💳 No credit cards

## SOMETHING SPECIAL

### 🍴 SIGALAS
$
PLATEIA MONASTIRAKI 2
TEL (210) 321 3036
For an authentic Athenian dining experience, Sigalas cannot be beaten. It is right on the busy Monastiraki Square, with the bustle extending into the warren of the restaurant itself. Waiters in red sweaters rush about, some looking as if they have been there since the restaurant opened at the end of the 19th century. It is a casual place, where arguments and laughter rage, old photos plaster every wall, and the food comprises good, inexpensive examples of standard Greek taverna fare. On

weekends, arrive early.

🚇 Monastiraki 🕐 Closed L
❄️ 💳 No credit cards

## PIREAS

### 🏨 IDEAL
**$**
NOTARA 142
TEL (210) 429 4050
Hotels in Pireas can be expensive or seedy, the Ideal is neither. Near the international ferry ports; newly renovated. Worth making advance reservations if you need to spend a night in Pireas.

🛏 31 🚇 Piraeus (long walk)/ airport bus ⬌ ❄️ 💳 AmEx, V

### 🏨 LILIA
**$**
ZEAS 131
TEL (210) 417 9108
E-MAIL INFO@LILIAHOTEL.GR
www.liliahotel.gr/en
Pleasant setting away from the noisy waterfront; clean, comfortable rooms. The closest harbor is Zea Marina, used by hydrofoils and catamarans to many destinations.

🛏 17 🚇 Piraeus (taxi from here advisable)/airport bus ⬌ ❄️ 💳 AmEx, V

### 🍴 ALLI SKALA
**$$$**
SERIFOU 57
TEL (210) 482 7722
A distinguished restaurant with a wonderful courtyard, but not overpriced for Pireas. Has a wider menu than just seafood, including meats and excellent examples of good Greek homecooking.

🚇 Piraeus 🕐 Closed L
❄️ 💳 All major cards

### 🍴 DOURAMBEIS
**$$$**
AKTI PROTOPSALTI 27
TEL (210) 412 2092
A simple restaurant but with outstanding—and expensive —fresh fish dishes from the Aegean Islands, including

a delicious crayfish soup. Established in 1932, this is one of the best in Pireas.

🚇 Piraeus ❄️ 💳 All major cards

### 🍴 VAROULKO
**$$$**
DELIYIORYI 14
TEL (210) 422 1283
Modern Greek and Continental cuisine, with an unusual menu including such surprises as grape leaves stuffed with fish. Monkfish is the chef's specialty. Reservations advised for this Michelin-starred place.

🚇 Piraeus 🕐 Closed L, Sun., & Aug. ❄️ 💳 All major cards

### 🍴 ACHINOS
**$$**
AKTI THEMESTOKLEOUS 51,
TEL (210) 452 6944
This split-level bar/restaurant has a stunning cliffside location, like a Pireas version of Santorini. The style is very modern Mediterranean with both simple and more creative fish dishes. There's an impressive wine list, too.

🚇 Piraeus ❄️ 💳 All major cards

### 🍴 KOLLIAS
**$$**
STRATIGOU PLASTIRA 3
TEL (210) 462 9620
Renowned Pireas fish restaurant, which ranges superbly from the conventional (mackerel, mussels, lobster) to the unusual (shrimp and tomato soup, scorpionfish).

🚇 Piraeus 🕐 Closed Sun.,

Aug., & L summer ❄️ 💳 All major cards

### 🍴 PLOUS PODILATOU
**$$**
AKTI KOUMOUNDOUROU 42, MICROLIMANO
TEL (210) 413 7910
Imaginative fresh seafood served overlooking the waterfront at Microlimano. Great

selection of wines.

🚇 Piraeus ❄️ 💳 All major cards

### 🍴 VASILAINAS
**$$**
ETOLIKOU 72
TEL (210) 461 2457
There are inexpensive places in Pireas if you forget fresh fish, which is always pricey in Greece. This taverna has been here since the 1930s and is noted for its set menu of 16 different dishes, a rainbow of Greek flavors.

🚇 Piraeus 🕐 Closed L & Sun.
❄️ 💳 All major cards

## ■ AROUND ATHENS

### AKRA SOUNION

### 🏨 GRECOTEL CAPE SOUNION
**$$$**
AKRA SOUNION
TEL 2292 069700
Superbly located 5-star resort hotel, with its own beach but backed by a pine forest on the edge of a national park. Lovely views of the Temple of Poseidon, good food, health club, and an outdoor pool; some of the private villas have their own swimming pools.

🛏 124 🅿️ ❄️ 💳 All major cards

### 🍴 ILIAS
**$$**
AKRA SOUNION
TEL 0292 39114
An alternative to the eating places outside the Temple of Poseidon is this fish taverna on the beach below. Less impressive view but slightly cheaper. No surprises on the menu, but lots of fresh fish.

❄️ 💳 No credit cards

### MARATHON

### 🏨 CLUB MEDITERRANEE ATHENIA

### $$$
**MARATHON BEACH**
TEL 22940 57100
www.clubmed.us
Close to the Marathon sites and right on the beach, this huge hotel is a first-class option for anyone wanting to be near, but not in, Athens. Has four pools, a nightclub, water-sports facilities, restaurants, and stores.
🛈 543 🅿 🛗 📶 🏊 📶
📶 All major cards

## VOULIAGMENI

### 🏨 ASTIR PALACE
### $$$
VOULIAGMENI
TEL (210) 890 2000
E-MAIL INFO@AEGEON-HOTEL.COM
www.astir-palace.com/en/
Luxury hotel complex that comprises three separate hotels, right by the sea, with superb views over the Aegean. Superior facilities, with central Athens accessible by day.
🛈 571 🅿 🛗 📶 🏊 📶 All major cards

### 🏨 ARMONIA
### $$
ARMONIAS 1
TEL (210) 896 3304
E-MAIL ARMONIA@ARMONIA.GR
www.armonia.gr
This A-class hotel has spectacular views over the Saronic Gulf and caters for the business traveler, with numerous well-equipped conference rooms. Rooms all have telephone, TV, air-conditioning, and piped music.
🛈 165 🅿 🛗 📶 🏊 📶 All major cards

## ◼ PELOPONNISOS

## ANDRITSAINA

### 🏨 THEOXENIA HOTEL
### $

ANDRITSAINA
TEL 26260 22219
The only hotel of any size in this mountain village. Facilities are basic but so are prices, and the rooms are clean and have telephones. Many also have splendid views of the surrounding mountains.
🛈 28 🕐 Closed Nov.–Feb.
🛗 📶 📶 No credit cards

### 🍴 O YIORGIS
### $
MAIN PLATEIA
TEL 26260 22004
The center of this mountain village is a perfect setting for this simple taverna. The staple is hearty fare such as grilled chops and beef dishes, but the local produce is delicious. Go for either a freshly grilled souvlaki, or a succulent oven-baked dish like *youvetsi*.
📶 📶 No credit cards

### 🍴 SIGOURI
### $
SOPHOKLEOS
Hearty Greek dishes that are created fresh each day in the kitchen of the owner. Specials might include moussaka or stuffed tomatoes, and there's wine from the barrel to drink.
📶 📶 No credit cards

## CORINTH

### 🏨 EFIRA
### $
ETHNIKIS ANTISTASSEOS 52
TEL 27410 24021
As in many of the mainland's most popular spots, there is a dearth of decent accommodations in Corinth, but the Efira is an acceptable option. It has typical clean and simple Greek rooms and its own restaurant.
🛈 45 🛗 📶 📶 No credit cards

## KITHERA

### 🍴 SOTIRIS
### $$

AVLEMONAS
TEL 27350 33922
Sotiris sits right on the main square in Avlemonas but only opens on summer weekends. When open, though, there is no better place to sample the best of the day's catch, such as tuna, mullet, and frequently obscure fish for which only the Greek name is known.
🕐 Closed Mon.–Fri. & winter
📶 📶 No credit cards

### 🍴 YDRAGOGEIO
### $$
KAPSALI
TEL 27350 31065
This excellent restaurant on the edge of Kapsali has something for everyone. Enjoy a beautiful view, regular live music, friendly service, a convenient location, and excellent food. Vegetarian options include stuffed peppers, while the staples of fresh fish and grilled meats are enhanced by mouthwatering spinach-and-cheese pies and other homemade dishes.
📶 📶 No credit cards

---

## KORONI

### ⊞ AUBERGE DE LA PLAGE
**$**

ZANGA BEACH
TEL 27250 22401

Given the superb views over Koroni's beautiful long bay of sandy beach and its castle, prices at the Auberge are surprisingly reasonable. All rooms have balconies and sea views.

🛏 43 🕐 Closed Nov.–Mar. 🅿 🔁 🕸 No credit cards

### 🍴 OUZERIE KANGELARIOS
**$$**

WATERFRONT
TEL 27250 22648

The perfect place for an early or late ouzo, with a snack from the range of unusual meze on offer. Grilled fish is good, and other seafood includes shrimps, mussels, squid, octopus, and a rare chance to try sea urchins.

🕸 🕸 No credit cards

## MANI

### ⊞ KARDAMYLI BEACH HOTEL
**$$**

KARDAMYLI BEACH, KARDAMYLI
TEL 27210 73180

Excellent location in this popular beach resort, right by the beach, with many of the rooms having either sea views or views to the mountains of the Mani behind.

🛏 29 🕐 Closed Nov.–Mar. 🅿 🔁 🕸 🌊 All major cards

### ⊞ LONDAS
**$$**

AREOPOLIS
TEL 27330 51360

The owners of this hotel are an artist and an architect, resulting in a sympathetic restoration from an old tower house into a comfortable A-class hotel. There are only four rooms, so advance reservations are essential.

The perfect base for exploring the Mani.

🛏 4 🕸 🕸 No credit cards

### ⊞ PORTO VITILO HOTEL
**$$**

KAROVOSTASSI, NEAR NEO ITYLO
TEL 27330 59270

This B-class hotel shows that in Greece you don't need luxury ratings to provide stylish and comfortable rooms. All have canopied beds, and all have balconies with views of either the sea or the mountains. All are also air-conditioned, and there is a convenient on-site taverna as the hotel is a little way out of the village center.

🛏 24 🕸 No credit cards

### ⊞ AKTAION
**$**

VASILEOS PAVLOU 39, GITHIO
TEL 27330 23500

Right on the waterfront, this bright and pleasant hotel has been converted from one of the old port mansions. Front rooms have balconies with pretty harbor and sea views.

🛏 22 🕐 Closed Nov.–March 🕸 🕸 No credit cards

### 🍴 KLIMATERIA
**$$**

PLATEIA POLYTECHNIOU
TEL 27330 31544

One of the best restaurants in the Peloponnisos, with lovingly prepared conventional Greek dishes, more imaginative gourmet options, a range of vegetarian meals, fresh fish and lobster, and fine wines. Choose whether you eat cheaply or more extravagantly.

🕐 Closed winter 🕸 🕸 All major cards

### 🍴 KOZIA
**$$**

VASILEOS PAVLOU 13, GITHIO
TEL 27330 24086

Excellent seafood taverna

with wide range of fresh fish along with meat dishes, vegetarian dishes, and salads as a cheaper option.

🕸 🕸 All major cards

### 🍴 NISSI
**$$**

MARATHONISI
TEL 27330 22830

Take a boat out to the little island of Marathonisi, and dine with a view back to the town at this taverna whose name means simply "island." The menu is a reasonably safe list of Greek staples, such as moussaka and squid, but they are well done.

🕸 🕸 No credit cards

### 🍴 LELA'S
**$**

SEA FRONT, KARDAMYLI
TEL 27210 73541

Family-run taverna where mother cooks excellent home recipes. Friendly service and views out to sea.

🕸 🕸 No credit cards

## METHONI

### ⊞ ACHILLES HOTEL
**$**

METHONI
TEL 27230 31819

A small and simple B-class hotel in this popular resort, which exemplifies Greek value for money. If you are prepared to forgo TV and telephone in your room, and settle for the basic comforts, cleanliness, and a friendly and relaxed atmosphere, then this is a real bargain. The only facilities are a bar and a breakfast room, but it is convenient to town.

🛏 13 🕸 🕸 No credit cards

## MONEMVASIA

### ⊞ MALVASIA
**$$**

KASTRO, MONEMVASIA

---

TEL 27320 61323
E-MAIL INFO@MALVASIA-HOTEL.GR
http://malvasia-hotel.gr/index-en.html
These converted old rooms are in the heart of the Monemvasia fortress, and staying here at night gives the feeling of having closed the drawbridge on the world. Very tasteful rooms, some suites available.

🛏 16 🛗 🏧 🏧 All major cards

### 🍴 KANONI
$

MAIN THROUGH ROAD OF OLD TOWN
TEL 27320 61387
Converted 17th-century mansion in the old town, where only the views can distract you from the good food.

🏧 🏧 All major cards

### 🍴 MATOULA
$

KASTRO
TEL 27320 61660
Situated in the old part of Monemvasia, the Matoula has a terrace setting with tables looking out across the sea and along the Peloponnesian coast. The food does justice to the view, with hearty oven-baked dishes such as lamb casserole alongside grilled pork, chicken, and fish.

🏧 🏧 No credit cards

## MYCENAE

### 🏨 OREA ELENI
$

15 HR. TSOUNTA
TEL 27510 76225
The long-established hotel in which archaeologist Heinrich Schliemann stayed while excavating Mycenae, up the road. Simple but clean, with five rooms, none en suite. Terrific character makes up for basic amenities. The restaurant is also the best bet locally (see below).

🛏 5 🕐 Closed Nov.–April
🅿 🛗 🏧 🏧 All major cards

### 🍴 LA BELLE HELENE
$$

TEL 27510 76225
Eat in Schliemann's hotel (see above) for a sense of place. No surprises on the menu, but the restaurant is better than—if slightly pricier than—the tourist-trap tavernas that abound in the area.

🏧 🏧 All major cards

## MYSTRAS

### 🏨 BYZANTION
$

MYSTRAS
TEL 27310 83309
E-MAIL BYZANHTL@OTENET.GR
www.byzantionhotel.gr/
The best place for an early morning start to a visit to Mystras, which is visible from some of the upper rooms. Though only a B-class hotel, it is clean and comfortable and has been recently renovated. It has its own restaurant, but there are a few other eating options nearby in this relaxed little village.

🛏 22 🕐 Closed Nov.–March
🏧 🏧 MC, V

## NAFPLIO

### 🏨 NAFPLIA PALACE
$$$

KASTRO ACRONAFPLIAS
TEL 27520 28981
E-MAIL RESERVATIONS@NAFPLIONHOTELS.GR
www.nafplionhotels.gr
This luxury hotel occupies a prime position overlooking Nafplio's harbor, the sea, and across to the Peloponnisos. It's an easy stroll down into the town, but a steep walk back up again, so take a car or a taxi. The 48 rooms, 3 suites, and 33 villas all have lovely sea views.

🛏 84 🏧 🏧 All major cards

### 🏨 VYREON
$$

2 PLATONOS

TEL 27520 22351
It's impossible to miss this brightly painted, intimate hotel in a quiet backstreet, opposite the entrance to the Agios Spiridon church. Great personality, rooms with character.

🛏 17 🛗 🏧 🏧 All major cards

### 🏨 KING OTHON
$

KING OTTO/OTHEAN 4
TEL 27520 27585
E-MAIL INFO@KINGOTHON.GR
www.kingothon.gr/
This old favorite has 12 simple, cheap rooms, some overlooking the courtyard garden where breakfast is served. There is now also an Otto II nearby.

🛏 12 🕐 Closed winter 🏧
🏧 AmEx, MC, V

### 🍴 OMORFI POLI
$$

BOUBOULINAS 75
TEL 27520 29452
An adventurous menu at this slightly more upmarket restaurant, to which there's also a charming, small nine-room

hotel attached. Try the stuffed pork fillet or stuffed potatoes. The flare extends to the wine list, which includes some of the local vineyards inland from Nafplio and producing remarkably good wine.

 Closed L & Sun.  No credit cards

### KARAMANLIS
**$**
BOUBOULINAS 1
TEL 27520 27668
Long-established Nafplio favorite, a plain and simple taverna on the waterfront and serving inexpensive but tasty Greek staples like chops, moussaka, country sausages, or slightly pricier fresh fish done on the grill.

 Most major credit cards

### STATHMOS CAFÉ
**$**
OLD RAILROAD STATION
Basic snacks, salads, and mezes, but a good shady setting for a quick meal or a lingering coffee or beer.

 No credit cards

### TA PHANARIA
**$**
STAIKOPOULOU 13
TEL 27520 27141
A small shaded area by the side of this taverna gives a charming spot for a meal. Good vegetarian dishes along-side the Greek staples single this taverna out.

 No credit cards

### O NOULIS
**$**
MOUTZOURIDOU 22
TEL 27520 25541
Most Greek eating places serve mezes of some kind, but places like the Noulis that spe-cialize in them are surprisingly rare. Dine Greek-style with a bottle of ouzo instead of wine, and keep ordering small plates of dishes like squid, octopus, or small deep-fried fish until

you're full. Order the special of ten different dishes and you certainly will be.

 Closed D & Sun.  No credit cards

## OLYMPIA

### EUROPA BEST WESTERN
**$$**
OLYMPIA
TEL 26240 22650
E-MAIL HOTELEUROPA@
HOTELEUROPA.GR
www.hoteleuropa.gr/en/
index.html
With a view from a hill overlooking ancient Olympia, this A-class hotel combines the comfort of a well-established chain with the personal touches that come from being family run. Walking and horse-back riding are available, and the hotel has its own tennis courts, too.

80 All major cards

### PRAXITELES
**$**
SPILIOPOULOU 7
TEL 26240 22592 OR
26240 23570 (RESTAURANT)
Small, affordable hotels like this are hard to find in the busy tourist town of Olympia. It is clean and extremely cheap, but don't expect frills. Justifiably popular eating place for locals and visitors alike. Do expect good food in the family restaurant of the same name.

10 AmEx, V

### KLADEOS
**$**
BEHIND RAILROAD STATION
TEL 26240 23322
Charming riverside setting for an old favorite serving seasonal specialties, from game to vegetarian and an excellent and substantial meze selection.

Closed L All major cards

### ZEUS RESTAURANT CAFÉ BAR
**$**
PRAXITELES STREET (HIGH STREET)
TEL 26240 23913
The accent is on fresh food, such as pork casserole, salads, or simply fresh orange juice. It is run by a friendly Greek-Australian couple.

No credit cards

## PATRA

### PRIMAROLIA HOTEL
**$$**
OTHONOS AMALIAS ST. 33
TEL 2610 629400
E-MAIL PRIMAROLIA@
ARTHOTEL.GR
www.arthotel.gr/primarolia/
The city's most stylish art hotel. Cool and comfortable rooms.

14 All major cards

### RANNIA
**$**
53 RIGA FEREOU
TEL 2610 220114
Delightfully quiet hotel in the busy port of Patra, located on a pleasant square well away from the port and waterfront. Not all rooms are en suite and amenities are basic, but the hotel is well taken care of.

30 All major cards

### PHAROS
**$$**
AMALIAS 48
TEL 2610 336500
Every port has a seafood restaurant named Pharos, or Lighthouse, and the one in Patra is especially good. There are meat and regular Greek options, but the fish is so fresh it would be a shame not to sample something from the daily catch.

All major cards

### MYTHOS
**$$**
TRION NAVARHON/RIGA

---

**FEREOU**

**TEL 2610 329984**

Charming and romantic yet inexpensive place whose speciality is the Mythos pie, made using chicken and feta cheese.

🕐 Closed L 🅴 🅰 All major cards

## PILOS

### 🍴 DIETHNES

$$

**PARALIA**

**TEL 27230 22772**

An ideal eating spot, right on the harbor, with fresh fish plucked from the sea that morning, perhaps mullet or swordfish, but with other Greek favorites too.

🅴 🅰 All major cards

### 🍴 O GRIGORIS

$

**MAIN SQUARE**

**TEL 27230 22621**

Attractive restaurant constructed of local stone, with a sheltered and shaded courtyard out back. It is noted for its grilled dishes, such as pork and chicken, as well as oven-baked stews such as *stifado*.

🅴 🅰 No credit cards

## SPARTA

### 🏨 MANIATIS

$

**PALEOLOGOU 72**

**TEL 27310 22665**

**www.arthotel.gr/primarolia/**

The main choice in central Sparta, this is an acceptable if uninspiring hotel with 80 en suite rooms. It has all the facilities, but this is a place in which to spend a night in order to see Mystras rather than spend a vacation.

🛈 80 🛗 🅴 🅰 All major cards

### 🍴 DIETHNES

$

**PALEOLOGOU 105**

**TEL 27310 28636**

Tables in the shady garden are popular with locals and the few tourists who venture here. Prices are kept low and standards high by the demands of the locals, but apart from a few daily specials expect no surprise choices on the menu.

🅴 🅰 No credit cards

## ■ CENTRAL GREECE, THESSALY, & EPIROS

### ARACHOVA

#### 🏨 APOLLON

$

**DELPHON 20**

**TEL 22670 31427**

Superb example of a reasonably priced and excellently run little hotel ideally placed for exploring Delphi and Parnassos. Clean and pleasant rooms (although not en suite) and friendly owners.

🛈 10 🅿 🛗 🅴 🅰 All major cards

#### 🍴 KARATHANASSI

$

**DELPHON 56**

**TEL 22670 31360**

You will dine much better in this long-established, family-run taverna (also known as Barba Yannis) than down the road in Delphi. Many hearty local specialties, including lamb, and an equally hearty range of wines.

🕐 Closed L in summer

🅴 🅰 No credit cards

#### 🍴 O SAKIS

$

**DELPHON 51**

**TEL 22670 31511**

Filling mountain food is on offer at this traditional old taverna on the main street. Strong on meat stews and grills, such as goat and lamb, and vast plates of tasty salads. Local wine from the barrel.

**PRICES**

**HOTELS**

An indication of the cost of a double room in the high season is given by **$** signs.

| | |
|---|---|
| **$$$$$** | Over $240 |
| **$$$$** | $160-240 |
| **$$$** | $110-160 |
| **$$** | $70-110 |
| **$** | Under $70 |

**RESTAURANTS**

An indication of the cost of a three-course meal without drinks is given by **$** signs.

| | |
|---|---|
| **$$$$$** | Over $65 |
| **$$$$** | $50-65 |
| **$$$** | $30-50 |
| **$$** | $20-30 |
| **$** | Under $20 |

🕐 Closed midsummer 🅴 🅰 All major cards

### DELPHI

#### 🏨 OLYMPIC

$$

**VAS. PAVLOU 53A**

**TEL 22650 82780**

**E-MAIL INFO@OLYMPIC-HOTEL .GR**

**www.olympic-hotel.gr/eng /index.htm**

Charming old-fashioned hotel with immaculate furnishings and stunning views. Has a central location, close to some of Delphi's better restaurants and the ancient site. Ideal for an early morning visit.

🛈 20 🛗 🅴 🅰 All major cards

#### 🏨 VARONOS

$

**FREDERIKIS 25**

**TEL 22650 82345**

**E-MAIL INFO@HOTEL-VARO NOS.GR**

**www.hotel-varonos.gr**

Small, family-run hotel, ideal for the independent traveler on a budget. Extremely friendly owners; basic but clean rooms with balconies and superb views. A short stroll to the ancient site of Delphi.

ⓘ 10 ⊟ 🅢 🅢 All major cards

### 🍴 INIOCHOS
$$

FREDERIKIS 19
TEL 22650 82710
Superb views over the valley and a very good and wide-ranging menu in a town where poor tourist fare is the norm: from mussels and fresh fish to lamb in pastry and several vegetarian dishes. Highly recommended.

🅢 🅢 No credit cards

### 🍴 TAVERNA SKALA
$$

ISAIA 11
TEL 22650 82442
This cosy wood-paneled taverna offers plain and simple Greek cooking and is not aimed at the tourist dollar but is popular year-round with local diners.

🅢 🅢 No credit cards

## IOANINA

### 🏨 EPIRUS PALACE HOTEL
$$$

TEL 26510 93555
E-MAIL INFO@EPIRUSPALACE.GR
www.epiruspalace.gr/
This new deluxe hotel, with gourmet restaurant and lagoon pool, is popular with weekending Athenians. All rooms luxuriously furnished with marble bathrooms. Four miles (7 km) from city center.

ⓘ 116 🅿 ⊟ 🅢 🅢 🅢 All major cards

### 🏨🍴 OLYMPIC
$$

MELANIDI 2
TEL 26510 25147
E-MAIL INFO@HOTELOLYMP.GR
www.hotelolymp.gr/en-index.html
Very good standards in this long-established central hotel, convenient for all the town's

attractions. The bright, clean rooms all have TVs, phones, and minibars. Popular La Fontantina restaurant (see below).

ⓘ 51 🅿 ⊟ 🅢 🅢 No credit cards

### 🍴 GASTRA
$$

1 MILE (1.5 KM) BEYOND AIRPORT
TEL 26510 61530
On the airport road, just before the turn for Igoumenitsa, this is one of the region's specialty restaurants where meat is cooked in an iron pot called a *gastra*. An iron lid is placed over the dish, which is covered in hot coals or wood. Slow cooking but mouthwatering when it arrives.

🕐 Closed Mon. 🅢 🅢 All major cards

### 🍴 LA FONTANTINA
$$

OLYMPIC HOTEL, MELANIDI 2
TEL 26510 25147
This Greek–Italian place, in the Olympic hotel, doesn't disappoint, as you can tell from the packed tables. Risotto is good, so too are the Greek bakes, like stuffed tomatoes.

🅢 🅢 All major cards

## SOMETHING SPECIAL

### 🍴 PAMVOTIS
$

NISSI ISLAND
TEL 26510 81081
If staying in Ioanina there can be no finer place to dine in the evening than on the little island in the lake. There are several similar fish restaurants here, and all can safely be recommended, but Pamvotis is one of the oldest and best. Choose your fish fresh from one of the tanks, and have it grilled for a sublime meal in surroundings that are both simple and romantic. Fish include trout from mountain hatcheries, as fish stocks in the

lake have dwindled.

🅢 🅢 All major cards

### 🍴 TO MANTELO
$

PLATEIA GIORGIOU 15
TEL 26510 25452
For the non-tourist experience, this Greek taverna serves generous helpings of local specialties such as fried peppers or eggplant, various *saganaki* dishes (including deep-fried Roquefort and feta), and *tsoutsoukakia* (slightly sweet, spicy sausages).

🅢 🅢 All major cards

## METEORA

### 🏨 EDELWEISS
$$

VENIZELOU 3, KALABAKA
TEL 24320 23966
Pleasant hotel in Kalabaka, close to the Meteora monasteries: some rooms offer distant views of them. Prices are reasonable, and it has its own swimming pool.

ⓘ 48 🅿 ⊟ 🅢 🅢 🅢 MC, V

### 🍴 METEORA
$

PLATIA DIMARCHIOU, KALABAKA
TEL 24320 22316
Simple but good, family-run taverna where the wife does the cooking and the husband and other relatives serve. Great moussaka, good choice of grilled meats.

🕐 Closed winter 🅢 🅢 No credit cards

## METSOVO

### 🏨 EGNATIA
$

TOSITSA 19
TEL 26560 41900
Moderately priced mountain hotel with traditional stone and woodwork decoration, right on the main street. Some rooms have mountain views, and the hotel has its own very good restaurant.

**1** 36 **P** **🔁** **🔂** **🔗** All major cards

## 🏨 GALAXY
**$**

MAIN SQUARE

TEL 26560 41202

Good, clean, family-run hotel, right in the heart of town. It has an adjoining restaurant, equally commendable and equally well run (see below).

**1** 10 **P** **🔁** **🔂** **🔗** MC, V

## 🍴 GALAXY
**$**

MAIN SQUARE

TEL 26560 41202

Good mountain dishes, with local cheeses and wine, served in a delightful traditional building in hotel of same name (see above) overlooking the main square. You will need a good appetite as portions are large.

**🔂** **🔗** All major cards

## 🍴 METSOVITIKO SALONI
**$**

TOSITSA

TEL 26560 42142

Attractive restaurant with mountain decor and mountain dishes, especially game. Veranda overlooks main street.

**🔂** **🔗** All major cards

## NAFPAKTOS

## 🏨 NAFPAKTOS HOTEL
**$$**

KORYDALIOU 4

TEL 26340 29551

Spotless hotel, handy for the harbor. Some rooms have sea views, so be sure to ask for one. All the rooms have balconies.

**1** 50 **P** **🔁** **🔂** **🔗** All major cards

## PARGA

## 🏨 PARADISSOS
**$**

PLATEIA AGIOU NIKOLAOU

TEL 26840 31229

Friendly hotel in a fully renovated old building on one of Parga's most attractive squares. In the center of town but only a short walk from the harbor with its restaurants, and the best town beach.

**1** 19 **P** **🔁** **🔂** **🔗** All major cards

## 🍴 FLISVOS
**$**

MAVROYENOUS 10

TEL 26840 31624

Located beyond the fortress away from the main waterfront tavernas. Has outstanding sunset views, good fish, good prices, good service.

**🕐** Closed in winter **🔂** **🔗** All major cards

## PILION

## 🏨 ARCHONTIKO MOUSLI
**$$**

MAKRINITSA

TEL 24280 99250 (MAIN OFFICE NUMBER, COVERING SEVERAL MANSIONS)

The restored Pilion mansions, with old furniture and decorated with embroidery and other wall hangings, make memorable but expensive places to stay. Advance reservations are recommended, as they are extremely popular.

**1** 8 **🔂** **🔗** No credit cards

## 🍴 OSTRIA TAVERNA
**$**

AGIOS IOANNIS

TEL 24260 31331

Serves some of the best regional food in the Pilion, such as an established favorite—rabbit stew.

**🕐** Closed Tues.–Thurs. L & winter **🔂** **🔗** All major cards

## VOLOS

## 🏨 PHILIPPOS
**$$**

SOLONOS 9

TEL 24210 37607

Modern hotel with all facilities, by main square in the center of Volos, convenient for the ferry harbor and for exploring the Pilion. Some rooms have sea views.

**1** 39 **🔁** **🔂** **🔗** No credit cards

## ZAGORIA

## 🏨 DIAS
**$$$**

MIKRO PAPINGO

TEL 26530 41257

Charming hotel in tiny, village off the beaten track, is built of stone with arched windows. Rooms are basic but clean, perfect for walkers exploring Vikos Gorge and Zagoria.

**1** 5 **P** **🔁** **🔂** **🔗** V

## 🏨 PAPAEVANGELOU HOTEL
**$$**

MEGALO PAPINGO

TEL 26530 41135

Exquisitely built rooms overlooking the gorge and Mount Smolikas. Romantic ambience and delicious homemade breakfasts.

**1** 11 **P** **🔗** No credit cards

---

---

🏨 Hotel   🍴 Restaurant   **1** No. of Guest Rooms   **P** Parking   🚇 Metro   🕐 Closed   🔁 Elevator

### SAXONIS HOUSES
**$$**

DASKA 11, MEGALO PAPINGO
TEL 26530 41615
A cluster of traditional Zagorian mansions converted into elegant, if somewhat expensive, hotel accommodations, retaining some original features such as fireplaces and painted ceilings.

ⓘ 10 🅿 🔁 🗗 🗗 No credit cards

### SPIROS TSOUMANIS
**$$**

MEGALO PAPINGO
TEL 26530 12108
Another hearty Zagorian place on the edge of the village, fortifying diners with its robust mountain cuisine. The grills are especially good, all the meat and vegetables being local and fresh.

🗗 No credit cards

### KATERINA'S ART
**$**

NEA VIKOS GORGE
TEL 26530 61233
Impressive restaurant in an old village mansion; some unusual Zagorian dishes, especially game.

🗗 🗗 No credit cards

### DIONYSOS
**$**

MONODENDRI
TEL 26530 71366
Sample real Epirot mountain food, including game dishes in season, and traditional local pies in this lively place on the main road and popular with hikers and climbers.

🗗 🗗 No credit cards

## MACEDONIA & THRACE

## ALEXANDROUPOLI

### ALKYON
**$**

MOUDANION 1
TEL 25510 23593
Simple, inexpensive, friendly hotel, tastefully done up and with good sea views. Although modern in design, it has a traditional feel inside, with old-fashioned furnishings.

ⓘ 32 🅿 🔁 🗗 🗗 All major cards

### KLIMATARIA
**$**

POLYTECHNIOU 18
TEL 25510 26288
On a busy square with many eating places, this is one of the best for fish. It has an extensive menu of traditional Greek dishes and more unusual ones, such as baked goat. Good choice of local wines, too.

🗗 🗗 All major cards

## CHALKIDIKI

### EAGLES PALACE
**$$$**

OURANOPOLIS
TEL 23770 31047
E-MAIL INFO@EAGLESPALACE
.GR
www.eaglespalace.gr/
Five-star luxury in large wooded grounds with a pool, tennis courts, bars, restaurants, and even its own luxury yacht. Most rooms have superb views out to sea, across to the Agion Oros peninsula. One of the best hotels in the region.

ⓘ 167 🅿 🔁 🗗 🞉 🗗
🗗 All major cards

### KOSTIS
**$$**

NEA FOKEA
TEL 23740 81379
Imaginative menu, with a tasty eggplant salad. Fresh fish is always available, with batter-fried cod in garlic sauce a specialty of the house.

🗗 🗗 All major cards

### TA PEFKA
**$**

NEOS MARMARAS WATERFRONT

TEL 23750 71763
Exquisite hilltop setting among pines and surprisingly good food given the reasonable prices. Seafood is popular—such as fresh sardines, octopus meze, or catch of the day—and more unusual dishes such as mussels in a red sauce or *saganaki* (deep-fried cheese).

🗗 🗗 All major cards

### TORONEOS
**$**

PEFKOHORI
TEL 23740 61495
Eat bread made to a special recipe by the local baker, and unusual dishes, especially fish, such as squid stuffed with feta and coriander, fried peppers and pumpkins; friendly service.

🕒 Closed winter 🗗 🗗 All major cards

## KASTORIA

### ORESTION
**$**

PLATEIA DAVAKI 1
TEL 24670 22257
Small, inexpensive option in center of town, just below the Old Town. There's a bar and breakfast room, all rooms are well cleaned and comfortable, and the owners are friendly.

ⓘ 20 🅿 🔁 🗗 🗗 All major cards

### TSAMIS
**$**

KOROMILA 3
TEL 24670 85334
Modern hotel but in old-fashioned style, a little out of the center in pleasant grounds and with good views of lake and town. All rooms have telephones, and there is a bar and restaurant, as well as water sports and other amenities.

ⓘ 80 🅿 🔁 🗗 🞉 🗗 All major cards

### OMONOIA
**$**

PLATEIA OMONOIA
TEL 24670 23964

---

🚭 Nonsmoking  🅰 Air-conditioning  🏊 Indoor Pool  🏊 Outdoor Pool  🞉 Health Club  🗗 Credit Cards

Tables outside on busy little square, a good place to people-watch and to enjoy the basic but well-prepared Greek food. Try the fish soup made from lake-caught fish.

 No credit cards

## KAVALA

###  GALAXY
$$$
VENIZELOU 27
TEL 25102 24521
Right by the port and therefore on the expensive side, this is a very good, modern hotel with spacious rooms. It is convenient for ferries and all of Kavala's attractions, including its waterfront restaurants.
① 149 🅿 ⮂ 🆂 🅰 All major cards

###  LUCY
$$
KALAMITSA BEACH
TEL 25102 42830
For those who desire a beachfront hotel this is the place, as it is right on the best beach in Kavala. It is modern and clean, and the rooms are well maintained. The prices are lower than in the center of town.
① 217 🕒 Closed winter ⮂ 🆂 🛆 🅰 All major cards

### 🍴 PANOS ZAFIRA
$$
KARAOLI DIMITRIOU 20
TEL 25102 27978
Of the many seafood restaurants situated in town, this has established a superior reputation, serving unusual items as well as the catches of the day, such as mullet or octopus. It is located near the harbor.
🆂 🅰 All major cards

## KOMOTINI

### 🏨 RODOPI
$$
ETHN MAKARIOU 3
TEL 25310 35988
Named for the mountains it looks out on, the hotel has

large, balconied rooms in a converted traditional Thracian mansion.
① 18 🅿 ⮂ 🆂 🅰 No credit cards

## LITOCHORON

### 🏨 DION PALACE RESORT
$$$
LITOCHORON BEACH
GRITSA
TEL 03520 61431
Handily placed on the Thermais Gulf for Dion and Mount Olympus, the Dion Palace has amenities like tennis courts, outdoor pool, watersports, horseback riding, bars, and a restaurant, and yet isn't expensive given the quality of the facilities on offer.
① 182 🅿 🆂 🅰 All major cards

### 🏨 MYRTO
$
AGIOS NIKOLAOS 5
TEL 23520 81398
Located close to the center of town, this modern hotel has good-size rooms, helpful staff, and a bright restaurant/breakfast room. Inexpensive for its standard and a good base for exploring the Olympus area.
① 31 🅿 ⮂ 🆂 🅰 All major cards

### 🍴 DAMASKINIA
$
KONSTANTINOU 4
TEL 23520 81247
Good, bustling family taverna, packed with locals on weekends and serving no-frills Greek food for hearty appetites. Charcoal grill for fresh meat and fish in summer.
🆂 🅰 No credit cards

## PRESPA LAKES

### 🍴 PARADOSI
$
PSARADES
One of several fish tavernas in the pretty fishing village

of Psarades, with an idyllic setting and an offering of excellent seafood.
🆂 🅰 No credit cards

## THESSALONIKI

### 🏨 CAPSIS BRISTOL
$$$$$
OLIMPIOU 2
TEL 23105 06500
One of the nicest—and priciest—boutique hotels in the city, the Capsis Bristol is small-scale and each room is individually decorated in traditional old style rather than modern chic. The facilities are modern, though, with a business center, internet and 24-hour room service.
① 20 🆂 🅰 All major cards

### 🏨🍴 MAKEDONIA PALACE
$$$$
MEGALOU ALEXANDROU 2
TEL 2310 897197
E-MAIL MKP@CLASSICAL HOTELS.COM
www.classicalhotels.com
The city's only deluxe hotel is the most comfortable in town, with excellent food served in its restaurant and a quiet

🏨 Hotel  🍴 Restaurant  ① No. of Guest Rooms  🅿 Parking  🚇 Metro  🕒 Closed  ⮂ Elevator

location that is a short walk from the center. All rooms come with balconies and most with views.

ℹ️ 288 🅿️ 📶 ❄️ 🏊 📶 🎾 All major cards

### 🏨 AMALIA
**$**
ERMOU 33
TEL 23102 68321
E-MAIL THESS@HOTELAM
ALIA.GR
www.hotelamalia.gr/
Central but not too expensive, this modern hotel has large rooms, all with phones and some with balconies. Noise can be a problem.

ℹ️ 66 📶 ❄️ All major cards

### 🏨 PARK
**$**
DRAGOUMI 81
TEL 23105 24121
www.parkhotel.com.gr/
index_en.html
Small, modern hotel with helpful staff in a fairly quiet setting but close to the city's main sights. Typical clean, efficient, mid-range hotel.

ℹ️ 56 📶 ❄️ All major cards

### 🍴 AIGLI
**$$$**
KASSANDROU/AYIOU NIKO-
LAOU
TEL 23102 70061
Under the dome of a former Turkish bathhouse, the Aigli's menu may sound conventional (*dolmades,* chicken kebab) but the standard is superb, and there's live music, too.

🕐 Closed Mon.–Wed. ❄️
No credit cards

### 🍴 DRAFT
**$$$**
LYCOURGOUS 3
TEL 23105 55518
One of Thessaloniki's chic eating and drinking places in the fashionable Ladadika district behind the port, where ouzo or beer (hence the name) are the main drinks

of choice, with plates full of superb mezes.

🕐 Closed Sun. ❄️ All major cards

### 🍴 ARISTOTELEOUS OUZERIE
**$$**
ARISTOTELEOUS 8
TEL 23102 30762
Fashionable and tasteful *ouzerie* hidden down an arcade, serving some of the best Greek dishes you will find, usually with a difference: cuttlefish stuffed with feta, or a spicy dip of feta, hot pepper, tomato, and oil.

🕐 Closed Sun. D ❄️ All major cards

### 🍴 TA NISSIA
**$$**
PROXENOU KOROMILAN 13
TEL 23102 85991
This unmistakable blue-and-white house, one street back from the waterfront, has one of the most imaginative menus around, such as shrimp with bacon, hare with onions, quince-and-walnut pie.

❄️ All major cards

### 🍴 STRATIS
**$**
NIKIS 19
TEL 23102 79353
Modern seafront restaurant with good service, traditional food, extensive wine list, imported beers, generous helpings; especially popular for lunch on Sunday.

❄️ All major cards

### 🍴 THANASIS
**$**
MODIANO KOMNENOU 32
TEL 2310 274170
There is no more authentic place than this long-established market taverna, usually packed with locals seeking the good home-cooked food. A unique eating experience.

❄️ No credit cards

### 🍴 TO MAKEDONIKO
**$**
GIORGIOU PAPADOPOULOU 32
TEL 23106 27438
Good, popular, basic Greek taverna in the Eptapyrgiou area of the upper town, with limited choice but good daily specials.

🕐 Closed Tues. ❄️ No credit cards

## XANTHI

### 🏨 SISSY
**$**
LEFKIPOU 14
TEL 25410 23242
Very central but not too expensive, this well-maintained and roomy hotel has with some rooms with good views over the town.

ℹ️ 27 🅿️ 📶 ❄️ No credit cards

## ◼️ EVIA

### 🏨 APOLLON SUITES
**$$$**
KARYSTOS
TEL 22240 22045
www.apollonsuiteshotel
.com/en
This classy, stylish, and modern small hotel is made up of several suites spread over a large area, overlooking the sea and the hotel's own water-sports facilities. The area around is beautiful, and the hotel is a delightful retreat.

ℹ️ 36 ❄️ 🏊 All major cards

### 🍴 KAVO D'ORO
**$$**
PARAODOS SACHTOURI,
KARYSTOS
TEL 22240 22326
Just off the main square, this taverna has been pleasing locals and visitors alike for many years. It serves local wine straight from the barrel and special Evian dishes known as *ladera* (cooked in olive oil). These include vegetable stews,

---

🚭 Nonsmoking ❄️ Air-conditioning 🏊 Indoor Pool 🏊 Outdoor Pool 🎾 Health Club ❄️ Credit Cards

such as *briam,* and meat stews.
⏱ Closed winter 🚡
🚫 No credit cards

### 🍴 O GOUVERIS
**$$**
BOUDOURI 22, HALKIDA
TEL 22210 25769
Right on the waterfront, this
taverna has a tasty range of fish
and seafood dishes, including
bream, sole, or whatever else
has been caught that day, along
with lobster, crayfish, and other
shellfish. Plenty of meat as well
as vegetarian options.
🚡 🚫 No credit cards

### 🍴 PYROFANI
**$**
LIMNI
TEL 22270 31640
This *ouzerie* near the main
square is noted for its fresh
seafood and shellfish, which
includes reasonably priced
lobster. Baked shrimps are a
specialty.
🚡 🚫 No credit cards

## ■ AEGEAN ISLANDS

### ARGO-SARONIC ISLANDS

## EGINA

### 🏨 EGINITIKO ARCHONTIKO
**$**
EGINA TOWN
TEL 22970 24968
Restored traditional mansion,
first built in 1820. Stronger
on atmosphere than quality
of rooms, but a perfectly ac-
ceptable economic option in
the center of Egina town, with
its two courtyards and a roof
garden.
ℹ 12 ⬔ 🚡 🚫 All major cards

### 🍴 TO STEKI
**$$**
PAN IRIOTI 45

TEL 22970 23910
Some of the best eating in
Greece is in little meze places
like this, where they do simple
things like fried sardines, squid,
and octopus really well. It's
right by the fish market and incredibly popular locally, so you
know they're doing it right.
🚡 🚫 No credit cards

## IDRA

### 🏨 BRATSERA
**$$$**
TOMBAZI, IDRA TOWN
TEL 22980 53971
E-MAIL BRATSERA@YAHOO
.COM
www.bratserahotel.com/
Stay in this former sponge
factory near the main harbor.
Excellent conversion of the
1860 building with traditional
island decor, pool, garden, and
dining area.
ℹ 14 ⬔ 🏊 🚡 🚫 All major
cards

### 🍴 KYRIA SOFIA
**$$$**
MIAOULI 60, IDRA TOWN
TEL 22980 53097
It's worth planning ahead and
booking a table at this old
Idra favorite, whose owner
used to work in New York
and serves really imaginative
Greek dishes, with some good
vegetarian choices.
⏱ Closed L, Jan.–Mar. 🚫 No
credit cards

### 🍴 KONDYLENIA'S
**$$**
COAST ROAD W OF IDRA TOWN
TEL 22980 53520
A short walk along the coast
west of Idra is this wonderful
taverna with terrific views
across to the Greek mainland.
It's a favorite place for watch-
ing the sunset. The menu is
pretty impressive too, catering
to the more sophisticated
Idra palates with dishes such
as spinach, squid, and shrimp
casserole, although fresh fish
simply grilled is also available.

⏱ Closed midwinter 🚡
🚫 No credit cards

### 🍴 TO STEKI
**$$**
MIAOULI, IDRA TOWN
TEL 22980 53517
This taverna satisfies patrons
all year in a pleasing setting
with old murals on the walls,
fresh fish on the menu, and
a limited number of daily
specials.
🚡 🚫 No credit cards

### 🍴 XERI ELIA
**$**
OFF MAIN SQUARE, IDRA TOWN
TEL 22980 52886
Down the narrow street near
O Kipos is this tucked-away
traditional taverna, which has
a garden dining area. Simple
menu of meats and fish, but
beautifully prepared and
friendly service.
🚡 🚫 No credit cards

## POROS

### 🍴 CARAVELLA
**$**
PARALIA

---

Very friendly, busy waterfront taverna with a typical Greek menu, prepared with care: moussaka, souvlaki, fish, octopus, *stifado*, vegetarian dishes.
🚭 🚫 All major cards

### 🍴 MARIDAKI AEGINA
$
DIMOKRATIAS
TEL 22970 25869
Lively waterfront restaurant/café where you can dine cheaply on salads or omelettes, moderately on grilled octopus or moussaka, or expensively on fresh fish.
🚭 🚫 No credit cards

## SPETSES

###  NISIA
$$$
DAPIA, SPETSES TOWN
TEL 22980 75000
The only luxury-class hotel on the island, the Nisia has 20 rooms and 10 suites in what was a 19th-century factory. Now the facilities are superb, with well-tended gardens, a magnificent swimming pool, a children's play area, and a highly regarded restaurant.
ⓘ 31 🚭 🏊 🚫 All major cards

### 🏨 POSSIDONION
$$$
DAPIA WATERFRONT, SPETSES TOWN
TEL 22980 72308
Poseidon himself would enjoy this, overlooking the harbor and across to the mainland. Delightfully old-fashioned hotel with slightly fading grandeur but great charm.
ⓘ 55 🕑 Closed winter 🚭 🚫 All major cards

### 🍴 EXEDRA
$$
PALEO LIMANI, SPETSES TOWN
TEL 22980 73497
Right on the old harbor; prices are a little high but the standard of the food makes it

worth paying. They do many of the island's seafood specialties, such as *argo*, a casserole of shrimp, lobster, and feta cheese.
🚭 🚫 All major cards

### 🍴 LAZAROS
$$
KASTELLI
TEL 22980 72600
This homely place serves its own retsina from the barrels on the walls, and there's a really lively atmosphere from the people who have climbed the hill behind the harbor to get here. It's worth it for delicious dishes like their goat in a lemon sauce, a popular local favorite.
🕑 Closed L, winter 🚫 No credit cards

### 🍴 LIRAKIS
$
MAIN HARBOR, SPETSES TOWN
TEL 22980 72188
Above the Lirakis supermarket with a fine view of the harbor, the Lirakis has an eclectic menu ranging from omelettes and vegetarian dishes such as *briam* (very like ratatouille) to more sophisticated but traditionally Greek meat and fish choices.
🕑 Closed winter 🚭 🚫 All major cards

## SPORADES

## ALONISSOS

### 🍴 TO KAMAKI
$$
IKION DOLOPON, PATITIRI
TEL 24240 65245
This *ouzerie* is the best eating in town, a couple of streets away from the waterfront. An impressive menu of seafood includes baked mussels and stuffed squid. You can either have them as mezes to whet the appetite with an early-evening ouzo, or even better, spend the night there and order several selections.

🕑 Closed Sept.–June 🚭 🚫 No credit cards

### 🍴 ASTROFENGIA
$
OLD ALONISSOS
TEL 24240 65182
Wonderful views at this popular restaurant, which is about as high as you can go in the Old Town. The evenings get lively with a festive atmosphere in summer. The food ranges from simple grilled fish steaks and stuffed tomatoes to the more sophisticated artichoke hearts with a cream-and-dill sauce.
🕑 Closed L 🚭 🚫 All major cards

## SKIATHOS

### 🏨 ATRIUM
$$$$
PLATANIAS
TEL 24270 49345
E-MAIL INFO@ATRIUMHOTEL.GR
www.atriumhotel.gr/Atrium/
Stylish new hotel, in a wonderful setting on a wooded hill and with an Olympic-size pool looking out over the Aegean. The rooms are large, and they, too, have good views from their balconies. Restaurant, bar, and water sports available.
ⓘ 75 🚭 🚭 🏊 🚫 All major cards

### 🍴 ASPROLITHOS
$$
MAVROYIALI, SKIATHOS TOWN
TEL 24270 23110
Taverna traditions are kept up here but in upscale style, and while they serve old favorites like moussaka, it's the lightest moussaka you've ever tasted. Specialties such as shrimp with artichokes are pricier.
🕑 Closed L 🚭 🚫 No credit cards

### 🍴 KAMPOURELI OUZERIE
$$
PARALIA, SKIATHOS TOWN

---

🚭 Nonsmoking  🚭 Air-conditioning  🏊 Indoor Pool  🏊 Outdoor Pool  💪 Health Club  🚫 Credit Cards

TEL 24270 21112

In the great bustling Greek *ouzerie* tradition, serving mezes (the Greek answer to the Spanish tapas)—a range of nibbles to eat with your ouzo, such as octopus, squid, and olives—and more substantial meals as well.

🅢 🅢 No credit cards

## 🍴 WINDMILL

**$$**

SKIATHOS TOWN

TEL 24270 24550

Right at the top of the eastern hill in the main town, this chic restaurant serves food just as special as the setting. Chicken with bourbon and chili is just one example of the unusual combinations. Desserts include poached pears.

🅢 🅢 No credit cards

## SKIROS

## 🏨 NEFELI

**$$**

SKIROS TOWN

TEL 22220 91964

This modern place, built in traditional fashion, is a mix of hotel rooms and larger apartments. At the edge of town, it's fairly quiet, but ask for a room with a view and make advance reservations. It is extremely popular.

🛈 14 🅢 🅢 All major cards

## 🍴 KRISTINA'S RESTAURANT

**$$**

SKIROS TOWN

TEL 22220 91123

Austrian Kristina is trying to combine a more nouveau touch, such as a generous number of vegetarian dishes and a good variety of breads, with Greek traditions. Her specialty is chicken fricassee.

🕑 Closed Sun. 🅢 🅢 All major cards

## SKOPELOS

## 🍴 ANATOLI OUZERIE

**$**

SKOPELOS TOWN

This is a place aimed at Greeks, with live music late at night. Dine on a selection of their exceptionally good meze. No phone, no address, so climb the hill and ask for Anatoli's. Locals will point the way.

🕑 Closed L & winter 🅢
🅢 All major cards

## 🍴 MOLOS

**$**

HARBOUR, SKOPELOS TOWN

TEL 24240 22551

There are several restaurants on the waterfront, offering good basic Greek food at inexpensive prices. Molos has fresh fish, grilled meats, as well as excellent casserole dishes.

🕑 Closed midwinter 🅢
🅢 No credit cards

## 🍴 TAVERNA T'AGNANTI

**$**

GLOSSA, SKOPELOS

TEL 24240 33606

This little, family-run taverna is one of those unpretentious places that are a delight to find in the islands. It has a great atmosphere, friendly hosts, inexpensive and well-prepared examples of standard Greek dishes: squid, grills, chops, and moussaka.

🅢 🅢 No credit cards

## NORTHEASTERN AEGEAN ISLANDS

## HIOS

## 🏨 GRECIAN CASTLE HOTEL

**$$**

HIOS TOWN

TEL 22710 44740

E-MAIL INFO@GRECIANCASTLE.GR

**www.greciancastle.gr/**

Restored factory, tastefully decorated and furnished, and with lovely gardens. Located on the seafront, it also offers a restaurant and bar.

🛈 55 🅢 🔃 🅢 All major cards

## 🏨 TA PETRINA

**$$**

VOLISSOS

TEL 22740 21128

Charming rural hilltop hamlet near beaches of northwest coast. A British-Greek couple have renovated the hotel to incredibly high standards; the terrace has barbecue facilities and a great view.

🛈 5 🅢 No credit cards

## 🍴 APOLAISI

**$$**

AGIA ERMIONI

TEL 22710 31359

Residents of Hios town happily travel the 6 miles (10 km) or so to this fishing village and its excellent fish taverna, which overlooks the water. It's a romantic setting, and you'll get the best of what's been caught in the village that day.

🕑 Closed L 🅢 🅢 All major cards

## PRICES

**HOTELS**

An indication of the cost of a double room in the high season is given by **$** signs.

| | |
|---|---|
| **$$$$$** | Over $240 |
| **$$$$** | $160-240 |
| **$$$** | $110-160 |
| **$$** | $70-110 |
| **$** | Under $70 |

**RESTAURANTS**

An indication of the cost of a three-course meal without drinks is given by **$** signs.

| | |
|---|---|
| **$$$$$** | Over $65 |
| **$$$$** | $50-65 |
| **$$$** | $30-50 |
| **$$** | $20-30 |
| **$** | Under $20 |

---

🏨 Hotel  🍴 Restaurant  🛈 No. of Guest Rooms  🅿 Parking  🔃 Metro  🕑 Closed  🛗 Elevator

### O MORIAS STA MESTA
$

MAIN PLATEIA, MESTA
TEL 22710 76400

It's well worth making the journey to this Mastic village to sample the traditional island fare at this simple taverna on the main square. The house specialty is pickled rock samphire (ask for *kritamo*). The local wine is made from raisins and has a sweet taste and thick consistency.

All major cards

### O PLATANOS TAVERNA
$

CHRISTOS RACHES

Wonderfully authentic tavern underneath a huge plane tree. Local specialties and delicious home-reared meat. Don't miss the cloudy red "Prammian" wine.

No credit cards

### TAVERNA HOTZAS
$

STEFANOU TSOURI 74, HIOS TOWN
TEL 22710 42787

The oldest taverna in town and one of the best loved, now in the fourth generation of the same family. Hotzas is an island institution and not to be missed. It is tricky to find in the backstreets, but everyone knows its name. It has a lovely garden eating area, which you share with the taverna's cats and hens, and the food is as wonderful as the rustic atmosphere. Simple dishes such as grilled fish or fried eggplant can be washed down with retsina from the barrel.

Closed Sun. & L
No credit cards

### THEODOSIOU OUZERIE
$

PARALIA, HIOS TOWN

If you are in the mood for casual dining by the waterfront, then this *ouzerie* offers a good selection of meze dishes,

which could make up a meal. Pastries and ice cream are also on offer.

Closed L     No credit cards

## LESVOS

### OLIVE PRESS
$$

MITILINI
TEL 22530 71646

Mitilini is an essential part of any visit to Lesvos, and you should try to reserve rooms here if you can. A traditional building right on the seafront, it really is where olives were pressed. There's a beautiful private courtyard and gardens too. Ask for a sea-view room.

53     All major cards

### VAFIOS
$$

VAFIOS, NEAR MITILINI
TEL 22530 71752

In the village of the same name, in the hills 3 miles (5 km) southeast of Mitilini, the taverna Vafios is a popular drive out in the evenings. Locals know it has a good range of pies and grills, with big helpings and low prices. Wine from the barrel.

Closed winter     No credit cards

### CAPTAIN'S TABLE
$

HARBOR, MITILINI
TEL 22530 71241

Right on the harbor. The house special is a huge "Captain's Plate" of mixed seafood, but there are also simple grills, vegetarian dishes, Italian choices, and more exotic dishes.

Closed winter     All major cards

### ERMIS
$

KORNAROU 2, MITILINI
TEL 22510 26232

This venerable *ouzerie* certainly

oozes atmosphere, the interior being like a cross between an antique store and a bar. It is a very popular local hangout, good for a quick drink or a full meal. Choose from the tasty meze dishes, such as fried cheese or squid.

No credit cards

### I SYKAMINIA
$

SKALA SYKAMINIAS
TEL 22530 55319

A taverna in a quiet setting, right on the picturesque harbor of this little fishing village. Take a table under the shade of the mulberry tree and sample the simple, delicious fish dishes such as squid or sardines. If there in late summer, try the regional dish of stuffed squash flowers.

No credit cards

## LIMNOS

### AKTI MYRINA
$$

MYRINA
TEL 22540 22310

This resort hotel is about half a mile (1 km) west of the main town, with its own private beach, three restaurants, water sports, and tennis. The well-equipped rooms are actually stone cottages set in the attractive surroundings.

125     Closed winter
All major cards

### O PLATANOS
$

KYDHA, MYRINA
TEL 22540 22070

Beautifully located on a little square just off the main street, O Platanos gets its name from the two huge plane trees that it shelters beneath. The food is simple but very tasty country fare, such as meat casseroles, oven-baked lamb. Some vegetarian options, too.

No credit cards

## SAMOS

### 🏨 FITO BUNGALOWS HOTEL
**$$**
PITHAGORIA
TEL 22730 61314
E-MAIL WELCOME@FITOBAY.GR
www.fitobay.gr/
A peaceful, low-level hotel, with its bungalows nestling in well-tended lawns and gardens crossed by shady paths. Whitewashed walls and pine furniture create an air of comfortable simplicity.
🛏 87  🕐 Closed winter  🅂 🖩
🅂 All major cards

### 🍴 VARKA
**$$**
PARALIA, PITHAGORIA
TEL 22730 61088
In this *ouzerie*, the food is as good as the setting is unusual. *Varka* means "boat," and this is a former fishing boat that has been converted. Expect the best of the local fish, and steaks are also available, but go for the mezes.
🕐 Closed winter  🅂 🅂 No credit cards

### 🍴 CHRISTOS
**$**
PLATEIA AYIOU NIKOLAOU
TEL 22730 24792
As simple as a Greek taverna can be, serving standard fare like chops, chicken, and fish, but all is well prepared and it certainly keeps the locals happy.
🅂 No credit cards

### 🍴 TAVERNA AVGO TOU KOKORA
**$**
KOKKARI
TEL 22730 92113
Fantastic waterfront location for this slightly more upscale eating place in Kokkari, 6 miles (10 km) west of Samos town. It offers a great variety of meze dishes that come highly recommended.
🅂 🅂 All major cards

## THASSOS

### 🏨 MAKRYAMMOS BUNGALOWS
**$$$**
MAKRYAMMOS
TEL 25930 22101
E-MAIL INFO@MAKRYAMMOS-HOTEL.GR
www.makryammos-hotel.gr
This resort hotel, with its own bar, restaurant, and tennis courts, is made up of cottages plus ten luxurious suites scattered around the lush green grounds. It has its own immaculate white sandy beach and one of the best settings you will find on Thassos.
🛏 206  🅿 🅂 🖩 🅂 AmEx, MC, Visa

### 🍴 O GLAROS
**$**
ALYKI
TEL 25930 53047
On the hill to the north of Alyki, with lovely views across the bay, O Glaros has an excellent local reputation for serving the best fish in the area. Enjoy fresh fish simply grilled over charcoal, or go for one of the delicious meat grills or roast chicken dishes.
🕐 Closed winter  🅂 🅂 No credit cards

## CYCLADES

## MIKONOS

### 🏨 MYKONOS GRAND HOTEL
**$$$$**
AGIOS YIANNIS
TEL 22890 25555
E-MAIL INFO@MYKONOS GRAND.GR
www.mykonosgrand.gr /page/
Beautiful hotel, located directly above three sandy coves with stunning sunset views of Dilos island. Spa suites are designed for couples on their honeymoon.
🛏 111  🅿 🔁 🖩 🎬 🅂 All major cards

---

### PRICES

**HOTELS**
An indication of the cost of a double room in the high season is given by **$** signs.

| | |
|---|---|
| **$$$$$** | Over $240 |
| **$$$$** | $160–240 |
| **$$$** | $110–160 |
| **$$** | $70–110 |
| **$** | Under $70 |

**RESTAURANTS**
An indication of the cost of a three-course meal without drinks is given by **$** signs.

| | |
|---|---|
| **$$$$$** | Over $65 |
| **$$$$** | $50–65 |
| **$$$** | $30–50 |
| **$$** | $20–30 |
| **$** | Under $20 |

---

### 🏨 HOTEL BELVEDERE
**$$$**
HORA, ROCHARI
TEL 22890 25122
E-MAIL CONTACT@BELVEDERE HOTEL.COM
www.belvederehotel.com/
Ideal resort-style hotel in the main town, convenient for shopping, eating, and clubbing. Rooms are small but cozy. Features newly opened Nobu Japanese restaurant. American breakfast.
🛏 48  🅂 🖩 🅂 All major cards

## SOMETHING SPECIAL

### 🍴 LA MAISON DE KAT'RINE
**$$$**
NIKI AGIOS GERASIMOS, CHORA
TEL 22890 22169
In the Greek islands there are very few restaurants that can combine atmosphere and top-quality cooking, but this is one of those rarities. It brings French flair to Greek cooking, so while the menu may say coq au vin, it will be Greek chicken cooked in Greek wine with a result that would grace a Parisian restaurant. Be prepared to

---

🏨 Hotel  🍴 Restaurant  🛏 No. of Guest Rooms  🅿 Parking  🖩 Metro  🕐 Closed  🔁 Elevator

pay much more than average, and make a reservation ahead to guarantee a table in the intimate dining room.
🕐 Closed L 🅲 ♿ All major cards

### 🍴 LA TAVERNE
$$$
HOTEL CAVO TAGOO, MIKONOS TOWN
TEL 22890 23692
Try and reserve a table (advance reservations are recommended) with a view over the bay for this stylish hotel restaurant where haute cuisine meets Greek menus for delicious results such as lamb chops with yogurt and mint sauce.
🅲 ♿ All major cards

### 🍴 SEA SATIN
$$
MIKONOS TOWN
TEL 22890 24676
The most fashionable place to dine, beneath the windmills and with a view of Little Venice and the sea. Fresh fish and vegetables are served with laid-back but quick service. Barbecued T-bones are delicious.
🕐 Closed L

### 🍴 KIKI
$
AGIOS SOSTIS
The ultimate beach taverna. There is no electricity and no phone, so Kiki closes at sundown. Juicy chops cooked on charcoal, excellent salads served in a shady courtyard.
🕐 Closed winter ♿ No credit cards

## NAXOS

### 🍴 ONEIRO
$$$
PLATEIA BRADOUNA, NAXOS TOWN
TEL 22850 23846
Probably the best restaurant in town, Oneiro commands

wonderful views from its roof garden, the atmosphere enhanced by the candlelit tables and a peaceful courtyard setting. The food matches the mood, with a menu that leans to the international but does not exclude Greek dishes such as lamb stuffed with garlic and bacon and cooked very slowly in the oven.
🕐 Closed L & winter 🅲
♿ No credit cards

### 🍴 FAROS
$$
PARALIA, CHORA
TEL 22850 23325
An example of a restaurant where foreign influence (in this case German) has combined with Greek tradition and ingredients to provide a wide menu. An old Greek standby, meatballs, is given a new lease on life with a goulash-style sauce.
🅲 ♿ All major cards

### 🍴 MANOLIS GARDEN TAVERNA
$
KASTRO, NAXOS TOWN
TEL 22850 25168
Right in the Old Town near the castle there are several restaurants catering to the tourist trade, but this delightful garden taverna maintains its reputation by serving traditional Greek dishes such as moussaka, deep-fried eggplant, and stuffed peppers and tomatoes.
🕐 Closed winter 🅲 ♿ No credit cards

### 🍴 NIKOS
$
PARALIA, CHORA
TEL 22850 23153
Nikos is owned by fisherman Nikos Katsayannis, so fish on the menu is guaranteed fresh, and there are generally some unusual varieties on offer. Plenty of other choices too, on a wide menu. The wine list concentrates on wines from

Naxos and the other Cycladic islands.
🅲 ♿ No credit cards

## PAROS

### 🏨 ASTIR OF PAROS
$$$$
KOLYMBITHRES BEACH, NEAR NAOUSSA
TEL 22840 51976
www.astirofparos.gr/
Paros's flagship hotel is almost a Cycladic village in its own right, with its own beach, small golf course, and an art gallery. The reception area displays modern Greek art. Well worth the outlay.
🛏 57 🅿 🕐 Closed winter
⬆ 🅲 🏊 🎾 ♿ All major cards

### 🍴 LALULA
$$
NAOUSSA
TEL 22840 51547
Greek island cooking is being influenced by the many overseas visitors who take up residence. This stylish German-run place does just that, adding more vegetarian choices and a lighter touch to the traditional meat and fish dishes.
🕐 Closed L 🅲 ♿ All major cards

### 🍴 ALIGARIA
$
PLATEIA ALIGARI, PARIKIA
TEL 22840 22026
This delightful little place is run by a gifted cook, Elizabeth Nikolousou. She knows how to serve up old favorites such as moussaka or stuffed tomatoes with an attention to detail that reminds you how good they can be when done properly.
🅲 ♿ No credit cards

### 🍴 TO KYMA
$
AYII ANARGHIRI BEACH
TEL 22840 52025
"The Wave" is run by two French women who serve up

an international menu, including Thai, Chinese, French, and even Scottish dishes alongside Greek favorites such as squid, stuffed vegetables, and lobster.

🔲 🔲 All major cards

### 🍴 LEVANTIS

$

PARIKIA

TEL 22840 23613

The name of this friendly little taverna, with its tables beneath trailing vines, indicates a nod toward the flavors of the Middle East with the use of yogurt, apricots, and nuts, and tender chicken dishes.

🕐 Closed L & Tues. 🔲 🔲 All major cards

## SANTORINI

### 🏨 ASTRA APARTMENTS

$$$$$

IMEROVIGLI

TEL 22860 23641

Absolutely delightful small village-like complex of rooms, suites, and villas with their own pools. The Astra is stunningly located on top of cliffs, with heavenly sunset views, and is easily one of the most comfortable yet relaxed places on the island.

🛏 85 🔲 🅿 🔲 🔲 All major cards

### 🏨 VEDEMA HOTEL

$$$$

MEGALOCHORI

TEL 22860 81796

E-MAIL INFO@VEDEMA.GR

www.vedema.gr/

The Vedema features Cycladic-style villas in a converted wine merchant's mansion. An extensive selection of Greek and international wines is offered in the century-old restaurant. The Cocoon spa has massage tents on the nearby beach.

🛏 36 🅿 🔲 🔲 All major cards

### 🍴 KATINA

$

OIA PORT

TEL 22860 71280

If you can face the trek down to the harbor at Oia—or rather face the climb back up again (though you can always phone for a taxi)—then Katina's is a great place for seafood, right by the sea.

🔲 🔲 No credit cards

### 🍴 SKARAMANGAS FISH TAVERN

$

MONOLITHOS BEACH

Most authentic shorefront taverna serving up the daily catch, such as red snapper on the grill.

🔲 No credit cards

## SIFNOS

### 🍴 TO LIOTRIVI

$$

ARTEMON

TEL 22840 32051

Sifnos is said to produce the best chefs in Greece, and the chef here, Yiannis Yiorgoulis, is said to be the finest one who has stayed on the island. Try a simple but unusual and delicious *kaparosalata* (caper salad), and you'll know why this place is so popular.

🔲 🔲 All major cards

### 🍴 CAPTAIN ANDREAS

$

BY THE BEACH, KAMARAI

TEL 22840 32356

If your needs are simple—the best local fish, grilled—then this restaurant on the beach is the place to come. The eponymous owner catches most of the menu himself, buys the best from his fellow fishermen, and the taste and setting don't come any better.

🔲 🔲 No credit cards

## SIROS

### 🏨 HOTEL OMIROS

$$

OMIROU 43, ERMOUPOLI

TEL 22810 84910

This elegant hotel in a pedestrianized street has

a charming, quiet setting and large rooms tastefully done out with traditional furniture. The roof garden offers terrific views across the harbor.

🛏 13 🔲 🔲 🔲 No credit cards

## TINOS

### 🍴 TO KOUTOUKI

$

G. GAGOU 5

TEL 22830 24857

This is what Greek eating is all about. You may get the same dishes that are on every other menu (if there is a menu) along this back street packed with dining options, but the Koutouki serves everything with freshness and friendliness. Dishes like veal stew or chicken in lemon sauce are made to perfection.

🔲 No credit cards

## DODECANESE

## KALIMNOS

### 🏨 PANORAMA

$

AMMOUDARA

TEL 22430 23138

Slightly back from the busy waterfront at the top of a steep hill, this modern hotel has very welcoming owners. Some of the rooms have terraces, and all have stunning sea views and are beautifully maintained.

🛏 13 ❄ 🚫 No credit cards

### ⫴ BARBA PETROS
$

PLATEIA DIAMANTIS, POTHIA
TEL 22430 29678

Full of character, this restaurant at the north end of the harbor offers fresh fish grilled on olive-wood charcoal, along with Greek island specialties such as squid stuffed with a delicious mix of spinach, cheese, and herbs.

❄ 🚫 No credit cards

### ⫴ DOMUS ROOF GARDEN
$

KANTOUNI
TEL 22430 47959

The Domus is located in a splendid setting—at Kantouni on the west coast, overlooking the beach and the Aegean—and has the food to match. Ordinary dishes such as *dolmades* and moussaka are exceptionally well done, and there are plenty of surprising inclusions too, such as Armenian lamb cooked with yogurt. A very warm welcome indeed.

❄ 🚫 All major cards

### ⫴ TAVERNA KSEFTERIS
$

CHRISTOS, POTHIA
TEL 22430 28642

This taverna is an island institution that has been handed down through several generations of the same family. You won't get nouvelle cuisine but you will get tasty *dolmades,* hearty stews, and a generous welcome.

❄ 🚫 No credit cards

## KOS

### 🏨 AFENDOULIS HOTEL
$

EVRIPILOU 1, KOS TOWN
TEL 22420 25321
E-MAIL INFO@AFENDOUL
ISHOTEL.COM
www.afendoulishotel.com/

A friendly, family-run hotel, this is the kind of place that the Greek islands are all about. Simple but spotless, close to the center and to the beach but in a quiet location. All rooms have balconies with views of the harbor.

🛏 23 ❄ 🚫 No credit cards

### ⫴ OLYMPIADA
$

KLEOPATRAS 2, KOS TOWN
TEL 22420 23031

In a town that is full of below-average tourist tavernas, here is a treat. It's a genuine no-nonsense Greek restaurant serving good food at cheap prices. Try a simple souvlaki or one of the many vegetable dishes.

❄ 🚫 No credit cards

### ⫴ PLATANOS
$

PLATEIA PLATANOS, KOS TOWN
TEL 22420 28991

With the best setting in town, the Platanos offers unusual Greek dishes such as octopus *stifado* and international variety such as Indonesian fillet steak. There's also live music on most evenings during the summer.

❄ 🚫 All major cards

### ⫴ TAVERNA MAVROMATIS
$

PSALIDI BEACH, KOS
TEL 22420 22433

The Mavromati brothers who run this taverna take no easy options but cater to Greek palates as well as those of overseas visitors. The deep-fried cheese is delicious, as are the tender grilled meat dishes, and of course there is always fresh fish.

⏱ Closed winter ❄ 🚫 All major cards

## PATMOS

### 🏨 AUSTRALIS
$

SKALA
TEL 22470 31576

This family-run hotel, owned by a couple who used to live in Australia, is in a very quiet location and surrounded by beautiful gardens. Breakfast is served on a terrace overlooking the harbor.

🛏 18 ⏱ Closed winter ❄ 🚫 No credit cards

### ⫴ VEGGHERA
$$$

NEA MARINA, SKALA
TEL 22470 32988

Vegghera is acknowledged as the best restaurant in town, set in an old mansion down at the marina. The owners combine Greek freshness with French flair and produce dishes like calamari in pesto, which brings a zing to an old standby. It's not cheap but it can justify the prices with the results.

⏱ Closed winter ❄ 🚫 All major cards

### ⫴ PATMIAN HOUSE
$$

CHORA, PATMOS TOWN
TEL 22470 31180

The best restaurant on the island. A beautifully restored 17th-century building is the backdrop to fine food. Conventional hors d'oeuvres such as *taramosalata* and spinach pie are homemade and mouthwateringly good, as are main dishes such as rabbit *stifado* with juniper berries.

⏱ Closed L ❄ 🚫 All major cards

### ⫴ TO PYROFANI
$

PARALIA, SKALA
TEL 22470 31539

This fish taverna buys direct from the local fishermen, so you may get lobster, swordfish, tuna, or mullet, depending

---

🚭 Nonsmoking  ❄ Air-conditioning  🏊 Indoor Pool  🏊 Outdoor Pool  🏋 Health Club  🚫 Credit Cards on what's in season—but whatever it is it will be fresh and simply grilled.

 All major cards

## RHODES

###  HILTON RODOS RESORT
**$$$**

LEOFOROS IALLYSOU, IXIA, RHODES TOWN

TEL 22410 75000

E-MAIL GM.RHODES@HILTON.COM

www1.hilton.com

This excellent five-star hotel, with its own splendid gardens and beach, is a few miles away from the noise of Rhodes town. Rooms are spacious and all have marble bathrooms, while facilities include restaurant, bar, sauna, tennis court, and Jacuzzi.

[1] 402 P 🔄 🔲 🏊 📺
🔲 All major cards

### 🏨 LINDOS MARE
**$$$**

LINDOS BAY, LINDOS

TEL 22440 31130

E-MAIL INFO@LINDOSMARE.GR

www.lindosmare.gr/

A luxury hotel on several levels leading down to a wonderful beach. It is in the more expensive bracket because rooms are quoted at half-board rate (including breakfast and dinner), but as it is over a mile (2 km) outside Lindos itself, most guests prefer to eat in and enjoy the many facilities.

[1] 123 P 🔲 🏊 🔲 All major cards

### 🏨 S. NIKOLIS HOTEL
**$$**

IPPODAMOU 61, RHODES OLD TOWN

TEL 22410 34561

An Old Town hotel that oozes history, incorporating stonework that goes back 800 years. Although some rooms are a little cramped, all of them are modern and have telephones. The owners also have rooms

to rent nearby.

[1] 30 🔲 🔲 All major cards

### 🍴 ALEXIS
**$$$**

SOKRATOUS 18, RHODES TOWN

TEL 22410 29347

One of the best fish restaurants in the Dodecanese. You will encounter seafood here not commonly seen on other menus (sea urchins, for example), and the best of the catch from the harbor. All vegetables are also organically grown by the owners.

🕐 Closed Sun. 🔲 🔲 All major cards

### 🍴 ARHONTIKO
**$$$**

LINDOS

TEL 22440 31992

It's worth journeying to Lindos to eat in this atmospheric old sea captain's mansion, where dishes such as plums stuffed with cream cheese and wrapped in bacon show the inventive level of the cuisine. There's an excellent wine list, too.

🔲 🔲 All major cards

### 🍴 KIOUPIA
**$$**

TREIS VILLAGE, RHODES TOWN

TEL 22410 91824

Make sure you come here with an appetite. After a choice of soups you will be faced with a table full of tempting meze dishes and hearty main courses. Remember, too, that there is a big and mouthwatering dessert menu.

🕐 Closed L & Sun. 🔲 🔲 All major cards

### 🍴 MAVRIKOS
**$$**

LINDOS

TEL 22440 31232

You get traditional Greek dishes here, such as oven-baked lamb or assorted mezes, but prepared with a flair that originated with the restaurant's

first chef, who cooked for many years in France. The flair and family tradition continue.

🔲 🔲 All major cards

### 🍴 PALIA ISTORIA
**$$**

MITROPOLEOS 108, AMMOS, RHODES NEW TOWN

TEL 22410 32421

This award-winning restaurant is one of the best in the town. Their meze dishes are renowned and include unusual dishes such as beets with walnuts, while main courses might range from a simple succulent roast pork to a pricier lobster spaghetti.

🕐 L 🔲 🔲 All major cards

## SYMI

### 🏨 ALIKI
**$$$**

YIALOS, SYMI TOWN

TEL 22460 71655

E-MAIL INFO@HOTELALIKI.GR

www.simi-hotel-aliki.gr/

Although it has changed hands in recent years, this venerable hotel on a quiet part of the Symi waterfront retains its

---

charm. A three-story neoclassical mansion, it was built in 1895, and rooms have been modernized so that they are comfortable without being stuffy. The best rooms are those upstairs at the front, with sea views and small balconies.

🚪 15 ❄ 🅴 No credit cards

### 🍽 MYLOPETRA
$$$
YIALOS
TEL 22410 72333
This former flour mill has become one of Symi's fine dining experiences, in an elegant old setting. The German owners transform mostly local ingredients to produce sophisticated dishes such as lamb in a hollandaise sauce, and they make their own bread, pasta, and cheeses.
🕐 Closed L, winter ❄ 🅴 Visa

## SOMETHING SPECIAL

### 🍽 GEORGIO'S
$
CHORIO, SYMI
There is no restaurant in the whole of Greece quite like Georgio's. It manages to be chaotic yet produce mouthwatering food night after night. The eponymous owner glides from kitchen to front of house, sometimes waiting on diners, or maybe taking his bouzouki from the wall to entertain, as the mood takes him. Efficiency is not the strong point, so do not be slow to ask for service, or the bill. Wander into the kitchen and ask to see what's cooking, then grab a table and sit back and watch the nightly drama unfold, as in a theater.
🕐 Closed L ❄ 🅴 No credit cards

### 🍽 MYTHOS MEZE RESTAURANT
$
YIALOS, SYMI TOWN

TEL 22460 71488
Stavros Godio is fast gaining an international reputation for his high-quality repertoire of Mediterranean cuisine. Mouthwatering bass in ginger sauce and oven-cooked pork in thyme and *balsamico* draw the gourmets to his waterside establishment and to his weekly cooking school.
🕐 Closed weekdays Nov.–Easter 🅴 All major cards

### 🍽 NERAIDA
$
YIALOS, SYMI TOWN
TEL 22460 71841
The Neraida looks no different from many other tavernas around Symi town harbor, but the standard of food is exceptional. Fresh fish is good, and the homemade spinach pies superb. Pop into the kitchen to see what's cooking.
❄ 🅴 No credit cards

### 🍽 THOLOS
$
NEAR PARADISE BEACH
TEL 22460 72033
This charming outdoor restaurant caters to vegetarians and those missing spicier foods. Home-cooked chickpea and mushroom bake and baby shrimps with green peppers are signature dishes.
🕐 Closed winter 🅴 No credit cards

## TILOS

### 🏨 IRINI
$
LIVADIA
TEL 22410 44293
Impeccably run family hotel with attractive, well-maintained gardens and a peaceful location. Front rooms have good sea views, and the breakfasts are generous. Nothing is too much trouble for the owners.
🚪 23 ❄ 🏊

## ■ CRETE

## AGIOS NIKOLAOS

### 🍽 PELAGOS
$$
CORNER KORAKA & KATEHAKI STREETS
TEL 28410 25737
Located in a two-story house, Pelagos offers a seductive choice of fresh seafood, including sea urchin salad. Outdoor street seating in addition to a secluded garden.
🅴 No credit cards

## ELOUNDA

## SOMETHING SPECIAL

### 🏨 ELOUNDA BEACH
$$$$$
ELOUNDA (1.2 MILES, 2 KM NORTH OF CENTER)
TEL 28410 41412
E-MAIL ELOHOTEL@ELOUNDA BEACH.GR
http://70.32.113.209/home.php
Easily the most luxurious hotel on Crete, and one of the finest in Europe, with room rates you might find in the center of New York or Paris. There are 301 rooms, some of which are actually private cottages with their own swimming pools, rented out to the mega-rich who value their privacy. For other guests there are a pool, beach, water sports, minature golf, sporting facilities, a sailing club, a health center, and an entertainment center.
🚪 301 🅿 🏊 🎾 🅴 All major cards

### 🏨 ELOUNDA MARE
$$$$
ELOUNDA (1.2 MILES/2 KM NORTH OF CENTER)
TEL 28410 41102
E-MAIL MARE@ELOUNDA-SA.COM
www.eloundamare.gr/
Exceptional gardens surround

this resort hotel that has a superb setting overlooking the Aegean. Whitewashed cottages surround the main building. Public areas have antique furnishings, and combine tradition with modern comfort.

🛈 108 🅿 ⬄ 🗢 🏊 🐾 All major cards

### 🍴 VRITOMARTES
$

G. SFIRAKI WATERFRONT
TEL 28410 41325

An unsophisticated and excellent taverna right on the harbor, where you dine gazing out over the sea. The fish on the menu was caught here just a few hours earlier, perhaps even by the owner himself. Meat and vegetable dishes are also available, but go for the fish every time.

🕒 Closed in winter 🗢
🐾 MC, V

## HANIA

### 🏨 VILLA ANDROMEDA
$$$

VENIZELOU 150
TEL 28210 28303
E-MAIL VILANDRO@OTENET.GR
www.villandromeda.gr/

This delightful, intimate hotel is in a restored neoclassical mansion from 1870. Its marble floors and elegant furniture give a grand impression, and rooms have views over sea and town, but can be noisy.

🛈 6 🗢 🐾 All major cards

### 🏨 AMPHORA
$$

PARODOS THEOTOKOPOU-
LOU 20
TEL 28210 93224
E-MAIL CONTACT@AMPHORA
.GR
www.amphora.gr/

First built around 1300, this restored mansion combines Venetian elegance, Turkish style, and modern comforts. The roof terrace has a great

view over Hania's beautiful harbor, and rooms are spacious, but there can be noise from the port.

🛈 21 ⬄ 🗢 🐾 All major cards

### 🍴 TAMAM
$$

ZAMBELIOU 49
TEL 28210 96080

One of the best places in town, as you can usually tell by the queues, serving dishes that range across the Mediterranean, such as risotto or Greek baked red peppers, but combined with Middle Eastern influences and the uses of spices, fruit, and yogurt.

🐾 All major cards

### 🍴 THE WELL OF THE TURK
$

KALINIKOU SARPAKI 1–3
TEL 28210 54547

Though there's no love lost between the Greeks and the Turks, this Middle Eastern restaurant thrives thanks to its imaginative cuisine, historic building, and stylish interior. Meatballs mixed with eggplant are one house specialty.

🗢 🐾 No credit cards

## IRAKLIO

### 🏨 CANDIA MARIS
$$$

AMMOUDARA
TEL 28103 314632

This luxury-class modern hotel was built in brick and marble using traditional Cretan styles, but the rooms (or rather cottages) all have modern facilities and sea views. The huge round swimming pool is an extra delight.

🛈 257 🅿 🗢 🏊 🐾 🗢 All major cards

### 🏨 LATO
$–$$

EPIMENIDOU 15
TEL 28120 228103

This attractive hotel is simple and modern, but its friendly

atmosphere and central location make it one of the best bets in the city. Some rooms have balconies overlooking the Venetian harbor, and the Archaeological Museum is close by.

🛈 50 ⬄ 🗢 🐾 All major cards

### 🍴 KYRIAKOS
$$

LEOFOROS DIMOKRATIAS 53
TEL 28120 24649

Some of the best food in Iraklio, with traditional Cretan dishes served with great style and attention to detail. Formal dress preferred, although it's a remarkably friendly place. Try the octopus with onions or the house specialty: snails.

🕒 Closed Wed. & sometimes in summer 🗢 🐾 All major cards

## LIMENAS HERSONISOU

### 🏨 ROYAL MARE VILLAGE
$$$$

LIMENAS HERSONISOU
TEL 28970 25025
E-MAIL RMV@ALDEMARHO-
TELS.COM

www.aldemarhotels.com/EN_
Crete-Royal-Mare-Village_
Welcome.html
One of Greece's only thalasso-
therapy centers is housed
within this luxury resort hotel
between Iraklio and Malia. In
addition to the main rooms,
there are a further 101 with
direct access to the center,
and 24 suites. Every comfort,
lovely gardens, and a private
beach.
ⓘ 390 🅿 🕭 🕭 🕭 🕭 All
major cards

## RETHIMNO

### 🏨 GRECOTEL CRETA PALACE
$$$$
MISIRIA BEACH
TEL 28310 55181
E-MAIL CONTACT@GRECOTEL
.GR
www.grecotel.com/
Surrounded by lush gardens,
this modern resort hotel has
been built simply but stylishly
in traditional Cretan fashion.
In addition to the rooms
there are 204 cottages and
villas, with every facility. Three
restaurants, four bars, tennis
court, and scuba diving.
ⓘ 355 🅿 🕘 Closed winter
🚭 🕭 🕭 🕭 All major cards

### 🏨 FORTEZZA
$$
MELISINOU 16
TEL 28310 55551
E-MAIL INFO@FORTEZZA.GR
www.fortezza.gr
This modern hotel incorpo-
rates traditional Cretan archi-
tectural styles and is wonder-
fully located in a quiet street
near the Venetian fortress. The
waterfront is only a short stroll
away from the hotel.
ⓘ 54 🕘 Closed winter 🔁
🕭 🚭 🕭 All major cards

### 🍽 AVLI
$$$
XANTHOUDIDOU 22/
RADAMANTHYOS
TEL 28310 26213

Try to get a table in the garden
courtyard with its palm trees
and art works, and the food
will do justice to the lush
setting. It's superior stuff, such
as one of their house specials:
wild kid goat in honey and
thyme. Explore the extensive
wine list too.
🚭 🕭 All major credit cards

### 🍽 CAVO D'ORO
$$
NEARCHOU 42
TEL 28310 24446
One of the better places on
the Venetian Harbor, popular
and always busy so reserve a
table in season. Good views
complement the food, which
is simple with an emphasis on
fish of the day, lobster, and
other seafood dishes.
🕘 Closed winter 🚭 🕭 All
major cards

## ◼ CORFU & THE IONIAN ISLANDS

## CORFU

### 🏨 HOLIDAY PALACE CORFU
$$$$
NAUSICAA, KANONI
TEL 26610 36540
E-MAIL RESERVATIONS@
CORFUHOLIDAYPALACE.GR
www.corfuholidaypalace.gr/
Luxury resort hotel close to
the airport and a taxi (or bus)
ride away from Corfu town.
Two restaurants, several bars,
snack bars, two pools, and a
casino are among the facilities.
ⓘ 256 🅿 🔁 🕭 🕭 🕭 🕭
🕭 All major cards

### 🏨 CAVALIERI
$$$
KAPODISTRIOU 4, CORFU TOWN
TEL 26610 39041
E-MAIL INFO@CAVALIERI-HOTEL
.COM
www.cavalieri-hotel
.com/eng/cavalieri.html
This is almost on the water-

front and upper front rooms
have good views of the Old
Fort and the sea. It's in an
old mansion that has been
restored without losing the
old-fashioned style. The rooms
are a little spartan but do have
all modern conveniences.
ⓘ 48 🔁 🚭 🕭 All major cards

## SOMETHING SPECIAL

### 🏨 BELLA VENEZIA
$
ZAMPELI 4, CORFU TOWN
TEL 26610 46500
E-MAIL BELVENHT@HOL.GR
www.bellavenezia
hotel.com/
This is a very modest C-class
hotel which has a charm and
character all its own, belying its
simple facilities. The building
is a 19th-century neoclassical
mansion that has been lovingly restored, with spacious,
high-ceilinged rooms. There is
also a beautiful garden. It is on
a quiet street a few minutes
walk from the center of
town. Staff are noted for their
friendliness.
ⓘ 32 🔁 🚭 🕭 All major cards

### 🍽 DIMARXION
$$$
GUILDFORD 71, CORFU TOWN
TEL 26610 39031
The best and most expensive
restaurant in town. Beautiful
location near Town Hall
Square, and food that ranges
from the conventional (but
superbly done) moussaka
to island specialties such as
bourdetto (fish in a tomato-
garlic sauce).
🚭 🕭 All major cards

### 🍽 AEGLI
$$
KAPODISTRIOU 23, CORFU
TOWN
TEL 26610 31949
A great place on Corfu town's
fashionable Liston, where peo-
ple come to see and be seen.
The location adds to the price,

---

🚭 Nonsmoking   🔁 Air-conditioning   🕭 Indoor Pool   🕭 Outdoor Pool   🕭 Health Club   🕭 Credit Cards but the food is exceptionally good, and includes many island specialties. Try their *sofrito* (veal in a garlic sauce).

🍽 🏧 All major cards

### 🍽 MOURAGIA
$$
ARSENIOU 15
TEL 26610 33815
This small *ouzerie* is usually full, especially at Sunday lunch when people come from a long way away to eat here. Grab an outside table if you can and go for a range of meze snacks, like deep-fried courgettes, stuffed squid, and whitebait.

🍽 🏧 All major cards

### 🍽 GRILL ROOM CHRISSOMALIS
$
THEOTOKI 6, CORFU TOWN
TEL 26610 30342
Very basic, much frequented by locals, and you will get the best of grilled meals at reasonable prices with friendly service.

🍽 🏧 No credit cards

### 🍽 IL POLLO
$
MITROPOLITON ATHANASIOU 71
TEL 26610 26210
Not too many tourists make their way along Garitsa Bay to places like Il Pollo, set back from the sea front. It's therefore very Greek, very animated, a large and simple dining room serving large and simple meals that are beautifully tasty. Try their grills, or ask for a range of mezes.

🕐 Closed L 🍽 🏧 All major cards

### 🍽 NIKOLAS
$
GIMARI, NEAR KALAMI
TEL 26630 91136
This traditional taverna is right on the beach in the quiet village of Gimari, 1 mile (2 km) west of Kalami. Busy at lunchtime with bathers and

families, in the evening it is quieter as diners enjoy both its peaceful setting and its excellent fresh fish dishes, such as mullet, swordfish, or tuna.

🕐 Closed winter 🍽 🏧 No credit cards

## ITHACA

### 🍽 LIBERTY
$$
MYLOS COASTAL RD., VATHI
TEL 26740 32561
Ultra-smart new restaurant around the main harbor, whose cool pale-gray decor contrasts the flavorful and colorful dishes, like seafood ravioli. There are 35 Greek labels on the wine list, too.

🕐 Closed Mon. in winter 🍽 🏧 All major cards

### 🍽 FATOURO
$
STAVROS
TEL 26740 31385
Well worth the trek up to Stavros, this homely family taverna is on the main square, not far from the bust of Odysseus. The food is unpretentious with no surprises, but simple dishes such as moussaka, stuffed grape leaves, and stuffed tomatoes are prepared with the best local ingredients.

🕐 Closed L 🍽 🏧 No credit cards

### 🍽 TREHADIRI TAVERNA
$
VATHI
TEL 26740 33066
Wonderful family-run place, where the wife cooks and the husband serves. Basic menu but prepared with great care and delicious.

🕐 Closed L 🍽 🏧 No credit cards

## KEFALONIA

### 🏨 WHITE ROCKS
$$$$$
PLATYS YIALOS, LASSI, ARGOS-

## PRICES

**HOTELS**

An indication of the cost of a double room in the high season is given by $ signs.

| | |
|---|---|
| $$$$$ | Over $240 |
| $$$$ | $160-240 |
| $$$ | $110-160 |
| $$ | $70-110 |
| $ | Under $70 |

**RESTAURANTS**

An indication of the cost of a three-course meal without drinks is given by $ signs.

| | |
|---|---|
| $$$$$ | Over $65 |
| $$$$ | $50-65 |
| $$$ | $30-50 |
| $$ | $20-30 |
| $ | Under $20 |

TOLI
TEL 26710 28332
One of the best hotels on the island, with its own private beach and another public beach nearby. It has good facilities and is not too far from Argostoli. In addition to the rooms it has 60 cottages.

🛏 102 🅿 🕐 Closed winter 🛗 🍽 🏧 All major cards

### 🍽 EMELISSE ART HOTEL
$$$
FISKARDO, KEFALONIA
TEL 26740 412000
Stylish Balinese furniture adorns these bungalows strewn over a peninsula. Wonderful homemade breakfasts.

🅿 🍽 🏖 🏧 All major cards

### 🍽 ANONYMOUS
$
ANTONI TRITSI 146, ARGOSTOLI
TEL 26710 22403
This little family-run place, right on the harbor, limits its menu to a few daily specials, plus the conventional grills and fresh fish. Friendly, relaxed service.

🍽 🏧 No credit cards

---

## 🍴 CAPTAIN'S CABIN

$

HARBOR, FISKARDO

TEL 26740 41007

Right on the harbor is this long-established family-run place where the friendly family produces a menu that caters to both locals and visitors alike. Fresh fish is always available and their versions of Greek staples such as stuffed tomatoes or fried squid are excellent.

All major cards

## 🍴 OLD PLAKA

$

METELAS, ARGOSTOLI

TEL 26710 24849

Typical open-all-hours Greek place, but a dressier clientele comes in the evenings. Reasonably priced but tasty Greek fare. Pork stuffed with garlic is a succulent house specialty.

All major cards

## 🍴 PATSOURAS

$

IOANNOU METAXA 32, ARGOSTOLI

TEL 26710 22779

On busy days in Argostoli, it's a relief to retreat to the quiet garden of this delightful and friendly little restaurant. The menu includes several island specialties, depending on the season, but Kefalonia meat pie is usually available.

No credit cards

## LEFKADA

## 🏨 LEFKAS HOTEL

$$

PAPAGOU 2, LEFKADA TOWN

TEL 26450 23916

The best bet if staying in the island capital, this hotel is large, central, and of a good standard. Spacious comfortable rooms and very accommodating staff and management.

93 All major cards

## 🍴 REGANTOS

$

DIMARHOU VERIOTI 17, LEFKADA TOWN

TEL 26450 22855

A restaurant that's popular in Lefkada town must be good, as there aren't too many foreign visitors around and the locals know what's what. Try the meat stews, sausages, and kebabs, for which Lefkada is noted.

Closed L No credit cards

## PAXI

## 🍴 REX

$

GAÏOS

TEL 26620 31268

If you want fresh fish then Rex has got it, simply grilled. The menu also includes basic Greek dishes such as moussaka and *dolmades* (stuffed grape leaves), but fish is the focus.

No credit cards

## 🍴 TAKA-TAKA

$

GAÏOS

TEL 26620 31323

A long-established favorite specializing in grilled meat and fresh fish. Friendly owners and a lovely outdoor eating area, covered in vines.

All major cards

## 🍴 VASSILI'S

$

WATERFRONT, LONGOS

TEL 26620 31587

Right on the picturesque little harbor at Longos, this restaurant looks very ordinary but serves up the best food on the island, backed up by an extensive wine list. Best to reserve a table at busy times of the year.

Closed some days L (phone to check) All major cards

## ZAKINTHOS

## 🏨 NOBELOS HOTEL

$$$

VOLIMES

TEL 26950 27632

E-MAIL INFO@NOBELOS.GR

www.nobelos.gr/

Four romantic suites—with traditional furniture and antiques—overlooks the sea. Greet the dawn with homemade breakfast. (The hotel restaurant is for guests only.)

4 All major cards

## 🏨 STRADA MARINA

$$$

LOMVARDOU 14, CHORA, ZAKINTHOS TOWN

TEL 26950 42761

E-MAIL HOTEL@STRADAMARIN.GR

www.stradamarina.gr/

Perfectly situated on the waterfront in the capital, this classy hotel has all the modern amenities and an attractive roof terrace with excellent views.

112 All major cards

## SOMETHING SPECIAL

## 🍴 MANTALENA

$

ALIKANAS

TEL 26950 83487

Arguably the best restaurant on the island, this is in a village south of the resort of Alikanas. It's family run, the menu made up of recipes collected from the owners' relatives over the years. Manager Tasos makes a charming maître d', with his good looks and impeccable English, while his mother produces delicious dishes from the kitchen. They serve water from their own well, wine from their own vineyards, and a complimentary glass of ouzo to every guest.

All major cards

# Shopping in Greece

Souvenir shops offer the usual knickknacks, with a heavy emphasis on ceramics. By looking around it is possible to find more unusual items made by craftspeople rather than settling for mass-produced goods. Leather is a good buy, from tiny purses to thick coats. Wool blankets are easily found, along with flokati, the handwoven wool rugs produced particularly in the northern mountains and in Thrace. However, since the euro was introduced in 2002, most Greek retailers have been forced to raise prices considerably—so don't expect any bargains.

Among the best buys are gold and silver jewelry—for which the Greeks have a reputation. There are exquisite rings, earrings, and necklaces. Other delicate work is seen in embroidery and handwoven items, lace, cotton skirts, and blouses. Many towns have folk museums displaying traditional clothing and decorative work, most with a gift shop selling modern examples. If there's no shop, the curators will be able to tell you where to find the local specialists. Other good souvenirs are tapes of Greek music and the *koboloi* (worry beads) you see hanging in most tourist shops. Generally Greek food and wine doesn't travel well, although some brand-name spirits are good bargains and so is the virgin olive oil.

## Where to Go

Different areas of Greece specialize in particular crafts. If you are keen on ceramics then the best examples are available in Rhodes, Sifnos, and Skiros, though you will find good work for sale almost anywhere in the country. For jewelry the place to go is Ioanina in Epiros, the traditional center of the silverworkers of Greece. Rhodes and Athens are both good for gold, but prices are high. Quality leatherwork is widely available, but the finest examples are available on Crete, and in particular the town of Hania. Wooden carvings and embroidery are especially good in Metsovo,

and quality embroidery is also to be found in the Ionian islands, especially Kefalonia and Zakinthos.

## Antiques

It is a criminal offense in Greece to buy, sell, own, or export any antique item. There is no clear definition of what is considered an antique item, but the law is aimed at protecting Greece's historical and cultural artifacts. If you are offered anything in an underhand manner that is obviously extremely old, then beware: If it is genuine, you could be in line for committing a criminal offense, and if it is not genuine then you are probably being ripped off. Better stick to obvious copies from museum shops.

That is not to say that you can't legally buy more recent antiques, such as books, paintings, engravings, and so on, and indeed you will see many such items for sale in markets such as at Monastiraki in central Athens and in Pireas on a Sunday morning, or in antiques shops around the country. However, there are not too many of these as Greeks tend to hold on to their family heirlooms rather than trade in them, and shopping for antiques is not as popular a pastime in Greece as in, say, the U.S.A. or Britain.

## Haggling

Haggling is acceptable in certain circumstances, notably in tourist areas such as the Plaka in Athens. Here store owners

will start you off on the process anyway by immediately quoting you a price less than the one on the ticket ("special price for today only"). The gullible tourist then accepts this as a bargain, rather than wondering if the price might have come down further: It usually will. Jewelry and craft shops often have room for maneuver, although by no means as much as is common farther east or in North Africa.

## ■ ATHENS

### Antiques, Arts, & Crafts

Artworks, old prints, and postcards can be bought in several good junk/antique shops at the very far end of Adhrianou: Keep walking and get beyond the souvenir shops of the Plaka.

**A.D. Gallery**, Pallados 3, tel (210) 360 2948. Tucked away in the newly fashionable Psirri district, this little gallery puts on changing exhibitions of contemporary art mixing painting, photography, and multimedia works. Opens lunchtime and evenings only, closed Sunday and Monday.

**Aidini**, Nikis 32, tel (210) 323 4591 or (210) 322 6088. An unusual basement craft shop/gallery located between Syntagma and the Plaka, where the owner makes distinctive metalwork sculptures, ranging from interesting fishes to pretty surreal objects.

**Alekos Kostas**, Abyssinia Square 3, tel (210) 321 1580. Antiques or junk? A little bit of both in this quirky shop in Monastiraki, whose owner has an eye for almost anything.

**L'Atelier,** Adrianou 116, tel (210) 323 3740. It is illegal to export genuine Greek antiquities, but here you can find good copies of vases, frescoes, and Cycladic statues. You might be lucky enough to see these instant "antiques" being made.

**Athens Gallery.** Pandrossou 14, tel (210) 324 6942 or (210) 894 0217. This stylish gallery is a cut above most of the surrounding Plaka souvenir shops. It represents a handful of contemporary Greek artists, which include sculptors, painters, potters, and jewelers. Even if you cannot afford to buy the more expensive items, they are well worth looking at.

**Gallerie Areta,** Pandrossou 31, tel (210) 324 3397 or (210) 894 0217. A small offshoot of the Athens Gallery selling mainly ceramics and paintings, including some delightful primitive artwork.

**Center of Hellenic Tradition,** Mitropoleos 59/Pandrossou 36, tel (210) 321 3023 or (210) 321 3842. In an arcade between the main Plaka street of Pandrossou and Mitropoleos is a selection of small stores devoted to Greek arts and crafts, including paintings, ceramics, woodwork, painted postcards, and icons. It also has a good café with a view down onto the passing throngs of the Plaka.

**EOMMEX,** Mitropoleos 9, tel (210) 323 0408. In this cooperative you can buy handmade rugs made by weavers from all over Greece, using traditional looms, materials, and techniques.

**Greek Women's Institution,** Ypatias 6, tel (210) 325 0524. This outlet highlights the Greek embroidery tradition, providing the more remote rural and island communities with some financial benefit from the country's popularity as a tourist destination—which they would not otherwise receive. A cause worth supporting.

**Iakovos Antiques,** Ifaistou 6, tel (210) 321 0169. Ceramics, paintings, and knickknacks old and new, not just from Greece but from around the world.

**Vassilios Kevorkian,** Ifaistou 6, tel (210) 321 0024. Handmade guitars, bouzoukis, and other stringed instruments produced in a tiny workshop in the bazaar. The friendly owner doesn't mind if you just look.

**Karamikos Mazarakis,** Voulis 31–33, tel (210) 322 4932. As well as traditional Greek flokati rugs and kilims, this large store between Syntagma and the Plaka sells wool and silk rugs from elsewhere in the world, and features unusual rugs using designs by famous artists.

**Takis Moraytis,** Adrianou 129, tel (210) 322 5208. Shop of a Plaka artist, with some good original Greek scenes. Expensive but good quality.

**Martinos,** Pandrossou 5, tel (210) 321 3110. There are some genuinely good antiques shops in among the Plaka's souvenir shops, and this is one of the best, offering antique furniture, old mirrors and kilims, and household antiques.

**Museum of Greek Children's Art,** Kodrou 9, tel (210) 331 2621. Delightful prizewinning paintings by Greek children are both on display and for sale. A chance to make an original purchase which will not only support the museum but bring a smile to the young artist's face.

**Nasiotis,** Ifaistou 24, tel (210) 321 2369. Look for the long display of old photos, engravings, books, magazines, and saucy postcards in this Aladdin's cave. Downstairs is a jumble of old books, mostly in Greek but some in other languages and worth a look.

**National Welfare Organization,** Ypatias 6, tel (210) 325 0524. This excellent cooperative offers for sale traditional craftwork

and practical items made by rural communities throughout Greece: embroidery, rugs, ceramics, icons. There is an especially good array of kitchenware, including coffeemakers, breadboards, and pots and pans. They are all attractive yet sturdily made and typically Greek, and buying here helps keep the craft traditions alive.

**Olive Wood Workshop,** Mnisikleous 8, tel (210) 321 6145. Small family shop in a Plaka side street selling beautiful olive wood carvings, including breadboards, cheeseboards, and bowls. The friendly young owner also makes many of the items and is usually at work in the corner of the shop.

**Panayiri,** Kleomenous 25, tel (210) 722 5369. Kolonaki shop with a good range of craft items, paintings, books, and—its specialty—model ships, carved by the owner, in wood taken from old ships.

**Pyromania,** Kodrou 14, tel (210) 325 5288. Tasteful examples of handblown glass, ceramics, and olive wood carvings, with a small workshop at the rear where the affable and talented artist-owner works. On the edge of the Plaka and easily spotted by its strikingly lit window displays.

**Mihalarias Arts,** Alopekis 1–3, tel (210) 721 3079. The shop itself is an antique, in Kolonaki, and from it the owner sells quality furniture, lamps, paintings, and other expensive items.

**Kostas Sokaras,** Adrianou 25, tel (210) 321 6826. Embroidery, jewelry, Greek folk costumes, and puppets from the traditional Greek art of the shadow theater.

## Books, Newspapers, & Magazines

**The Booknest,** Panepistimiou 25–29, tel (210) 323 1703. Great jumble of a bookstore covering hardbacks and paperbacks, old and new, guidebooks and fiction, in many languages.

**Compendium,** Nikis 28, tel (210) 322 1248. English-language books, magazines, guides, fiction, books about Greece, maps, and a large secondhand section for exchanging your used paperbacks. There are sometimes readings from local or visiting authors—check the notice board for details.

**Pantelides,** Amerikis 11, tel (210) 362 3673. This is the biggest English-language bookstore in Athens, with everything from popular blockbuster paperbacks to obscure specialist works. There is a good section of books about Greece, plus dictionaries, art books, cookbooks, and history. The English-speaking owner is always pleased to help.

**Raymondos,** Voukourestiou 18, tel (210) 364 8189. You will find a wide range of foreign magazines here, and it's a good source of magazines about Greece, as well as Greek fiction in English and guidebooks.

## Clothes

The car-free Ermou Street has a range of international clothing stores such as Benetton, Lacoste, and Marks & Spencer, as well as many Greek equivalents. More exclusive designer stores can be found in the fashionable Kolonaki district, at the foot of Lykavittos.

**Artisti Italiani,** Kanari 5, Kolonaki, tel (210) 339 0254. Italian designs for women and men and appropriately priced.

**Stavros Melissinos,** Pandrossou 89, tel (210) 321 9247. Now a Plaka institution, Melissinos has been making sandals and writing poetry since the 1960s. He made sandals for John Lennon and will do the same for you.

## Food & Drink

Visit the **Central Market** south of Omonoia on Athinas to buy herbs, spices, nuts, olives, cheeses, and other delicacies.

**Aristokratikon,** Karayiori Servias 9, tel (210) 322 0546. Greeks like really sweet sweets and this upmarket store has been supplying the city with chocolates and other indulgences for decades.

**Bachar,** Evripidou 31, tel (210) 321 7225. Specialist store near the Central Market, with spices and herbs for both culinary and medicinal use.

**Brettos,** Kydathinaion 41, tel (210) 323 2110. Well-stocked and colorful liquor store in the Plaka, with own-brand spirits and liqueurs as well as numerous Greek drinks.

**The Mastiha Shop,** Panepistimiou Street/Kriezotou Street, tel (210) 363 2750. This lovely little shop near Syntagma sells everything made from the mastic plant—which grows on the island of Hios—including sweets, juices, cosmetics, medicines and many other items, all said to be health-giving.

## Jewelry

Athens has a long tradition of silversmiths, and a number of stores can be found in the district around Lekka and Praxitelous Streets. Some have huge, garish silver displays, but there are smaller stores that include more tasteful items. Several of the more expensive jewelry stores are along the Voukourestiou shopping street.

**Borell's,** Ypsilandou 5, tel (210) 721 9772. Modern and some antique jewelry, just off Kolonaki Square.

**Ilias Lalaounis Jewelry Museum,** Karyatidon-Kallisperi 12, tel (210) 922 1044. See copies of works by this world-famous Greek jewelry designer, in a stylish museum. Originals can be ordered,

at a price. The Lalaounis store is at Panepistimiou 6, tel (210) 361 2429.

**Marathianakis,** Voukourestiou 21, tel (210) 362 7118. Stunning Greek gold pieces based on Byzantine designs.

**Marianna Petridi Jewellery,** Haritos 34, tel (210) 363 4295. Boutique showcasing Marianna's talents with semiprecious stones—plus a handful of emerging designers like Katerina Anesti.

**Nisiotis,** Lekka 28, tel (210) 324 4183. Excellent store specializing in upscale silverware.

**Zolotas,** Stadiou 9, tel (210) 322 1222. One of Greece's leading jewelers, with work worth seeing in its own right, whether you buy or not. Also has a store in the Plaka at Pandrossou 8.

## Museum Reproductions

Several of the major museums in Athens sell copies of their most appealing items, and these can range from small and inexpensive to life-size reproductions. The standard is generally high. The main stores are at the National Archaeological Museum (see pp. 82–85), the Benaki Museum (see pp. 74–75), and the Goulandris Museum of Cycladic Art (see pp. 78–79).

## Music

In the **Monastiraki flea market** there are several specialist record stores, with a particular emphasis on 1960s and 1970s music, from the popular to the obscure. Good selection of vinyl as well as CDs.

**Museum of Popular Instruments,** Diogenous 1–3, tel (210) 325 0198. The museum shop sells recordings of every type of musical tradition from all over Greece. Vast stock, plus books (mostly in Greek).

## PELOPONNISOS

### NAFPLIO

**To Enotio,** Staikopoulou 40, tel 27520 21143. The Greeks have a great tradition of shadow puppet shows and you can buy examples of the puppets here, both old and new, in this delightful shop with a fun window display.

**Odyssey,** Plateia Syntagmatos, tel 27520 23430. Good selection of books, newspapers, and magazines in several languages. Books include guidebooks and Greek fiction, or fiction set in Greece.

## CENTRAL GREECE

### OANINA

**Athanasias Daktylithos,** Pirsinela 14, tel 26510 28005. Good stock of Greek and foreign-language newspapers and magazines; newspapers are usually available the day after publication.

**Kasa Makis,** Plateia Eleuthezotou 2, tel 26510 22502. Wine merchant selling a worldwide range as well as many good-quality Greek wines, of the type that seldom make it onto the limited menus of many restaurants. Also sells a tasty selection of Greek cakes and candy.

**Nikos Xaritos,** Anexartisias 2, tel 26510 29200. There are plenty of stores selling silver in Ioanina, but only a handful of workshops remain. This one sells the young owner's handmade plates, cups, jewelry, and decorative items, mainly in silver and brass.

## MACEDONIA & THRACE

### THESSALONKI

**Marina,** Mitropoleos 62, tel 23102 38361. The eponymous Marina once worked for Greece's most celebrated jeweler, Ilias Lalaounis, whose work has influenced her own designs. Not cheap—but certainly cheaper than her former teacher.

**Molho,** Tsmiski 10, tel 23102 75271. If you want to find a book, newspaper, or magazine in English or any other foreign language in Thessaloniki, then this is the place to look. If you cannot find it here it probably cannot be found—from conventional guides to archaeology, history, poetry, and fiction. A good selection of Greek titles, too.

**Adelphi Kazanzidi,** Klissouras 12, tel 23102 62741. If you like the Greek copper wine jugs and coffeemakers, then head for this copper workshop that has been family-owned for several generations, and one of the finest in the city preserving a traditional craft that is more commonly seen in the Middle East and Central Asia.

## AEGEAN ISLANDS

### ARGO-SARONIC ISLANDS

**Elefteris Diakoyiannis,** Vas-Georgiou 39, Egina town, tel 22970 24593. A good selection of ceramics from all over Greece. Also has a selection of jewelry and reproductions of Greek sculpture.

## SPORADES

### Skiathos/Skopelos

**Archipelago,** Skiathos town & Skopelos town, tel 24270 22163 & 24270 23127. These two stores have a mix of antiques, unusual arts and crafts items, and clothing—well worth browsing through.

**Galerie Varsakis,** Plateia Trion Ierarchon, Skiathos town, tel 24270 22255. Owned by an artist whose surreal paintings are for sale, this arts and crafts treasure trove includes jewelry, embroidery, carvings, and carpets.

### Skiros

**Faltaïts Museum,** Palaiopyrgos, Skiros town, tel 22220 91232 (museum); 22220 92158 (Argo). Small museum of folk art with a workshop and gift shop attached where you can buy the work of modern craftsmen and women, doing your part to help keep the island traditions alive. The museum has an outlet, called Argo, on the main street.

**Andreou's,** Agoras, tel 22220 92926. This woodcarving workshop sells hand-crafted furniture in time-honored Skyrian style, along with kitchen utensils and other smaller household items that are rather easier to take home.

### NORTHEASTERN AEGEAN ISLANDS

### Hios

**The Mastiha Shop,** Aigeou 12, tel 22710 40223. Sells products made from the sap that oozes from the mastic trees here on Hios, which gets turned into cosmetics, balms, sweets, health drinks, shampoos and other healthy items.

## Lesvos

**The Lesvos Shop,** Pavlou Kountourioti 22, tel 22510 26088. This fine shop is worth supporting as it's a community project which helps keep island traditions alive by selling local produce, from ouzo and olive oil to soaps and ceramics.

## CYCLADES

### Andros

**Batsi Gold,** Bats, tel 22820 41575. In this south coast resort, find a good collection of jewelry inspired by ancient Greek myths and legends: bracelets, earrings, necklaces, pins, rings.

**Paraporti,** Plateia Kairi, Andros town, tel 22820 23777. Craft items, especially ceramics, from Andros, as well as embroidery, some jewelry, and model ships.

### Mikonos

**Center for Contemporary Art,** Kouzi Yorgouli 43, Mikonos town, tel 22890 26868. You could shop till you drop in Mikonos, as a great number of artists, producing quality arts, crafts, and clothing, have set up shop here. This center concentrates on modern Greek artists.

**Galatis,** Polykandrioti Street, Mikonos town, tel 22890 22255. Mykonian clothes designer whose modern creations were once worn by Brigitte Bardot and Sophia Loren.

**Ilias Lalaounis,** Polykandrioti 14, Mikonos town, tel 22890 22444. The most famous jeweler in Greece, with his own museum in Athens, has an outlet on Mikonos. His work is priced accordingly.

**The Rarity Gallery,** Kalogera 22, Mikonos town. The oldest gallery on the island, showing works of many famous Greek artists. Beautiful veranda.

### Naxos

**Tirokomika Proionia Naxou,** Papavasiliou, Naxos town, tel 22850 22230. Fantastic food and drink store on Naxos, an essential visit if you want to take anything home or simply prepare a fine picnic with local cheeses, all kinds of olives, and local wines.

### Paros

**Enosis,** Plateia Mando Mavrogenous, Paros town, tel 22820 22181. This is a fine enterprise selling all local produce such as cheeses and wines, honey, olive oil, and even Parian pasta.

### Santorini

**Canava Roussos,** Kamari, tel 22860 31278. They make some good wine on the island of Santorini, and here is a chance to sample at the source, and buy a few bottles at reasonable prices.

### Sifnos

**Antonis Kalogirou,** Harbor, Kamares, tel 22840 31651. This potter sells his own distinctive work, in Sifnos style, and also sells paintings of island life, which are much better than many of the mass-produced prints on sale everywhere.

### Tinos

**Harris Prassas Ostria-Tinos,** Evangelistrias 20, Tinos town, tel 22830 23893. This jeweler has produced an eclectic collection of work, incorporating ancient and modern styles, in both silver and gold. Much of it has a religious theme, appropriate to Tinos as a pilgrimage site.

## DODECANESE

There are many shops selling sponges in the Dodecanese, and almost all tourist shops will have at least a few on display. In order to know what you're buying, you should first visit a specialist center (some are listed below). Experts there will explain what to look for in a good sponge and allow you to test several types before making up your mind. Some points to remember are that naturally colored brown sponges are stronger than artificially colored yellow ones, smaller holes make better sponges, and cut sponges do not last as long as whole sponges.

### Kalimnos

**Astor Workshop of Sea Sponges,** Pothia, tel 22430 29815. See the whole process of sponge production, then buy some of the best quality sponges on the island known for them.

### Patmos

**Katoi,** Chora, tel 22470 31487. Good choice of jewelry, icons, and ceramics of the island.

### Rhodes

**Ministry of Culture Museum Reproduction Shop,** Ippitou, Rhodes Old Town. This is the official government shop where you can pick up top-quality reproductions of statuary and other items on display in Greek museums.

### Symi

**Aegean Sponge Center,** Harbor, Yialo. There are thousands of sponges for sale on an island that once made part of its wealth from sponge fishing. The owners of the Sponge Center will show how to tell good sponges, and talk about the life of the sponge fishermen.

## CRETE

Embroidery and weaving have been traditional crafts on Crete, going back to Minoan times, and you can pick up some fine examples in the larger towns and villages on the Lasithi Plateau. Leatherwork is also good.

**Eleni Kastrinoyanni,** Ikarou 3, Iraklio, tel 28210 26186. Exclusive store selling modern examples of many of the Cretan folk arts, such as weaving, embroidery, pottery, and jewelry.

**Leather Alley,** Odos Skridlof, Hania. Close to the market, the street known as Leather Alley is lined with stores selling leather goods, including sandals, boots, handbags, backpacks, belts, and wallets.

**Elixir,** Koundourou 15, Agios Nikolaos, tel 28410 82593.
Elixir stocks examples of fine Cretan produce such as olive oil, soap, and honey, that make beautiful souvenirs, for yourself and your friends.

**Petrakis Icon Workshop,** Elouda 72053, tel 28410 41669. A young married couple keep the Greek icon-painting tradition alive with superb skill at their workshop. The owners also display conventional paintings and other craft work.

## CORFU & THE IONIAN ISLANDS

### CORFU

**Mironis,** Spyridon 65, tel 26610 40364. One of several olive-wood workshops in Corfu town. The kitchen, decorative, and other items on offer here at Mironis are handmade by the family.

**Symposium,** Near Nisaki, tel 26630 91094. As you enter Nisaki look for this wonderful food store, stocking the best food and drink products from the island and other parts of Greece. Food lovers' eyes will light up.

**Elli,** Theotki 88, Corfu Town, tel 26610 26283. An outlet for the hand-embroidered tablecloths and other items produced by the island women. Good quality work is expensive, but the shop's owner will explain how many months of work go into some of the items. Smaller items are also for sale, all exquisitely made.

**Mavromatis Distillery,** 8 miles (13 km) from Corfu town on road to Palaiokastritsa, tel 26630 22174. See the manufacturing process for the company's three main products: brandy, ouzo, and the unique local liqueur made from kumquats. A chance to buy them, too, of course.

**Terracotta,** Filarmonikis 2, Corfu town, tel 26610 45260. Good-quality outlet for arts and crafts items made only by Greek artists. These are excellent examples of work, such as sculptures and ceramics, and while it may be expensive, it is of the best quality.

**Vassilakis,** Opposite Achilleion Palace, tel 26610 52440. One of the largest stocks of Greek wines, spirits, and liqueurs that you will find anywhere, with tastings before you buy.

### KEFALONIA

**Alexander's,** Vergoti, Argostoli, tel 26710 23057. Large and varied collection of Greek handicrafts, including jewelry handmade by the store's owner, plus ceramics, dolls in island costumes, embroidery, and unusual handmade glass items.

**Gentilini Vineyard,** Minies, tel 26710 41618. This small-scale vineyard does not conduct organized tours so be sure to telephone to check before visiting. If convenient, you will get a personal tour of the vineyard and a chance to sample and buy some of the high-quality wine.

### ZAKINTHOS

**Handicraft Cooperative,** Lombardou 42, Zakinthos town. On the waterfront, this excellent store sells a range of island-made products including rugs, clothing, embroidery, and tablecloths.

# Entertainment

Entertainment is often impromptu: Someone is inspired to get up and sing or dance in a bar or taverna; there's a party to mark one of the many feast days scattered throughout the Greek calendar; or maybe it's someone's name day (the Greek equivalent of a birthday), when everyone sharing the same name will jointly host a party. However, there are also some more organized events and festivals.

## ■ ATHENS

### Arts Festivals

An annual festival of music, dance, drama, and other arts is held in Athens every summer, throughout the months of June–October. Events take place at Herodes Atticus Theater, tel (210) 322 1459 or (210) 323 2771.

### Feasts

January 6 is a national holiday, the Feast of the Epiphany, but is also the day for the **Blessing of the Waters,** to bring good fortune to this maritime nation for the forthcoming year. This is done at Pireas, and throughout the country. March 25 is **Independence Day,** when Athens hosts parades and other special festivities to celebrate the 1821 War of Independence against the Turks.

### Folk Dance

Dora Stratou was a renowned dancer and enthusiast for Greek music and culture, and the dance troupe she founded performs nightly from May to the end of September in a delightful open-air theater, the **Dora Stratou Theater** on Philoppapou Hill, tel (210) 324 4395.

### Sound & Light Show

Held on the Pnyx Hill opposite the Acropolis from April to October. There are different language shows each evening so check the current program, tel (210) 322 1459.

## ■ PELOPONNISOS

### Arts Festivals

A festival including classical music, drama, and other arts is held in the charming town of **Nafplio** every summer. For details call 27520 28607.

Each summer, **Patra** hosts a festival devoted to classical music, theater, and traditional music and dance.

### Drama Festival

Held in conjunction with the Athens Arts Festival, this festival of drama in the stunning setting of the ancient theater at **Epidavros** runs throughout the summer. Performances are not held every night, so obtain a current program, tel (210) 322 1459.

### Feasts

July 18–20 is the **Feast of Profitis Ilias,** celebrated with services and festivities at many monasteries throughout the country bearing that name. The biggest celebration by far takes place on the high peak of **Mount Taygettus,** near the town of Sparti.

### Wine Festival

**Patra** is renowned for its Carnival celebrations and for a big annual wine festival that runs from late August to mid-September, tel 26102 79866.

## ■ CENTRAL GREECE, THESSALY, & EPIROS

### Feasts

On April 23, the **Feast of St. George** is celebrated with traditional music, dancing, and costumes in the mountain village of **Arachova,** near Delphi.

## ■ MACEDONIA & THRACE

### Arts Festivals

A festival concentrating on **drama** is held in the ancient theater at **Philippi** during the summer months.

In **Thessaloniki,** the annual **Dimitria Festival** includes music, theater, and opera, and takes place at various venues around the town in late October and early November. The festival is timed to correspond with October 26, the feast day of the city's patron saint.

### Feasts

On May 21, at the **Feast of Agios Konstantinos,** there are fire-walking ceremonies in some of the villages near Thessaloniki, most notably at **Lagkadas.** October 26 is the **Feast of Agios Dimitrios** in **Thessaloniki** (see above).

In villages across **Thrace,** a tradition takes place on January 8 that turns this male-dominated society on its head: The men remain at home and do housework, and the women relax in the cafés.

## AEGEAN ISLANDS

### ARGO-SARONIC ISLANDS

#### Feasts

September 8 marks the **Battle of the Straits of Spetses**, a battle that is reenacted in the town's harbor each year. The same date is the **Feast of the Birth of the Virgin Mary,** celebrated all over Greece.

The **Independence Day** celebrations of March 25 are celebrated with particular fervor and exuberance on **Idra.**

### SPORADES

#### Feasts

February 25 is celebrated on **Skopelos** as the **Feast of Agios Riginos,** the island's patron saint.

St. George is **Skiros's** patron saint, so his **festival** on April 23 is enthusiastically celebrated there with music and feasting.

### NORTHEASTERN AEGEAN ISLANDS

#### Drama Festival

A festival devoted to the ancient drama of Greece takes place every July in **Thassos town.**

#### Feasts

**Ikaria** island is famous for **panayiri,** or fiestas, which take place all summer. Some last three days.

In the village of **Agia Paraskevi,** on Lesvos, there are festivities on the **feast day** of that name, which falls on July 26. On August 15 the **Feast of the Assumption** is best observed in **Ayiassos.**

On **Samos,** the **Feast of Agia Paraskevi** is especially celebrated in the village of that name on July 26.

There is a tradition on **Limnos** of horse racing to celebrate the **Feast of St. George,** on April 23.

## CYCLADES

#### Feasts

There are big celebrations on **Tinos** on March 25, **Independence Day,** and August 15, the **Assumption of the Virgin.**

#### Music Festival

A music festival is held on Santorini every August.

### DODECANESE

#### Feasts

The mountain village of **Olympos,** near Karpathos, is a great place to be on August 15, the **Feast of the Assumption.**

The **Feast of Agia Marina** on July 17 is a big day in the village of that name on the island of **Kasos.**

On **Kos,** the **Feast of St George,** April 23, is traditionally celebrated with horse racing.

The **Feast of Agia Marina,** July 17, is a big celebration in the village of Agia Marina on **Leros.**

July 18–20 is when the **Feast of Profitis Ilias** is celebrated in the numerous monasteries named after the prophet. Celebrations are particularly colorful at the monastery on **Rhodes,** about half a mile (1 km) SE of Kameiros.

The islanders of **Simi** travel to the offshore island of Agia Marina to celebrate the **Feast of Agia Marina** on July 17.

On **Tilos** on July 27, villagers travel to the monastery of Agios Pandelimon for the annual **feast** of food, music, and dancing.

#### Folk Dance

In **Rhodes Old Town** there are nightly performances during the week, from May to October (currently 9:15 p.m. Mon., Wed., & Fri.), by the **Nelly Dimoglou Company** at the Old Town Theater, near Plateia Arionos, Rhodes town, tel 22410 20157.

#### Sound & Light Show

Held in **Rhodes'** Municipal Garden, next to the Palace of the Grand Masters, from April to October. Shows are in different languages, check for details tel 22410 21922.

## CRETE

### Arts Festival

A major **arts festival** takes place in **Iraklio** each August, with drama, dance, and music concerts featuring international names as well as Greek stars.

Every August/September the **Renaissance Festival** in **Rethimnon** includes lively music and theater events, tel 28310 22245 or 28310 53583.

### Wine Festival

**Rethimno** also holds an annual wine festival, usually held throughout most of July.

## CORFU & THE IONIAN ISLANDS

### Cricket

In **Corfu,** July is the time of the annual **Cricket Week,** the island's odd British sporting legacy. Matches take place on the Esplanade in Corfu town. Participants include island teams, visiting English village teams, and anyone else who cares to make up a team.

### Feasts

The **Unification of the Ionian Islands** on May 21 is celebrated throughout the island group, but especially in and around **Corfu town.**

### Sound & Light Show

This is held in the Old Fortress, **Corfu town,** from May until the end of September. Check locally for details, tel 26610 37520.

# Activities in Greece

Greece offers a wide array of activities, with water sports featuring prominently. Most resorts have a choice of sports available, such as windsurfing, waterskiing, pedaling boats, jet skiing, and paragliding. Activities such as walking and cycling tend to be unorganized and left to the individual. Tennis, soccer, and basketball are popular, and there are a few golf courses.

## Golf

Avid golfers may be interested in the following courses: **Glyfada Golf Course,** Konstantinou Karamanli, Glyfada, Athens, tel (210) 894 6820. A 150-acre (60 ha), 18-hole, par 72 course. The best in Greece, with a clubhouse and full facilities.

**Afantou Golf Course,** Rhodes, tel 22410 51255. An 18-hole, par 72 course. This is not a particularly good course but is still enjoyable for its setting.

**Corfu Golf Club,** Ermones, Corfu, tel 22610 94220. An 18-hole, par 72 course, suitable for all levels. Coaching is given, and there is a restaurant and a shop with equipment for rent.

**Crete Golf Club,** Hersonnisos, tel 28970 26000. An 18-hole, par 72 course, overlooking stunning Cretan landscape. Restaurant and clubhouse facilities.

## Horseback Riding

Not very big in Greece, but for details of clubs in Athens, Thessaloniki, and around the country, contact: **Hellenic Riding Club,** Maroussi, Athens, tel (210) 682 6128.

## Marathon Running

The original marathon route is run twice a year. Details from: **SEGAS,** Syngrou 137, Athens, tel (210) 935 9302.

## Mountaineering

There are numerous mountaineering clubs around Greece that can provide information on activities, mountain trails, and the many mountain huts and refuges that can be reserved

through them. For an up-to-date list contact: **Hellenic Federation of Mountaineering Clubs,** Miloni 5, 10673 Athens, tel (210) 364 5904.

## Sailing

Sailing enthusiasts, whether experienced or not, will find the variety of sailing conditions in the Greek seas most satisfying. For general information contact: **Hellenic Professional Yacht Owners Association,** A8–A0 Marina Zea, 18536 Piraes, tel (210) 452 6335.

## Scuba Diving

Diving is permitted only in certain areas during daylight hours, so check locally. The permitted areas are on or near Corfu, Kalimnos, Kos, Lefkada, Mikonos, Paxi, Rhodes, and Zakinthos. For details, contact: **Union of Greek Diving Centers,** tel (210) 922 9532.

## Skiing

Information on skiing in Greece is available from the **Hellenic Federation of Skiing Clubs,** Karayoryi tis Servias 7, 10563 Athens, tel (210) 323 0182.

Skiing centers include: **Kalavrita Ski Resort,** Xirokambos, Kalavrita, tel 26920 22174 or 26920 22661. In the Peloponnisos, 12 runs totaling 15.5 miles (25 km) and covering all levels, at altitudes between 5,578 and 7,700 feet (1,700 and 2,347 m). Restaurant, shop, clinic, mountain refuge.

And in Central Greece: **Metsovo Ski Center,** Karakoli and Politses-Profitis Ilias Metsovo, tel 26560 41312/41211. Open Christmas to Easter. Good facilities for Greece, but not up to Western

European or U.S. standards.

**Parnassos Ski Center,** Fterolakka and Kellaria, tel 22340 22693. Twelve runs ranging from two green to two black runs, at an altitude of 5,750 feet (1,750 m) at Kellaria and 5,900 feet (1,800 m) at Fterolakka. Store, ski school, chalet for meals. Open around December to Easter.

**Pilion Ski Center,** Agriolefkes, Pilion, tel 24210 25696/73719. Usually open from late November to late April, with three main slopes, beginners' slopes, and cross-country trails.

## Spectator Sports

Soccer remains Greece's sporting obsession, but it has been matched by basketball, since the Greek team won the 1987 European Championships. It may be hard to get served in a bar or taverna when all eyes are glued to sport on TV.

## Waterskiing

For general information on Athens-area facilities contact: **Greek Water Skiing Federation,** Posidonos Avenue, Elliniko, Athens, tel (210) 894 7413.

## Windsurfing

Experienced windsurfers who want the best facilities should look to the Ionian Islands (Corfu, Lefkada, and Zakinthos in particular), and to Kos, Lesvos, Naxos, Paros, and Samos.

# Menu Reader

## General terms
the check  *o logariasmos*
bottle  *boukali*
glass  *potiri*
water  *nero*

## Basics
bread  *psomi*
cheese  *tyri*
eggs  *avga*
fish  *psari(a)*
honey  *meli*
meat  *kreas*
oil  *lathi*
  without oil  *khoris lathi*
pepper  *to piperi*
salt  *alati*
seafood  *thalassina*
sugar  *zakhari*
vegetables  *lakhanika*
vegetarian  *khortofagos*
yogurt  *yiaourti*

## Hors d'Oeuvres
cod roe pâté  *taramosalata*
eggplant dip  *melitzanosalata*
garlic dip  *skordalia*
mixed hors d'oeuvres  *mezedes*
olives  *elies*
soup  *soupa*
stuffed grape leaves  *dolmades*
yogurt, cucumber, and garlic dip
  *tzatziki*

## Vegetables
beans (green)  *fasolakia*
beans (lima)  *koukia*
beans (white)  *gigantes*
cabbage  *láhano*
cucumber  *angòri*
eggplant  *melitzana*
  eggplant (stuffed)  *papoutsakia*
Greek salad  *khoriatiki*
lentils  *fakes*
lettuce  *marouli*
okra  *bamies*
peppers  *piperies*
potatoes  *patates*
  french fries  *patates tighanites*
ratatouille  *briam*
rice  *rizi/pilafi*
salad  *salata*

spinach  *spanaki*
tomato  *domates*
zucchini  *kolokithakia*

## Fish & Seafood
anchovy  *gavros*
bream  *kefalas*
clams  *kidonia*
cod  *bakaliaros*
crayfish  *karavides*
cuttlefish  *soupia*
lobster (Aegean variety)  *astakos*
mackerel  *skoumbri*
mussels  *mydhia*
octopus  *oktapodi*
oysters  *streidia*
red mullet  *barbouni*
sardines  *sardelles*
sea bass  *lavraki*
shrimp/prawns  *garides*
sole  *glossa*
squid  *kalamaria*
  baby squid  *kalamarakia*
swordfish  *xifias*
tuna  *lakerda/tonnos*
whitebait  *marides*

## Meat
chicken  *kotopoulo*
chop (pork or beef)  *brizola*
hamburger  *bifteki*
lamb  *arni*
liver  *sikoti*
meatballs  *keftedes*
pork  *khirino*
rabbit  *kounelli*
veal  *moskhari*

## Desserts
custard  *krema*
custard pie  *galaktoboureko*
honey-and-nut pastries  *baklava*
ice cream  *pagoto*
rice pudding  *rizogalo*
sesame-seed sweetmeat  *halva*
walnut cake  *karydopita*

## Fruit
apples  *mila*
cherries  *kerasia*
figs  *syka*
grapes  *stafylia*

kiwi fruit  *aktinida*
lemon  *lemoni*
melon  *peponi*
oranges  *portokalia*
peaches  *rodakino*
pears  *akladia/krystalia*
quince  *kydoni*
strawberries  *fraoules*
watermelon  *karpouzi*

## Drinks
beer  *bira*
chocolate milk  *galakakao*
coffee  *kafes*
lemonade  *limonada*
milk  *gala*
orangeade  *portokalada*
tea  *tsai*
water  *nero*
  mineral water  *metaliko nero*
wine  *krasi*
  red wine  *kokkino/mavro*
  rosé wine  *kokkinelli/roze*
  white wine  *aspro*

## Some common dishes/terms
*kleftiko*  meat wrapped in thick
  parchment paper and baked in
  the oven with potatoes and
  vegetables
*loukanika*  spicy sausage
*loukoumades*  deep-fried dough-
  nuts soaked in honey
*moussaka*  baked layers of
  eggplant, potato, and meat
*pastitsio*  macaroni baked with
  meat
*scharas*  from the grill
*souvlaki*  small pieces of meat
  grilled on a skewer
*souzoukakia*  ground beef
  patties
*stifado*  beef or other meat stew,
  with tomatoes and onions
*youvetsi*  lamb or other meat
  baked in the oven with
  pasta or potatoes in a clay
  casserole dish or sometimes,
  aluminum foil

# Language Guide

## Greek Alphabet

| | | |
|---|---|---|
| Alpha | A, α | *a*, as in m*a* (short for m*a*ma) |
| Beta | B, β | *v*, as in *v*ery |
| Gamma | Γ, γ | *y*, as in *y*es |
| Delta | Δ, δ | *th*, as in *th*at |
| Epsilon | E, ε | *e*, as in y*e*s |
| Zita | Z, ζ | *z* |
| Eta | H, η | *ee*, as in m*ee*t |
| Theta | Θ, θ | *th*, as in *th*ing |
| Iota | I, ι | *i*, as in m*ee*t |
| Kappa | K, κ | *k* |
| Lambda | Λ, λ | *l* |
| Mu | M, μ | *m* |
| Nu | N, ν | *n* |
| Xi | Ξ, ξ | *ks* |
| Omicron | O, o | *o*, as in b*o*ne |
| Pi | Π, π | *p* |
| Rho | P, ρ | rolling *r* |
| Sigma | Σ, σ | *s* (mid-word) |
| | ς | (end of word) |
| Tau | T, τ | *t* |
| Upsilon | Y, υ | *e* as in m*ee*t |
| Phi | Φ, φ | *f* |
| Chi | X, χ | *h*, as in *h*at |
| Psi | Ψ, ψ | *ps*, as in cor*ps*e |
| Omega | Ω, ω | *o*, as in b*o*ne |

## Pronunciation

| | |
|---|---|
| αι | *e*, as in m*e*t |
| αυ | *av/af* |
| ει | *ee*, as in r*ee*d |
| ευ | *ev/ef* |
| ου | *ou*, as in t*ou*r |
| γγ | *ng*, as in a*ng*ora |
| γκ | *g*, as in *g*oat, at beginning of a word; *ng* in the middle |
| μπ | *b* at beginning of a word; *mb* in the middle, as in e*mb*argo |
| ντ | *d* at beginning of word; *nd* in the middle, as in e*nt*omology |
| σι | *si*, as in *si*phon |
| τζ | *j*, as in *J*ohnny |

## Time

| | |
|---|---|
| in the morning | *to proí* |
| in the afternoon | *to mesiméri* |
| in the evening | *to vrádhi* |
| at night | *ti níchta* |
| this morning | *símera to proí* |
| this afternoon | *símera to mesiméri* |
| this evening | *símera to apóyevma* |
| tonight | *apópse* |
| last night | *timberasméni níchta* |
| this week | *avtí tin evdhomádha* |
| next month | *ton epómeno mína* |
| What time is it? | *Ti óra íne?* |
| What time? | *Ti óra?* |

## Numbers

| | |
|---|---|
| zero | *midhén* |
| 1 | *éna* |
| 2 | *dhío* |
| 3 | *tría* |
| 4 | *téssera* |
| 5 | *pénde* |
| 6 | *éxi* |
| 7 | *eftá* |
| 8 | *ochtó* |
| 9 | *enyá* |
| 10 | *dhéka* |
| 100 | *ekató* |
| 1000 | *hílya* |

## Days of the Week

| | |
|---|---|
| Monday | *deftéra* |
| Tuesday | *tríti* |
| Wednesday | *tetárti* |
| Thursday | *pémpti* |
| Friday | *paraskeví* |
| Saturday | *sávato* |
| Sunday | *kiriakí* |

## Useful Phrases

Could you help me, please? *Boríte na me voithísete, parakaló?*

Could I ask you something? *Boró na rotíso káti?*

Do you know..? *Xérete...?*

Where's the toilet? *Poo íne i twaléta?*

Who? *Pyós?*

Who's that? *Pyós íne?*

What? *Ti?*

Why? *Yatí?*

How? *Pos?*

How far is that? *Póso makriá íne?*

How long does that take? *Pósi óra dhiarkí/kratái?*

How long is the trip? *Póso kratái to taxídhi?*

Which? *Pyo? Pya?*

When? *Póte?*

Where are you from? *Apó poo érhesthe?*

I'd like a kilo of apples, please. *Tha íthela éna kiló míla.*

How much? *Póso?*

How much is this? *Póso káni?*

Can I take this? *Boró na to páro mazí moo?*

I'm just looking, if that's all right. *Tha ríxo mya matyá, an epitrépete.*

Could you giftwrap it, please? *Boríte na to tilíxete ya dhóro, parakaló?*

Yes, of course *Ne, vévea/vevéos*

No, I'm sorry *Óhi, lipáme*

All right *Kalá*

Okay *Endáxi*

I don't know *Dhen xéro*

Thank you *Efcharistó*

You're welcome *Parakaló*

Thank you very much *Efcharistó polí*

Very kind of you *Polí evyenikó ek méroos sas*

Thank you for your trouble *Efcharistó ya tongópo*

Sorry! *Sighnómi*

Excuse me *Me sinchoríte*

I do apologize *Me sinchoríte*

I'm sorry *lipáme*

Never mind *Endáxi étsi*

Do you like it? *Soo arési?*

Wonderful! *Thavmásio!*

It's really nice here! *Ti oréa poo íne edhó!*

I'm American *Ime amerikos*

Do you speak English? *Miláte angliká?*

I (don't) understand *(dhen) Katalavéno*

Do you understand me?    *Me katalavénete?*

Could you repeat that, please?    *Boríte na to epanalávete, parakaló?*

Could you speak more slowly, please?    *Boríte na miláte pyo arghá, parakaló?*

How do you pronounce that?    *Pos proférete aftó?*

Help!    *Voithiá!*

Could you call/fetch a doctor, please?    *Parakaló, kaléste/id-hopiíste ghríghora éna yatró?*

Call an ambulance!    *Idhopiíste éna asthenofóro!*

## Dining Out

Is the restaurant open yet?    *Ine anichtí i koozína?*

What time does the restaurant open/close?    *Póte aníyi/klíni i koozína?*

I'd like a table for two, please.    *Tha íthela éna trapézi ya dhío átoma.*

We've/we haven't made a reservation.    *(dhen) Klísame trapézi.*

Can we wait for a table?    *Boróome na periménoome ya éna trapézi?*

Is this seat taken?    *Ine eléftheri aftí i thési?*

Could we sit here/there?    *Boróome na kathísoome edhó/ekí?*

Can we sit by the window?    *Boróome na kathísoome kondá sto paráthiro?*

Can we eat outside?    *Boróome na fáme éxo?*

Do you have another chair for us?    *Mas férnete akóma mya karékla?*

Waiter!/Madam!/Sir!    *Garsóni!/Kiría!/Kírie!*

Could we see the menu/wine list, please?    *Boróome na dhóome tongatálogho/tongatálogho krasyón?*

Do you have a menu in English?    *Éhete éna katálogho sta angliká?*

Do you have a dish of the day?/

tourist menu?    *Éhete pyáto tis iméras/tooristikó menóo?*

What are the specialties of the region/the house?    *Pyes íne i spesialité tis periohís/too maghazyóo?*

What's this?    *Ti íne aftó?*

Is this a hot or a cold dish?    *Aftó to fayitó íne krío i zestó?*

Is this sweet?    *Aftó to fayitó íne ghlikó?*

Is this spicy/hot?    *Aftó to fayitó íne pikándiko/piperáto?*

I'll/we'll have what those people are having.    *Théloome to ídhyo fayitó poo tróne ekíni i ánthropi, parakaló.*

Could I have some more bread, please?    *Parakaló, lígho psomí akóma?*

a bottle of water/wine    *Parakaló, éna bookáli neró/krasí akóma*

some salt and pepper    *Mas férnete to alatopípero, parakaló?*

a napkin    *Mas férnete mya chartopetséta, parakaló?*

a spoon    *Mas férnete éna kootaláki, parakaló?*

some toothpicks    *Mas férnete odhondoghlifídhes, parakaló?*

a glass of water    *Mas férnete éna potíri neró, parakaló?*

a straw (for the child)    *Mas férnete éna kalamáki (ya to pédhi), parakaló?*

How much is this dish?    *Póso káni aftó to fayitó?*

Could I have the bill, please?    *To loghariazmó, parakaló?*

Could you warm up this bottle/jar for me?    *Boríte na moo zestánete avtó to biberó/vazàki?*

Is there somewhere I can change the baby's diaper?    *Ipárhi kápyos chóros ópoo boró na aláxo to moró?*

The child will share what we're having.    *To pedhí tha fái lígho apó to dhikó mas fayitó.*

## Accommodations

Do you have a single/double room available?    *Éhete éna*

eléfthero monó/dhipló dhomátyo?

Does that include breakfast/lunch/dinner?    *Me to proinó/to mesimeryanó/to vradhinó?*

Could I see the room?    *Boró na dho to dhomátyo?*

Could we have two adjoining rooms?    *Boróome na échoome dhío dhomátya dhípla-dhípla?*

with/without toilet/bathtub/shower    *me/chorís twaléta/bányo/doos*

(not) facing the street    *(óhi) apó ti meryá too dhrómoo*

with/without a view of the sea    *me/chorís théa pros ti thálasa*

Is there an elevator in the hotel?    *To xenodhohío éhi asansér?*

Do you have room service?    *To xenodhohío éhi exipirétisi dho-matíoo/room sérvis?*

What time's breakfast?    *Ti óra íne to proinó?*

Can I have breakfast in my room?    *Boró na écho to proinó sto dhomátiómoo?*

Where's the emergency exit/fire escape?    *Poo íne i éxodhos kindhínoo/i skála pirkayás?*

The key to room..., please    *To klidhí too dhomatíoo..., parakaló*

Is there drinking water?    *Ipárchi pósimo neró?*

Could you put in a crib?    *Boríte na válete kyéna pedhikó kreváti sto dhomátiómas?*

Could you find a babysitter for me?    *Boríte na moo vríte mya béibi-síter?*

Could you put it on my bill?    *Boríte na to ghrápsete sto logha-riazmómoo?*

Does this amount include the tip?    *(Sto posó aftó) simberilamvánete i exipirétisi?*

Can I pay by credit card?    *Boró na pliróso me pistotikí kárta?*

Can I pay with foreign currency?    *Boró na pliróso me xéno sinálaghma?*

Could I have a receipt, please?    *Boró na écho mya apódhixi/to loghariazmó?*

## Directions

Where?   *Poo?*
here/there   *edhó/ekí*
to the right/left   *pros ta dhexyá/
   aristerá*
on the right/left of   *dhexyá/
   aristerá apó*
straight ahead   *ísya*
via   *méso*
in   *se*
opposite   *apénandi*
next to/near   *dhípla se/kondá se*
in front of   *brostá*
in the center   *sti mési*
down   *(pros ta) káto*
up   *(pros ta) páno*
inside   *(pros ta) mésa*
outside   *(pros ta) éxo*
behind   *(pros ta) píso*
at the front   *brostá*
at the back   *píso-píso*
in the north   *sto vorá*
to the south   *pros to nóto*
from the west   *apó ti dhísi*
from the east   *tis anatolís*
north/south/west/east of
   *vórya/nótya/dhitiká/
   anatolitiká apó*
address (street/number)
   *idhiéfthinsi (odhós/arithmós)*

## Traveling Around

Where does this train go
   to?   *Poo piyéni aftó to tréno?*
Does this boat go to...?   *Aftó to
   plío piyéni se ...?*
Can I take this bus to...?   *Boró na
   páo se ... me to leoforío?*
Does this train stop at...?   *Aftó to
   tréno stamatái se ...?*
Is this seat taken/free/reserved?
   *Aftí i thési íne pyazméni/
   eléftheri/klizméni?*
Could you tell me where I have
   to get off for...?   *Moo léte poo
   prépi na katevó ya...?*
Could you let me know when
   we get to...?   *Boríte na me
   proidhopiísete ótan tha ftánoome
   kondá se...?*
Could you stop at the next stop,
   please?   *Boríte na stamtísete
   stin epómeni stási, parakaló?*
Where are we now?   *Poo ímaste
   edhó?*

Can I come back on the same
   ticket?   *Ine me epistrofí aftó
   to isitírio?*
Can I change on this ticket?   *Boró
   na sinechíso maftó to isitírio?*
How long is this ticket valid
   for?   *Ya póso kyeró ischíi aftó
   to isitírio?*
Where can I...?   *Poo boró na...?*
   buy a ticket?   *Poo boró na
   aghoráso isitírio?*
   make a reservation?   *Poo boró
   na klíso thési?*
   make a flight reservation?
   *Poo boró na klíso thési sto
   aeropláno?*
Could I have a...to..., please?   *Thélo éna...ya...*
   a one-way   *Thélo éna apló
   isitírio ya...*
   a round-trip   *Thélo éna
   metepistrofís ya...*
   second class   *dhéfteri thési*
   tourist class   *tooristikí thési*
Do you also have...?   *Mípos éhete
   ke...?*
   season tickets?   *Mípos éhete ke
   kárta polaplón dhiadhromón?*
   weekly tickets?   *Mípos éhete
   ke kárta ya mya evdhomádha?*
I'd like to reserve a seat/sleeping
   berth/cabin   *Thélo na klíso
   thési/kreváti/kabína*
   by the window   *sto paráthiro*
   smoking/no smoking   *kapní-
   zondes/mi kapnízondes*
   single/double   *ya éna átomo/
   ya dhío átoma*

Where's...?   *Poo íne...?*
Where's the information
   desk?   *Poo íne to ghrafío
   pliroforyón?*
Do you have a city map with the
   bus/the subway routes on
   it?   *Mípos éhete éna chárti tis
   pólis me to dhíktio leoforíon/
   too metró?*
Do you have a schedule?   *Mípos
   éhete to orário ton dhromoloyíon?*
How much is a one-way/round-
   trip?   *Póso káni éna apló
   isitírio/éna metepistrofís?*
Do I have to pay a supple-
   ment?   *Prépi na pliróso

simbliromatikó isitírio?*
How much baggage am I al-
   lowed?   *Póses aposkevés boró
   na páro mazímoo?*
Do I have to change trains/
   buses/boats? Where?   *Prépi
   naláxo tréno/leoforío/plío? Poo?*
Does the plane touch down anywhere en route?   *To aeropláno
   káni endhiámeses prosyiósis?*
Does the boat call in at any ports
   on the way?   *To plío pyáni
   skála ke sála limánya?*
Does the train/bus stop
   at...?   *Káni stási se... to tréno/
   to leoforío?*
Is there a connection to...?
   *Ipárchi andapókrisi ya...?*
How long do I have to
   wait?   *Pósi óra prépi na
   periméno?*
When does...leave?   *Póte févyi...?*
Could you get me a taxi,
   please?   *Boríte na kalésete éna
   taxí ya ména?*
Where can I find a taxi around
   here?   *Poo boró na vro éna taxí
   edhó kondá?*

## Banks

Where can I find a bank/
   an exchange office around
   here?   *Ipárchi edhó kondá
   kamyá trápeza/kanéna ghrafío
   sinaghmatos?*
Where can I cash this traveler's
   check?   *Poo boró na exaryiróso
   aftí tin taxidhiotikí epitayí?*
Can I withdraw money on my
   credit card here?   *Boró na
   páro leftá edhó me mya pistotikí
   kárta?*
I've had some money trans-
   ferred here. Has it arrived
   yet?   *Ékana éna tileghrafikó
   émvazma. Eftase to émvazma?*
I'd like to change some money   *Tha íthela naláxo chrímata
   dollars into...   *dholária ya...*
What's the exchange rate?   *Pya
   íne i isotimía?*
Could you give me some small
   change with it?   *Boríte na moo
   dhósete ke lígha psilá, parakaló?*

# INDEX

Boldface indicates illustrations.
CAPS indicates thematic categories.

## ILLUSTRATIONS CREDITS

Abbreviations for terms appearing below: (t) top; (b) bottom;(c) center; (l) left; (r) right:

National Geographic
TRAVELER
# Greece

### Published by the National Geographic Society

John M. Fahey, Jr., *President
  and Chief Executive Officer*
Gilbert M. Grosvenor, *Chairman of the Board*
Tim T. Kelly, *President, Global Media Group*
John Q. Griffin, *President, Publishing*
Nina D. Hoffman, *Executive Vice President;
  President, Book Publishing Group*

### Prepared by the Book Division

Kevin Mulroy, *Senior Vice President and Publisher*
Leah Bendavid-Val, *Director of Photography Publishing
  and Illustrations*
Marianne R. Koszorus, *Director of Design*
Barbara Brownell Grogan, *Executive Editor*
Elizabeth Newhouse, *Director of Travel Publishing*
Carl Mehler, *Director of Maps*
Barbara A. Noe, *Series Editor*
Cinda Rose, *Series Art Director*

### Staff for 2009 Edition

Caroline Hickey, Elliana Speigel, *Project Managers*
Kay Kobor Hankins, *Art Director*
Diane Nelson, *Designer*
Robin Currie, *Text Editor*
Jane Sunderland, *Editorial Consultant*
Steven D. Gardner, Michael McNey, Nicholas P.
  Rosenbach, and Mapping Specialists, *Map Research
  & Production*
Al Morrow, *Design Assistant*
Connie D. Binder, *Indexer*
Richard Wain, *Production Project Manager*
Hunter Braithwaithe, Bridget A. English, Maura
  Walsh, *Contributors*
Meredith Wilcox, *Illustrations Specialist*

Jennifer A. Thornton, *Managing Editor*
R. Gary Colbert, *Production Director*

### Manufacturing and Quality Management

Christopher A. Liedel, *Chief Financial Officer*
Phillip L. Schlosser, *Vice President*
Chris Brown, *Technical Director*
Nicole Elliott, *Manager*
Monika D. Lynde, *Manager*
Rachel Faulise, *Manager*

**National Geographic Traveler: Greece (Third Edition)**
**ISBN: 978-1-4262-0396-1**

First edition: Edited and designed by AA Publishing (a
trading name of Automobile Association Developments
Limited, whose registered office is Norfolk House, Priest-
ley Road, Basingstoke, Hampshire, England RG24 9NY.
Registered number: 1878835).

Founded in 1888, the National Geographic Society is
one of the largest nonprofit scientific and educational
organizations in the world. It reaches more than 285
million people worldwide each month through its
official journal, *National Geographic,* and its four other
magazines; the National Geographic Channel; television documentaries; radio programs; films; books; videos and DVDs; maps; and interactive media. National
Geographic has funded more than 8,000 scientific
research projects and supports an education program
combating geographic illiteracy.

For more information, please call 1-800-NGS LINE
(647-5463) or write to the following address:

National Geographic Society
1145 17th Street N.W.
Washington, D.C. 20036-4688 U.S.A.

Visit us online at www.nationalgeographic.com/books.

For information about special discounts for bulk
purchases, please contact National Geographic
Books Special Sales: ngspecsales@ngs.org.

For rights or permissions inquiries, please contact
National Geographic Books Subsidiary Rights:
ngbookrights@ngs.org.

The Library of Congress catalogued the first edition as follows:
**Library of Congress Cataloging-in- Publication Data**
Gerrard, Mike.
  National Geographic traveler. Greece/Mike Gerrard.
       p       cm
  Includes index.
  ISBN 0-7922-7946-8 (alk. paper)
  1. Greece—Guidebooks.  I. Title: Greece. II. Title.

  DF716.G48  2001
  914.9504′76—dc21                                    00-069562
CIP

Printed in China

The information in this book has been carefully
checked and to the best of our knowledge is accurate.
However, details are subject to change, and the
National Geographic Society cannot be responsible for
such changes, or for errors or omissions. Assessments
of sites, hotels, and restaurants are based on the
author's subjective opinions, which do not necessarily
reflect the publisher's opinion.

# NATIONAL GEOGRAPHIC
# TRAVELER

- **Alaska** (2nd Edition)
- **Amsterdam**
- **Arizona** (3rd Edition)
- **Australia** (3rd Edition)
- **Barcelona** (3rd Edition)
- **Beijing**
- **Berlin**
- **Boston & environs**
- **California** (3rd Edition)
- **Canada** (2nd Edition)
- **The Caribbean** (2nd Edition)
- **China** (2nd Edition)
- **Costa Rica** (3rd Edition)
- **Cuba** (2nd Edition)
- **Dominican Republic**
- **Egypt** (2nd Edition)
- **Florence & Tuscany** (2nd Edition)
- **Florida**
- **France** (2nd Edition)
- **Germany** (2nd Edition)
- **Great Britain** (2nd Edition)
- **Greece** (3rd Edition)
- **Hawaii** (3rd Edition)
- **Hong Kong** (3rd Edition)
- **India** (2nd Edition)
- **Ireland** (2nd Edition)
- **Italy** (3rd Edition)
- **Japan** (3rd Edition)
- **London** (2nd Edition)
- **Los Angeles**
- **Madrid** (2nd Edition)
- **Mexico** (2nd Edition)
- **Miami & the Keys** (3rd Edition)
- **Naples & Southern Italy**
- **New York** (2nd Edition)
- **New Zealand**
- **Panama**
- **Paris** (2nd Edition)
- **Peru**
- **Piedmont & Northwest Italy**
- **Portugal**
- **Prague & the Czech Republic**
- **Provence & the Côte d'Azur** (2nd Edition)
- **Romania**
- **Rome** (3rd Edition)
- **St. Petersburg**
- **San Diego** (2nd Edition)
- **San Francisco** (3rd Edition)
- **Shanghai**
- **Sicily** (2nd Edition)
- **South Africa**
- **Spain** (3rd Edition)
- **Sydney**
- **Taiwan** (2nd Edition)
- **Thailand** (3rd Edition)
- **Venice**
- **Vietnam**
- **Washington, D.C.** (3rd Edition)

AVAILABLE WHEREVER BOOKS ARE SOLD